OXFORD WORLD'S CLASSICS

WILLIAM SHAKESPEARE

The History of King Lear

Edited by
STANLEY WELLS

ON THE BASIS OF A TEXT PREPARED BY GARY TAYLOR

OXFORD
UNIVERSITY PRESS

OXFORD

UNIVERSITY PRESS

Great Clarendon Street, Oxford OX2 6DP

Oxford University Press is a department of the University of Oxford.
It furthers the University's objective of excellence in research, scholarship,
and education by publishing worldwide in

Oxford New York

Auckland Bangkok Buenos Aires Cape Town Chennai
Dar es Salaam Delhi Hong Kong Istanbul Karachi Kolkata
Kuala Lumpur Madrid Melbourne Mexico City Mumbai Nairobi
São Paulo Shanghai Singapore Taipei Tokyo Toronto

with an associated company in Berlin

Oxford is a registered trade mark of Oxford University Press
in the UK and in certain other countries

Published in the United States
by Oxford University Press Inc., New York

First published by the Clarendon Press 2000
First published as an Oxford World's Classics paperback 2001

British Library Cataloguing in Publication Data

Data available

Library of Congress Cataloging in Publication Data

Shakespeare, William, 1564–1616.
[King Lear]
The history of King Lear / edited by Stanley Wells on the
basis of a text prepared by Gary Taylor.
(Oxford world's classics)
Includes bibliographical references and index.
1. Lear, King (Legendary character)—Drama.
I. Wells, Stanley, W., 1930– . II. Taylor, Gary, 1953– . III. Title.
PR2819.A2W47 2000 822.3'3—dc21 00–034005

ISBN–13: 978–0–19–283992–3
ISBN–10: 0–19–283992–6

7

Printed in Great Britain by
Clays Ltd, St Ives plc

PREFACE

ANY Shakespeare editor must incur immense debts to generations of predecessors. In working on *King Lear* I have been fortunate to be able to draw on a long and distinguished editorial and scholarly tradition extending back beyond Nicholas Rowe to Heminges and Condell or their assignees who worked on the First Folio, and to the anonymous but intelligent workmen who tried to make sense of the first Quarto in preparing copy for the reprint of 1619. Above all I have had the advantage and stimulus of being able to consult excellent recent, fully annotated editions by three good friends, the late Kenneth Muir, Jay Halio, and R. A. Foakes. I have done what I can to make my edition complement rather than rival theirs. My text is heavily indebted to that prepared, with my collaboration, by Gary Taylor for the Oxford Complete Works of 1986, but I have rethought a number of its readings.

A General Editor contributing to his own series is rather in the position of an actor who directs himself in a leading role. For the kind of direction that I should normally hope to provide to a member of my company I am especially indebted to Roger Warren, Robert Smallwood, John Jowett, and M. J. Kidnie, each of whom has offered helpful criticism of substantial stretches of my performance. Among other scholars who have been generous in sharing their expertise I should mention Jeremy Barlow, J. M. Binns, Anthony Burton, Paul Edmondson, Melvin Earles, Richard Knowles, Joan Lane, the late Peggy Munoz Simons, Steve Sohmer, Marvin Spevack, and Martin Wiggins. I have benefited greatly from the willing assistance of library staff at the Shakespeare Centre and the Shakespeare Institute, and am especially grateful to Sylvia Morris at the former and James Shaw at the latter. Kate Welch has compiled the index. Jessica Wells helped with a tedious piece of keyboarding, and Clemency Wells advised on a point of horsemanship.

In putting the edition through the press I have been fortunate once again to have Christine Buckley as a scrupulous copy editor. At Oxford University Press Frances Whistler has been an unfailing and immensely generous source of wise advice and practical help.

Stanley Wells
The Shakespeare Birthplace Trust
Stratford-upon-Avon
July 2000

CONTENTS

LIST OF ILLUSTRATIONS

INTRODUCTION

ONCE upon a time, probably in 1605, a man called William Shakespeare, using a quill pen, wrote a play about the legendary British King Lear and his three daughters. How often he drafted and redrafted his script we do not know; the version that reached print in 1608, and which seems to have been his first completed manuscript of the play, contains some 25,000 words.

Shakespeare's penning of these words has had consequences that he cannot have foreseen. It has resulted in countless theatrical performances, many of them in languages that he cannot have known and in countries of which he can have had no inkling. It has enhanced—and occasionally diminished—the reputations of innumerable actors. It has stimulated other writers—playwrights, novelists, poets, essayists—to produce an enormous body of work. It has generated a multiplicity of works by artists in other media—visual art,[1] music,[2] opera,[3] film and television.[4] It has provoked, especially in the twentieth century, a vast body of scholarly and critical writing.[5] And it produced a work which, at least since the Romantic period (with its admiration for the Sublime), has come to be regarded not only as its author's finest literary achievement, but also as one of the most profound and challenging examinations ever undertaken of what it means to be human, an examination

---

[1] There is no comprehensive study. William L. Pressly, in *A Catalogue of Paintings in the Folger Shakespeare Library* (New Haven and London, 1993), notes that the play proved popular with artists for over a hundred years, beginning in the 1760s. He reproduces (fig. 58) Robert Smirke's fine oil of the reunion scene. Some works, such as Peter Van Bleeck's painting of Susanna Cibber of 1755, are clearly derived from the theatre, others, such as James Barry's 'King Lear and Cordelia' (Pressly's fig. 2) represent scenes not performed during the period, when Tate's adaptation held the stage, and still others may be either purely imaginary or only obliquely influenced by stage practice.

[2] *The Shakespeare Music Catalogue*, ed. B. N. S. Gooch and D. Thatcher, 5 vols. (Oxford, 1991), is noted on p. 290 below.

[3] Probably the most successful operatic version is that by Aribert Reimann, published in 1978 and written for Dietrich Fischer-Dieskau, who performed and recorded it. A number of great composers have contemplated operas on the theme without actually writing them (p. 290 below).

[4] Reference works listing film and television versions are noted on p. 290 below.

[5] Many of these writings are referred to in the remainder of this Introduction; surveys of scholarship and criticism are noted on p. 286 below.

conducted not discursively but in a text that requires actors to represent men and women in action that is often violent, in extremes of suffering, and in repose. In imaginative scope and in its power to generate intellectual and emotional response, *King Lear* has been compared with the greatest masterpieces of art, literature, and music. Coleridge wrote of the storm scenes: 'O, what a world's convention of agonies is here! . . . surely such a scene was never conceived before or since. Take it but as a picture for the eye only, it is more terrific than any which a Michel Angelo, inspired by a Dante, could have conceived, and which none but a Michel Angelo could have executed.'[1]

A. C. Bradley took up the theme, writing that when he thinks of the play as 'the fullest revelation of Shakespeare's power' he finds he is grouping it 'with works like the *Prometheus Vinctus* [by Aeschylus] and the *Divine Comedy* [by Dante], and even with the greatest symphonies of Beethoven and the statues [by Michelangelo] in the Medici Chapel' (p. 244).

Such praise of the text as a work of literature has not always been matched by equal admiration of its qualities as an actable drama. Charles Lamb, complaining that, in the theatres of his time, 'the Lear of Shakespeare cannot be acted', wrote 'The contemptible machinery by which they mimic the storm which he goes out in, is not more inadequate to represent the horrors of the real elements, than any actor can be to represent Lear: they might more easily propose to personate the Satan of Milton upon a stage, or one of Michael Angelo's terrible figures.'[2] And even Bradley qualified his admiration by writing that though *Lear* is 'Shakespeare's greatest achievement, it seems to me *not* his best play'. For centuries, however, no one, including Bradley, had had the chance to see the play performed in anything like a full and unadapted text, or in conditions remotely approximating to those for which it was written. During the twentieth century, when many productions have played much fuller texts than in earlier times, and when the theatre has learnt to adapt itself to play

<hr />

[1] Coleridge's remarks are conveniently reprinted in Bate, *Romantics*; the quotation is from p. 393.

[2] Lamb's essay 'On the Tragedies of Shakspeare, considered with reference to their fitness for stage representation' (1811), is excerpted in Bate, *Romantics*, pp. 111–27; the quotation is from p. 123.

texts of the past rather than adapting them to suit itself, complaints that the play is unactable have receded, and *King Lear* has come to be seen as the height of its author's achievement as a dramatist as well as a poet: a poetic drama whose poetry can be fully apprehended only through performance. Performance has also humanized it, so that it seems equally great but less formidable than some earlier accounts might suggest, a colossus of a play still, but one that is shot through with irony and tenderness, a play that may arouse laughter as well as terror, tears as well as awe.

This volume offers an edited text of the play based on its first printing, explanatory notes printed below the text, and an introductory essay sketching the play's genesis, reception, and influence. It is necessary first to say something about what happened to the text after Shakespeare originally wrote it in order to explain how this edition differs from others. (A more technical discussion of the text is offered on pages 81–93.)

What Shakespeare Wrote

The play was first printed in 1608, in a volume described as *The True Chronicle History of King Lear* and known as the First Quarto, a technical term describing a book made up of a number of sheets of paper that have been folded twice, producing four leaves each. The text resembles others that are believed to have been printed from Shakespeare's original papers in that it represents a manuscript intended for performance but bearing no indications of revision, or even annotation, as a result of performance. This is the base text. All other versions of the play adapt this, more or less radically, and none of the play's progeny could have existed without it. It was reprinted with minor changes, all probably deriving from the printing house, in 1619. Like all editions of Shakespeare's plays printed in his lifetime, it is not divided into acts and scenes. This edition, like that printed in the Oxford Complete Works, numbers the scenes into which it falls naturally, but does not impose act divisions on the text.

Not long after Shakespeare first wrote the play, and before the script was printed, the company of players, the King's (formerly the Lord Chamberlain's) Men, in which he was an actor and shareholder, and for which he had already written at least twenty

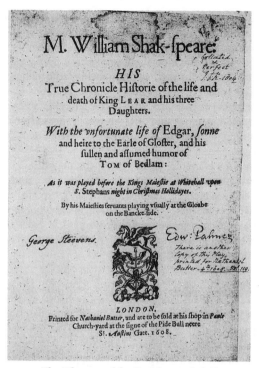

1. The title-page of the First Quarto (1608).

plays, put it into performance.[1] They are likely to have done so first at their regular theatre, the Globe. No doubt they used stage business and sound effects, including music, beyond those indicated in the original manuscript, and they may well have made changes to the dialogue, too. The title-page of the Quarto (fig. 1) gives us the only precise date of an early performance, stating that 'His Majesty's servants playing usually at the Globe on the Bankside' acted the play before King James, not in a public theatre but in his palace at Whitehall. The year must have been 1606, since the

---

[1] Arguments for the date of the revision printed in the Folio are summarized in *TC*, p. 131; they are presented in detail in 'The Date and Authorship of the Folio Revision', by Gary Taylor, *Division*, pp. 351–451.

Stationers' Register entry on 26 November 1607 states that the play had been given 'upon St Stephen's night'—26 December, now known as Boxing Day—'at Christmas last'. (The title-page of the 1608 Quarto allows for the passage of time by adjusting this to 'upon St Stephen's night in Christmas holidays'.) The performance took place in either the Great Chamber or the Hall.[1]

Before long—probably in 1610—the same company put on performances also based on the script that Shakespeare had first written, but with many differences, which included the addition of around one hundred lines, omissions (including a whole scene) amounting to some three hundred lines, changes of words and of phrasing within speeches, shifts of speeches from one character to another, and alterations in the action.

Though we have no documentary record of these performances, it is virtually certain that they took place. A text incorporating the major changes was printed in 1623 in the collected edition known as the First Folio, seven years after Shakespeare died, and it is unlikely that anyone would have made these changes—apparently transcribed on to a copy of the second edition, published in 1619, of the text first printed in 1608[2]—unless they had been intended for performance; similarly, those responsible for printing them in 1623 would have been unlikely to do so unless they had actually been performed. It is not absolutely certain that the person responsible for the changes was the play's original author, but they display the same level of literary and dramatic accomplishment, and as Shakespeare continued to write for the company of actors who had originally performed the play, it is reasonable to assume that

---

[1] The Great Chamber was made ready 'for the plaies' in December 1606 (Malone Society, *Collections*, vol. 6 (Oxford, 1961 (1962), p. 101); preparations for a masque performed on Twelfth Night may have precluded use of the Hall. The wooden-floored Chamber was 'a rectangular room roughly sixty feet long by thirty feet wide', with two points of entry and 'a large bay window looking out to the west', and 'heated with a fireplace, in the centre of the eastern wall' (J. Astington, *English Court Theatre, 1558–1642* (Cambridge, 1999), p. 51). Adaptation of the text may have been necessary, at least for Edgar's descent at 6.19.1, since there was no upper level.

[2] The thorny question of the copy used for the Folio is discussed by Gary Taylor, 'Folio Compositors and Folio Copy: *King Lear* and its Context', *Papers of the Bibliographical Society of America*, 79 (1985), 17–74. Further discussion is offered in HalioF (pp. 63–8) and Foakes (pp. 123–8), who concur that, though 'The evidence . . . is very difficult to interpret . . . there is at present a consensus that the text in F has a significant relation with Q2, and no direct link with Q1' (Foakes, p. 124).

he made the changes, even if in doing so he may well have responded to suggestions made by his colleagues. The First Folio text, then, represents the first known theatrical adaptation of the play, and the only one in which Shakespeare himself had a hand.

Throughout the seventeenth century, Shakespeare's play of *King Lear* continued to be represented in print by two separate versions deriving from the texts of 1608 and 1623. The former was reprinted, more or less accurately, in 1655 as well as in 1619. The First Folio was reprinted with no major changes to its texts in 1632, 1663 (with a second issue in 1664 in which a number of plays supposedly by Shakespeare were added), and 1685. In 1709, however, the Folio was effectively rendered out of date on the publication of an edition of Shakespeare's plays prepared by the playwright Nicholas Rowe. Rowe based his text on the Fourth Folio, of 1685, but undertook a certain amount of textual editing designed to make the plays more intelligible to readers and to reflect theatre practice of his own time. Even more significantly, in 1723–5 the poet Alexander Pope published a new edition of the Complete Works (based largely on Rowe's revised edition of 1714) in which he added to the text of *King Lear* derived from the Folio certain passages unique to the Quarto, and omitted a few lines found only in the Folio. In doing so he began a tradition of conflating the two early texts into one, a process that was effectively completed by Lewis Theobald in his collected edition of 1735, and which was followed by all editors until 1986.[1]

The assumption behind this procedure was that the Quarto and Folio editions each represented imperfectly a single text which can be hypothetically reconstructed by collapsing the two variant versions into one, adding passages that occur in only one of them, and making a choice among the local variants in passages that are common to both. Most editors took the Folio as the basis for their editions, often believing that the Quarto was seriously corrupt. During the 1970s and early 1980s, however, a mass of bibliographical and other evidence was brought forward to support the theory that the Quarto and Folio texts, so far from representing a single lost play, are independent witnesses to two distinct

---

[1] The only exceptions are in facsimile editions normally designed for scholarly purposes. Treatment of the text by eighteenth-century editors is charted by Steven Urkowitz, 'The Base Shall to th' Legitimate: The Growth of an Editorial Tradition', *Division*, pp. 23–43.

Shakespearian versions, the earlier printed from his original manuscript before the play had been put into rehearsal, and the other from a text incorporating changes made for performance. In 1986, the Oxford Complete Works, responding to a growing body of scholarly opinion, printed two texts of the play, one based on the Quarto, the other on the Folio. Since then, new editions have appeared, some, such as the third Arden edition of 1997, continuing the conflationary process, others based on either the Quarto or the Folio.

When choices such as these exist, it is the general policy of this series to base an edition on the text that lies closest to performance. So, for example, G. R. Hibbard's Oxford Shakespeare edition (1987) of *Hamlet*, unlike most editions of the play, offers a text firmly based on the Folio, to the extent of omitting from the body of the text passages found only in the 1604 Quarto. Since the Folio text of *King Lear*, too, brings us closer to performance than the Quarto, it might have seemed logical to present an edited text of that version, too. In fact, however, this edition is based on the Quarto. One reason for this departure from the series principle is quite simply that while editors have generally preferred the Folio text as a basis for their editions, and while many excellent annotated editions have been prepared in this way, the Quarto text has rarely been edited in its own right.[1] The only two published editions offering Quarto-based texts with anything like the kind of annotation expected of a modern scholarly edition are those prepared by René Weis (published in 1993), whose commentary is principally given over to comparison with the Folio-based text, which he prints in parallel, and who does not offer collations, and Jay L. Halio (1994, in the New Cambridge 'Early Quartos' series), whose commentary is devoted principally to textual matters. Graham Holderness's edition, in the 'Shakespearean Originals: First Editions' series (1995), has only a slight commentary and no textual collations. I hope that this edition will seem complementary to other modern editions, offering insight into the text of Shakespeare's greatest play as he first conceived it.

[1] An exception is M. R. Ridley, in his lightly annotated New Temple edition of 1936, who anticipated later scholars in stating that 'the "accepted" text of the play is a conflation which makes the worst of both worlds and has no authority whatever' (p. xi). He may have been influenced by Granville Barker (p. 72 below). Ridley's text, based on the Quarto, adds Folio-only passages in brackets.

Another, more pressing reason for choosing the Quarto is that it does not simply represent the play before it was acted, but must for several years have served as the basis for performances given before the text as preserved in the Folio was prepared, and that that revised text, prepared we believe several years after the play had been first composed, was so far removed from the Quarto as to constitute virtually a separate play. In a sense, admittedly, any change, however small, has this effect; but of all the Shakespeare plays surviving in two authoritative texts *King Lear* is the one in which the differences are greatest.

Although this edition is based on the Quarto rather than the Folio, it necessarily incorporates a number of the Folio's alternative readings. The two texts are verbally identical at many points, but the Quarto is particularly badly printed. Even if the Folio did not exist, an editor's corrections would in many cases be identical with the Folio readings. At other points the Folio offers readings which are arguably superior to those of the Quarto without necessarily being the exact words that the Quarto printers misread in the manuscript from which they were setting. The aim here has been to preserve Quarto readings where they can be justified and, in emending where they cannot, to give no more weight to Folio alternatives than to other possibilities. The Folio is, after all, a derivative, adapted, and edited text.

Although many of the Folio's readings are the result of revision undertaken several years after initial composition, others are either certain or likely to be the result of decisions taken in the initial act of translating the Quarto text into performance.[1] This is clearly true of, for example, the Folio's provision of music cues demanded by the Quarto but not present in it; but it is also perfectly possible that some of the cuts, additions, and variants in both dialogue and action that the Folio records were made when the play was first staged. This poses a nice philosophical problem. How is the editor to distinguish between, on the one hand, changes likely to have been made for performances deriving from the manuscript that lies behind the Quarto, and, on the other hand, changes made at the time of major revision?

---

[1] It is also, of course, theoretically possible that some of the Folio changes record performance decisions made at various points after the initial performances based on the Quarto, but before the major revision, but since there seems no way of identifying such changes, the question is incapable of resolution.

The ultimate answer is that there is no way in which this can be done. An editor can only surmise, and the safest basis of surmise is theatrical need. As a result, this edition adopts Folio changes (and makes a few others) when they seem necessary, or highly desirable, to the theatrical realization of the Quarto text but rejects others which, even if they might be regarded as improvements to that text, might reasonably be thought to be changes made after initial performance.

In view of its concentration on the integrity of the Quarto text, this edition does not collate Folio variants, or reprint passages unique to the Folio, except when they are germane to the purpose of establishing the Quarto text. A Folio-based text prepared according to the principles of this edition is available in the Oxford Complete Works (1986, etc.), and the variants are collated in the *Textual Companion* (1987).

The commentary to this edition follows the general principles of the series in offering discussion of textual problems and decisions, lexical and syntactical notes, explanation of classical and other allusions, and discussion of points of staging in terms of the theatres of Shakespeare's time. At the start of each scene it lists necessary properties (apart from costume except where this is especially significant). In allowing for the possibilities of variant interpretation of both language and staging it draws at times on the play's later critical and theatrical history, but makes no attempt to offer anything like comprehensive coverage of these matters. Since the Quarto has only just entered the editorial tradition, particular attention is paid to readings in Halio's and Weis's editions based on that text even when they are not accepted.

When Shakespeare wrote 'King Lear'

The challenge of determining when Shakespeare wrote the manuscript that underlies the printed Quarto of 1608 is of interest and importance, especially to critics who wish to examine the play as a product and reflection of its time. It is complicated by a number of uncertainties. Before the Quarto was published it was entered in the register of the Stationers' Company—a standard prelude to publication—on 26 November 1607 as 'A booke called. Mr William Shakespeare his historye of Kinge Lear as yt was played before the King*es* maiestie at Whitehall vppon St Stephans knight at

Christm^as Last by his ma^ties servant*es* playinge vsually at the globe
on the banksyde'. There is no reason to doubt the claim made in
the entry, and repeated in substance on the title-page of the printed
book, that the play had been performed at Whitehall 'vppon St.
Stephans knight at [Christmas] Last'—that is to say, on 26 December 1606. This is unlikely to have been the first performance,
as plays were normally tried out in the public theatres before being
offered at court. We have no more relevant evidence relating directly to performance. On this basis, the play was probably written
several months, at least, before December 1606.

Working backwards from this in the effort to find a date before
which the play could not have been completed, we can use the evidence of what Shakespeare read in composing it. Here the clearest
guidance is provided by the publication in 1603 of both Samuel
Harsnet's *Declaration of Egregious Popish Impostures* (entered on
16 March) and John Florio's translation of Montaigne's *Essais*,
both of which, it is generally agreed, influenced the play's language at a number of points. That takes us back to 1603 (always
assuming, of course, that Shakespeare did not read these works in
manuscript[1] before then).

Another unquestionable source is the play published anonymously as *The True Chronicle History of King Leir and his three daughters, Gonorill, Ragan, and Cordella* in 1605, having been entered in
the Register on 8 May, and stated on its title-page to have been
'divers and sundry times lately acted'. This is presumably the play
recorded in Philip Henslowe's papers, where it is not marked as
new, as having been performed twice at the Rose by the combined
Queen's and Sussex's Men in April 1594.[2] There had apparently
been a plan to publish it soon afterwards, since 'The moste famous
Chronicle historye of Leire kinge of England and his Three Daughters' was entered in the Stationers' Register on 14 May 1594, but
no copy survives, and the presumption is that the plan came to
nothing. If, as some scholars, including R. A. Foakes (p. 90),
argue, Shakespeare necessarily used the printed text, this would
mean that he was writing no earlier than May 1605. It is certain
that Shakespeare had a close knowledge of this text, but not at all

---

[1] Florio's translation had been entered in 1595 and may well have circulated in
whole or in part in manuscript.

[2] Philip Henslowe, *Henslowe's Diary*, ed. R. A. Foakes and R. T. Rickert (Cambridge, 1961), p. 21.

certain that this knowledge was derived from reading it in print. It is possible, as Sir Walter Greg conjectured, that Shakespeare had access to a manuscript.[1] He may have seen the play acted, perhaps more than once; and he may even, as Muir (p. xxix) acknowledged, have acquired familiarity with it by acting in it himself.

The claim that the old play had been recently performed may not be true: title-page evidence is often unreliable, and the fact that no company is named arouses suspicion. It is possible that publication occurred after Shakespeare's play had been acted, and that the publishers hoped, as Muir wrote, 'that it would be mistaken for Shakespeare's new play, or at least derive some reflected glory from it'.[2]

This would mean that Shakespeare would have to have read it in manuscript or to have derived his knowledge of it either from seeing it performed long before, or from acting in it. Though these possibilities may seem unlikely, they cannot be ignored. Shakespeare clearly had an exceptional memory, and the nature of his indebtedness to this text suggests easy familiarity rather than close consultation.[3] As W. W. Greg wrote, 'it would seem that as he wrote, ideas, phrases, cadences from the old play still floated in his memory below the level of conscious thought, and that now and again one or another helped to fashion the words that flowed from his pen' (p. 397).

There is reason to suggest that *King Leir* lodged in Shakespeare's memory at a much earlier stage in his career than has been commonly supposed. Scholars have looked to it primarily in relation to *King Lear*. Though Geoffrey Bullough, in his collection of Shakespearian source materials, notes resemblances to other plays, especially *Richard III* and *As You Like It*, he does not follow this up with the deduction that, if these resemblances indicate indebtedness, Shakespeare must have known the old play before it reached print. And an examination of the text without concentrating on

[1] W. W. Greg, 'The Date of *King Lear* and Shakespeare's Use of Earlier Versions of the Story', *The Library*, Fourth Series, 20 (1940), 377–99. Greg does not consider the possibility that Shakespeare performed in the play.

[2] The principal support for this theory is the Stationers' Register entry of the play as a 'Tragedie' (altered to 'Tragecall historie'), whereas it is more properly described as a tragicomedy. Bullough discusses the matter, pp. 269–70.

[3] Greg, in the article cited in n. 1 above, and Bullough note verbal and other parallels. The commentary to this edition notes parallels only when they help to explain the text.

Lear reveals resemblances to other plays, including *The Taming of the Shrew*, *Richard II*, *Much Ado About Nothing*, and *Hamlet*, not noted by Bullough.[1] Some of these resemblances may be accidental (just as some of the resemblances to *King Lear* would not individually demonstrate indebtedness), but collectively they suggest that Shakespeare knew the play virtually from the start of his writing career, and the natural conclusion is that he may well have acted in it when it was performed, in or before 1594, probably by the Queen's Men.[2] This belief may be supported by resemblances between *King Lear* and another play, *Selimus*, also acted by the Queen's Men in the early 1590s.[3] Long familiarity with *King Leir* does not, however, preclude the possibility that Shakespeare wrote his play after *Leir* had appeared in print, and that he consulted the text afresh at this point, so his indebtedness to it does not certainly help with the dating.

Other evidence is also contentious. At a number of points in the play, it has been suggested, Shakespeare alludes to dateable events. Gloucester's reference to 'These late eclipses in the sun and moon' (2.103) may allude to the eclipses, at least partially witnessed in England, of the moon in April and September and of the sun on 2 October 1605; Greg indeed could not 'see any escape from this conclusion',[4] which Taylor, among others, also endorses (*TC*). Muir, however, notes eclipses of both sun and moon in 1601 'that would still be remembered by the audience', and there was a partial eclipse of the moon in May 1603. In *Othello*, too, written

[1] Scholars who study *Leir* only in relation to *Lear* ignore its apparent influence on earlier plays by Shakespeare. There is no comprehensive study, but M. A. Skura brings together some of the evidence for the play's influence on e.g. *Titus* and *Richard II* in her *Shakespeare the Actor and the Purpose of Playing* (Chicago, 1993), pp. 285–6, and M. Mueller, noting parallels with *Richard III*, *Merchant*, *AYLI* and *Hamlet*, writes suggestively on 'the pervasive presence of the Leir play in Shakespeare's memory' as 'evidence of a long-standing intention to write a play about Lear' ('From *Leir* to *Lear*', *PQ* 73 (1994), 195–217; quotation from p. 213). Shakespeare's familiarity with the old play from long before it was published adds substance to Muir's suggestion (p. xxix) that he may have acted in it, and reinforces the idea (discussed in *The Queen's Men and their Plays*, by Scott McMillin and Sally-Beth MacLean (Cambridge, 1998), pp. 160–6) that he was a member of the Queen's Men before he joined the Chamberlain's Men in 1594.

[2] McMillin and MacLean discuss the play's provenance, p. 88.

[3] The parallels, of 'situations and ideas, pointing to a recollection not from a printed page but from the theatre', are discussed in '"King Lear" and "Selimus"', by Inga-Stina Ekeblad (Ewbank), *N & Q*, NS 4 (1957), pp. 193–4.

[4] 'The Date of *King Lear*', p. 377.

probably in late 1603 or early 1604, Shakespeare had already alluded to double eclipses:

> Methinks it should be now a huge eclipse
> Of sun and moon, and that th'affrighted globe
> Should yawn at alteration.
>
> (5.2.108–10)

Eclipses were a topic of much interest in the early years of the century;[1] those of 1605 had been forecast in, for instance, John Harvey's *Discoursive Probleme Concerning Prophesies* of 1588,[2] and in 1604 Himbert de Billy, in *Certaine wonderful predictions*, had written of 'many great eclipses' which would result in the 'spoil and ruin of the common society'.[3] A sceptical view would allow the possibility that, while Shakespeare knew that he could rely on a reference to eclipses to produce a response in his audience, he did not expect them to connect such a reference with any particular event. As G. I. Duthie remarks, 'Why should it be supposed that if Shakespeare makes a character refer to "these late eclipses" he must needs have in mind eclipses that had actually occurred in the recent experience of himself and his audiences?'[4] The eclipses cannot be regarded as watertight evidence for dating the play.

Gary Taylor has argued that Shakespeare was influenced by the play *Eastward Ho!*, written by George Chapman, Ben Jonson, and John Marston early in 1605 and published in that year after it had been entered in the Stationers' Register on 4 September.[5] If it is accepted that Shakespeare knew the play in performance this would imply composition of *Lear* no earlier than April 1605. Taylor also argues that Shakespeare was influenced by George Wilkins's play *The Miseries of Enforced Marriage*, based on a pamphlet describing a murder committed on 23 April 1605 which was entered for publication on 12 June of that year. The play can have been written no

---

[1] F. G. Butler, 'Novas, Eclipses and the English Stage, 1598–1608', *Shakespeare in South Africa*, vol. 10 (1997), 33–43.

[2] Cited by Furness, p. 379.

[3] Johnstone Parr, 'A Note on the "Late Eclipses" in *King Lear*', *Shakespeare Association Bulletin*, 20 (1945), 46–8.

[4] Introduction to the Cambridge edition, p. xiv.

[5] The evidence is set out in Gary Taylor's article, 'A New Source and an Old Date for *King Lear*', *RES* 132 (1982), 396–413. HalioF does not deny the possibility of influence; Foakes (p. 108) finds the argument 'not convincing'. Charles Nicholl briefly discusses affinities between the plays in *The Chemical Theatre* (1980), p. 182.

earlier than June 1605, and the presence in its text of numerous oaths strongly suggests composition before the passing of the 'Act to Restrain Abuses of Players', forbidding profanity, of May 1606. Since the play was performed, and probably written for, Shakespeare's company, he may well have read it soon after it was written, sometime between June 1605 and May 1606.

This combined evidence, then, suggests that Shakespeare wrote all or most of *King Lear* in the later part of 1605, and the fact that it was not given at court during the Christmas season of that year seems to indicate that, though by then it may have been played at the Globe, it was not yet ready for the court.[1] If it is accepted that there is a reference to the eclipse of the sun in October, the date of composition is pushed still further forward, though of course the passage in question, while it occurs early in the play, could date from a late stage of composition—Shakespeare did not necessarily start writing at the beginning and work steadily through to the end.

Where the Play Came From

At the time Shakespeare started to write *King Lear* he already had a large body of work to his credit, and this experience certainly affected the process of composition.[2] To give only a few examples, in *Titus Andronicus* he had already portrayed an elderly tyrant who goes mad;[3] *The Comedy of Errors* portrays a man who, finding himself denied by those nearest and dearest to him, fears he will go mad as a consequence; the *Henry VI* plays are concerned with divisions

[1] I discount G. Ashe's suggestion (*N & Q* 195 (1950), 508–11) that Shakespeare was influenced by William Strachey's sonnet 'On *Sejanus*' (reprinted by Muir, p. xx), printed after 6 August 1605; this depends mainly on the parallel between Lear's 'Vaunt-couriers to oak-cleaving thunderbolts' (9.5) and Strachey's use of the word 'vaunt-curring' in conjunction with lightning; but, as *OED* makes clear, the word 'vaunt-courier' was in common use at the time (indeed, it appears in Harsnet, p. 213), so the resemblance may well be coincidental. Chambers argues (*William Shakespeare: A Study of Facts and Problems*, 2 vols. (Oxford, 1930), i. 468) that a scene in Edward Sharpham's play *The Fleire* (registered 13 May 1606) is influenced by *Lear*, but the parallel does not necessarily indicate influence in either direction.

[2] *Lear*'s affinities with earlier plays are discussed by e.g. Emrys Jones in *Scenic Form in Shakespeare* (Oxford, 1971), 163–94, and Mack, pp. 51–6, etc.

[3] Affinities with *Titus* are discussed by Thomas P. Harrison, ' "Titus Andronicus" and "King Lear": A Study in Continuity', in *Shakespearean Essays*, ed. Alwin Thaler and Norman Sanders (Knoxville, Tenn., 1964), pp. 121–30.

in the kingdom; in the figure of Constance in *King John* Shakespeare had shown an enfeebled but eloquent grieving parent;[1]
there are so many resemblances with *As You Like It* that the
comedy has been described as 'Anti-Lear';[2] *Twelfth Night* has a
common concern with the paradoxical relationship of wit and
folly; and fathers outraged by their daughters' behaviour are stock
figures in Shakespearian comedy and extend to Brabanzio in *Othello*. Links with earlier plays include structural and poetic devices,
and even verbal repetitions (at, e.g., 9.75–8, 11.41–2 and
20.166). But Shakespeare never simply repeats himself, and the
tragedies immediately preceding *Lear*—*Hamlet* and *Othello*—are
very different in tone, structure, and effect.

King Lear is a pseudo-historical figure whose story had been told
often before Shakespeare came to write his play. But this is not one
of those plays—like, for example, *Romeo and Juliet*, *Julius Caesar*, or
The Winter's Tale—for which we can point to a single piece of writing that Shakespeare must have had open on his desk as he wrote,
a work which provided the overall outline of the play's narrative
along with something, at least, of its dramatic structure. Still less is
it a play in which a major source stimulated much of its language,
as, conspicuously, Sir Thomas North's translation of Plutarch did
for the Roman plays. Though Shakespeare certainly drew on
many existing literary, dramatic, and historical writings in composing *King Lear*—and also, no doubt, though less definably, on
personal experience—it seems likely that these fed his imagination
over many years rather than that he, as it were, sat down with the
open-minded intention of basing a play on a particular, existing
work and then looked around for material he might use to reshape
and modify it to suit his purpose.

There is reason to suspect that Shakespeare had been thinking
about dramatizing the story of King Lear for many years before he
started to write it. Its basic situation is curiously adumbrated in
what may well be his first work for the stage, *The Two Gentlemen of
Verona*. There, the Duke is planning to marry his daughter, Silvia,
to the foolish Thurio; responding to Valentine's question 'Cannot
your grace win her to fancy him?', he complains:

---

[1] Jones, pp. 167–9.
[2] M. Mueller (in the article cited in p. 12 n. 1) discusses '*As You Like It* as Anti-
Lear', pp. 198–202.

No, trust me. She is peevish, sullen, froward,
Proud, disobedient, stubborn, lacking duty,
Neither regarding that she is my child
Nor fearing me as if I were her father.
And may I say to thee, this pride of hers
Upon advice hath drawn my love from her,
And where I thought the remnant of mine age
Should have been cherished by her child-like duty,
I now am full resolved to take a wife,
And turn her out to who will take her in.
Then let her beauty be her wedding dower,
For me and my possessions she esteems not.

$$(3.1.68–79)$$

As the Duke 'thought the remnant of [his] age | Should have been cherished by her child-like duty', so Lear 'thought to set [his] rest | On [Cordelia's] kind nursery'; as the Duke is resolved to 'turn [Silvia] out to who will take her in', so Lear tells Cordelia that he will 'as a stranger to my heart and me | Hold thee from this for ever'; as the Duke says 'let her beauty be her wedding dower', so Lear will say 'Thy truth then be thy dower'; and like the Duke, Lear is to accuse his daughter of pride and to withdraw his love from her because of it. The tone of the Duke's words is comic because he is, unknowingly, addressing Silvia's successful suitor, but the situation he describes is, apart from his resolution to remarry, very much that of King Lear as he banishes Cordelia. As this passage looks forward to Shakespeare's play of *King Lear*, so also it looks backwards—or at least sideways—to the anonymous play of *King Leir*, because in that play too the King is planning to marry his youngest daughter to a man whom 'she ne'er could fancy' (l. 141).

The Lear story itself is a complex, inextricably entangled mixture of elements deriving from myth,[1] legend, and history. Numerous oriental and European precursors and analogues have been identified;[2] their main interest lies in the awareness they create that the story Shakespeare tells springs from deep roots in the human consciousness.

---

[1] Sigmund Freud, in 'The Theme of the Three Caskets' (in *The Penguin Freud Library*, Vol. 14: Art and Literature (Harmondsworth, 1985), pp. 235–47), proposes that the opening scene is based on an ancient myth of a man's having to choose among three women, the third of whom represents death.

[36] The still-standard work is *The Story of King Lear from Geoffrey of Monmouth to Shakespeare* by Wilfrid Perrett (Berlin, 1904), summarized in e.g. Bullough.

Legend. As a pseudo-historical narrative attached to the name of Leir, legendary founder of the city of Leicester (whose name was supposed, erroneously, to derive from 'Lear'), the tale first appears in England during the twelfth century in *Historia regum Britanniae*, written by the learned and imaginative monk Geoffrey of Monmouth, who purports to tell the story of British kings from the time of Brut, great-grandson of Aeneas and legendary founder of the British race. This work was not available in print in Shakespeare's time, but it was widely distributed in manuscript.[1] Shakespeare may have read it, or have picked up details from it transmitted by other writers. A summary of the story told by Geoffrey of Monmouth will give an indication of the pre-Shakespearian version of the tale:

Leir, who had governed for sixty years, had three daughters, Gonorilla, Regan, and Cordeilla. Growing old, he planned to divide his kingdom among them, and to find them suitable husbands. To see who deserved the best part of the kingdom, he asked who loved him best. Gonorilla and Regan flattered him, but Cordeilla said 'Look how much you have, so much is your value, and so much I love you.' Lear disinherited her and married off her sisters, Gonorilla to the Duke of Cornwall, Regan to the Duke of Albania, or Albany, the northern part of Britain. Later Aganippus, King of the Franks, married the dowerless Cordeilla for love. Later still, his elder daughters' husbands usurped his power, allowing him and sixty soldiers to live with the Duke of Albania. After two years Gonorilla reduced his followers to thirty men, dismissing the rest. Leir went to live with his other daughter, but after a quarrel she reduced his train to five. So he went back to Gonorilla, who made him manage with just one follower. In high dudgeon, he departed for Gaul to try his fortunes with Cordeilla, while fearing a cold reception. But she, hearing of his condition, wept, and commanded that he should be attended by forty men and generously provided for. Aganippus raised an army to restore him to his kingdom; they succeeded, and three years later Lear died. (By this time he must have been very old indeed.) Cordeilla, widowed, buried her father at Leicester. Some years later her nephews rebelled against her, captured her, and put her in prison, where she committed suicide.[2]

---

[1] A heavily abridged version, still in Latin, by Virunius Ponticus, was printed in 1585; it is mentioned by J. H. Binns in his *Intellectual Culture in Elizabethan and Jacobean England: The Latin Writings of the Age* (Leeds, 1990), who tells me that it names Leir only in passing.

[2] Summarized from the translation by Aaron Thompson published in 1718 and excerpted in Bullough, pp. 311–16.

2. Imaginary portraits of Leir and Cordeile (Lear and Cordelia), from *The Genealogy of the Kings of England* (?1560).

One way or another, this story as told by Geoffrey came to be widely disseminated and, inevitably, modified, appearing in a number of works that Shakespeare is likely or certain to have read either for pleasure or in the process of gleaning material for earlier plays. Though the historicity of Geoffrey's account was often questioned, Leir and his daughter and successor Cordeile (the name appears in variant forms) were regularly listed in genealogies of the English sovereigns, and imaginary portraits of them were printed. The images reproduced in fig. 2 are from a *Genealogy of the Kings of England* printed around 1560. Their story is told in the early pages of Raphael Holinshed's chronicle *History of England*, of 1577, which includes a different, beefier portrait of Cordelia (fig. 3). Shakespeare

3. Imaginary portraits of Leir and Cordeilla from Holinshed, *The Chronicles of England*, vol. 1 (1577).

knew this work well and used it throughout his career. Republished in an enlarged version in 1587, it formed staple reading for his English history plays. Its account of Leir, though apparently derived through intermediaries, closely resembles Geoffrey's and had little specific influence on Shakespeare (Bullough, p. 274).

The 1574 edition of the voluminous and frequently reprinted *Mirror for Magistrates* includes a verse complaint written by John Higgins and supposedly spoken by Cordila (or Cordell). Again the story is basically the same, but here, as in a slightly later retelling in William Warner's verse chronicle *Albion's England*, first published in 1584, the names of the elder sisters' husbands are reversed. An accretion which may have influenced Shakespeare (and which Higgins seems to have derived from Polydore Vergil's *Anglicae Historiae* of 1534) is Cordila's statement (found first in the 1587 edition) that

> . . . nature so doth bind and duty me compel
> To love you, as I ought my father, well;
> Yet shortly I may chance, if Fortune will,
> To find in heart to bear another more good will.

So Cordelia will ask 'Why have my sisters husbands if they say | They love you all?' (1.90–1). Shakespeare is very likely to have read the version printed in 1590 in Book 2, Canto 10 of Edmund Spenser's epic poem *The Faerie Queene*, in which, for the first time,

the youngest daughter's name appears as Cordelia and she dies by
hanging.

A complete catalogue of minor variations on the story would be
of little critical value, nor would it necessarily demonstrate indebtedness since Shakespeare himself might have introduced changes
independently of other writers. Of more interest is the relationship
between *King Lear* and its undoubted main source, the tragicomedy of *King Leir*, if only because the two works, though clearly
interrelated, are so radically different in effect.

'*King Leir*'. *King Leir* enjoyed modest success in its own time. The
recorded performances of 1594 drew receipts of thirty-eight and
twenty-six shillings respectively, indicating good houses, and unlike many plays of the period it reached print, but to later ages it has
been of interest only in relation to Shakespeare.[1] It is, so far as we
know, the first version of the tale in dramatic form, and, partly for
that reason, the longest thus far. The basic story is slightly modified, and the anonymous author (or authors) invents additional detail and pads it out with extraneous material. The play's ethos is
explicitly and strongly Christian: a feature against which Shakespeare reacted vigorously. Plotting is leisurely and discursive, the
style generally plain with occasional flights of rhetoric, the tone
often deliberately, sometimes rather coarsely, comic, while occasionally rising to eloquence. Characterization is generally two-
dimensional. *King Leir* left Shakespeare plenty of scope for originality.

Its opening stretch of action, extending to over 740 lines of blank
verse with occasional couplets and a little prose, expounds material
that Shakespeare compresses, but also adds to, in his first scene.
This Leir is grieving for his recently dead wife; weary of the world,
he determines to resign the crown and divide his kingdom equally
among his three daughters as a dowry. He tells his courtiers that
Gonorill and Ragan are being successfully wooed by the Kings of
Cornwall and Cambria, but that Cordella does not fancy any of her

[1] It is reprinted in for instance the Malone Society Reprints (Oxford, 1907), in
Joseph Satin's *Shakespeare and his Sources* (Boston, 1966; a modernized, lightly annotated text) and, most accessibly, in Bullough's collection of Shakespeare's narrative and dramatic sources. An edition by Donald M. Michie (New York, 1991)
includes a section on the relationship between the two plays, arguing that Shakespeare read *Leir* in manuscript, that his play 'was completed and on stage early in
1605' (p. 26), and that this led to the publication of *Leir*.

suitors. Leir decides to play a trick on her: he will ask his daughters
which loves him best, and when, as he expects, Cordella claims it is
she, will require her, as proof, to marry a husband of his choosing,
the King of Ireland. Leir's faithful servant Perillus, a forerunner of
Shakespeare's Kent, foresees disaster. The wicked Skalliger spills
the beans to the elder sisters, who rejoice in the opportunity to
thwart Cordella. In the scene of the love test, the elder sisters make
grotesquely exaggerated protestations; Cordella (like Cordelia after
her) comments in asides, then, when her turn comes, simply says

> I cannot paint my duty forth in words.
> I hope my deeds shall make report for me;
> But look what love the child doth owe the father,
> The same to you I bear, my gracious lord.

Lear renounces her and resolves to divide the kingdom between
her sisters.

Only when this episode is complete do we meet the Gallian
(French) king—the equivalent of Shakespeare's King of France—
who, having heard of the beauty of Leir's daughters, plans to sail
to Britain to win one of them, accompanied by his servant Mumford, both in the guise of pilgrims. Mumford's declaration that he
is 'some kin to the Blunts, and, I think, the bluntest of all my kin-
dred' (ll. 386–8) anticipates Shakespeare's characterization of
Kent, who can 'deliver a plain message bluntly' (4.31). In Scene 5
we meet for the first time Cornwall and Cambria, who encounter
each other as they ride post-haste to claim their brides. The episode
is comically presented. In the following scene the elder sisters gloat
over Cordella's misfortune 'Because she doth surpass us both in
beauty'. Leir enters, soon followed by the suitors, who are greeted
fulsomely by their future brides. Leir invites them to draw lots to
determine which half of the kingdom each shall have, and declares
that, having dispossessed himself, he will live with Gonorill. Perillus, Kent-wise, puts in a word for Cordella, but Leir quashes him in
lines that anticipate Shakespeare's rebuke to Kent (1.145):

> Urge this no more, an if thou love thy life.
> I say she is no daughter that doth scorn
> To tell her father how she loveth him.
> Who ever speaketh hereof to me again
> I will esteem him for my mortal foe.
>
> (ll. 569–73)

In Scene 7 the Gallian King and Mumford, disguised, overhear Cordella lamenting her plight while accepting it as God's will. In an episode tinged with comedy, the King successfully woos her. This ends the play's first movement.

In a moralizing speech of choric narrative addressed to the audience, Perillus then tells how Gonorill has turned against her father, who, 'the mirror of all patience [a quality that Lear will wish within himself: 7.429, 9.37] | Puts up all wrongs, and never gives reply' (ll. 755–6). The statement that she 'sets her parasites on purpose oft | In scoffing wise to offer him disgrace' may have suggested Oswald's insolence (4. 74–87). But Perillus—like Kent—will remain loyal. Next, Gonorill complains to Skalliger of the 'quips and peremptory taunts' which, she claims, she suffers from her father. There are likenesses here to Lear's speech beginning 'O reason not the need', especially between Lear's

> If only to go warm were gorgeous,
> Why, nature needs not what thou, gorgeous, wearest
>
> (7.426–7)

and Gonorill's

> I cannot make me a new-fashioned gown
> And set it forth with more than common cost
> But his old doting doltish withered wit
> Is sure to give a senseless check for it.
>
> (782–5)

Shakespeare's Lear, indeed, is closer to Gonorill's slanderous caricature of her father than to Leir himself. When Skalliger advises her to halve Leir's allowance she says she has already done so, and will now deprive him of all so that he has to look elsewhere. Left alone, Skalliger hypocritically vilifies her while also admitting his own guilt. In the next scene Cornwall (somewhat anticipating his counterpart, Albany, in Shakespeare) defends Leir to his wife, who shows contempt for him. Leir prays for death, but Perillus, in an episode of some eloquence, seeks to console him, saying that he has two other daughters who will welcome him—and thus reminding him of his unkindness to Cordella. ('To think of my unkindness to Cordella', says Leir; 'I did her wrong', Lear will say: 5.23.) Leir agrees to try his luck with Ragan, whom we forthwith see alone, proclaiming that, rather than put up with the tribulations that Gonorill complains of, she would 'send him packing somewhere else to go'.

Cornwall expresses concern to Gonorill about Leir's absence; she seeks to mollify him, but, alone, wishes her father's death, saying she will pursue him with slanders to exonerate herself. In a lively episode anticipative of Shakespeare's Scene 19, but different in plot function, Gonorill intercepts a letter from her husband addressed to Leir that a messenger is taking to Ragan's house, and persuades the messenger not only to replace it with one addressed to her sister in which she vilifies her father, but also to agree to 'make him away' if Ragan thinks that 'convenient'. The familiarity between Gonorill and the messenger here anticipates Gonoril's relationship with Edmund as well as Oswald.

In soliloquy, Cordella piously expresses gratitude for her good fortune along with intense desire for her father's forgiveness. We see Leir and the loyal Perillus limping exhaustedly to Ragan's house; Leir declares himself 'but the shadow of myself' just as Lear—but at a different point in the action—will call himself 'Lear's shadow' (4.223). Ragan hypocritically 'dissemble[s] kindness' to his face but, left alone, declares that 'ere't be long his coming he shall curse' (1153). The messenger delivers Gonorill's letter and agrees 'to give a stab or two if need require' (1211). Ragan complains that her husband is in league with her father, whereas in *Lear* Regan has Cornwall's full support. The virtuous Cordella continues to grieve for her father's plight, in spite of his unkindness, and her husband promises to send ambassadors to invite him to visit them; if he refuses, they will 'sail to Cornwall for to visit him' (1287). Ragan commissions the messenger to kill both Leir and Perillus.

Meanwhile the Gallian ambassador arrives at the court of Cornwall and Gonorill, expecting to find Leir there, and is hypocritically welcomed. In a complex scene, Leir and Perillus persuade the messenger not to kill them, Leir comes to recognize the truth about his three daughters, and the loyal Perillus urges him to go to France to seek succour from Cordella. Two claps of thunder heard during this scene may have given Shakespeare a cue for the storms during which his Lear, too, learns hard truths. Penniless, Leir and Perillus make their way to France where they encounter Cordella and her husband, disguised, on their way to England. At the climax of this scene Cordella reveals herself to Leir; the episode in which they are reconciled, absurd though it is in its excessive patterning, un-questionably influenced Shakespeare in its image of the father kneeling to his daughter for forgiveness, though not in verbal expression:

> LEIR
>
> O, no men's children are unkind but mine.
>
> CORDELLA
>
> Condemn not all, because of others' crime.
> But look, dear father, look, behold and see,
> Thy loving daughter speaketh unto thee.   *She kneels*
>
> LEIR
>
> O, stand thou up, it is my part to kneel,
> And ask forgiveness for my former faults.   *He kneels*
>
> CORDELLA
>
> O, if you wish I should enjoy my breath,
> Dear father, rise, or I receive my death.   *He riseth*
>
> LEIR
>
> Then I will rise to satisfy your mind,
> But kneel again, till pardon be resigned.   *He kneels*
>
> CORDELLA
>
> I pardon you—the word beseems not me,
> But I do say so for to ease your knee.

In the closing stretch of action, the French King invades England with his army. Again there are occasional pre-echoes of Shake-speare; Perillus's rebuke of Gonorill as a 'fiend in likeness of a human creature' (l. 2582), for instance, anticipates Albany's 'See thyself, devil. | Proper deformity shows not in the fiend | So horrid as in woman' (16.58–60); but the play ends in victory for the French King's party, with Leir 'again possessed of [his] right' (l. 2632) and conscious of the true value of each of his daughters.

Clearly, Shakespeare picked up hints from *King Leir* for his treatment of plot and dialogue. The old play's black-and-white characterization had its effect, too: of all his plays, *King Lear* is the one in which the characters can most easily be considered in terms of moral absolutes.[1] This may be thought of as one aspect of a common debt to the morality tradition and to developing conventions

---

[1] G. Wilson Knight opens his classic essay 'The Lear Universe' (*The Wheel of Fire*, 1930, pp. 194–226) with 'It has been remarked to me that all the persons in *King Lear* are either very good or very bad', and explores this theme in the rest of the essay.

of character portrayal.[1] The Earl of Kent, for example, with his mixture of comic bluster and devoted loyalty, has a lineage that can be traced back to the clever trickster and faithful servant of Roman comedy,[2] and John Reibetanz remarks that at times Edgar and Edmund 'appear like back to back pictures of Vice and Virtue in an emblem book'.[3] Edmund, in his direct address to the audience and his self-conscious amorality, has antecedents in the Vice of medieval drama, and also in the stage machiavel and in earlier stage bastards, including those in Shakespeare's own *King John* and *Much Ado About Nothing*; the Quarto's prefixes, and some of its directions, call him simply 'bastard'.[4]

The contrast between the brothers has often been emphasized in performance, particularly because it is important, and difficult, to establish an identity for Edgar before he adopts disguise. So, in Adrian Noble's production of 1993, Simon Russell Beale's Edgar was initially 'a naïve bookish scholar, reading in the midst of the court hubbub', an interpretation that made all the more terrifying his transformation when he was 'so traumatised by the blinding of his father that he repeatedly sought to revenge it, blinding Oswald with his staff as he killed him and trying to gouge Edmund's eyes with his thumbs at the end of their savage duel'.[5] Similarly in Richard Eyre's 1997 production, Paul Rhys was seen 'before the play began making observations through smoked glass of an eclipse of the moon . . . and carefully making notes in his earnest, scholarly way'.[6]

The women characters too, as Marianne L. Novy notes, owe 'something to the traditional tendency in Western literature to

[1] Mack (pp. 56–63) writes on the play's affinities with the morality tradition. Marcus (p. 152) considers the Quarto text 'closer . . . to the structure of a traditional morality play' than the Folio.

[2] Mark Thornton Burnett, *Masters and Servants in English Renaissance Drama and Culture* (Basingstoke, 1997), p. 83.

[3] John Reibetanz, *The 'Lear' World: A Study of 'King Lear' in its Dramatic Context* (Toronto, 1977), p. 45.

[4] Alison Findlay, *Illegitimate Power: Bastards in Renaissance Drama* (Manchester, 1994), remarking on 'the form of conspiratorial confidence, characteristic of bastard villains who follow on the tradition of the Vice character' (p. 225), notes that 'Edmund begins to lose touch with the audience when he is legitimised as a "Loyal and natural boy" [6.84]' (p. 219).

[5] Holland, p. 170.

[6] Robert Smallwood, 'Shakespeare Performances in England', *SS* 51 (1998), 219–55; p. 251.

split the image of woman into devil and angel, Eve and Mary. Goneril and Regan are much less psychologically complex than most Shakespearean characters of comparable importance.'[1]

Shakespeare drew on many other direct as well as traditional sources, too, and his transmutation of his inherited material is so radical that his play creates a far greater impression of originality than of derivativeness.

'*Arcadia*'. Conspicuously, Shakespeare chose to weave alongside and into the story of Lear and his three daughters the parallel narrative of the Earl of Gloucester and his two sons, Edgar and Edmund. He found the seeds for this in a work of far higher literary and intellectual quality than *King Leir*, Sir Philip Sidney's romance *Arcadia*, written mainly in prose but interspersed with many poems, first printed posthumously in 1590.

This was one of the great books of the time. In reading it, Shakespeare must have been struck by the relation between the Lear story and the episodes in *Arcadia* telling of a Paphlagonian king deposed and blinded by a wicked, illegitimate son but cherished by the natural son whom, under the influence of the bastard, he has cast off with orders—not obeyed—that he be killed. Shakespeare is indebted to *Arcadia* for plot motifs and atmospheric effects rather than for language. The king comes into the story in Book 2, Chapter 10, during an 'extreme and foul' winter storm; the princes who witness his plight are 'compelled by the hail that the pride of the wind blew into their faces to seek some shrouding place within a certain hollow rock'—a passage that seems to lie behind Shakespeare's storm and its sheltering hovel (though the transformation, at a different part of the plot, of 'the hail that the pride of the wind blew into their faces' into Albany's contemptuous 'O Gonoril, | You are not worth the dust which the rude wind | Blows in your face' (16.29–31) is typical of Shakespeare's eclectic opportunism). From there the princes see the king and his virtuous son 'both poorly arrayed, extremely weather-beaten, the old man blind, the young man leading him', as Edgar leads the blind Gloucester. Like Gloucester, the miserable and penitent king asks his son to leave him after guiding him 'to the top of [this] rock,

[1] Marianne L. Novy, *Love's Argument: Gender Relations in Shakespeare* (Chapel Hill, 1984), p. 153.

thence to cast himself headlong to death', and like Edgar, the son circumvents his father's plan to destroy himself. The bastard's attempts to kill his brother have an imprecise counterpart in Shakespeare's tournament between Edmund and Edgar. In Sidney it is not until after the virtuous son has been crowned that his father dies; grieving over 'his own fault' but rejoicing in 'his son's virtue', he weeps tears 'both of joy and sorrow' and, 'his heart broken with unkindness and affliction, stretched so far beyond his limits with . . . excess of comfort as it was able no longer to keep safe his royal spirits', dies, as Gloucester dies ''Twixt two extremes of passion, joy and grief' (24.195).

In filling out this tale to make it more suitable for his purposes, Shakespeare drew on another episode in *Arcadia*, from Book 2, Chapter 15, in which the hypocritical machinations of a wicked stepmother to trick her husband into thinking that her stepson seeks his death resemble Edmund's plot against Edgar.[1]

Other Influences. King Leir and *Arcadia*, then, gave Shakespeare important plot material, and as he drew it together and shaped it into tragic form, his imagination was fed also by other writings not specifically concerned with the Lear story. Florio's translation of essays by Montaigne and Samuel Harsnet's *Declaration of Egregious Popish Impostures*, both published in 1603, were mentioned in connection with the play's date of composition. The links with Montaigne are demonstrated partly by correspondences of rare words, or at least of words that Shakespeare had not previously used, such as 'auricular', 'compeer', 'derogate', and 'handy-dandy'; individually such correspondences could easily be coincidental, but cumulatively they are difficult to dismiss.[2] More potentially fruitful, but even harder to demonstrate beyond question, are resemblances of thought, but the very title of one of Montaigne's essays, 'Of the Affections of Fathers to their Children', is enough to indicate a shared interest. Leo Salingar, who has written a subtle and learned essay on the links between Montaigne and *King Lear*, considers that 'the coincidence of verbal echoes and variations on identical moral themes is so strong between the essay and the first

---

[1] Bullough, pp. 408–11. The chief resemblances are with Shakespeare's Scenes 2 and 6.

[2] Muir (p. 236) prints a list of 96 words, which he admits 'should be received with caution', many of them in common use at the time.

two acts in *King Lear* as to imply that Shakespeare was not merely recalling the essay here and there while he was penning the play but that he had been considering it in detail about the same time as he was planning the scenes of exposition and had altered his narrative source-material accordingly'.[1] But Shakespeare interrogated what he read: though Montaigne's scepticism may well have influenced, for instance, Edmund's cast of mind as expressed in Scene 2, its expression from the mouth of so villainous a character is enough to indicate that Shakespeare did not adopt an unquestioning attitude to the work.

Harsnet's *Declaration of Egregious Popish Impostures* attacks the attempts by Jesuit missionaries to win converts by persuading gullible servingmaids and young men that they were possessed by devils, sometimes physically abusing them in the process, and then conducting pretended exorcisms on them, and reprints the testimonies of some of the victims. A major contribution to a controversial debate of intense topical interest at the time of its publication, it is vividly written in an idiosyncratic, linguistically innovative style which affected the vocabulary of Shakespeare's play even more decisively than Montaigne. The names of the devils invoked by Edgar when, as Mad Tom, he simulates possession, clearly derive from the *Declaration*; indeed, when he declares 'Five fiends have been in Poor Tom at once, as of lust Obidicut, Hobbididence prince of dumbness, Mahu of stealing, Modo of murder, Flibbertigibbet of mocking and mowing, who since possesses chambermaids and waiting-women' (15.56–60) he is not merely picking up names from Harsnet, but, in the final phrase, alluding obliquely to the book itself. Lear's use of the term 'hysterica passio' is only one of numerous links with Harsnet, whose language is also reflected in, especially, the imagery of the storm scenes. Harsnet writes satirically, sometimes cruelly, of the sufferings, mental and physical, of under-privileged people; his portrayal of an unfortunate young woman 'sitting bound in a chair' while she was tortured resembles the binding of Gloucester to a chair to have his eyes put out. More generally, the profound response to human suffering which pervades Shakespeare's play may represent his sensitive

---

[1] Leo Salingar, '*King Lear*, Montaigne and Harsnett', in his *Dramatic Form in Shakespeare and the Jacobeans* (Cambridge, 1986), pp. 107–39; p. 113. This essay offers an excellent discussion of philosophical links between Montaigne and *King Lear*.

reaction to Harsnet's more adversarially detached attitude to the horrors he writes about. It is because Edgar adopts the persona of one of the least privileged members of society, a mad beggar, that Harsnet surfaces most clearly in his language, but Edgar is only the central figure in a network of men—Lear and Gloucester, Kent and even the Fool—displaced from a position of privilege and forced to contemplate the privations of homeless outcasts, who in the process learn to understand and to feel compassion for society's victims.[1]

Like Florio's Montaigne, then, the *Declaration* seems to have exerted a pervasive as well as a local influence; indeed, its editor argues that 'Shakespeare read Harsnet before he wrote *Lear*, and the reading so affected his conception of the central themes, scenes, and characters of the play that it may have been the determining influence upon his decision to write the play at all' (Brownlow, p. 118). This hypothesis adds weight to the belief that *King Lear* grew slowly in Shakespeare's mind, and, for all the literariness of its origins, is finally the product of deep personal meditation.

Many other written sources for the language of *King Lear* have been certainly or conjecturally identified, and some of them are referred to in the notes to this edition. The Bible exerted a strong influence, even though Shakespeare has been at pains to locate his action in a non-Christian, pagan society; indeed, both the Book of Job and the parable of the Prodigal Son have been regarded as deep sources of the play.[2] The dialogue draws exceptionally

---

[1] Recognition of Harsnet's influence on *Lear* extends back to Theobald, but was greatly extended by Kenneth Muir's essay 'Samuel Harsnett and *King Lear*', *RES*, NS 2 (1951), 11–21, reworked in his Arden edition and his book *The Sources of Shakespeare's Plays* (1977). In *Shakespeare, Harsnett, and the Devils of Denham* (Newark, London and Toronto, 1993) F. W. Brownlow offers a thorough study of Harsnet, including consideration of the relationship of his work to Shakespeare, along with an edition of the *Declaration*. Harsnet also figures in Stephen Greenblatt's eloquent 'Shakespeare and the Exorcists', in his *Shakespearean Negotiations* (Oxford, 1988).

[2] These and other analogues are discussed by e.g. Rosalie L. Colie, 'The Energies of Endurance: Biblical Echo in *King Lear*', in Colie and Flahiff, pp. 117–44, Susan Snyder, '*King Lear* and the Prodigal Son', *SQ* 17 (1966), 361–9, and Harold Fisch, Chapter 4 of *The Biblical Presence in Shakespeare, Milton and Blake* (Oxford, 1999). More generally, Naseeb Shaheen identifies specific parallels in his *Biblical References in Shakespeare's Plays* (Newark, Del., 1999, superseding his *Biblical References in Shakespeare's Tragedies* (1987)), and Peter Milward finds numerous biblical echoes, some rather faint, in his determinedly Christian *Biblical Influences in Shakespeare's Great Tragedies* (Bloomington, 1987).

heavily also on the proverbial, folk language of the time: R. W. Dent, in his index to Shakespeare's proverbial language, has more citations to *King Lear* than to any other play except *Romeo and Juliet*.[1]

Visual influences, too, have been detected, such as the paintings of the Day of Judgement commonly found in churches of the time—though the one in the Guild Chapel in Stratford-upon-Avon may have been defaced in Shakespeare's boyhood by his father on the orders of the Town Council as a remnant of popish superstition.[2] And there may have been a catalysing external influence in the case of Sir Brian Annesley, a rich old man with three daughters.[3] When he made his will, in 1600, the two elder were married; he bequeathed the bulk of his estate to his youngest, to whom he had taken the precaution of giving the same name as Leir's— Cordell. He became senile in 1603, when his eldest daughter, Grace, and her husband Sir John Wildgoose tried to show that he had been mad when he made his will, as a way of laying hands on his estate. Cordell protected him and inherited most of his wealth. News of the case seems likely to have spread among the circles in which Shakespeare moved; an executor of Annesley's will was Sir William Harvey, third husband of the Dowager Countess of Southampton, mother of the Earl to whom Shakespeare had dedicated his narrative poems.

What brought all these and many other elements together in the crucible of Shakespeare's imagination can only be conjectured. He must have been motivated partly by sheer professionalism: the need to provide his company with a steady supply of plays. But there must also have been a profound creative urge that impelled him to write so intellectually ambitious and passionately expressed a play, one that makes fewer concessions to the need to entertain, in any easy sense of the word, than anything he wrote before or after.

---

[1] Dent, pp. 3–4.

[2] The theme is explored, with special reference to nakedness and 'Lear's preoccupation with Judgement', in '*King Lear* and Doomsday', by Mary Lascelles, *SS 26* (1973), pp. 69–79.

[3] Geoffrey Bullough studied the case in '*King Lear* and the Annesley Case: A Reconsideration', *Festschrift Rudolf Stamm*, ed. E. Kolb and J. Hasler (Berne, 1969), pp. 43–50. Richard Wilson offers a revisionary account in his *Will Power* (1993), surmising that 'the name of Kent, substituted for Perillus, was suggested by the county where the modern Lear was persecuted and tormented' (p. 49).

Shaping the Play

Professionalism shaped the parameters within which he worked. He knew that his play would be presented primarily in a particular theatre, the Globe, with clearly defined resources: a theatre whose open stage encouraged an emblematic, even symbolical mode of representation. He does nothing to stretch these resources: the play needs an upper level for Scene 6, but otherwise could be played entirely on the main stage. Nor does it call for exceptional properties: a throne, a few chairs, a pair of stocks, torches, weapons, a map, regalia including a coronet, purses, and rather a lot of letters are all that the play requires.[1] Musical and other sound effects, though important, are nothing extraordinary: hunting horns are called for at 3.10; the flourishes and sennets for ceremonial entrances and exits, and the 'alarms' of 23.0 and 23.4, would have been played on brass and drums;[2] drums might well also have helped to mimic thunder. The sound of a distant drum is called for at 20.276, two on-stage trumpeters are needed for the combat between Edmund and Edgar in the final scene, and the 'soft music' (21.0) of the reunion scene probably sounded from bowed and plucked stringed instruments, and from recorders.

Shakespeare knew that the play needed to be capable of being acted in locations other than the Globe: at court (as it was in 1606), and on tour. He knew the size of the company and both the capabilities and the limitations of the actors who constituted it, he knew that women's parts would be played by young male actors, and he knew—up to a point—what he could expect of his audience. He had inherited, and himself helped to develop, conventions of playwriting which he could adopt and adapt as he thought fit. Meditating on the Lear story as it already existed, he made decisions that would recast it from prose chronicle, verse complaint, poetic narrative, and theatrical tragicomedy into high, philosophical tragedy, decisions in which artistic aims were controlled and stimulated by practical needs.

---

[1] Use of properties is studied in Frances Teague's *Shakespeare's Speaking Properties* (Lewisburg, 1991); Foakes (p. 5) points out that her list is incomplete.

[2] Sohmer, stating that 'Shakespeare certainly knew the Roman festal calendar included an important rite of purification of their war trumpets', suggests that the 'elaborate rite of trumpets and martial combat' of the final scene 'not only leads to Edmund's death but seems to depurate him as well' (paragraphs 20, 21).

The most basic decision was to adopt tragic form. This is the end to which the action was to be directed, and to bring it about required an adjustment of the end of the story. The old play concludes happily with the reconciliation of Lear and Cordelia, but in pseudo-historical versions of the tale Lear, 'made ripe by eld' (as Spenser puts it[1]), dies naturally, and years later Cordelia, dispossessed of her kingdom and imprisoned by her nephews, kills herself. Centring the tragedy on Lear, and avoiding the suicide motif—or rather, transferring it to Gonoril—Shakespeare causes Cordelia to die, murdered and still young, before Lear, and then, stressing the bond between them, has the father die over his daughter's body, of grief no less than age. Lear's journey towards death, adumbrated in his opening speech,[2] forms one of the play's links with the morality tradition in which 'the hero is humbled and made to recognize his own weakness and vulnerability, which are the necessary conditions of his existence'.[3]

Seeking intensity of effect, Shakespeare pared away much of the action of the old play, especially its scenes of bawdy comedy, and reorganized and compressed much of the narrative that he retained, as for example in the opening scene. In Shakespeare's play, Lear's division of the kingdom has a ritualistic quality. Avoiding simplistic explanations of human behaviour, he reduces the motivation by which Leir, widowed, sets up the love test as a way of ensuring the succession. This has been seen as a fault. Coleridge commented on the 'nursery-tale' character of the scene;[4] notoriously, Tolstoy, with the instincts of a great romantic novelist, preferred the old play to what Shakespeare made of it;[5] and more recently even Frank Kermode appears to align himself with critics who 'have openly admitted that the anonymous author

---

[1] *The Faerie Queene*, Book 2, Canto 10, 32.2.

[2] More obviously in the Folio, where he says he will 'Unburdened crawl toward death' (1.1.41), than in the Quarto, but implicit there in his statement that he intends 'To shake all cares and business off our state | Confirming them on younger years' (1.40–1).

[3] Emrys Jones, *Scenic Form in Shakespeare* (Oxford, 1971), p. 158. Jones offers an excellent analysis of the play's structure.

[4] Bate, *Romantics*, p. 389.

[5] 'Shakespeare and the Drama', in *Tolstoy on Shakespeare* (n.d. [1904], 7–81): 'the whole of [*King Leir*] . . . is incomparably and in every respect superior to Shakespeare's adaptation', p. 43. George Orwell discusses resemblances between Tolstoy and Lear in 'Lear, Tolstoy and the Fool', in *Shooting an Elephant and Other Essays* (New York, 1945), pp. 32–52.

manages the opening scene better than his successor'.[1] It might on the contrary be argued that Shakespeare's opening scene is a masterpiece of dramatic exposition—almost a little play in its own right—and that its reduction and simplification of motive is one of the ways in which it establishes a mode in which symbol and emblem will have as important a part to play as psychological verisimilitude. Constantly the play's language—verbal and gestural—will relate its action to moral and philosophical concepts, and its mode of characterization will be prepared, when necessary, to subordinate plausibility to broader patterns of dramatic discourse. To say that Shakespeare was writing a straightforward morality play would be a gross over-simplification, but he was aware of the morality tradition, his use of abstract nouns as personifications reflects its conventions (at e.g. 1.138–40), and he is unafraid of allowing his characters to draw attention to the unreality of their own behaviour—'Why I do trifle thus with his despair | Is done to cure it' (20.33–4), says Edgar as he plays his part in the elaborate morality play in which he acts as moral tutor to his suicidal father. A remark like this transparently shows us a dramatist putting his own words into a character's mouth in order to guide his audience's reactions, and there are others like it, especially when Shakespeare feels the need to rein back a potentially comic response to the absurdity of madness: 'O thou side-piercing sight!' (20.85) from Edgar as he sees Lear crowned with weeds and flowers, and 'A sight most pitiful in the meanest wretch, | Past speaking in a king' from the Gentleman, just in case we are merely amused by Lear's running exit (20.193–4).

Another technique by which Shakespeare opens up the play's action, replacing specificity by multiplicity of suggestiveness, is delocalization. In the old play, movements are plotted with some care: 'Now happily I am arrivèd here, | Before the stately palace of the Cambrian King', says the messenger (ll. 1158–9); in *King Lear*, however, it is often impossible to assign the action to any specific location. The only town mentioned by name (with the possible exception of Gloucester at 5.1) is Dover, thought of as the closest place in England to France—and even that (rather like Moscow in Chekhov's *Three Sisters*) is an ideal rather than a reality. The play's action, writes Jodi Mikalachki, 'staggers toward a Dover it

---

[1] Riverside, p. 1250.

will never reach, smelling its way to the sea whose other shore is the distant and yet-to-be encountered civility of Europe' (p. 70). Yet Dover is the gateway through which civilizing virtues, embodied first in the King of France and later in his queen, Cordelia, enter upon the barbarity of Britain. As 'the place where Lear will see Cordelia, or the place where Gloucester will have the satisfaction of suicide' the town is, as Jonathan Goldberg has written, 'a site of desire, the hope for recovery or, at least, repose, restoratives to answer "eyeless Rage" [8.7], or the final closing of the eyes in a sleep without end'.[1]

Equally, Shakespeare withdraws, or muddies, the sense of period. Charles Edelman (p. 152) remarks that 'those who would perform *King Lear* soon realise that there is simply no one era for the costume and scene designers to employ which is not rendered inconsistent elsewhere'. To give just one example, according to Holinshed Lear lived 'in the year of the world 3105', that is, around 656 BC, 'three generations prior to the founding of Rome'; nevertheless, Shakespeare's characters swear by Roman deities,[2] and Edgar became king some 1,700 years later, in AD 959. (This assumes, of course, that the Edgar of the play is to be equated with the historical king of that name; but since such a king existed, some members, at least, of the audience may have made the connection, especially since other aspects of the play may relate to the Anglo-Saxon king.[3]) Shakespeare denies the old play's strongly explicit Christian frame of reference; 'In contrast to *Hamlet*', W. R. Elton has written, 'a Christianized version of the pre-Christian Amleth story, *Lear*, in Shakespeare's hands, becomes a paganized version of a Christian play' (p. 70). But it might be argued that this demonstrates a concern for authenticity beyond that of the author of the old play, which Shakespeare short-circuits in adopting a pagan setting.

To say this is not necessarily to deny that the play can promulgate Christian values or that it draws on the language and associations of Christianity, as it manifestly does in, especially, the

[1] Jonathan Goldberg, 'Perspectives: Dover Cliff and the Conditions of Representation', in *Shakespeare and Deconstruction*, ed. G. D. Atkins and D. Bergeron (New York, 1988), pp. 245–65.

[2] Sohmer, paragraph 2.

[3] Links between *Lear* and the story of King Edgar are explored in 'Anglo-Saxon Elements of the Gloucester Sub-plot in *King Lear*', by Tony Perrello, *English Language Notes*, 35 (1997), 10–14.

portrayal of Cordelia; but Shakespeare was clearly anxious not to place the action within a specific philosophical or religious context. The replacement of God by the gods, the frequent invocation of pagan deities, may, as some critics have argued,[1] enhance the earnestness of the play's concern with fundamental human issues. Stripped of the consolations of received religion, it gains in mystery, in the sense of life as a battle with the elements, a struggle for survival against wind and rain in a world where humanity has to compete with animal forces both within and outside itself. Shakespeare turns the play into a kind of anti-pastoral by his addition of the storm that is external to Lear and of the tempest that rages in his mind. As in *As You Like It*, the 'winter wind' is 'not so unkind | As man's ingratitude' (*AYLI* 2.7.175–7).[2]

Absence of specificity in the play's geographical and temporal setting would have been enhanced by the neutrality of its original staging on the bare boards of the Globe, a staging which in itself encouraged non-naturalistic interpretation of action. Later stagings of the play have often sought a similar effect. Many productions from Macready's in 1838 up to and including the Elliott–Olivier television film (discussed on pp. 78–9) have placed part or all of the action in a Stonehenge-like setting of vast, primitive blocks of stone and dressed the characters in druidic robes. More adventurous directors have found different ways of suggesting that the play belongs to no specific time or place. So Komisarjevsky in his 1936 Stratford production used a single set composed of stairs and platforms with the declared intention of suggesting the play's 'elemental quality',[3] and Isamu Noguchi's cubist settings and bizarre costumes for the 1955 Stratford production directed by George Devine, with John Gielgud as a heroically loyal Lear, were designed to be 'free of historical or decorative associations so that the timeless, universal, and mythic quality of the story [might] be

---

[1] S. L. Bethell, for instance, wrote 'may we not at least suspect Shakespeare of deliberately intending to present a world without revelation, in order to determine how far human nature could penetrate its mysteries and achieve religious and moral order apart from the gift of supernatural grace' (*Shakespeare and the Popular Dramatic Tradition* (1944), p. 54). Bethell also offers an analysis of Cordelia's associations 'with theological terminology and Christian symbol', pp. 59–60.

[2] Mueller, in the article referred to in p. 12 n. 1, discusses '*As You Like It* as Anti-Lear', pp. 198–202. Emrys Jones has suggestive remarks on the comedy as a source for the tragedy (*Scenic Form*, pp. 171–3).

[3] Ralph Berry, 'Komisarjevsky at Stratford-upon-Avon', *SS* 36 (1983), 73–84; p. 78.

4. Jonathan Hyde as Edgar as Tom o'Bedlam in Adrian Noble's RSC production, 1982.

clear'. ('No revival', wrote J. C. Trewin, 'was so calculated to withdraw the mind from the timeless, universal, and mythical quality of the narrative and from Shakespeare's text.'[1])

But the play is not simply abstract. Many features of the text link it to Shakespeare's time, notably Edgar's disguise as a Tom o'Bedlam, a figure that would have been as familiar to Jacobean audiences as homeless derelicts and bagladies today and that might similarly have aroused dismay as well as pity. 'Edgar', writes Michael Goldman, 'must be filthy, grotesque, very nearly naked, and bear on his body evidence of horrible mutilation. He is the kind of beggar who *enforces* charity—so repellent, nasty, and noisy that you pay him to go away.'[2] Though the play's landscape is pagan

---

[1] J. C. Trewin, *Shakespeare on the English Stage 1900–1964* (1964), p. 221.

[2] Michael Goldman, *Shakespeare and the Energies of Drama* (Princeton, 1972), p. 97.

and Lear reigned many centuries before the Christian era, it can accommodate references to 'spectacles' (2.35), a godson (6.91), items of contemporary clothing such as the codpiece (9.27), and even—if only by oversight—steeples with weathercocks (9.1–3). In Shakespeare's time, indeed, the play would, so far as we can tell, have been performed in contemporary costume, though not necessarily in the everyday dress of members of the audience. Theatre companies spent lavishly on splendid costumes, and sometimes acquired them at little cost: a Swiss visitor to London in 1599, Thomas Platter, noted that 'The play-actors are dressed most exquisitely and elegantly, because of the custom in England that when men of rank or knights die they give and bequeath almost their finest apparel to their servants who, since it does not befit them, do not wear such garments, but afterwards let the play-actors buy them for a few pence.'[1] This meant that distinctions of social rank could be indicated visually. It is all too easy to forget, when reading the play—and consequently also when staging it— that, for example, characters baldly referred to as Gloucester and Kent are senior members of the aristocracy, and that this would have meant a great deal to the play's first audiences. Post-Restoration stagings up to and beyond the time of Garrick also used costume of the time of performance; from when Garrick first played the role, in 1756, till early in the nineteenth century, Lear was traditionally costumed in scarlet trimmed with ermine for most of the action, and he is so portrayed in paintings not directly based on theatrical performance.[2]

Many modern directors have sought to emphasize the play's relevance to audiences of today by the use of modern dress—as in Deborah Warner's National Theatre production of 1990—and, sometimes, specifically contemporary settings. Not uncommonly this has resulted in a blurring of social distinctions, and consequently in a diminution of the play's political dimension. In its own time the play would have touched contemporary concerns, political and philosophical, in ways that are difficult to identify precisely but which it has been the endeavour of much historicist criticism to tease out. So for example Leah S. Marcus has probingly

---

[1] Ernest Schanzer, 'Thomas Platter's Observations on the Elizabethan Stage', *N & Q*, NS 3 (1956), 465–7; p. 466.

[2] Foakes, p. 13.

investigated liturgical and political significances that the Quarto text may have held for King James and his court in the performance given, as we know, on St Stephen's Night, 1606—a feast day on which 'the high were to look out in pity on the tribulations of the low' (p. 154). More simplistically, Annabel Patterson has proposed that the audience at that performance 'would quickly have realized that the archaic setting was a ruse to permit analysis of a particular style and ideology of monarchy', regarding the issue of the union of England and Scotland as 'one major form of the topicality in which *King Lear* is saturated', and the bulk of the play as 'a critique of the socioeconomic system of Jacobean England'.[1]

The constitution of the acting company available to Shakespeare inevitably helped to shape the play. *Leir*, it has been estimated, could be acted by a group of eleven men and three boys;[2] by the time Shakespeare came to write *King Lear* companies were larger, and the quarto text of this play requires at least thirteen men (nine playing major roles) and three boys.[3] We know too little about individual actors, but there is no question that Richard Burbage was the company's principal tragedian, and Shakespeare must have had him very much in mind as he wrote. Born in 1568, he was under forty years old when he first played the octogenarian Lear. It is a demanding role, physically as well as mentally, and many of the best performances in later times have been given by actors much younger than the character. Shakespeare was careful too to write challenging and rewarding roles for other members of his company: this is not a one-man play. Gloucester and Kent are strong supporting roles; Edgar provides virtuoso opportunities for a young actor both in his protean shifts of identity and in his reflectiveness when he speaks in his own persona, which can make him

---

[1] *Shakespeare and the Popular Voice* (Oxford, 1989), pp. 106, 107, 108.

[2] McMillin and MacLean, p. 191; David Bradley (*From Text to Performance in the Elizabethan Theatre* (Cambridge, 1992), p. 232), using a slightly different method of calculation, estimates a minimum cast of thirteen or more, with a probable sixteen, including five or six boys.

[3] This is David Bradley's figure (p. 237); he estimates from three to five boys, presumably allowing for the possibility that the Fool and one other role might have been played by a boy. T. J. King's estimate is nine men and three boys, with extras for the minor roles (*Casting Shakespeare's Plays* (Cambridge, 1992), pp. 223–4). In 'Attendants and Others in Shakespeare's Margins: Doubling in the two texts of *King Lear*' (*Theatre Survey*, 32 (1991), 187–213), Skiles Howard finds that the Quarto text 'can be performed throughout without exceeding the number of players [i.e. 14] in the opening scene', and distributes the roles on this basis.

a moral centre of the play;[1] by contrast, Edmund's cheerful amorality suits an actor of strongly defined, virile personality. We do not certainly know which of Shakespeare's actors played other roles than Lear.

The number of female characters is the same as in *Leir*, and so, broadly, are their functions, though the wicked sisters do not actually plot to murder their father, and Cordelia is not as conventionally pious as her forebear. As often, Shakespeare adds to the choric element, especially in the character of the Fool (not required by the plot, as is demonstrated by its omission in the version by Nahum Tate which held the stage from 1681 to 1838), in aspects of the role of Edgar, and in his development of the role of Kent.

The Fool is another dramatic stereotype on which Shakespeare plays highly original variations.[2] The character has antecedents in both life and drama; indeed, Will Sommers, court jester to Henry VIII, is the presenter of Thomas Nashe's pageant-play *Summer's Last Will and Testament*, published in 1600. Many of Sommers's japes are recounted in a lively little book published in 1600 as *Fool upon Fool* (revised in 1608 as *A Nest of Ninnies*), and written by Robert Armin, a comic actor who joined Shakespeare's company in 1599 and for whom Shakespeare may have intended the role of the Fool.[3] This possibility, however, is not compatible with the idea that he meant the Fool and Cordelia to be doubled, since Cordelia must have been played by a boy, and Armin (born around 1568) was in his late thirties when *King Lear* was first performed. W. P. Ringler Jr. argues that Armin is more likely to have played Edgar, partly on the grounds that the Fool is a 'boy',

[1] The complexities of Edgar's role are illuminatingly examined by Michael E. Mooney in '"Edgar I Nothing am": *Figurenposition* in *King Lear*', *SS 38* (1985), 153–66.

[2] The pioneering study is Enid Welsford's *The Fool: His Social and Literary History* (1935, etc.). Later criticism includes R. H. Goldsmith, *Wise Fools in Shakespeare* (East Lancing, Mich., 1955), pp. 60–7, 95–9.

[3] The case for Armin having played the Fool is argued by e.g. Leslie Hotson, *Shakespeare's Motley* (1952), Chapter 7, and C. S. Felver, *Robert Armin, Shakespeare's Fool* (Kent, Ohio, 1961). S. Booth argues for doubling the roles in modern productions, without noting that this would require the Fool to be played by a female (or Cordelia by a male) actor: 'Speculations on Doubling in Shakespeare's Plays', in *Shakespeare: the Theatrical Dimension*, ed. P. C. McGuire and D. A. Samuelson (New York, 1979), pp. 103–31. Armin's writings are reprinted in facsimile in *The Collected Works of Robert Armin*, with introductions by J. P. Feather, 2 vols. (New York, 1992).

and also because Armin appears to have been a master of the kind of multiple impersonations required from the performer of Edgar.[1]

Armin distinguishes between natural fools—half-wits who provide entertainment which is, to a greater or lesser degree, involuntary—and artificial fools: professional entertainers whose simulated folly is part of their act. Shakespeare had already made use of the type figure, most notably in Touchstone in *As You Like It*, and Feste in *Twelfth Night*. The fool characteristically wore a distinctive, multi-coloured patchwork costume, the 'motley' referred to at Scene 4.139, along with a coxcomb, and carried a bauble—a stick with a carved head, sometimes with a bladder on the end with which he belaboured the victims of his wit, and which often assumes phallic significance.[2] Court fools had special privileges; as the Duke says of Touchstone, 'He uses his folly like a stalking-horse, and under the presentation of that he shoots his wit' (*As You Like It* 5.4.104–5). But they were also vulnerable to punishment if they went too far in criticism of their betters. Once, we are told, Cardinal Wolsey threatened Will 'A rod in the school | And a whip for a fool | Are always in season'; so Lear will warn 'Take heed, sirrah—the whip' (4.104), and may threaten him with one, as Wolfit did.[3]

The character type was valuable particularly because it could serve a quasi-choric function while remaining within the framework of the action. It can speak for the author or, more subtly, express a dissentient point of view which increases the complexity of the portrayal. The fool can act as a kind of safety-valve for the audience, expressing their feelings and mediating between them and the action. Being classless, he can move easily between one set of characters and another. And as an entertainer, he can amuse the audience in the theatre as well as those on stage. His characteristic behaviour was vividly described by Thomas Lodge in his book *Wit's Misery*, of 1596: 'give him a little wine in his head, he is continually flearing and making of mouths; he laughs intemperately

[1] Ogden and Scouten, pp. 129–32.

[2] Whereas Leslie Hotson considered that Lear's Fool 'belonged to the contemporary scene' (*Shakespeare's Motley* (1952), p. 100), David Wiles (p. 190) regards Shakespeare's use of the traditional fool's appurtenances as deliberately historicizing; 'Lear's fool belongs to a vanished world, and not to the social reality of 1605'.

[3] Donald Wolfit's performance is reconstructed by Ronald Harwood in his *Sir Donald Wolfit: His Life and Work in the Unfashionable Theatre* (1971), pp. 160–4; repr. in Wells, *Theatre*, pp. 224–30.

at every little occasion, and dances about the house, leaps over tables, outskips men's heads, trips up his companions' heels, burns sack with a candle, and hath all the feats of a lord of misrule in the country . . . it is a special mark of him at the table, he sits and makes faces.'[1] But Lear's Fool has cause to be more melancholy; and we are told that he has 'much pined away' even before we see him.

Court and domestic fools died out in the later part of the seventeenth century, and the absence of an obvious social counterpart in later ages has caused difficulty in representing Lear's Fool—which may be why Tate omitted him. In 1838, when Macready (at the last minute) ventured to restore the role, it was played by a woman, Priscilla Horton, a practice which has recurred, reflecting the asexuality of the role (at least in Macready's shortened text). He has no personal name. He is a function as much as a character, and so peculiarly liable to openness of interpretation. Lear often addresses him as 'boy' (and once as 'lad'), and if, as has been conjectured, he was originally doubled with Cordelia, he would have been played by a boy in Shakespeare's company. But the form of address could be a remnant of a long-standing relationship, validating the common practice of playing him as a man of Lear's generation. Directors have often brought the Fool on stage in the opening scene as a silent partner to his master; but this detracts from the dramatic and symbolic impact of his entry after Lear has repeatedly called for him in Scene 4. His role as entertainer has been recognized by costuming him as a circus clown[2] or a broken-down old comedian.[3]

Actors are apt to compare the Fool to a pet monkey—hyperactive, attached to its master but chatteringly irreverent both to him and to those around him. So in an anecdote whose truth may be metaphorical rather than literal, Rosenberg reports that Michael Williams, in Trevor Nunn's 1968 production, saw the Fool's loyalty to Lear 'as almost instinctive, animal-like. He decided to choose a monkey for his model, and was studying the monkey

---

[1] Quoted by Shickman, p. 76.

[2] e.g. Ottavia Piccolo (another woman) in Giorgio Strehler's 1972 Italian production (discussed by Pia Kleber in *Foreign Shakespeare*, ed. D. Kennedy (Cambridge, 1993), pp. 152–3), and Antony Sher in Adrian Noble's 1982 RSC production.

[3] e.g. Michael Williams in Trevor Nunn's RSC production of 1976.

5. Ian Talbot (who took over from Antony Sher) as the Fool in Adrian Noble's RSC production, 1982.

house at the zoo, when he saw a familiar figure in front of him—Alex Clunes [*in error for* Alec McCowen], Scofield's stage Fool. Clunes [*sic*] pointed to a monkey at the top of the house and said, "That was mine."' (Rosenberg, p. 109.) Similarly Antony Sher, whose essay on playing the Fool to Michael Gambon's Lear in Adrian Noble's 1982 RSC production is an illuminating study of the role from the actor's point of view, declares that in rehearsal the director 'asked each of the actors involved to find an animal to play, in order to release the savagery and wildness of the situation. I chose a chimpanzee, chattering and clapping hands, hurling myself around in forward rolls, and found this very liberating for the role. That weekend I hurried to London Zoo to watch the chimps and became even more convinced that they had all the requisite qualities for the Fool—manic comic energy when in action, a disturbing sadness when in repose. A delightful coincidence that day at the zoo was rounding a corner to discover that Michael Gambon was also there, presumably also in search of his character, leaning against the plate-glass of the gorillas' cage, man and beast locked in solemn contemplation of one another.'[1]

Shakespeare's addition to the Lear story of the parallel story of Gloucester and his two sons—largely of his own invention in spite of having its origins in Sidney—is in part a response to the need, 'On a stage where the progress of the story is advanced by the momentary clearing of the stage and where continuous playing is the rule',[2] for the dramatist to provide more than one set of characters. But as usual Shakespeare made artistic capital out of practical necessity: the addition adds to both the implicit and the explicit commentary on the Lear story. This is his only tragedy to have a fully developed plot parallel to that of the main action: he juxtaposes the story of a man who is driven mad with that of one who has his eyes torn out. It seems misleading to refer to the Gloucester story as a subplot, or underplot, because it adds to the Lear story, with which it soon becomes inextricably intertwined, rather than simply supports it. Parallels of situation are clear, but there are also differences which extend the play's range of reference.[3]

Both Lear and Gloucester are men of power, but Lear's royalty means that his fate has dynastic implications, whereas Gloucester's remains on a more domestic level. Lear has two hypocritical, self-seeking, rationalist daughters and a virtuous one; the superstitious Gloucester has one hypocritical, self-seeking, rationalist son and a virtuous one. Gloucester, as we learn at the very beginning of the play, has transgressed sexually; both his younger son and Lear's elder daughters seek to do so, with each other, in the course of the action. Lear too displays faults of character—irascibility, self-centredness, blatantly false judgement ('Come, noble Burgundy')—on his first appearance. During the course of the action, Lear's elder daughters and Gloucester's younger son will turn against both their fathers and their siblings, and will pay for it

---

[1] A. Sher, 'The Fool in *King Lear*', in *Players of Shakespeare 2: Further Essays in Shakespearean Performance by Players with the Royal Shakespeare Company*, ed. R. Jackson and R. Smallwood (Cambridge, 1988), pp. 151–66; pp. 154–5.

[2] D. Bradley, work cited in p. 38, n. 2, p. 34.

[3] D. Bradley states 'It is really a misnomer . . . to speak of "sub-plots" or "double-plots" in Elizabethan plays', pointing to 'the Gloucester family . . . whose history is fully explored and whose life-lines are interwoven, both in actuality and in the tightest thematic way, with those of the main characters' (p. 35).

6. David Bradley as Gloucester and Robert Stephens as Lear in Adrian Noble's RSC production, 1993.

with their deaths. Lear's youngest daughter and Gloucester's elder son, on the other hand, will remain loyal to their parents, and take offensive action on their behalves in the play's closing episodes. Whereas Cordelia, banished, is absent for much of the action, Edgar, disguised, is able to set his virtue to work on behalf of Lear as well as his own father. He will survive, but Cordelia will die a cruel and unmerited death. Both Gloucester and Lear will undergo great suffering, but Lear's is primarily of the mind, Gloucester's of the body.

Lear's madness is one of Shakespeare's additions to the story, heightened and complicated by Edgar's impersonation of a serv-ingman, possessed by devils, 'whose sexual conquest of his mis-tress has made him run mad',[1] and also by the 'natural' folly of the Fool. As in *Hamlet* the hero's feigned madness sets off and gives

---

[1] Duncan Salkeld, *Madness and Drama in the Age of Shakespeare* (Manchester, 1993), p. 103.

reality to the actual madness of Ophelia, so the manifest if skilful 'daubings' of Edgar counterpoint and heighten the pathos and credibility of Lear's loss of reason.[1] But Hamlet contains both the feigned madman and the fool within himself; in Lear, their polarization increases the emphasis on 'reason in madness' (20.164). By causing Lear to go mad, Shakespeare greatly extends the character's emotional range (and therefore his theatrical power); in his madness the King challenges not only his court and family but the universe around him. But madness also enhances the intellectual and political range of the play in the opportunities it affords for satire. Before Lear goes mad, the Fool satirizes him in snatches of verse and song that have a more than local resonance. The Fool leaves the play after Lear is sent to seek 'welcome and protection' (13.85) at Dover, but then Lear subsumes the Fool's role within himself, directing against others, and against society in general—especially in his scene (Sc. 20) with the blind Gloucester—the kind of satire that the Fool had directed against him.

Lear's climactic expression of mental suffering comes as the elemental tempest beats around him, and he declares

> This tempest in my mind
> Doth from my senses take all feeling else
> Save what beats there: filial ingratitude.
> (11.12–14)

But the suffering diminishes when madness comes upon him. As Gloucester is to realize later in the play, madness can bring relief from suffering:[2]

> Better I were distraught;
> So should my thoughts be fencèd from my griefs,
> And woes by wrong imaginations lose
> The knowledge of themselves.

(20.273–6)

[1] Howard Felperin writes 'Edgar's "madness", as a role based upon a wholly traditional and external view of madness as demonic possession, is actually the antithesis of the true madness of Lear, since the latter arises from the breakdown of roles whereas the former is itself a role and therefore a protection against a maddening overperception' (*Shakespearean Representation: Mimesis and Modernity in Elizabethan Tragedy* (Princeton, 1977), p. 101).

[2] Felperin takes a contrary view: Gloucester 'naïvely wishes he could go mad like Lear, mistaking madness for a protection against pain when it is in fact an exposure to it' (p. 101).

The climax of Gloucester's physical suffering comes later than Lear's, with his blinding—'All dark and comfortless' (14.83)— and he too is made horribly aware of 'filial ingratitude' when, as he calls upon Edmund to take revenge, Regan enlightens him that it is Edmund who betrayed him. Suffering teaches both men how they have misvalued their offspring, and leads them to acknowledge their own faults and to express humility. Finally, each will die, both reconciled to their virtuous children: Gloucester, off stage, happy in Edgar's love; Lear, before our eyes, grieving over the body of his dead daughter.

Although the plot of *King Lear* is intricately woven, it is nevertheless open enough to admit the inclusion of speeches and episodes which, inessential to the story line, add to and illuminate its system of ideas. Prominent among these are much of the Fool's role, including the bulk of the scene (Sc. 5) in which Lear first experiences intimations of madness; Lear's mock-trial of Gonoril and Regan (13.31–75); Edgar's moralizing speech at the end of Scene 13 ('When we our betters see bearing our woes . . .'); the scene (Sc. 17) in which we hear of Cordelia's reaction to her father's plight;[1] and, most conspicuously, the encounter between mad Lear and blind Gloucester (Sc. 20). Some of these episodes are absent from the Folio text, but all throw light on the ideas provoked in Shakespeare's mind as he first wrote the story of King Lear and the Earl of Gloucester.

In refashioning this story Shakespeare was influenced by contemporary notions of dramatic genre, but by no means in thrall to them. The entry of the play in the Stationers' Register refers to it as a 'history', and the title-page of the Quarto calls it a 'true chronicle history'; I adopt this title for convenience, to distinguish it from the text printed among the tragedies in the Folio, but there is no doubt that from the start Shakespeare was determined to reshape his chronicle sources into tragic form. This was, however, a fluid concept. It permitted the inclusion of comedy and satire, associated especially with the roles of the Fool, Edgar as Tom o'Bedlam, Kent in his brusqueness, and Oswald as the butt of Kent's scorn.[2] It

---

[1] Described by Granville Barker as, 'as far as the mere march of the action is concerned', a 'wholly unjustifiable scene' (p. 275).

[2] The seminal study is G. Wilson Knight's essay '*King Lear* and the Comedy of the Grotesque', in *The Wheel of Fire* (1930), pp. 160–76. Susan Snyder develops the theme in *The Comic Matrix of Shakespeare's Tragedies* (Princeton, 1979), pp. 137–79.

permitted too a development of the narrative that links it to the romance tradition.[1] Although Shakespeare's protagonist undergoes suffering far greater than that portrayed in the old play, there is a point of the action at which it seems possible that his play, like *King Leir*, will end as a tragicomedy, concluding with what Nahum Tate was to call 'a success to the innocent distressed persons'. Rescued by the forces of Cordelia, now Queen of France, Lear is restored at once to sanity and to the love of the daughter whom he had banished.[2] The scene of their reunion and mutual forgiveness links this most tragic of plays to the comic tradition, to the reunion of the living with the supposedly dead—fathers and daughters, brothers and sisters, husbands and wives—in plays from each stage of Shakespeare's career, ranging from *The Comedy of Errors* to *The Tempest*. In all those plays one of the relatives believes that the other has come back from the dead; Lear, however, believes that he himself has been resurrected, and regrets it: 'You do me wrong to take me out o'th' grave . . .' (21.43). (It is not clear whether at this point Lear believes that he has been brought back to life on earth, or that, somehow, his dead body has been taken out of the grave and made sentient even though his soul is 'bound upon a wheel of fire'.)

Any sense of a happy ending that this episode may create is rapidly dispelled. The play's closing stages present a sequence of events in which the slow struggle towards success of the political and military movement headed by Cordelia, Albany, and Edgar suffers repeated setbacks as a result of a series of hammer blows directed against those on whose behalf they are fighting. The disguised Edgar's delivery of a challenge to Albany (22.42–52) raises hope, but then Edmund declares that Lear and Cordelia 'shall never see [Albany's] pardon'. After the oddly stylized and foreshortened off-stage battle (23.0–5) we hear that 'King Lear

[1] Reibetanz writes suggestively on the play's links with romance (article cited in p. 25 n. 3, pp. 116–17).

[2] Shakespeare leaves vague Cordelia's motives for her return to England and its place in the play's time scheme. R. Knowles discusses the topic in 'Cordelia's Return' (*SQ* 51 (1999), 33–50), arguing for deliberate indeterminacy 'carefully calculated so as not to raise questions in the audiences' minds about the event's verisimilitude while allowing for maximum dramatic effect, particularly in preserving the integrity and intensity of Lear's madness and in propelling the action to its denouement' (p. 50).

hath lost' and has been taken prisoner along with Cordelia. Lear's vision of a timeless life with Cordelia in which they will take upon themselves 'the mystery of things' as if they were God's spies is immediately followed by Edmund's sinister instructions to the Captain to 'follow them to prison' on a 'great employment' which 'Will not bear question'.

The outlook for those engaged in the countermovement brightens with Albany's arrest of Edmund and Gonoril, his challenge to Edmund and Edmund's counter-challenge, followed by the disguised Edgar's successful fight against his brother, though the scene is darkened again by Edgar's narrative of their father's death and of Kent's grief, so strong that 'the strings of life | Began to crack'. Edmund shows signs of relenting—'This speech of yours hath moved me, | And shall perchance do good'—and although the appearance of a Gentleman 'with a bloody knife' may arouse fears for Lear and Cordelia, it emerges that Regan has stabbed herself and poisoned Gonoril, and their bodies are brought on stage. Edmund's determination to do good in spite of his own nature raises hope that it may not be too late to save Lear and Cordelia, but hope is shattered by Lear's entry bearing his youngest daughter's body. The stage picture here creates a grim echo of the opening scene. There, Lear on his throne had been flanked by his three daughters. Now, as Granville Barker pointed out, 'The same company are here, or all but the same, and they await his pleasure. Even Regan and Goneril are here to pay him a ghastly homage. But he knows none of them—save for a blurred moment Kent whom he banished—none but Cordelia' (pp. 277–8). The structural echo can be reinforced by stage patterning, as it was in Nicholas Hytner's 1990 RSC production when the placing of stage furniture for the sisters in the opening scene was echoed in both the mock trial and the final scene. News of Edmund's death completes the annihilation of the anti-Lear party, and we are given cause to think that the play may still be going to end with Lear at least alive, as Albany resigns the kingdom to him, promises honour to Edgar and Kent, and seems to be wrapping the play neatly up with an assignment of poetic justice.

> All friends shall taste
> The wages of their virtue, and all foes
> The cup of their deservings.

But he has not rhymed.[1] Something happens to draw attention to Lear—'O see, see!'—and the play achieves its tragic consummation with his death. Only then are we ready for the couplets in which Albany reassigns rule to Kent and Edgar, Kent declares that he too is ready to die, and Albany speaks a subdued epitaph.

The Play's Language

The use of rhymed couplets to close a play is conventional. Shakespeare was indebted to convention, but not subservient to it, for the language of his play. The old play of *King Leir* is typical of its time in its mingling of verse for the high characters with prose for the low—messengers and watchmen, for instance. This convention underlies, but does not determine, Shakespeare's practice. As in almost all plays of the period, blank verse is his norm, and he handles it with the flexibility that characterizes his use of the medium in his later work. To give but one example, the sonorous formality of Lear's opening speech (1.36–48) is very different from the fractured suspensions of 'O, reason not the need! . . .' (7.422–44). And although, when recollected from a distance, the play may give the impression of being written in a relatively uniform, generally austere style, when more closely examined it reveals a wide range of verbal registers and a remarkable degree of stylistic self-consciousness. With a virtuosity deriving from long experience, Shakespeare varies the blank verse as occasion arises with rhymed couplets—sometimes to define exits and scene endings—a variety of lyric measures and octosyllabics for the Fool's homilies and snatches of song, and prose.[2]

The play's linguistic artifice is not entirely unselfconscious. Although the playwright's art lies partly in the success with which he conceals art so as to create the impression of spontaneous utterance, at times he causes characters to express awareness of the manipulative and affective powers of what they say and of the way they say it. In the opening scene, Gonoril and Regan find themselves in the position of the playwright in being required to

[1] Almost all Shakespeare's plays end with a rhymed couplet, followed in *Hamlet*, *Timon*, *Coriolanus*, and *2 Henry IV* by a half-line of command or interrogation, and occasionally by a rhymed song or a prose epilogue. The exceptions are *Two Gentlemen*, *1 Henry VI*, *LLL*, *Much Ado*, and *Winter's Tale*.

[2] Vickers, *Prose*, pp. 351–71, offers a fine study of the play's use of prose.

articulate emotions that they do not feel. Shakespeare causes them to speak in a self-conscious, hyperbolical style, creating set speeches which give the impression of having been thought out in advance and which are delivered as on-stage performances—as may be emphasized by the manner of their delivery and by formality of staging. He directs the audience's attention to their falsity through Cordelia's asides and her explicit criticism of her sisters' 'glib and oily art'. As a result, Cordelia's relative inarticulacy may acquire its own kind of eloquence, making us 'imagine that she feels much more than she says'.[1] Kent is proud of his ability to 'deliver a plain message bluntly' (4.31), while Cornwall accuses him of affecting 'A saucy roughness' (7.92), whereupon Kent deliberately goes 'out of his dialect' to speak in high-flown terms. The blind Gloucester is defensively aware of Edgar's improvement in 'phrase and matter' even though Edgar suggests that his father's other senses may have grown 'imperfect | By [his] eyes' anguish' (20.5–8), Edmund recognizes that his disguised brother's 'tongue some say of breeding breathes' (24.140), and the end of the play returns to its beginning as Albany declares we should 'Speak what we feel, not what we ought to say.'

Unlike people in real life, he says so in verse, not in prose. Nevertheless, roughly 25 per cent of the play is written in prose.[2] Its use may be determined by situation as much as character. The courtly prose spoken at the play's opening by the aristocratic Gloucester and Kent heightens the formality of Lear's first utterances, establishing the verse rhetoric of his opening speech as a norm, and the return of prose in the scene's closing dialogue between Gonoril and Regan is both appropriate to their cold rationality and rounds off the scene with aesthetically pleasing shapeliness. Prose occurs frequently in scenes where the emotional temperature is relatively low, such as the exposition of the Gloucester plot (Sc. 2), and in the rough comedy of Lear's conversation with the disguised Kent (Sc. 4) and the baiting of Oswald (Sc. 4 and 7). It can help to convey the pathos of inarticulacy, as when Lear first embarks on the process of self-examination in the presence of the Fool:

---

[1] Marianne L. Novy, *Love's Argument* (cited in p. 26 n. 1), p. 154.

[2] Vickers, *Prose*, table on p. 433, based on Alfred Hart, 'The Number of Lines in Shakespeare's plays', *RES* 8 (1932), 19–28.

FOOL . . . Thou canst not tell why one's nose stands in the middle of his face?

LEAR No.

FOOL Why, to keep his eyes on either side's nose, that what a man cannot smell out, a may spy into.

LEAR I did her wrong.   (5. 19–24)

Here, emotion exists between rather than in the lines; silences are as expressive as speech. In this scene, departing from the standard conventions of poetic drama, Shakespeare creates a dialogue of non-communication anticipative of the methods of Beckett or Pinter in its approach to psychological realism, a dialogue as concerned with failure of communication as with the direct expression of meaning or emotion. Edgar's prose as he adopts the roles of Poor Tom and, later, the 'bold peasant' with a rustic accent whom Oswald makes the mistake of challenging (20.223–42), helps Edgar to assume a linguistic as well as a physical disguise.[1]

Prose marks Lear's increasing understanding of common humanity:

Is man no more but this? Consider him well. Thou owest the worm no silk, the beast no hide, the sheep no wool, the cat no perfume. Here's three on 's are sophisticated; thou art the thing itself. Unaccommodated man is no more but such a poor, bare, forked animal as thou art. (11.92–7)

It charts his descent into madness, but also points the poignancy of his resumption of verse as he recalls his lost kingly dignity: 'When I do stare, see how the subject quakes!' (20.106). The mixing of prose with verse helps to maintain dramatic impetus as the action develops, but it is unsuited to the relentless intensity of the closing scenes; from the episode of Lear's reunion with Cordelia to the end, only the Herald's challenge (24.109–13) is in prose.

Both the prose and the verse of the play are underpinned by the rigorous training in rhetoric that Shakespeare must have received at school, but his method of using it is a far cry from the patterned formality apparent in earlier plays such as *Richard III* and *A Midsummer Night's Dream*. Paradoxically, *King Lear*—a play that revels in paradox[2]—is at one and the same time both the most and

---

[1] Vickers, p. 352.

[2] Rosalie L. Colie writes on paradoxes in *King Lear* in her *Pseudodoxica Academica* (Princeton, 1966), pp. 461–81. Brian Vickers offers a critical investigation of

the least poetical of Shakespeare's tragedies. Remarking that 'one reason why *King Lear* has been mistaken for an unactable play is that it is so nearly an unreadable play', Winifred Nowottny noted the absence of 'poetry that survives quotation out of context'.[1] The passage that might most be thought to do so, the Gentleman's description of Cordelia's reaction to news of her father's plight beginning 'You have seen | Sunshine and rain at once . . .' (17.18–19), forms part of the entire scene omitted in the Folio text, as if it were considered an indulgence. The absence of 'beauties' is a measure of the subordination of poetic to dramatic effect.

The same critic also wrote 'the play is inexhaustibly patterned',[2] and the patterning of its language forms a nervous system for the play, linking all its parts into a single intercommunicating organism.[3] In this sense the play is pure poetry, but poetry in which language, action, stage effect, and even silence[4] are inextricably interwoven. The essentially dramatic nature of the language is apparent in the way that verbal and visual images interact. So, for example, the intricate patternings of imagery of sight initiated by Gonoril's claim that she loves Lear 'dearer than eyesight' emerge into the action with the blinding of Gloucester when he is not merely deprived of eyesight but has his eyes torn out and cast upon the stage; the play's concern with justice and punishment is emblematized in the stage property of the stocks in which Kent is confined; and its implicit investigation of what it is to be a man is conducted partly through a multiple series of allusions to animals, from Lear's comparison of himself to a dragon (1.113) to his posing

Shakespeare's reading in collections of paradoxes in '*King Lear* and Renaissance Paradoxes', *MLR* 63 (1968), 305–14.

[1] Winifred M. T. Nowottny, 'Some Aspects of the Style of *King Lear*', *SS 13* (1960), 49–57.

[2] 'Lear's Questions', *SS 10* (1957), 90–7; p. 90.

[3] Use on the text of a computer search facility brings home the fact that many words are repeated throughout; so for example 'father' occurs 78 times in the dialogue, 'man' and 'men' 73 (and 'gentleman' 8), 'see' and its cognates 68, 'love' 65, 'king' 64, 'speak' 63, 'eye' 56, 'fool' and 'folly' 56, 'daughter' 55, 'nature', 'natural' and 'unnatural' 48, ' old' 46, 'night' and 'tonight' 39, ' nothing' 27, 'lady' 23, 'fiend' 21, 'wise' and 'wisdom' 19, 'feel' 17, 'wind' 15, 'dog' 13, 'rain' 10, and 'thunder' 9.

[4] Jill Levenson writes on silence in the play in 'What the Silence Said: Still Points in *King Lear*', in *Shakespeare 1971: Proceedings of the World Shakespeare Congress in Vancouver, August 1971*, ed. C. Leech and J. M. R. Margeson (Toronto, 1972), pp. 215–29.

over Cordelia's body of the unanswerable question 'Why should a dog, a horse, a rat have life, | And thou no breath at all?' (24.301–2).

To its early audiences, the language of *King Lear* must have seemed very strange, as original in its day as that of James Joyce or Dylan Thomas in theirs. The commentary to this edition notes over a hundred words or compounds which either represent or predate *OED*'s first recorded use (absolutely or in this sense), and though this is not entirely reliable it gives some idea of the innovativeness of the play's vocabulary. There are also many rare words and expressions, some literary, others deriving from specialist vocabularies that defeat scholarly investigation. The language constantly strains meaning beyond its normal limits. Margreta de Grazia notes its 'inclination to superfluity', its use of 'superlatives and super-superlatives' and 'pejor-pejoratives', and links this with the way 'the play itself goes to extremes, pushing beyond the bounds of tragedy, particularly in its superfluous addition of Cordelia's death'.[1] Frequently, too, syntax is strained to the point of contortion, and (even allowing for textual problems) characters express themselves so cryptically that they risk becoming incomprehensible. This is germane to the dramatic purpose in, especially, many of the Fool's oracular rhymes and songs in which he tries obliquely to convey harsh truths, and also in the calculated dissociations of Edgar's assumed and Lear's real madness. Sometimes too it helps movingly to convey the difficulty that characters themselves experience in expressing themselves. But it seems almost wanton when, for example, Gonoril says of her sister

> But being widow, and my Gloucester with her,
> May all the building on my fancy pluck
> Upon my hateful life   (16.83–5)

or when she warns Lear that unless he is careful

>   the fault
> Would not scape censure, nor the redress sleep
> Which in the tender of a wholesome weal
> Might in their working do you that offence,

---

[1] 'The Ideology of Superfluous Things; *King Lear* as Period Piece', in *Subject and Object in Renaissance Culture*, ed. M. de Grazia *et al*. (Cambridge, 1996), 17–42; reprinted in *Shakespeare's Tragedies*, ed. S. Zimmerman, New Casebooks (1998), 255–84; p. 282.

7. 'Bound upon a wheel of fire': from Giovanni Ferro, *Teatro d'imprese*
(Venice, 1623).

> That else were shame, that then necessity
> Must call discreet proceedings.
>
> (4.200–6)

It is almost as if she wished to provide food for commentators.

To say all this, however, is not to deny that the language of the
play can rise to incomparable heights of calculated eloquence in
both verse and prose, or indeed that it may at times speak with a
sublime simplicity that seems all the more powerful for the knotted
tortuosities that have gone before. Both qualities are supremely
present in the scene of the reunion between Lear and Cordelia. We
had last seen Lear as, in his madness, he ran to escape capture with
the words 'Nay, an you get it, you shall get it with running'
(20.191–2). After the grotesquery of that exit, his dignity is re-
established with a cosmic image linking earth, heaven, and hell,
fusing the Christian belief in resurrection of the body with classical
mythology (in its recollection of Ixion):

LEAR

> You do me wrong to take me out o'th' grave.
> Thou art a soul in bliss, but I am bound
> Upon a wheel of fire, that mine own tears
> Do scald like molten lead.
>
> (21.43–6)

Vast in imaginative scope and elevated in poetic tone though these lines are, they are plain in diction and contain only two words of more than one syllable. This simplicity is sustained throughout the episode that follows. It contains little overt expression of feeling. It is written in verse, but many of the phrases that have proved most moving in performance are so far from being consciously 'poetic' that we ourselves might use them in everyday conversation with no feeling that we were being literary: such phrases as 'I feel this pin prick', 'You must not kneel', 'Do not laugh at me', 'I know you do not love me', even 'You must bear with me'. Though Cordelia says little during the episode, her actions and reactions as she kneels to her father, begs his blessing, weeps, and denies that she has had cause to do Lear wrong, demand from the performer an eloquent if often silent depiction of a highly emotional state, and do much to direct the audience's reactions. They are part of the performative poetry of the scene. A comparison of this scene with the parallel one in the play of *King Leir* provides an object lesson in the superiority of Shakespeare's artistry.

The intellect and imagination of Shakespeare's audience are challenged not only by the language but also by the inventive audacity with which he laid out his plot material. Some episodes, such as Lear's mock-trial of his absent daughters, Gloucester's leap from a cliff that exists only in Edgar's brilliant word-painting, and the conversation between the mad King and the blind Gloucester—often seen in recent times as an anticipation of Beckett[1]—are bizarre in their surreality. Violence was common in the theatres of Shakespeare's time, but the blinding of Gloucester followed by the stabbing of Cornwall exceeds in horror even the more sensational brutalities of *Titus Andronicus* because of the sophisticated craftsmanship with which Shakespeare leads up to and away from the blinding itself.[2] Readers and audiences have often found the scene too painful to bear; it was omitted in some nineteenth-century performances, including Irving's,[3] and even in our own time Jonathan Miller—like Garrick before him—had it played off stage.[4]

---

[1] Notably by Jan Kott in *Shakespeare our Contemporary* (1964), '*King Lear* or *Endgame*', pp. 101–37.

[2] I discuss this and similar episodes in 'The Integration of Violent Action in *Titus Andronicus*', in *Shakespearean Continuities: Essays in Honour of E. A. J. Honigmann*, ed. J. Batchelor, T. Cain, and C. Lamont (1997), pp. 206–37.

[3] Halstead, xiii. 486.

[4] At the Old Vic in 1989, discussed in S. Wells, 'Shakespeare Production in England in 1989', *SS 43* (1991), pp. 188–9.

Early Performance

The mock-trial (13.16–51) is not present in the Folio text. Perhaps
Burbage himself found it too much of a challenge in its treading of
the knife-edge between pathos and absurdity; or perhaps its early
audiences could not measure up to it. We know little about the reception of the play in Shakespeare's time. The fact that it was performed at court indicates at least initial success, and an epitaph on
Burbage, who died in 1619, lists 'kind Lear' among his finest roles.[1]
The prominence accorded to the role of Edgar on the title-page of
the Quarto may mean that the actor of this virtuoso role scored a
hit. A provincial touring company of recusant actors performed a
number of plays, including 'Perocles prince of Tire' and 'king
Lere', in 1610 at Gowthwaite Hall, in Yorkshire. It is of interest
that they worked from printed copies, not manuscripts. Repeatedly since C. J. Sisson drew attention to the court case in which
they were involved it has been stated that they played Shakespeare's *King Lear*, but this is not certain; the old play was also
available in print.[2] Before long, however, a version of Shakespeare's play was acted in Germany: a company of English actors
playing in Dresden in 1626 acted among other plays with Shakespearian connections 'Tragoedia von Lear, König in Engelandt'.
Identification of the play as a tragedy indicates that it was based on
Shakespeare.[3]

There is also an early offshoot of the play—the first of its many
subsequent adaptations into media other than that for which it
was composed—which, though modern editors ignore it, is of

---

[1] Cited in C. M. Ingleby *et al.*, *The Shakspere Allusion-Book*, revised version,
2 vols. (Oxford, 1932), p. 272.

[2] Sisson mentions the case briefly in his *Lost Plays of Shakespeare's Age* (Cambridge, 1936), p. 4, and discusses it at greater length in 'Shakespeare Quartos as
Prompt-copies', *RES* 18 (1942), 129–43. Sisson writes 'There is no good reason for
suspecting that it might have been the old Chronicle History of *King Leir*', but produces no real arguments on either side of the question. Among those who similarly
assume that the play was Shakespeare's are Muir (p. xl), Foakes (p. 90) and Halio
(F, p. 34) in their editions, and Barbara Mowat in her fine essay 'The Theater and
Literary Culture', in *A New History of Early English Drama*, ed. J. D. Cox and D. S.
Kastan (New York, 1997), pp. 213–48. It is true that a comic actor, William Harrison, said in evidence that he had played the clown's, or fool's, part in both *Pericles*
and the *Lear* play, but this might apply as well to the role of Mumford in *Leir* as to the
Fool in *Lear*.

[3] Albert Cohn, *Shakespeare in Germany in the Sixteenth and Seventeenth Centuries*
(1865), p. cxvi.

interest for more than one reason. This is the ballad 'A Lamentable Song of the Death of King Lear and his Three Daughters' (reprinted with commentary on pp. 277–85). Though the first known printing is in a volume dated 1620, it was probably composed well before that date. By its very existence the ballad tells us that the play was popular enough to generate a song likely to have been sung in the streets of London. Like many later offshoots, it compounds elements from the play with material drawn from elsewhere. In its descriptions of Lear in his madness and his death over Cordelia's body it gives us what may well be unique eyewitness impressions of moments from the play as performed by Shakespeare's company.

The fact that Shakespeare took the trouble to revise his play suggests both that he was not entirely satisfied with it in its original form, and that it nevertheless continued in the repertoire—a fact which surely indicates that the original Globe audiences were capable of a profundity of response with which they are not always credited. There are, however, far fewer early allusions to *King Lear* than to, say, *Hamlet* or *Othello*.[1] It seems likely that the play's challenges were too great to win easy popularity for it in its own time.

'*King Lear*' as a Text for Readers

At the opening of this Introduction I referred briefly to the continuing, and growing, impact that Shakespeare's text has exerted through the centuries. Any text operates by virtue of latent energies released as the result of a process of interaction between the words on the page and people who read them. With plays, these energies are most properly mediated through performance—and even actors have to read the text before they can perform it. Nevertheless, Shakespeare was writing in a period which was exceptional in that much of the finest verse and prose was composed for the theatre, and as a result his plays, like those of his contemporaries, have continued to offer much to readers as well as to playgoers. John Keats, one of Shakespeare's best readers, described the experience as purgatorial in lines that reflect a common response:

[1] *The Shakspere Allusion-Book*—admittedly imperfect—lists only four allusions before 1640. Echoes of *Lear*—whether derived from text or performance—in the anonymous, manuscript play *Tom o' Lincoln* (*c.*1611; Oxford, Malone Society Reprints, 1992), known only since 1973, bear witness to the contemporary impact of Lear's sufferings.

> Once again, the fierce dispute
> Betwixt damnation and impassioned clay
> Must I burn through; once more humbly assay
> The bitter-sweet of this Shakespearean fruit.[1]

For Keats, as for many others, the play induces humility, offering an experience almost too intense to bear. A vast body of scholarly and critical literature, too, is based either entirely or mainly on reading experience.

The tools of scholarship and of criticism are constantly changing. Critics have analysed the play's structure, its techniques of characterization, its dramaturgy, its imagery and symbolism, and its other verbal techniques. They have worried over the ethical and moral issues that it raises, its relation to systems of thought in its own and later times, the social and philosophical resonances it may have evoked in contemporary audiences, and that it continues to evoke today; and they have endlessly, sometimes heatedly, discussed whether it is open to Christian interpretation. They have applied to it the techniques of formalist, structuralist, deconstructionist, historicist, New Historicist, feminist, humanist, Marxist, and many other types of criticism. They have investigated the play's performance history, criticized its critical history, charted its fluctuating popularity and influence, and considered its effect on both readers and audiences whether performed in 'authentic' or adapted texts, in English or in translation. All this bears witness to the richness and density of Shakespeare's text, and to the force of its impact over the centuries, not only on those who regard it as one of the landmarks of Western civilization, but even on those who have found it technically faulty and ideologically distasteful. An attempt to summarize even the principal writings about *King Lear* would inevitably be superficial; some are cited elsewhere in this Introduction. Guides to criticism, and anthologies, frequently appear, and some of the landmarks are listed on pp. 286–90.

Performance always, and obviously, belongs to its present. Though criticism may seek to create the impression that it reaches back to objective truths, it too belongs to the time in which it is

[1] 'On Sitting Down to Read *King Lear* Once Again' (1818). Keats's letters, too, bear witness to the profundity of his response to the play. The significance of his sonnet in relation to his development as a poet is discussed in R. S. White's *Keats as a Reader of Shakespeare* (1987), pp. 23–30. A broader study is D. G. James's 'Keats and *King Lear*', *SS* 13 (1960), 58–68.

written. It is inescapably subjective, reflective of the personality of the writer, the intellectual and social preoccupations of the age that gives rise to it, governed by its own rules and conventions. Though it proceeds through intellectual analysis, it often aspires to the condition of art, and much criticism of *King Lear* especially tries to convey something of the emotional impact the play has had upon the writer. In the hands of writers such as Charles Lamb, A. C. Bradley, Wilson Knight, Stephen Greenblatt and many others, criticism achieves its own kind of literary distinction, irrespective of the validity of its arguments.

As will be clear from the discussion of the text (pp. 3–9), however, what people read as *King Lear* has been far from constant over the centuries. Even those editions which aim to present the play in its purity vary according to editorial theory and practice, so that for example Malone's edition of 1790 makes different choices in its selection of variant readings and its emendations from Craig's of 1901 or Kenneth Muir's of 1952, and more recently Quarto and Folio have been disentangled. In addition, some aspects of the text lie within the domain of the editor in ways that impact on the nature of the reading experience. In its first printing the text was presented continuously, with none of the divisions into acts and scenes that were added in the Folio, let alone the indications of locality introduced first by eighteenth-century editors. Editions of the second half of the twentieth century give far less typographical prominence than their predecessors to editorially imposed act and scene divisions, and the practice, going back to Rowe (1709), of heading each scene with a statement of its supposed location—'A Room in the Duke of Albany's Palace', or 'A Chamber in a Farmhouse adjoining the Castle', to quote from Muir's edition—has slowly been abandoned[1] but still influences thinking about the play: it is common to speak of the heath scenes even though the precise word 'heath' occurs nowhere in the text.[2]

[1] Some editors, however, continue the practice in their notes, e.g. Riverside, second edition (1997), and Norton (1997). It seems reasonable to do so when a location for the action is clearly implied, and provided it is understood that this need not be, and in Shakespeare's theatre would not have been, realistically represented. This and related topics are discussed in S. Wells, 'To Read a Play', in *Reading Plays: Interpretation and Reception*, ed. P. Holland and H. Scolnicov (Cambridge, 1991), pp. 30–55.

[2] A heath appears to have been represented by a stock piece of scenery in Tate's adaptation, and to have entered the editorial tradition via Tate through

Stage directions vary greatly from one edition to another in the extent to which they attempt to flesh out the often inadequate directions of the early texts, helping the reader to envisage stage action. The physical presentation varies too, ranging from plain text editions (especially useful to actors) to heavily annotated ones such as Furness's New Variorum (1880), and from the most utilitarian of school editions and paperbacks, through reprints adorned with illustrations and theatrical photographs, to the typographical splendour of A. H. Bullen's ten-volume Shakespeare Head edition of 1904–7 and the elegance of Folio Society reprints (such as that of 1956, which offers an introduction by Donald Wolfit along with reproductions of Noguchi's designs for the 1955 Stratford production). All this has its effect on the reading experience.

Performance Texts of 'King Lear'

For theatre practitioners from members of Shakespeare's company onwards the act of reading has been an essential preliminary to performance, and an early step in the process of releasing the theatrical energies of the text has often been an acknowledgement of the need to alter it to suit changing theatrical exigencies, including the abilities of individual actors, the nature of the performance space, the expectations of the audience, and so on. This process is seen at work in the play's first surviving theatrical adaptation, that printed in the 1623 Folio. Since then it has resulted in a stream of theatre texts published and unpublished, prompt books and acting editions, which have received relatively little scholarly attention but which bear witness to the metamorphoses the text has undergone in performance, and to the philosophical impossibility of regarding the play of *King Lear* as anything approaching a fixed entity.

Prompt books are essentially working documents, invaluable to the theatre historian but often cryptic and deceptively partial witnesses to the theatrical event.[1] Published theatre editions fall into two principal categories. Some are offered as practical guides to putting on the play. An extreme example is the Samuel French

Rowe. James Ogden discusses the effect of the tradition in 'Lear's Blasted Heath', Ogden and Scouten, 135–45.

[1] The standard reference work on English-language prompt books to 1961 is Charles H. Shattuck's *The Shakespeare Promptbooks: A Descriptive Catalogue* (Urbana, 1965), which describes 116 items for *Lear* and lists others.

Acting Edition of 1967, prepared by an actor, George Skillan, which is furnished with astonishingly detailed instructions for the kind of performance that might have been given in English provincial theatres during the earlier years of the twentieth century, and with an elaborate, theatrically-interpretative commentary. Other theatre editions present themselves rather as souvenirs of particular productions.[1] The first major example is John Bell's collection of 1774–5 offering the plays 'as they are now performed at the Theatres Royal in London', in which *Lear* appears in Garrick's version of Tate's adaptation, with an engraving of 'Mr Reddish in the Character of Edgar' and of Lear removing his 'lendings' in the storm—one of the most frequently illustrated points of the play. During the nineteenth century, texts of the play as acted were available for audiences of, for example, Charles Kean's 1858 production and Henry Irving's Lyceum version of 1892, with a statement in the latter that the play 'is necessarily reduced to reasonable length to suit the exigencies of the present time' and that 'In the curtailment, all superfluous horrors have been omitted'. Both versions entirely omit the blinding scene, and (like Macready's acting edition of 1838, which probably influenced them) end virtually with Lear's death, on Kent's words 'He hates him | That would upon the rack of this tough world | Stretch him out longer'.

Theatre editions, like theatre programmes, are mostly ephemeral. They serve a purpose at the time of the production which gives rise to them, and they pass into the province of the theatre historian when it is over. Occasionally, however, the printed text of an acting edition usurps the authority of the original text, and so it was with the first surviving English theatre version of *King Lear* (unless that label belongs to the Folio text), Nahum Tate's adaptation of 1681. Shakespeare's play had been acted on the Restoration stage before Tate's version appeared: according to the prompter John Downes, *Lear* was given 'exactly as Mr Shakespeare wrote it' in London probably in the 1663–4 season,[2] but nothing else is known

---

[1] Much detailed information about changes made both to Tate's text and to Shakespeare's in a large number of English and American prompt books and acting editions up to 1974 is given in Halstead, vols. 11 (unpaginated) and 13, pp. 463–91. Chaotically organized and far from reliable, this work may nevertheless be useful for initial guidance.

[2] *Roscius Anglicanus* (1708), ed. J. Milhous and R. D. Hume (Society for Theatre

of these performances, and the fact that they were succeeded by a heavily adapted version suggests that they had no great success.

Nahum Tate's Adaptation

The History of King Lear. Acted at the Duke's Theatre. Reviv'd with Alterations. By N. Tate was printed in 1681 with a cast list naming the great actor Thomas Betterton as Lear.[1] Tate made far more changes than the adapter of the Quarto text printed in the First Folio, and, like him, did so in the belief that he was effecting improvements. In his introductory epistle he professes great admiration for 'our Shakespeare's creating fancy', while criticizing the play as 'a heap of jewels unstrung and unpolished, yet so dazzling in their disorder that I soon perceived I had seized a treasure'. Restringing the jewels he shortens the text by around eight hundred lines, removing entirely the character of the Fool; he modernizes the language at many points; he adds a love story of his own composition, removing the King of France and turning Edgar and Cordelia into virtuous lovers who come together at the end; most notoriously, he makes 'the tale conclude in a success to the innocent distressed persons', preserving the lives of Lear, Kent, and Gloucester and sending them off into peaceful retirement. Edgar ends the play optimistically, declaring to Cordelia:

> Thy bright example shall convince the world,
> Whatever storms of fortune are decreed,
> That Truth and Virtue shall at last succeed.

What Tate did to Shakespeare was not essentially different from what Shakespeare had done to *King Leir*: Shakespeare had turned an old tragicomedy into a tragedy, Tate reversed the process. In doing so he created a new, different play which, critics have increasingly argued, has its own artistic validity. Admittedly, he

---

Research, 1987), p. 72. The date is more firmly established by a journal entry quoted in *The London Stage, 1600–1800*, Part 1, 1660–1700 (Carbondale, 1965), ed. W. van Lennep *et al*., p. 75.

[1] Tate's *Lear* has been frequently reprinted, e.g. in *Shakespeare Made Fit: Restoration Adaptations of Shakespeare*, ed. S. Clark (Everyman, 1997). The most thoroughly edited text is in Christopher Spencer, ed., *Five Restoration Adaptations of Shakespeare* (Urbana, 1965); there is a helpful edition by A. J. Black, Regents Restoration Drama series, 1975.

rather asked for trouble by retaining as much of Shakespeare as he did, thereby inviting odious comparisons with verse that he wrote himself.[1] But at the time Tate wrote, Shakespeare was not thought of as an immortal classic, but as a dramatist whose works, however admirable, required adaptation to fit them for the new theatrical and social circumstances of the time, as well as to changes in taste. William Davenant had already composed successful new plays on the basis of, for example, *The Two Noble Kinsmen* (as *The Rivals*, 1664), *The Tempest* (with Dryden, 1667) and *Macbeth* (1673). Now Tate did the same for *King Lear*, and in the process created a text which, though it operates on a far lower level of artistic aspiration than its source play, has to be acknowledged as one of the longest-lasting successes of the English drama: it supplanted Shakespeare's play in every performance given from 1681 to 1838.

As Shakespeare rose in esteem, however, invidious comparisons came to be made, and Tate's text, frequently vilified, was itself subjected to adaptation. As early as 1711, Addison complained that, 'reformed according to the chimerical notion of poetical justice', the play had 'lost half its beauty'.[2] David Garrick used unaltered Tate for his first appearances as Lear in 1742, in his twenty-fifth year, but in 1743 playbills advertised performances at Lincoln's Inn Fields 'with restorations from Shakespeare' (Lear was played by an anonymous 'Gentleman'). Later Samuel Foote urged Garrick to play the original, 'fool and all', but the great actor prepared a new version of Tate for performances given from 1756, still without the Fool, though with considerable restoration in the earlier part of the play.[3] In 1756 the poet and playwright Frances Brooke

---

[1] N. K. Maguire studies and defends the play as 'part of the Tory counter-propaganda campaign' in reaction to the 1678–83 Exclusion crisis in 'Nahum Tate's *King Lear*. "the king's blest restoration"', in *The Appropriation of Shakespeare*, ed. J. Marsden (Hemel Hempstead, 1991), pp. 29–42; M. Dobson supports this view in his *The Making of the National Poet: Shakespeare, Adaptation and Authorship* (Oxford, 1992), esp. pp. 80–6.

[2] *Spectator*, 41 (16 April 1711).

[3] Garrick's successive changes are summarized in *The Plays of David Garrick*, vol. 3, ed. H. W. Pedicord and F. L. Bergmann (Carbondale, 1981), pp. 447–50. According to Halstead Garrick 'played 1567 lines of Shakespeare compared to Tate's 1116'. His production is discussed by G. W. Stone, 'Garrick's Production of *King Lear*, A Study in the Temper of the Eighteenth-Century Mind', *Studies in Philology*, 45 (1948), 89–103, and Peter Holland writes on Garrick's evolving view of the role in *Shakespeare: An Illustrated Stage History*, ed. J. Bate and R. Jackson (Oxford, 1996), pp. 82–6.

(1724–89), writing of a performance with Garrick's great rival, Spranger Barry, as Lear, found it 'matter of great astonishment' that actors, above all Garrick, 'who professes himself so warm an idolater' of Shakespeare, should prefer Tate to 'Shakespeare's great original'. Nevertheless she acknowledged that the performance 'moved the whole house to tears'.[1] A version prepared by George Colman for Covent Garden in 1768 omitted Tate's love story, and did not succeed. Garrick continued to play Lear with enormous success till the end of his career, and even though he deprived himself of the death scene, tears continued to dominate audiences' responses. This won him praise in competition with Barry. A contemporary wrote:

> The town has found out different ways
> To praise the different Lears.
> To Barry they give loud huzzas,
> To Garrick—only tears.

And another added:

> 'A King? Nay, every inch a king'
> Such Barry doth appear,
> But Garrick's quite a different thing:
> He's every inch King Lear.[2]

At Garrick's farewell performance in 1776, we learn,

The curse at the close of the first act, his frenetic appeal to heaven at the end of the second on Regan's ingratitude, were two such enthusiastic scenes of human exertion that they caused a kind of momentary petrifaction through the house, which he soon dissolved as universally into tears. Even the unfeeling Regan and Goneril, forgetful of their characteristic cruelty, played through the whole of their parts with aching bosoms and streaming eyes. In a word, we never saw before so exquisite a theatrical performance, or one so loudly and universally applauded.[3]

---

[1] Cited in B. Vickers, *Shakespeare: The Critical Heritage*, vol. 4 (1976), pp. 247–9.

[2] Percy Fitzgerald (*The Life of David Garrick* (1899)) ascribes the first epigram to Richard Berenger (d. 1782), and quotes the second anonymously, saying that Theophilus Cibber maliciously pretended to believe that Garrick wrote it himself.

[3] Henry Bate in *The Morning Post*, 22 May 1776, repr. in Wells, *Theatre*, pp. 28–9. No doubt the response was provoked in part by the audience's knowledge that this was a farewell performance.

8. Detail from George Romney (1734–1802), *King Lear in the Tempest Tearing off his Robes*.

Though touching, this is also faintly ludicrous. Garrick was un-questionably a great Lear, but neither descriptions nor theatrical illustrations do much to preserve the impact that he and other ac-tors of his time achieved in the role. Nor is there much critical or lit-erary response of any distinction from this period; the arts of both theatrical and literary criticism were still relatively undeveloped. More profound responses to the play survive, however, in some of the more private visual art that it inspired. George Romney's extraordinary oil painting (fig. 8)—an early work, dating from around 1760—is intensely dramatic, and, like the theatre of his time, shows the characters in contemporary costume. It was painted at the height of Garrick's career, but before Romney had left his native Lake District to seek his fortune in London. Though the painting apparently has no direct relationship to performance, it is curiously close to a description of Garrick written by Thomas Wilkes around the time that Romney painted the picture: 'I never see him coming down from one corner of the stage, with his old grey hair standing, as it were, erect on his head, his face filled with horror and attention, his hands expanded, and his whole frame actuated by a dreadful solemnity, but I am astounded, and share in all his distress . . . Methinks I share his calamities, I feel the dark drifting rain and the sharp tempest.'[1] Nevertheless, Romney's painting is closer to Shakespeare than to contemporary acting editions. The demented Lear, his head bare, is beginning to tear off his clothes. Gloucester is there to the left of the painting, with his torch, and Edgar, wrapped in his blanket, to the right. Behind Edgar, Kent looks on in dismay, and at the far right is a middle-aged looking personage who may or may not be the Fool. In Shakespeare, Kent, Edgar and the Fool are with Lear as he starts to strip, and Gloucester enters just after; at the corresponding moment in Garrick's version of Tate, there is of course no Fool, and Gloucester comes on considerably later.

If Romney's skeletally grotesque portrayal of Lear anticipates Wilson Knight's essay on '*Lear* and the Comedy of the Grotesque', John Runciman's no less fine oil *King Lear in the Storm*, of 1767 (fig. 9), looks forward, in its introduction into the scene of a storm at sea, to the imagery criticism also of the 1930s. Here again the costumes resemble those used on the stage in the artist's time. W. Moelwyn Merchant, in his study of the painting, remarks that Lear 'wears the full Van Dyck dress which had become common for actors in the eighteenth century who represented pre-Tudor characters', and 'the figures of Kent and Edgar are rembrandtesque'; on the other hand, Lear is not represented as a king. The most original aspect of the painting is the fact that 'The greater part of the canvas . . . is occupied by stormy sea and sky.' As Merchant remarks, Runciman, with 'the visual penetration of a painter . . . has isolated the imagery which most effectively depicts the King's mental chaos'.[2] Less symbolic but no less vivid is a drawing (fig. 10) by John

[1] *A General View of the Stage* (1759), pp. 234–5.

[2] W. Moelwyn Merchant, *Shakespeare and the Artist* (Oxford, 1959), pp. 190–8; quotations from pp. 191, 193, 196.

9. John Runciman (1744–68), *King Lear in the Storm* (1767).

Runciman's brother Alexander (1736–85) done in Rome, also in 1767, which provides an early depiction of the Fool, with coxcomb and bauble, and apparently wearing a phallus.

The continuing success of Tate's adaptation, even in modified form, reflects aspects of the neoclassicism that prevailed in both theatrical practice and critical thought during the later part of the seventeenth century and much of the eighteenth, both in England and overseas. Even Samuel Johnson, writing over eighty years after the adaptation first appeared, gave his guarded approval to the popularity of its happy ending:

Cordelia from the time of Tate has always retired with victory and felicity. And if my sensations could add anything to the general suffrage, I might relate that I was many years ago so shocked by Cordelia's death that I know not whether I ever endured to read again the last scenes of the play till I undertook to revise them as an editor.[1]

A French play based on the story and successfully performed on a number of occasions from 1783 to 1800 also neoclassicized it. This

[1] From Johnson's notes on the play, conveniently reprinted in *Samuel Johnson on Shakespeare* (Harmondsworth, 1989), ed. H. Woudhuysen.

10. Alexander Runciman (1736–85), *King Lear on the Heath* (1767).

is J.-F. Ducis's *Le Roi Léar* (1783), written in rhyming alexandrines, which restructures the narrative even more comprehensively than Tate, and owes relatively little to Shakespeare, whose name is not mentioned in the published text.[1] In Germany, Friedrich Schröder played Lear in a long-lived adaptation of 1778 less drastic than Tate's; Lear is allowed to die, of a heart attack brought on by the false belief that Cordelia is dead; she recovers and 'finishes the play mourning for him'.[2]

---

[1] There is a full account and analysis of the adaptation in *Shakespeare for the Age of Reason: the earliest stage adaptations of Jean-François Ducis, 1769–1792*, by John Golder (Oxford, 1992), pp. 112–53. Golder writes 'it is hard to believe that audiences failed to identify in Léar the hapless Louis XVI' (p. 153), rather as in England somewhat later parallels were drawn between Lear and the supposedly mad King George III.

[2] Simon Williams, *Shakespeare on the German Stage: Volume 1, 1586–1914* (Cambridge, 1990), p. 83.

Even in the Romantic period, with its very different criteria of taste, and in spite of growing scorn for Tate, his version remained the starting point for performances on the English-speaking stage. Though Charles Dibdin vigorously defended Shakespeare in his *Complete History of the Stage* (1800),[1] John Philip Kemble, in 1809, dropped some of Garrick's restorations 'and put back a corresponding amount of Tate'.[2] His great rival and successor Edmund Kean, whose acting style was far more romantic than Kemble's, used Tate at first but, declaring that 'No one . . . could know what he was capable of until they had seen him over the dead body of Cordelia', restored the tragic ending for a few performances in 1823; they failed, and he regretfully reverted to Tate.[3] In America, too, where the play had first been performed in 1754, Tate's was the standard version until 1875 when Edwin Booth's became 'the first Lear-without-Tate to be performed by any important American actor'.[4] A 'happy ending' was also adopted at the Burgtheater, Vienna, in 1822 in a relatively faithful adaptation by Josef Schreyvogel in which, after Lear's last words (in the Folio text) 'Look there, look there!', Cordelia miraculously revived, and the curtain fell on an additional reunion scene.[5]

Return to Shakespeare

The major breakthrough on the English stage came at Covent Garden in 1838, when William Charles Macready, after much hesitation, abandoned Tate altogether in favour of a shortened and somewhat rearranged version of Shakespeare's text, even including the Fool, played by a young woman, Priscilla Horton.[6] This was a successful production in which, according to John Forster, Macready's Lear was 'heightened by this introduction of the Fool to a surprising degree'.[7] Nevertheless, *Lear* was the least popular of

---

[1] Vol. 3, pp. 320–6; cited by Carlisle, pp. 270–1.   [2] Odell, ii. 52.

[3] From 1814 to 1819, Kean, playing in Wroughton's adaptation of *Richard II*, had what must have been the galling experience of hearing Lear's words over the dead Cordelia spoken by the Queen over himself (Odell, ii. 74–5).

[4] C. J. Shattuck, *Shakespeare on the American Stage*, vol. 2 (Cranbury, NJ, 1987), p. 33.

[5] Williams (p. 68 n. 2), p. 116.

[6] Odell describes Macready's text, ii. 195–7, and the staging, ii. 210–11. Lacy's acting edition shows that on his first entry on the vast stage, Lear was accompanied by some sixty extras.

[7] Forster's appreciative review (often mistakenly ascribed to Charles Dickens),

Shakespeare's major tragedies on the Victorian stage, and though Tate did not return, Shakespeare's text continued to be rearranged and shortened in ways that reduced its emotional and intellectual challenge. The German novelist Theodor Fontane, who saw Samuel Phelps's Sadler's Wells production when it visited Berlin in the winter of 1858, remarked that 'The manager's scissors had done their worst' while nevertheless admiring the skill of the cutting. Attempting to define the difference between German and English attitudes to the play he wrote that

> an English performance lays more emphasis on its pathetic elements. The German performance gives a Lear who is mad and a king, the English above all the old, abused and abandoned man; the German emphasises the consequences of illness and a broken heart, but through the raging of the English Lear there always sounds the grief that created that madness, the lamenting of an old man and a heartbroken father. . . . there is always a danger that the high tragic and royal elements will be watered down to the sentimental and petty-bourgeois.

And, he added, 'that Oswald is played as a clown goes without saying. Like it or not, every Shakespeare play has to have some kind of comic man.'[1]

As English actors travelled abroad, so foreign actors came to England. The Italian Tommaso Salvini gave a virtuoso performance as Lear in a severely abbreviated and rearranged Italian translation which toured in England and America from 1882; the effect, especially on English-speaking audiences, must have been operatic.[2]

The late nineteenth century was a low water mark in the play's reputation. Henry James, writing in 1883, found it 'impossible to imagine a drama that accommodates itself less to the stage' (p. 90). At the time of Henry Irving's production in 1892, newspaper writers declared that 'Shakespeare is, as a poet and playwright, at

which pays especial attention to the role of the Fool, is reprinted in e.g. Wells, *Theatre*, pp. 72–7.

[1] Theodor Fontane, *Shakespeare in the London Theatre, 1855–8*, translated by R. Jackson (1999), p. 102.

[2] The performance is described in *The Italian Shakespearians*, by Marvin Carlson (Washington, DC, 1985), pp. 101–8; Henry James's review of a performance in Boston in 1883 is reprinted in his *The Scenic Art*, ed. A. Wade (1949), pp. 178–80. Carlson also writes on Ernesto Rossi's Lear, which he toured from the 1870s to 1896, occasionally speaking a few lines, sometimes even the whole of the last act, in English.

his worst in *King Lear*' and that the play 'would not be tolerated if produced without the name of Shakespeare'.[1] A. C. Bradley's reservations about the play's theatrical potential, expressed in the course of the most sustained piece of analytically appreciative criticism that Shakespeare's tragedies had so far received, have already been quoted (p. 2). Irving, in the attempt to improve the play according to the standards of his day, cut some 46 per cent of the lines, streamlined the action, reduced its violence and sexuality, increased the prominence of his own role, and rearranged episodes to suit the illusionistic scenic conventions of the theatre of his time.[2] For all this, it was one of his least successful performances.

At the time of Irving's production, the counterwave to Victorian spectacular theatre was just beginning to make itself felt in pseudo-Elizabethan productions by William Poel which were to result in a greatly increased understanding of Shakespeare's stagecraft and consequently in a revolution in staging by which, to put it simply, staging methods were adapted to the plays rather than play texts to the conventions and physical conditions of the current theatrical scene. Poel's emphasis on continuity of action is paralleled in André Antoine's 1904 production at the Théâtre Antoine in Paris. This was the first French production of the unadapted text, given in a translation by Pierre Loti.[3] In Berlin, too, a production by Max Reinhardt of 1908, and in London a Haymarket Theatre production of 1909 with designs by Charles Ricketts, anticipated the more fluent staging methods adopted by Harley Granville Barker in Savoy Theatre productions of 1912 to 1914 (which did not include *Lear*).[4] Poel was anything but a textual purist, but Barker, who played Richard II and other roles for him, mediated his ideas into the English theatrical mainstream and developed them in ways that encouraged the use of full, unadapted texts.

---

[1] *The Idler* and *The Illustrated London News*, cited by A. Hughes, *Henry Irving, Shakespearean* (Cambridge, 1981), p. 118. Similar criticism continued to appear; as late as 1955, Margaret Webster expressed disbelief that *Lear* 'ever was or ever will be a good play in the sense of a theater piece' (*Shakespeare Without Tears* (Cleveland), pp. 214–23), cited Carlisle, p. 278.

[2] Hughes, pp. 118–19.

[3] The production is described in *André Antoine*, by Jean Chothia (Cambridge, 1991), pp. 134–43. According to Robert Speaight (*Shakespeare on the Stage* (1973) pp. 183) it was the first Paris production of a complete Shakespeare play.

[4] Dennis Kennedy, *Granville Barker and the Dream of Theatre* (Cambridge, 1985), p. 152; Bratton, p. 43.

Barker's *Preface* of 1927, one of the most practically efficacious pieces of drama criticism ever written, is a landmark in the history of the reception of *King Lear* because of its successful and calculated refutation of Charles Lamb's claim that 'Lear is essentially impossible to be represented on a stage'.[1] Lamb, as Barker writes, had never seen the play acted; and even at the time Barker wrote there had been few opportunities to judge the stageworthiness in performance of anything like a full version of Shakespeare's text. All criticism of the play up to the end of the nineteenth century and beyond is based either on reading, or on theatre experience of adapted, re-arranged, and truncated versions of the text, or on one modified by the other. Barker, urging the need for close study of the play as a product of Shakespeare's skills as a practical dramatist, is at pains especially to counter Bradley's belief (developing Charles Lamb's criticism of 'The contemptible machinery by which' the actors 'mimic the storm') that in the theatre 'The storm scenes in *King Lear* gain nothing and their very *essence* is destroyed'.[2] Combating the tradition that prevailed throughout the nineteenth century of representing the storm with a battery of sound and light effects, Barker insists that the storm is not in itself 'dramatically important, only in its effect upon Lear', and that the actor should 'impersonate both Lear and—reflected in Lear—the storm'.[3] Barker himself was among the earlier opponents of conflation, writing that 'Where Quarto and Folio offer alternatives, to adopt both versions may make for redundancy or confusion' (p. 329). Overall he regarded the Folio as the more satisfactory text, but clearly believed that a director would be best advised to make considered choices among variants. This is what Theodore Komisarjevsky did in his acclaimed, though quite heavily cut, Stratford production of 1936, in which he also made textual transpositions and, in part, turned the Knights into 'a Chorus commenting on the futility of the old king's aims. They repeated, in unison, the Fool's songs and sayings.'[4]

It was not until 1940 that Barker at last had the opportunity to

---

[1] Lamb's essay, also referred to in p. 2 n. 2, is an eloquent tribute to the play for all its anti-theatrical bias.

[2] Bradley, p. 269.

[3] p. 266. Bratton describes successive stagings of the storm, pp. 26–30.

[4] Ralph Berry, 'Komisarjevsky at Stratford-upon-Avon', *SS* 36 (1983), 73–84; p. 79.

11. The reunion of Lear and Cordelia in the production by John Gielgud and Anthony Quayle, Shakespeare Memorial Theatre, 1950. Left to right: Andrew Cruickshank as Kent, Peggy Ashcroft as Cordelia, John Gielgud as Lear, Peter Norris as the Doctor, and Robert Hardy as a Knight.

translate his *Preface* into theatrical practice and to show that it was possible to perform an almost complete text, in Elizabethan costume, with great theatrical success when, in collaboration with Lewis Casson, he directed John Gielgud as Lear at the Old Vic.[1] Gielgud acknowledged Barker's influence when, collaborating this time with Anthony Quayle, he directed himself as Lear at Stratford-upon-Avon in 1950. T. C. Worsley described this production as one that 'might convert those, if there still are any, who prefer reading *Lear* to seeing it':

---

[1] Unfortunately Barker's theatre text appears not to have survived. Gielgud writes briefly about the production in his *Stage Directions* (1965), pp. 51–5, and prints rehearsal notes along with letters from Barker, pp. 121–33. Dennis Kennedy discusses the production in *Granville Barker and the Dream of Theatre*, pp. 156–8, drawing on an unpublished account by Hallam Fordham, with notes by Gielgud, housed in the Folger Shakespeare Library, Washington. Gielgud, who had already played Lear at the Old Vic in 1931, at the age of 27, did so again at Stratford in 1950 and 1955; he recorded it for radio and audio cassette (Random House, ISBN 1–85686–202–X) in a Renaissance Theatre Company production celebrating his ninetieth birthday in 1994.

I have never seen the recognition scene [fig. 11] . . . so movingly played. The bewildered waking, the ghost of a voice speaking as if from some other dimension, the fall on to his knees that is half a fall from the bed, and then the stumbled, pleading recognition—I should not believe that anyone, however visually imaginative, could in his study bring the tears to his own eyes as Mr Gielgud does to ours here.[1]

Since Barker's time there has been a general tendency in the British theatre and elsewhere not to work from pre-existing acting editions but to create prompt books from full, edited—which has almost invariably meant conflated—texts, cutting no more than a few hundred lines.[2] Of course, any cutting has an effect on meaning, and while some directors cut for mainly practical reasons— ease of comprehension, length of performance, etc.—others do so in order to further their own interpretative ideas.[3] Peter Brook, in his Stratford-upon-Avon production of 1962, was accused of slanting the text towards a bleakness reminiscent of the plays of Samuel Beckett, whose work is invoked by Jan Kott in the chapter '*King Lear* and *Endgame*' in his book *Shakespeare Our Contemporary*.[4] Brook offered overall an exceptionally full text, but two of his principal changes, the omission of the servants' comforting of Gloucester after his blinding (14.97–105) and of Edmund's repentance and last-minute attempt to save Cordelia (24.196–214), added to the production's sense of a hostile universe.[5] The vehemence of the criticism centring on these changes—even though the former is made in the Folio—was a measure of the impact of what has come to be recognized as one of the most challenging productions the play has ever received.

[1] *The Fugitive Art* (1952), pp. 152–5.

[2] At Stratford-upon-Avon the New Temple , and later the New Penguin, editions have been popular, mainly no doubt because they offer a clean page. In recent years directors have sometimes made statements about textual policy; for example Adrian Noble's Stratford production of 1993, with Robert Stephens as Lear, stated in its programme that about four hundred lines were cut, while leaving the reader to assume that this was from the conflated version. In 1974 Buzz Goodbody directed a two-and-a-half hour studio production, entitled simply *Lear*, which was explicitly described as 'a cut version . . . devised for schools and public performances'; it featured an original Prologue concerned with social injustice.

[3] The roles of the Fool and Edgar, especially in his persona of Poor Tom, have often been abbreviated, doubtless on grounds of comprehensibility.

[4] Whether Brook was, as some assumed, actively trying to put Kott's interpretation into practice is disputed: Leggatt, p. 46.

[5] The prompt book shows that Brook adjusted the final scene to go straight from Kent's 'Is he not here?' (24.232) to 'Howl, howl, howl . . .' (24. 253), omitting the

Debate about the relationship between the Quarto and Folio texts, followed by the publication of unconflated editions, has renewed interest in the critical and theatrical implications of textual choices. Directors have become more liable to acknowledge which text they are using, and in what ways they have altered it, and there have been consciously experimental productions based firmly on one text or the other. At the University of Rochester in 1985 a semi-professional cast aimed 'honestly to explore the Quarto, to determine to the best of our ability what would work on our stage with our actors', while admitting conflation with the Folio 'if certain words or passages could not be given a satisfactory stage life'.[1] The fully professional theatre, on the other hand, has favoured the Folio text. So for example Nicholas Hytner, in 1990 at Stratford-upon-Avon, claimed in his programme 'The text is that of the First Folio.' Whereas prompt books normally adapt a printed text, his uses a special typescript which includes Q's mock-trial along with an inserted, printed text of Edgar's 'When we our betters . . .' speech (13.95–108), also found only in Q—presumably a late insertion.[2]

Interpretation in Performance

But textual choices and decisions are only the first of the processes by which the energies of a dramatic text are released through performance. Theatrical realization of the text calls for collaboration from many participants and is subject to a wide range of variables, including the personality and styles of the performers, the constraints of the performance space, and, less definably, the intellectual and social climate of the time. No production can be neutral, but some are more clearly interventionist than others. So, for

carrying on of Goneril's and Regan's bodies. Maynard Mack is strongly critical of Brook's interpretation and the way it was achieved: pp. 30–2, 38–41. Alexander Leggatt, who (like me) was present at the first performance, offers a full, balanced, and appreciative account of the production, which he (like many others of his generation) found revelatory, and of the varying reactions that it evoked. Although in Brook's film based on this production the text is very heavily cut, the comforting of Gloucester is restored to the extent that a servant is seen to break an egg and apply its contents to Gloucester's eye-socket.

[1] David Richman, 'The *King Lear* Quarto in Rehearsal and Performance', *SQ* 37 (1986), 374–82.

[2] Peter Holland discusses the production in *English Shakespeares*, pp. 37–44.

example, when Peter Brook caused Lear's knights to behave as Gonoril says they do, in a debauched and riotous fashion (4.232–8), he was consciously breaking with tradition in a manner that reduced sympathy for Lear. The production device affected interpretation no less than his textual changes, and he was as severely criticized for it as for them.[1] Scofield's performance as Lear matched Brook's direction. It was an austere reading of the role, understated in suffering, denying to both the character and the audience the emotional release afforded by actors who rage more extrovertly against the coming of the dark. 'Lay him to rest,' wrote Kenneth Tynan, 'the royal Lear with whom generations of star actors have made us reverently familiar . . .'[2] But the effect of Scofield's austerity on many members of the audience was no less devastating than the overt emotionalism of a Wolfit. And no one present at the first night will forget the sight of the cruelly blinded Gloucester groping his way toward the wings as the house lights slowly rose to signal the interval.

If Brook attempted to interpret the play through ideas current at the time, he did so without drawing explicit parallels with modern society. Other directors have used production devices to force the audience to make connections. In Deborah Warner's Royal National Theatre production of 1990, which used a full (conflated) text, Lear whizzed on in a wheelchair wearing a red nose for his first entry, clearly celebrating his eightieth birthday. The chair became a symbolic prop; later, 'bundled up with a rug over his knees, Lear looked old and vulnerable, a geriatric out-patient waiting for the ambulance to take him home'.[3] A production by Helena Kaut-Howson seen first at the Leicester Haymarket in 1997 presented the play 'as the dream, or hallucination, of a dying patient in a geriatric hospital' with 'wheelchairs becoming chariots, a

---

[1] 'Lear's knights literally demolished the set, throwing plates and tankards, upending the heavy table on which presumably the king's dinner was soon to be served, and behaving in general like boors—as if the visible courtesy of their spokesman earlier, Albany's significant unawareness of what Goneril is complaining about, and Lear's explicit description of his knights . . . had no existence in the play.' (Mack, pp. 30–1.)

[2] The opening sentence of a review, originally printed in *The Observer*, reprinted in *Peter Brook: A Theatrical Casebook*, ed. David Williams (1988, revised 1991), pp. 23–7. This volume also includes 'Lear Log' by Charles Marowitz (pp. 6–22), a revealing account of rehearsals for the production based on his experience as Assistant Director.

[3] Holland, p. 48.

bathtub Tom's hovel, and the hospital bed the one in which Lear awakened to Cordelia'.[1] Lear was played by a woman, Kathryn Hunter.

Other directors have been bolder with text as well as setting. Sometimes indeed, especially when given in translation, the play has been virtually rewritten—as it was by Tate, though to very different ends. In Germany in 1974 Peter Zadek, rejoicing in the liberations of the age, set it in circus tents; Lear sexually assaulted Cordelia in the reunion scene and carried her on stark naked in death. Ingmar Bergman, directing the play in Stockholm in 1984, used expressionist devices to restructure the action, emphasizing an alliance between power and sex: Goneril seduced Oswald, on stage, and the sisters' desire for Edmund was obsessive.[2] In Japan, Tadashi Suzuki created his own text for *The Tale of Lear* (1984), producing 'a distillation of the play to its spiritual and emotional essence'. Here, as in some Western productions, Lear's throne became a wheelchair.[3] And on film, experimentation reaches an extreme in Jean-Luc Godard's postmodern *King Lear* (1987), 'in which William Shakespeare Junior the Fifth goes to Hollywood to produce his ancestor's plays, which end up being edited by Woody Allen'.[4]

Alongside such experimental versions, directors have continued to present the original text in more straightforward ways which justify Granville Barker's faith that Shakespeare's stagecraft, properly understood, can be successfully translated into modern theatrical terms. In 1997, Peter Hall's uncut Folio text played in Jacobean dress at the Old Vic was disappointingly unengaging, but Richard Eyre's National Theatre version, in which Ian Holm played Lear, offering a virtually complete conflated text played in 'timeless' costumes—'hints of Renaissance here, of the First World War there', as Robert Smallwood wrote—'presented the play's seething emotional relationships unrelentingly before the audience's examination'.[5] Both Edgar and Lear genitally exposed

[1] Quotations are from Robert Smallwood's review, *SS* 51 (1998), 219–55; p. 246.

[2] Bergman's production is reviewed by I. Lindblad, *SQ* 36 (1985), 458–60.

[3] A. J. Nouryel, 'Shakespeare and the Japanese Stage', in *Foreign Shakespeare* (cited in p. 41 n. 2); quoted from p. 265.

[4] L. Boose and R. Burt, 'Totally Clueless? Shakespeare goes Hollywood in the 1990s', in *Shakespeare the Movie*, ed. L. Boose and R. Burt (1997), pp. 8–22; p. 9.

[5] Smallwood, p. 251.

their bodies to the storm: more than anywhere else in the Shakespeare canon, full nakedness is justified in the play's portrayal of 'unaccommodated man'.

During the twentieth century, energies deriving from the text of *King Lear* have been released in performances given in media other than theatre—film, television, radio and sound recordings. Although these are no less of their own time than stage productions, they reach far wider audiences over a longer period of time. Not all of them necessitate textual adaptation. Sound recordings, such as that in which an immensely distinguished cast headed by John Gielgud—playing Lear for the last time over sixty years after his earliest performances in the role—enact a full Folio text, can reach a wide audience; but absence of a visual dimension means that the experience offered lies somewhere between that of reading the play and of seeing it realized in stage terms.

Film and its close relative television are potentially highly flexible media offering great opportunities for experimentation, but generally so far working within traditions of naturalistic presentation related to those of nineteenth-century theatre, which also encourage textual adaptation.[1] Peter Brook's film of 1971, deriving (though also differing greatly) from his stage production and with some of the same cast, abbreviates the text no less drastically than Irving had in 1892, and employs more ostensibly naturalistic settings than Brook's Stratford production.[2] Michael Elliott's television film released in 1983, with Laurence Olivier as Lear, is avowedly theatrical in its origins, recalling nineteenth-century productions in its naturalistic settings and drawing on a 1946 Old Vic production in which Olivier had directed himself.[3] Just as

---

[1] Screen versions from 1909 onwards are studied in Kenneth S. Rothwell's *A History of Shakespeare on Screen: A Century of Film and Television* (Cambridge, 1999).

[2] Michael Birkett, who produced the film, made in Denmark, discusses the transition from stage to screen in an interview printed in R. Manvell's *Shakespeare and the Film* (1971), pp. 136–43. Leggatt offers a critical appreciation, pp. 95–106, and also of other film and television adaptations. Brook had directed Orson Welles in a 73-minute American television film made in 1953, discussed by Tony Howard, 'When Peter Met Orson: The 1953 CBS *King Lear*', in *Shakespeare the Movie*, pp. 121–34.

[3] *Shakespeare on Television*, ed. J. C. Bulman and H. R. Coursen (Hanover, New Hampshire, and London, 1988), includes essays comparing the Elliott–Olivier version with the production directed for BBC television by Jonathan Miller, with Michael Hordern as Lear, along with selections from reviews of these and other televised productions.

Garrick's 1776 performances were all the more affecting because audiences knew that they would be his last, so Olivier's gains in poignancy because of the aged and ailing actor's self-evident frailty. Nevertheless his performance constantly illuminates the role, not simply in the pathos of the reunion with Cordelia, but especially in the unsentimental lightness of touch with which he plays the Dover Cliff scene. This Lear has passed beyond the tempestuous madness of the storm into a precarious serenity that looks forward to his vision of singing, with Cordelia, 'like birds i'the' cage' (24.9). Though intimations of reality lurk beneath the surface, his woes 'by wrong imaginations' have lost the 'knowledge of themselves' (20.275–6).

Increasingly, Shakespeare's international appeal has resulted in the translation and transmutation of his plays into foreign language versions. Grigori Kozintsev's powerful film of 1970, using a translation into Russian by Boris Pasternak, was issued in Britain with subtitles using Shakespeare's language. The spectator is able simultaneously to hear Pasternak and to read Shakespeare.[1] Still more radical in adaptation was Akira Kurosawa's great film *Ran* (the title means both 'chaos' and 'civil war') of 1984, in which Shakespeare's play, transferred to feudal Japan, and with Lear's daughters metamorphosed into sons, became the basis for an essentially new work of art, just as Shakespeare himself had transformed the old play. So interpretation moves into adaptation, which in turn moves into re-creation. The work of art begets others in a cycle of response and counter-response.

I wrote at the beginning of this Introduction of some of the ways in which what Shakespeare wrote has created a stream of influence productive of new works of art. Some of them, such as Turgenev's long short story *A King Lear of the Steppes* (1870), Gordon Bottomley's verse play *King Lear's Wife* (1915), Edward Bond's play *Lear* (1971), or Elaine Feinstein's *Lear's Daughters* (1987), explicitly acknowledge in their titles a debt to the original, however far they depart from it. In others, such as Jane Smiley's novel *A Thousand Acres* (1991), the debt is no less great if less readily

---

[1] Kozintsev writes powerfully about play and film in *King Lear: The Space of Tragedy: The Diary of a Film Director* (1977). Context as well as appreciation is provided in *Shakespeare in Eastern Europe*, by Zdeněk Stříbrný (Oxford, 2000), who also discusses a number of East European productions and adaptations of the play.

apparent.[1] Sometimes, as in Balzac's novel *Le Père Goriot* (1834), it is buried deep beneath the surface, and no doubt there are works in which influence is present though unidentifiable. In 'Offshoots of *King Lear*' (pp. 286–92) I give information about a selection of the more important manifestations of the stream of influence set flowing by Shakespeare's penning of those 25,000 or so words in 1605.

---

[1] Smiley writes about the creation of her novel in 'Shakespeare in Iceland', *Shakespeare and the Twentieth Century*, ed. J. Bate *et al.* (Newark, NJ, 1998), pp. 41–59.

TEXTUAL INTRODUCTION AND
EDITORIAL PROCEDURES

THIS section provides a more technical supplement to information about the text provided on pp. 3–9. It is based in large part on the *Textual Companion* (Oxford, 1988) to the Oxford edition of the Complete Works, pp. 509–11. The prime editor of the play in that edition was Gary Taylor, working in collaboration with Stanley Wells.

There are two early quartos, known as Q1 and Q2. The earlier is said on its title-page (reproduced as fig. 1) to have been printed for Nathaniel Butter in 1608.[1] The printer was Nicholas Okes. Fig. 12 reproduces a page from this edition, with notes drawing attention to characteristic features of its presentation of the text.

Q2, also printed for Butter, bears the same date. The priority of Q1 was not established until 1866; between 1908 and 1910 W. W. Greg, A. W. Pollard, and others demonstrated that Q2 was one of a group of plays printed with false dates in 1619 by William Jaggard for Thomas Pavier.[2] Printed directly from Q1, it has no independent authority. Though it introduces error, its printers attempted, with some success, to correct typographical mistakes, to make punctuation more intelligible, and to supply needed stage directions. As explained in the General Introduction (pp. 3–9), Q1 has only recently been edited in its own right. The first fully critical edition is an unpublished one by P. W. M. Blayney who kindly allowed access to its text to the Oxford editors; a number of his emendations are followed here. Changes from Q2 accepted in our edition are recorded in our collation notes, printed immediately below the text.

Blayney, in his monumental study of the texts of the play,[3] demonstrates that printing of Q1 probably began in December 1607 and continued into 1608 (p. 85). Two compositors set the

---

[1] *King Lear* is No. 265 in W. W. Greg's *Bibliography of the English Printed Drama to the Restoration*, 4 vols. (1970), i. 264–6.

[2] *TC*, p. 49.

[3] *The Texts of 'King Lear' and Their Origins, Vol. 1, Nicholas Okes and the First Quarto* (Cambridge, 1982)—surely one of the most impressive works of scholarship and of scholarly printing ever published. (Vol. 2 has not appeared.)

The Hiſtorie of King Lear.

Duke. What is the matter ſir?

Lear. Ile tell thee, life and death!I am aſham'd that thou haſt
power to ſhake my manhood thus, that theſe hot teares that
breake from me perforce,ſhould make the worſt blaſts and fogs
vpon the vntender woundings of a fatherscurſſe, peruſe euery   5
ſence about the old fond eyes, beweepe this cauſe againe, ile
pluck you out,& you caſt with the waters that you make to temper clay, yea, i'ſt come to this? yet haue I left a daughter,whom
I am ſure is kind and comfortable, when ſhee ſhall heare this of
thee, with her nailes ſhee'l ſlea thy woluiſh viſage, thou ſhalt   10
find that ile reſume the ſhape,which thou doſt thinke I haue caſt
off for euer, thou ſhalt I warrant thee.

Gon. Doe you marke that my Lord?

Duke. I cannot bee ſo partiall *Generill* to the great loue I
beare you,   15

Gon. Come ſir no more, you, more knaue then foole, after
your maſter?

Foole. Nunckle*Lear*, Nunckle *Lear*, tary and take the foole
with a fox when one has caught her, and ſuch a daughter ſhould
ſure to the ſlaughter, if my cap would buy a halter, ſo the foole   20
followes after.

Gon. What *Oſwald*, ho.   *Oſwald.* Here Madam,

Gon. What haue you writ this letter to my ſiſter?

Oſw. Yes Madam.

Gon. Take you ſome company, and away to horſe, informe   25
her full of my particular feares, and thereto add ſuch reaſons of
your owne, as may compaſt it more,get you gon,and after your
returne now my Lord,this mildie gentlenes and courſe of yours
though I diſlike not, yet vnder pardon y' are much more alapt
want of wiſedome, then praiſe for harmfull mildnes.   30

Duke. How farre your eyes may pearce I cannot tell, ſtriuing
to better ought, we marre whats well,

Gon. Nay then.   *Duke.* Well,well,the euent,   *Exeunt*
                              Enter Lear.

Lear. Goe you before to *Gloſter* with theſe letters , acquaint   35
my daughter no further with any thing you know, then comes
from her demand out of the letter, if your diligence be not ſpee-
die, I ſhall be there before you.

                                                          Kent.

12. A page (sig. D2 verso) from Q1, illustrating characteristic features of
the text:

1 a character identified by rank rather than name (common in plays of the period):
'*Duke*' for '*Albany*'

2 absence of entry direction

2–12 verse set as prose

4 obvious error: 'make the worst blast'; see also 18–19, 'take the foole with a fox
when one has caught her'; 30, 'then praise'

5 running together of words: 'fatherscursse'

5, 31 different spellings of the same word: 'peruse', 'pearce'

7 inversion of words: 'you cast' for 'cast you'

13 wrong case punctuation: italic question mark

15, 33 speeches ending with a comma

16 'then' for modern 'than' (noted particularly at 4.114–23); see also 29, 'y' are'
for 'you're'   17 question mark for exclamation

22, 33 two short speeches set on a single line

25–30, 35–8 light punctuation, e.g. commas between complete sentences

32 idiosyncratic spelling: 'ought' for 'off', resulting in misleading punctuation

34 no indication of scene break (common in plays of the period)

34 deficient stage direction (Kent also should enter)

book seriatim—i.e. working straight through from the beginning
to the end of the manuscript, not dividing up separate sections of
the text between them so that they could work simultaneously.
They are identified by Blayney as Okes's B and C. C set 17.0 to
18.30; 20.95 to 205; 20.263 to 21.55; and 24.118 (after 'summons') to the end. B set the rest of the play.

Lear appears to have been the first play printed by Okes. It clearly
made heavy demands on his limited supply of type: for instance,
the question mark often appears in italic after a word set in roman,
and the ampersand is often used for 'and'. Even after allowance is
made for the possibility that differences between the Quarto and
the Folio texts may reflect changes of mind on Shakespeare's part
rather than mistakes by the compositor, Q1 is exceptionally unreliable in its distinctions between prose and verse and in its arrangement of verse. Unfamiliarity with this kind of manuscript, mistakes
on the part of the compositors, and ambiguity and alteration in the
manuscript may account for all such errors of lineation, though it
may be difficult to distinguish between these causes in any given
instance. Changes of lineation made in this edition are recorded on
pp. 293–302. Explanations of some of them are provided in the
Textual Companion, 'Lineation Notes', pp. 654–8.

It seems clear that the copy from which the printers worked was
hastily written. At points, for example, the compositors have apparently been faced with abbreviations which they have incor-
rectly expanded—at 16.15 '*Edgar*' for 'Edmund', probably written
'*Ed*.', the opposite error at 20.0.1, and at 19.4, 'Lady' for 'Lord',
probably written 'L.'

Twelve copies of Q survive. Many corrections were made while
the book was going through the press, resulting in a large number
of differences from one copy to another.[1] Lists and discussions of
these press variants can be found in Greg, *Variants*, and Blayney,
Texts, pp. 592–7. The corrected state is not necessarily to be preferred since the compositor may have guessed at a correct reading
without consulting the manuscript. In this edition each variant is
considered in its own right, but an attempt has always been made
to make sense of the uncorrected reading in the belief that this may
be closer to the original manuscript than the supposed correction.

[1] The classic study is W. W. Greg's *The Variants in the First Quarto of 'King Lear'*
(1940).

The variants, along with the many clear errors, show that the handwriting of the manuscript from which the compositors worked presented difficulties. They show too that the manuscript could easily have been misread in ways associated with the sections of the manuscript play *Sir Thomas More* believed (along with a few signatures on legal documents) to constitute the only surviving evidence of Shakespeare's handwriting, and also with other quartos believed to have been set up from Shakespeare's own papers. In the frequent inadequacy of its stage directions and the inconsistency of its designations of characters this quarto also appears to have been set up from an author's draft rather than a fair copy made by a scribe, or a theatrical manuscript. Such evidence suggests that the underlying manuscript was a late draft. The bibliographical evidence tends to confirm literary arguments that the Quarto represents a legitimate early version of the play rather than a corruption of it, as earlier critics believed.

Unlike the Folio, the Quarto version contains many obviously nonsensical or inadequate readings. The chief problem for an editor is the extent to which these should be corrected by reference to F. In this edition, Q1 is followed when it seems defensible. When it seems not to make sense, an effort has been made to seek the most plausible explanation of the error and the most economical restoration of sense without presuming that the Folio reading necessarily offers the most valid correction of the Q1 text. Nevertheless, readings of the Folio are accepted if, as frequently happens, they appear to offer the best solution to errors in Q.[1]

Like all the texts of Shakespeare printed in his lifetime, Q1 has no act or scene divisions. It was written for continuous performance, and since it stands outside the eighteenth-century editorial tradition, no convention of act-scene reference has been established. In this edition the scenes are numbered continuously, with no interpolation of act divisions, reflecting the way it would originally

---

[1] There is a myth, circulated even among textual scholars, that the Oxford edition wilfully follows Q when that edition could easily and certainly be corrected from F. So for example E. A. J. Honigmann writes 'Why . . . refuse help from the alternative version, which may supply the uncorrupted reading?' (review of the Norton edition, *N & Q* 244 (1999), p. 114). In fact the Oxford text based on the Quarto adopts around 120 readings from F in the dialogue, along with others in stage directions. Not all these readings are accepted in the present edition.

have been performed. The scene divisions pose no problems except at the point where Kent falls asleep in the stocks (7.166). In Q—as in F—Kent remains on stage asleep during Edgar's soliloquy, waking up shortly after Edgar exits and Lear enters. The stage is not cleared; F marks no scene division before Edgar's entrance or after he leaves; both texts envisage the same sequence of action. Eighteenth-century editors were nevertheless troubled by the apparent reappearance of the fugitive Edgar before Gloucester's home, and by the apparent compression of time. Steevens therefore made Edgar's soliloquy a new scene, followed by yet another scene in which Lear and his party discover Kent in the stocks. This arrangement makes unwarranted assumptions about consistency of time and place in the pre-Restoration theatre. The present edition follows the early texts in regarding as one uninterrupted scene the action from Kent and Oswald's entrance to the exeunt of Cornwall, Regan, Gonoril, Oswald, and Gloucester.

Collations

The collations attempt to record all substantive departures—i.e. those affecting meaning—from Q1 along with a selection of the more plausible editorial emendations not adopted here. Changes to the wording of Q1's stage directions, interpretations of its spelling which might be questioned, and substantive changes of its punctuation are recorded but not normally ascribed. Otherwise, changes are normally attributed to the first edition in which they appear. Readings adopted from the Folio are recorded, along with others which might be corrections of Q1 rather than changes to its text, but, treating F as an independent text, we make no attempt to record all the many points at which it differs from Q1. These are listed in the collations to e.g. Jay L. Halio's edition of *The First Quarto of King Lear* (Cambridge, 1994). Non-substantive printing errors (i.e. self-evident printing errors that do not affect meaning) in Q1 are listed in the *Textual Companion*, 'Incidentals', pp. 540–1, where they are keyed to the Oxford original-spelling edition of the Complete Works. The present edition differs at certain points from that printed in the Complete Works. Apart from a few changes of modernization, punctuation, wording of directions, and minor corrections, it reverts to Q1 for substantive readings at 1.257 (instead of adopting Rowe's emendation), 2.125, 8.9

(for Muir's emendation), 11.4, 11.165, 15.57, 20.130, and 20.174. At 1.176.1 it adds a direction from F, at 2.126 and 5.29 it follows F instead of Q1, and at 11.54–5 it adopts an emendation by Halio.

Q1's punctuation is very light and erratic, often employing commas when modern usage prefers heavier punctuation such as semicolons, colons, and stops. Question marks and full stops are often used for exclamations. Such punctuation is characteristic of texts believed to be printed directly from Shakespeare's papers, and of the sections of *Sir Thomas More* generally supposed to be in Shakespeare's own hand. It is not necessarily an indication of how words should be spoken; a sequence of clauses separated only by commas does not necessarily imply that Shakespeare wished them to be delivered breathlessly. This edition attempts to punctuate in a manner that will increase comprehensibility for the modern reader without being over-prescriptive for the actor. Changes of the original punctuation which manifestly affect meaning are recorded, as for instance at 1.250.1, where Q1 reads 'Bid them farewell *Cordelia*, though vnkind | Thou loosest here, a better where to find.', which implies, at least to a modern reader, that it is Cordelia who is unkind, not her sisters. Though the collations attempt to indicate alternative interpretations when, for example, a sentence might be intended as either a plain statement or an exclamation or question (as at 1.98 and 2.25), they do not record changes, such as addition of a question mark when the words preceding it are clearly interrogative, which simply interpret for a modern reader the sense that seems implicit in the original. Modernizations of spelling are noted when Q1 might be suspected of ambiguity, e.g. at 1.91, where 'Happely' is altered to 'Haply'.

The reading to the left of the square bracket is that of this edition. The reading to the right is that of Q1 unless otherwise stated. Qa refers to the uncorrected, Qb to the corrected state of the Quarto. Quotations from early editions are given in the original spelling, but long s (ſ) and wrong fount letters are not reproduced as such. A wavy line or 'swung dash' (~) to the right of the bracket signifies a word that is substantively the same as that to the left; the caret (∧) indicates absence of a punctuation mark. Quotations from Blayney's edition are ascribed to him and modernized when appropriate. BL2 refers to an annotated copy of Q in the British Library, shelfmark C.34.k.17.

Other Editorial Procedures .

This edition follows the Editorial Procedures common to volumes in the Oxford Shakespeare series. Spelling is modernized according to the principles set out by Stanley Wells in *Modernizing Shakespeare's Spelling, with Three Studies in the Text of 'Henry V'*, by Stanley Wells and Gary Taylor (Oxford, 1979). Quotations from printed texts by Shakespeare's contemporaries are given in modern spelling unless there is reason to preserve the original spelling. References to works of Shakespeare are to the Oxford Complete Works (1986, etc.). Throughout the play, directions for speeches to be spoken 'aside' and to a particular character are editorial, as are numerals ('First', etc.) preceding the word 'Gentleman' in speech-prefixes and directions. All other departures from Q1's stage directions are noted in the collations but not in the text. Directions whose content and/or placing are uncertain, and disputable speech prefixes, are printed in broken brackets ⌈ ⌉: so, for example, '*To Cordelia*' at 1.115, since it is possible that the following words should be addressed to Kent rather than to Cordelia, and '*Edmund*' in the direction at 1.255, since (as explained in the commentary to 1.36, '*Exit*') he may have left the scene earlier.

Shakespeare draws heavily on proverb lore, transmitted orally as well as in writing. The standard compilation of proverbs and commonplaces of his time is M. P. Tilley's *A Dictionary of the Proverbs in England in the Sixteenth and Seventeenth Centuries* (Ann Arbor, 1970); this includes a 'Shakespeare Index' which was heavily revised and expanded in *Shakespeare's Proverbial Language: An Index* by R. W. Dent (Berkeley, etc., 1981), using references relating to Tilley's. I draw on this in the commentary, citing references in the form 'Dent E26'. The language of Shakespeare's time was permeated by the Bible. Identification of biblical influence in the commentary is indebted to Naseeb Shaheen's *Biblical References in Shakespeare's Plays* (Newark, Del., 1999). Quotations from the Bible are normally from the 1582 reprint of the Geneva (or 'Breeches') Bible, the version with which Shakespeare seems to have been most familiar (discussed by Shaheen, pp. 38–48). Quotations from Harsnet are modernized from and refer to Brownlow's edition; the form 'Harsnet' is preferred to the alternative Harsnett. In the notes, as in the stage directions, the play is thought of primarily as a text to be performed in the theatres of Shakespeare's time, though from time to time the notes also record decisions made in later performances.

Abbreviations and references

EDITIONS OF SHAKESPEARE

Q, Q1	The First Quarto, 1608
Q2	The Second Quarto, 1619
F, F1	The First Folio, 1623
F2	The Second Folio, 1632
F3	The Third Folio, 1663
F4	The Fourth Folio, 1685
Alexander	Peter Alexander, *Works* (1951)
BL2	Anonymously annotated copy of Q1, British Library C.34.K.17
Bratton	J. S. Bratton, *King Lear*, Plays in Performance (Bristol, 1987)
Capell	Edward Capell, *Comedies, Histories, and Tragedies*, 10 vols. (1767–8)
Collier	John Payne Collier, *Works*, 8 vols. (1842–4)
Craig	W. J. Craig, *The Tragedy of King Lear*, Arden Shakespeare (1901)
Duthie	G. I. Duthie, *Shakespeare's 'King Lear': A Critical Edition* (Oxford, 1949)
Duthie–Wilson	G. I. Duthie and John Dover Wilson, *King Lear*, New Shakespeare (Cambridge, 1960)
Dyce	Alexander Dyce, *Works*, 6 vols. (1857)
Foakes	R. A. Foakes, *King Lear*, The Arden Shakespeare, Third Series (1997)
Furness	H. H. Furness, *King Lear*, New Variorum Shakespeare (Philadelphia, 1880)
HalioF	Jay L. Halio, *The Tragedy of King Lear*, New Cambridge Shakespeare (Cambridge, 1992)
HalioQ	Jay L. Halio, *The First Quarto of King Lear*, New Cambridge Shakespeare, Early Quartos (Cambridge, 1994)
Hanmer	Thomas Hanmer, *Works*, 6 vols. (Oxford, 1743–4)
Horsman	E. A. Horsman, *The Tragedy of King Lear* (Indianapolis, 1973)
Hudson	H. N. Hudson, *Works*, 11 vols. (Boston, 1851–6)

Hunter	G. K. Hunter, *King Lear*, New Penguin Shakespeare (Harmondsworth, 1972)
Jennens	Charles Jennens, *King Lear* (1770)
Johnson	Samuel Johnson, *Plays*, 8 vols. (1765)
Kittredge	G. L. Kittredge, *King Lear*, The Kittredge Shakespeare (Boston, 1940)
Malone	Edmond Malone, *Plays and Poems*, 10 vols. (1790)
Muir	Kenneth Muir, *King Lear*, Arden (1952, etc.)
Norton	Stephen Greenblatt (general editor), *The Norton Shakespeare Based on the Oxford Edition* (New York, 1997)
Oxford	Stanley Wells, Gary Taylor, John Jowett, and William Montgomery, *Complete Works* (Oxford, 1986)
Pope	Alexander Pope, *Works*, 10 vols. (1723–5)
Ridley	M. R. Ridley, *King Lear*, New Temple Shakespeare (1935)
Riverside	G. Blakemore Evans (textual editor), *The Riverside Shakespeare* (Boston, 1974; 2nd edn, 1997)
Rowe	Nicholas Rowe, *Works*, 6 vols. (1709)
Rowe 1714	Nicholas Rowe, *Works*, 8 vols. (1714)
Singer 1856	Samuel W. Singer, *Dramatic Works*, 10 vols. (1856)
Staunton	Howard Staunton, *Plays*, 3 vols. (1858–60)
Steevens	Samuel Johnson and George Steevens, *Plays*, 10 vols. (1778)
Theobald	Lewis Theobald, *Works*, 7 vols. (1733)
Warburton	William Warburton, *Works*, 8 vols. (1747)
Weis	René Weis, *King Lear: A Parallel Text Edition* (1993)

OTHER ABBREVIATIONS

Abbott	E. A. Abbott, *A Shakespearian Grammar* (1869)
Armstrong	E. A. Armstrong, *Shakespeare's Imagination* (1946)
Barker	Harley Granville Barker, *Prefaces to Shakespeare*, 2 vols. (1958). The Preface to *King Lear*, first printed in 1927, revised 1935, is in Vol. 1; it has been variously reprinted.
Bate	Jonathan Bate, *Shakespeare and Ovid* (Oxford, 1993)
Bate, *Romantics*	Jonathan Bate, ed., *The Romantics on Shakespeare*, New Penguin Shakespeare Library (Harmondsworth, 1992)
BlayneyQ ('Blayney' in collations)	Unpublished 'reference text' (1979) of Q1, consulted and cited by the Oxford editors

Blayney, *Texts*   Peter W. M. Blayney, *The Texts of 'King Lear' and their Origins: Vol. I: Nicholas Okes and the First Quarto* (Cambridge, 1982)

Bradley   A. C. Bradley, *Shakespearean Tragedy* (1904)

Bullough   Geoffrey Bullough, *Narrative and Dramatic Sources of Shakespeare*, vol. vii, Major Tragedies (1975)

Carlisle   Carol Jones Carlisle, *Shakespeare from the Greenroom: Actors' Criticisms of Four Major Tragedies* (Chapel Hill, 1969)

Cercignani   Fausto Cercignani, *Shakespeare's Works and Elizabethan Pronunciation* (Oxford, 1981)

Chambers, *Elizabethan Stage*   E. K. Chambers, *The Elizabethan Stage*, 4 vols. (Oxford, 1923)

Colie and Flahiff   Rosalie L. Colie and F. T. Flahiff, eds., *Some Facets of 'King Lear': Essays in Prismatic Criticism* (Toronto and London, 1974)

Dent   R. W. Dent, *Shakespeare's Proverbial Language: An Index* (Berkeley, 1981)

Dessen, *Conventions*   Alan Dessen, *Elizabethan Stage Conventions and Modern Interpreters* (Cambridge, 1984)

Dessen, *Recovering*   Alan Dessen, *Recovering Shakespeare's Theatrical Vocabulary* (Cambridge, 1995)

Division   Gary Taylor and Michael Warren, eds., *The Division of the Kingdoms: Shakespeare's Two Versions of King Lear* (Oxford, 1983, 1986)

Edelman   Charles Edelman, *Brawl Ridiculous: Swordfighting in Shakespeare's Plays* (Manchester, 1992)

ELR   *English Literary Renaissance*

Elton   W. R. Elton, *King Lear and the Gods* (San Marino, Calif., 1966; repr. Lexington, Ky., 1988)

Greg, *Collected Papers*   W. W. Greg, *The Collected Papers of Sir Walter W. Greg*, ed. J. C. Maxwell (Oxford, 1966)

Greg, *Variants*   W. W. Greg, *The Variants in the First Quarto of 'King Lear': A Bibliographical and Critical Inquiry* (1940)

Gurr and Ichikawa   A. J. Gurr and Mariko Ichikawa, *Shakespeare and the Theatres of his Time* (Oxford, 2000)

Hall   Joan Lane, *John Hall and his Patients: The Medical Practice of Shakespeare's Son-in-Law* (Stratford-upon-Avon, 1996)

Halstead   William P. Halstead, *Shakespeare as Spoken*, 12 vols. (Ann Arbor, 1977), and its supplements, vols. 13 and 14, *Statistical History of Acting Editions of Shakespeare* (1983)

Harsnet	F. W. Brownlow, *Shakespeare, Harsnett, and the Devils of Denham* (Newark, 1993); includes an edition of Harsnet's *Declaration of Egregious Popish Imposters* ('Harsnet' is an alternative spelling)
Heilman	R. B. Heilman, *This Great Stage* (Baton Rouge, 1948)
Henn	T. R. Henn, *The Living Image: Shakespearean Essays* (London, 1972)
Hoeniger	F. David Hoeniger, *Medicine and Shakespeare in the English Renaissance* (Newark, London and Toronto, 1992)
Holland	Peter Holland, *English Shakespeares: Shakespeare on the English Stage in the 1980s* (Cambridge, 1997)
Hulme	Hilda M. Hulme, *Explorations in Shakespeare's Language* (1962; repr. 1977)
Johnson	Samuel Johnson, *Johnson on Shakespeare*, ed. Arthur Sherbo, 2 vols. (New Haven and London, 1968); notes on *King Lear*, ii. 659–705
Knowles	Richard Knowles, 'Cordelia's Return', *SQ* 50 (1999), 33–50
Leggatt	Alexander Leggatt, *King Lear*, Shakespeare in Performance series (Manchester, 1991)
(*King*) *Leir*	Anon., *The True Chronicle Historie of King Leir and his three Daughters* (1605); quotations modernized from the reprint in Bullough, pp. 337–402
Mack	Maynard Mack, *King Lear in Our Time* (Berkeley, Calif., 1965; London, 1966)
Marcus	Leah Marcus, *Puzzling Shakespeare: Local Reading and its Discontents* (Berkeley, etc., 1988); reprinted in part in Ryan, *New Casebook*, pp. 114–29 (references are to the original)
Mikalachki	Jodi Mikalachki, *The Legacy of Boadicea: Gender and Nation in Early Modern England* (1998)
Milward	Peter Milward, *Biblical Influences in Shakespeare's Great Tragedies* (Bloomington, 1987)
MLN	*Modern Language Notes*
MLR	*Modern Language Review*
N & Q	*Notes and Queries*
Odell	G. C. D. Odell, *Shakespeare from Betterton to Irving*, 2 vols. (New York, 1920)
OED	*The Oxford English Dictionary*, second edition, 20 vols. (Oxford, 1989), Compact Disk (1992)

Ogden and Scouten   James Ogden and Arthur H. Scouten, eds., *'Lear'*
from Study to Stage: Essays in Criticism (Madison, 1997)

Onions   C. T. Onions, *A Shakespeare Glossary*, rev. R. D. Eagleson
(Oxford, 1986)

Opie   Iona and Peter Opie, eds., *The Oxford Dictionary of Nursery*
Rhymes (Oxford, 1951)

Percy, *Reliques*   Thomas Percy, *Reliques of Ancient English Poetry*,
ed. H. B. Wheatley, 3 vols. (1886?, repr. New York,
1966)

Perrett   Wilfrid Perrett, *The Story of King Lear from Geoffrey of*
Monmouth to Shakespeare (Berlin, 1904)

PQ   *Philological Quarterly*

RES   *Review of English Studies*

Rosenberg   Marvin Rosenberg, *The Masks of King Lear* (Berkeley,
1982)

Ryan   Kiernan Ryan, ed., *New Casebooks: King Lear: Contem-*
porary Critical Essays (1993)

Rydén   Mats Rydén, *Shakespearean Plant Names: Identifications and*
Interpretations (Stockholm, 1978)

Salingar   L. C. Salingar, *Dramatic Form in Shakespeare and the*
Jacobeans (Cambridge, 1986)

Schmidt   Alexander Schmidt, *Shakespeare-Lexicon* (1874–5), rev.
G. Sarrazin, 6th edn., 2 vols. (Berlin, 1971)

Seng   Peter J. Seng, *The Vocal Songs in the Plays of Shakespeare: A*
Critical History (Cambridge, Mass., 1967)

Shaheen   Naseeb Shaheen, *Biblical References in Shakespeare's Plays*
(Newark, Del., and London, 1999)

Shickman   Allan R. Shickman, 'The Fool's Mirror in *King Lear*', *ELR*
21 (1991), 75–86

Smith   Bruce R. Smith, *The Acoustic World of Early Modern*
England: Attending to the O-factor (Chicago, 1999)

Sohmer   Steve Sohmer, 'The lunar calendar in Shakespeare's *King*
Lear', *Early Modern Literary Studies*, 5.2 (September
1999); Internet http://purl.oclc.org/emls/05–2/sohm-
lear.htm, 15 December [*sic*] 1999

Spurgeon   Caroline F. E. Spurgeon, *Shakespeare's Imagery and What*
it Tells Us (Cambridge, 1935)

SQ   *Shakespeare Quarterly*

SS   *Shakespeare Survey*

S.St.   *Shakespeare Studies*

Sternfeld   F. W. Sternfeld, *Music in Shakespearean Tragedy* (1963)

Stone   P. W. K. Stone, *The Textual History of 'King Lear'* (1980)

Sugden   E. H. Sugden, *A Topographical Dictionary to the Works of Shakespeare and his Fellow Dramatists* (Manchester, 1925)

Taylor, 'Four Readings' Gary Taylor, 'Four New Readings in *King Lear*', *N & Q*, NS 29 (1982), 121–3

Taylor, *Moment by Moment* Gary Taylor, *Moment by Moment by Shakespeare* (1985)

TC   Stanley Wells, Gary Taylor, John Jowett, and William Montgomery, *William Shakespeare: A Textual Companion* (Oxford, 1987)

Teague   Frances Teague, *Shakespeare's Speaking Properties* (Lewisburg, London and Toronto, 1991)

Urkowitz   Steven Urkowitz, *Shakespeare's Revision of 'King Lear'* (Princeton, 1980)

Vickers, *Prose*   Brian Vickers, *The Artistry of Shakespeare's Prose* (1968)

Walker   W. S. Walker, *A Critical Examination of the Text of Shakespeare*, ed. W. N. Lettsom, 3 vols. (1860)

Wells, *Theatre*   Stanley Wells, ed., *Shakespeare in the Theatre: An Anthology of Criticism* (Oxford, 1997)

Wiles   David Wiles, *Shakespeare's Clown* (Cambridge, 1987)

Williams, *Dictionary* Gordon Williams, *A Dictionary of Sexual Language and Imagery in Shakespearean and Stuart Literature*, 3 vols. (1997)

Williams, *Glossary* Gordon Williams, *A Glossary of Shakespeare's Sexual Language* (1998)

The History of King Lear

THE PERSONS OF THE PLAY

LEAR, King of Britain

GONORIL, Lear's eldest daughter

Duke of ALBANY, her husband

REGAN, Lear's second daughter

Duke of CORNWALL, her husband

CORDELIA, Lear's youngest daughter

King of FRANCE
Duke of BURGUNDY } suitors of Cordelia

Earl of KENT, later disguised as Caius

Earl of GLOUCESTER

EDGAR, elder son of Gloucester, later disguised as Tom o'Bedlam

EDMUND, bastard son of Gloucester

OLD MAN, a tenant of Gloucester

CURAN, Gloucester's retainer

Lear's FOOL

OSWALD, Gonoril's steward

Three SERVANTS of Cornwall

DOCTOR, attendant on Cordelia

Three CAPTAINS

A HERALD

A KNIGHT

A MESSENGER

Gentlemen, servants, soldiers, followers, trumpeters, others

The History of King Lear

Sc. 1   *Enter the Earl of Kent, the Earl of Gloucester, and*
          Edmund the bastard

KENT I thought the King had more affected the Duke of
Albany than Cornwall.

GLOUCESTER It did always seem so to us, but now in the division of the kingdoms it appears not which of the Dukes he
values most; for equalities are so weighed that curiosity
in neither can make choice of either's moiety.

Title] M. William Shak-speare HIS Historie, of King Lear. Q
  1.0.1–2 Enter . . . bastard] Q (Enter Kent, Gloster, and Bastard.)   2, 33.2, 61, 118 Cornwall]
Cornwell Q

Title The play's entry in the Stationers' Register (see Introduction, p. 4) describes it
as a history (which could mean simply a
narrative), and this term recurs in the
Quarto's head title and running titles as
well as on its title-page (fig. 1).

1 This is a formal court scene. At the Globe
the stage may have been set with a chair
of state—a throne mounted on a plat-
form with steps, which Lear would have
mounted on his first entrance. It seems
likely that royal characters, at least,
would be distinguished by costume and
headdress, and that the male courtiers
would wear swords. Other properties
required are a coronet (l. 33.1) and a map
(l. 37).

0.1 *Earl of Kent* There were historical Earls
of Kent, but Shakespeare invents the
character for this play, while taking hints
from the counsellor Perillus in *King Leir*.
Kent is a large county in the south-east of
England, in which Dover is a principal
town. Earls rank below dukes and mar-
quises in the Norman and subsequent
aristocratic hierarchy. At 4.37 Kent says
he is 48 years old.
Earl of Gloucester Q's spelling, 'Gloster',
reflects the pronunciation current both
in Shakespeare's time and today.
Shakespeare imported the name into the
story. Gloucester, prosperous in Roman
times, is the principal city of the county
of Gloucestershire, in south-west

England. There were earls of Gloucester
from the twelfth century to the
fourteenth, and dukes from 1385, but
both titles were extinct in Shakespeare's
time. His choice of earl rather than duke
may represent an effort at historicization,
even though either title would have
been anachronistic in relation to the
supposed dates of Lear's reign. Gloucester is old enough to have two grown-up
sons.

0.2 *Edmund* Gloucester's illegitimate son,
younger by *some year* (1.18–19) or *some
twelve or fourteen moonshines* (2.5)
than his brother. Like Edgar, Edmund
was the name of several Saxon kings,
probably chosen for this reason (though
possibly suggested by its occurrence in,
e.g., Holinshed, Harsnet, and Camden)
rather than because Shakespeare had a
brother (who died in 1607) of the same
name.

1 **affected** favoured, loved

4 **kingdoms** may refer to the territories already ruled by Albany and Cornwall
along with the rest of the 'kingdom'—
F's word; but could mean 'kingly authorities' (*OED sb.* 1). The implications of the
word are more fully discussed in *Division*,
p. vi.

5–6 **equalities . . . moiety** correspondences
are so nicely balanced (or pondered) that
minute observation of neither share (*moiety*) can determine grounds for preference

KENT Is not this your son, my lord?

GLOUCESTER His breeding, sir, hath been at my charge. I
have so often blushed to acknowledge him that now I am
brazed to it. *Shameless*   10

KENT I cannot conceive you.

GLOUCESTER Sir, this young fellow's mother could, where-
upon she grew round-wombed and had indeed, sir, a son
for her cradle ere she had a husband for her bed. Do you
smell a fault?   *offspring*   15

KENT I cannot wish the fault undone, the issue of it being so
proper. *handsome*

GLOUCESTER But I have, sir, a son by order of law, some
year elder than this, who yet is no dearer in my account.
told [Though this knave came something saucily into the   20
son he's world before he was sent for, yet was his mother fair,
a son there was good sport at his making, and the whoreson *bastard*
of a must be acknowledged.] (*To Edmund*) Do you know this
whore noble gentleman, Edmund?

EDMUND No, my lord.   25

GLOUCESTER (*to Edmund*) My lord of Kent. Remember him
hereafter as my honourable friend.

EDMUND (*to Kent*) My services to your lordship. *gesture of respect*

KENT I must love you, and sue to know you better. *seek*

EDMUND Sir, I shall study deserving.   30

25 EDMUND] *Bast*. Q (*subs. throughout*)

between the portions allocated to each.
The implication is that Lear has already
divided the kingdom between them.

8 **breeding** may play on the senses
'begetting' and 'bringing up',
'educating'.
at my charge at my expense; or, more
generally, my responsibility

10 **brazed** brazened, made shameless

11 **conceive** understand. Gloucester forces a
pun on 'become pregnant (by)'.

15 **smell a fault** detect a transgression, with
possible wordplay on *fault* as 'lost scent'
(in hunting) and female genitals
(Williams, *Glossary*)

16 **issue** result, offspring

17 **proper** fault*less* (substantially *OED a*. 8a),
handsome (*OED* 9)

18 **by order of law** by legal arrangement
(*OED, order, sb*. 16), i.e. legitimate

19 **elder** Edgar's seniority (emphasized again
at 2.5–6) indicates that Edmund was
adulterously begotten.

20 **knave** fellow (jocular)
saucily wantonly, cheekily (Shakespeare
usually uses the word seriously: *OED,
saucy, a.*[1] 2b)

22 **whoreson** bastard (jocular as well as
literal)

28 **My services . . . lordship** A bow or other
gesture of respect is called for.

29 **sue** seek

30 **study deserving** seek to earn favour

GLOUCESTER (*to Kent*) He hath been out̲ nine years, and
away he shall again.
   Sound a sennet
The King is coming.
   Enter one bearing a coronet, then King Lear, then the
   Dukes of Albany and Cornwall; next Gonoril, Regan,
   Cordelia, with followers

32.1 *Sound a sennet*] Q (*after* 'coming', *l.* 33)   33.1 *King*] *not in* Q

31 **out** away, for an unexplained reason:
perhaps, as was common in Shakespeare's time, to be brought up in
another nobleman's household, or
abroad on an educational or military mis-
sion. An actor might draw significance
from Gloucester's apparently cheerful ac-
quiescence in Edmund's absences, in
contrast to his treatment of Edgar.

32.1–33.3 The directions demand a ritualistic and hierarchical entry, probably
through the central entrance at the
Globe. Lear presumably sits centre-stage
before speaking. Cordelia, who later
speaks aside to the audience, may well
stand downstage. Some directors bring
on the Fool with Lear. In naturalistic
terms this would help to explain his later
awareness of what happened in the
scene, but his entry in 1.4 is so elabo-
rately built up as to suggest that he has
not been seen before.

32.1 **sennet** A trumpet call heralding a ceremonial entry.

33.1 **coronet** small crown worn by one
below the rank of king (so Casca in *Caesar*: "twas not a crown neither, 'twas
one of these coronets', 1.2.237–8), here
probably intended for Cordelia's successful suitor. Lear himself would wear the
royal crown, and Albany and Cornwall
would wear coronets (A. J. Gurr, 'Staging at the Globe', in *Shakespeare's Globe
Rebuilt*, ed. R. Mulryne and M. Shewring
(Cambridge, 1997), 159–68; p. 165).
Lear This is the regular spelling in the
Quarto, a phonetic variant of the previously more common 'Leir'. According to
John Higgins in *The Mirror for Magistrates*
(1574), this legendary King of Britain
ruled some 880 years before the birth of
Christ; Holinshed (Bullough, vii. 316)
says he 'made the town of Caerleir now
called Leicester'. At 21.59 he claims to be
aged *Fourscore and upward*.

33.2 *Duke of Albany* According to Holinshed (i. 144 in the six-volume reprint of
1807), Albany, or Albania, was the
whole of Britain 'beyond the Humber
northward', named after Albanect,
youngest son of Brutus. The name was
current in Shakespeare's time; King
James's younger son, Prince Charles, became Duke of Albany on his baptism in
1600. The Duke's age is not specified.
The first syllable of his name is pronounced 'Orl-' or 'Ol-'. 'Duke' is the
highest title of the aristocracy, ranking
immediately below royalty.
Duke of Cornwall Cornwall is, and was,
a large area in the south-west of England,
an independent kingdom until it came
under Anglo-Saxon rule in the tenth century. From the time of Edward III the
duchy has been hereditary to the Prince
of Wales, so when Shakespeare wrote the
play it belonged to James I's eldest son,
Prince Henry, born 1594. This means
that if Shakespeare were thinking in
terms of his own time, Cornwall would
have had to be Lear's son, not his son-in-
law. There is a Duke of Cornwall in *King
Leir*, married not to Regan but to Gonoril.
Shakespeare does not specify his age.
Gonoril In Q, as in *King Leir*, the name is
spelt Gonorill, closer to Holinshed's
'Gonorilla' than F's 'Gonerill'. We follow the usual practice of omitting the re-
dundant final letter. She is Lear's eldest
daughter, but her age is not specified.

33.2 *Regan* Lear's middle daughter. This is
Holinshed's spelling; in *Leir*, she is
Ragan. Her age is not specified.

33.3 *Cordelia* Lear's youngest, and
unmarried, daughter. Her name is
'Cordella' in Holinshed, 'Cordeilla' in
Leir. Shakespeare adopts Spenser's form,
perhaps, in view of his practice of giving
his heroines significant names—Marina,
Perdita, Miranda—in his late plays,

LEAR

Attend my lords of France and Burgundy, Gloucester.

GLOUCESTER I shall, my liege.					[*Exit*]			35

LEAR

secret

Meantime we will express our darker purposes.

most pressing

The map there. Know we have divided

In three our kingdom, and 'tis our first intent

Responsibility

To shake all cares and business off our state,

establishing

Confirming them on younger years.					40

The two great princes, France and Burgundy—

Great rivals in our youngest daughter's love—

not actually
who
loves him
but who
will say
_it._

Long in our court have made their amorous sojourn,

And here are to be answered. Tell me, my daughters,

[Which of you shall we say doth love us most,]			45

declaration of
daughters'
devotion /
Respect?

That we our largest bounty may extend

Where merit doth most challenge it?

Gonoril, our eldest born, speak first.

GONORIL

Sir, I do love you more than words can wield the matter;

Dearer than eyesight, space, or liberty;					50

---

35 *Exit*] F; *not in* Q; *Exeunt Gloucester and Edmund* CAPELL   39 off] Q (of)   48 first.] Q (~?)

'having in mind an association with the heart' (Foakes)—'cor' in Latin; but Foakes's further suggestion of a significant anagram of 'ideal' in '-delia' seems strained.

34 **Attend** wait upon, escort. The implication is that they are waiting to be summoned to the royal presence.

35 **liege** liege lord, the superior in a feudal system to whom allegiance is due
Exit Edmund also may leave here; he has nothing to say in the rest of the scene, but will later be affected by what occurs, and may reasonably swell the crowd. J. L. Halio argues for his continuing presence in 'Staging *King Lear* 1.1 and 5.3', in *Shakespearean Illuminations*, ed. J. L. Halio and H. Richmond (Newark, NJ, 1998), pp. 102–9; p. 105.

36 **darker** more secret, inward. Perhaps referring to his previously unannounced plan to add his unmarried daughter, Cordelia, to the married ones as recipients of his bounty. The opening dialogue

could imply an understanding that the kingdom was to be shared only between Gonoril and Regan; if so *In three* (l. 38) would come as a surprise.

37 **The map there** Apparently Lear calls for a map to be produced (as explicitly in F), though in many productions it has been made conspicuous on his entry. The midline pause allows for action.

38 **first** most pressing (*OED a.* 4a)

39 **business** could mean (*OED* 5) the same as *care*; anxiety, responsibility.
state (physical) condition, status, high rank

40 **Confirming** establishing

41 **France and Burgundy** It was customary for rulers to be addressed simply by the name of their territory.

44 **answered** given a decision

46 **largest** most generous

47 **challenge** lay claim to (*OED v.* 5)

49 **wield** express (*OED v.* 4d)

50 **eyesight, space, or liberty** Key concepts of the play: Gonoril will command *Pluck out his eyes* (14.4); *liberty* may mean

Beyond what can be valued, rich or rare;
No less than life; with grace, health, beauty, honour;
As much as child e'er loved, or father, friend;
A love that makes breath poor and speech unable.
Beyond all manner of so much I love you.   55

CORDELIA (*aside*)
What shall Cordelia do? Love and be silent.

LEAR (*to Gonoril*)
Of all these bounds even from this line to this,
With shady forests and wide-skirted meads,
We make thee lady. To thine and Albany's issue
Be this perpetual.—What says our second daughter?   60
Our dearest Regan, wife to Cornwall, speak.

REGAN   Sir, I am made
Of the self-same mettle that my sister is,
And prize me at her worth. In my true heart
I find she names my very deed of love—   65
Only she came short, that I profess
Myself an enemy to all other joys
Which the most precious square of sense possesses,
And find I am alone felicitate
In your dear highness' love.

---

53 as] F; a Q   father, friend] Q (~‿ ~)   59 Albany's] Q (*Albaines*)   63 mettle] Q (mettall)
64 worth. In] Q (~‿ ~)

'domain' or 'property' (*OED sb.*[1] 7c) as well as 'freedom'.

51 **what** whatever
53 **father, friend** (e'er loved; *friend* could mean relative, or lover); possibly an error for F's 'father found' (so HalioQ)
54 **makes breath poor** outruns the power of expression
unable inadequate
55 **Beyond . . . much** 'beyond any "so much", any comparison, of whatever kind it may be' (Schmidt)
56 **Love . . . silent** The idea that we can say least to those we love best was proverbial (Dent L165 cites, e.g., 'She remembered it was one of the properties of love to be silent', Pettie, *Palace of Pleasure* (1576)), and recurs in Shakespeare.
57 **this . . . to this** Lear gestures to, or draws on, the map.

58 **forests** F's addition, 'and with champains riched, | With plenteous rivers' is added in HalioQ on the grounds that it may have been omitted as the result of eyeslip.
wide-skirted meads wide-bordered, extensive meadows
63 **Of the** 'elided as one syllable'
mettle spirit, substance (not distinct in Shakespeare's time from 'metal')
64 **prize me** value myself
65 **deed** bond
66 **came** HalioQ regularizes the metre by adding 'too' from F.
that to the extent that
68 **square of sense** Variously explained; the general sense is 'area' or 'criterion' (from the carpenter's square) of sensibility; there may be a hint of 'genital area'.
69 **felicitate** made happy (*OED*'s only instance)

CORDELIA (*aside*)   Then poor Cordelia—   70
  And yet not so, since I am sure my love's
  More richer than my tongue.
LEAR (*to Regan*)
  To thee and thine hereditary ever
  Remain this ample third of our fair kingdom,
  No less in space, validity, and pleasure   75
  Than that confirmed on Gonoril. (*To Cordelia*) But now
        our joy,
  Although the last, not least in our dear love:
  What can you say to win a third more opulent
  Than your sisters?
CORDELIA Nothing, my lord.   80
LEAR
  How? Nothing can come of nothing. Speak again.
CORDELIA
  Unhappy that I am, I cannot heave
  My heart into my mouth. I love your majesty
  According to my bond, nor more nor less.
LEAR   *obligation*
  Go to, go to; mend your speech a little   85
  Lest it may mar your fortunes.
CORDELIA   Good my lord,
  You have begot me, bred me, loved me.
  I return those duties back as are right fit—
  Obey you, love you, and most honour you.
  Why have my sisters husbands if they say   90

70 Cordelia] Q (*Cord.*)

72 **More** much
73 **hereditary** by inheritance
75 **validity** value
77 **last** Both 'last-born' and 'last to be asked'.
78 **third** one of three (not necessarily equal) parts. Seemingly Lear has reserved the best for Cordelia.
81 **Nothing . . . nothing** Proverbial (Dent N285).
82–3 **heave . . . mouth** 'The heart of fools is in their mouth: but the mouth of the wise is in their heart' (Ecclesiasticus 1: 26). In *Leir*, Cordella says 'I cannot paint my duty forth in words' (l. 277).
84 **bond** obligation, duty. The word's range

of reference is discussed by Salingar, pp. 96–7. He finds 'something cold and measured in Cordelia's use of the word'.
85 **Go to** A general expression of disbelief or rebuke; 'Come, come!'.
87 **begot . . . bred** begotten . . . brought up, raised, educated
88 **return . . . fit** pay back (*OED*, *return*, *v.*[1] 21a) 'those duties that are most fitting' (Kittredge), i.e. those mentioned in the following line.
89 **Obey . . . love . . . honour** The passage echoes the Christian catechism: 'To love, honour, and succour my father and mother'; Shaheen, p. 607, records biblical parallels.

Maybe

They love you all? <u>Haply</u> when I shall wed
That lord whose hand must take my plight shall carry
Half my love with him, half my care and duty.
Sure, I shall never marry like my sisters,
To love my father all.   95

LEAR But goes this with thy heart?

CORDELIA Ay, good my lord.

LEAR So young and so untender?

CORDELIA So young, my lord, and true.

LEAR

Well, let it be so. Thy truth then be thy dower;   100
For by the sacred radiance of the sun,
The mysteries of Hecate and the night,
By all the operation of the orbs _activity/influence of celestials_
From whom we do exist and cease to be,
Here I disclaim all my paternal care,   105

Close Relationship: Propinquity, and property of blood,
And as a stranger to my heart and me
Hold thee from this for ever. The barbarous Scythian,
Or he that makes his generation
Servings of food Messes to gorge his appetite,   110

91 Haply] Q (Happely)   98 untender?] Q (~,)   102 mysteries] F2; mistresse Q; miseries F1
night] F; might Q

91 **Haply** maybe, perhaps (merges with 'happily'; Q spells 'Happely')
92 **plight** troth-plight (sealed by handclasp), pledge
96 **goes** accords
98 **So . . . untender?** Q follows with a comma, F with a question mark (which could be interpreted as an exclamation mark): this could be either a question, an exclamation, or a statement. *OED* records no previous use of 'untender'; it has been calculated that Shakespeare coined 93 latinate words beginning in un- (B. A. Garner, 'Shakespeare's Latinate Neologisms', *S. St.* 15 (1982), 149–70; pp. 165–6).
102 **mysteries** mysterious rites
Hecate Two syllables (hecket); pagan goddess of the underworld and of night; makes a personal appearance in the scenes of *Macbeth* attributed to Middleton.
night Q's 'might' 'could be defended—"the mysteries and the might of

Hecate"—but the construction would be awkward; the proposed easy misreading produces more natural syntax and a more explicit contrast with "the sun"' (*TC*).
103 **operation . . . orbs** activity and influence of the celestial bodies
105 **paternal** *OED*'s first instance of the adjective (the adverb is recorded in 1603).
106 **Propinquity** close relationship
property . . . blood family attributes
108 **Scythian** inhabitant of uncivilized regions of Asia, proverbially barbarous: 'Was never Scythia half so barbarous', *Titus* I.I.131. Shakespeare's audience might have heard a reference to Tamburlaine, the Scythian tyrant of Marlowe's popular two-part play, in which Scythians are twice called 'barbarous' (Part I, 3.3.271; Part 2, 3.4.19).
109 **generation** offspring, or (his own) kind
110 **Messes** servings of food

Shall be as well neighboured, pitied, and relieved
As thou, my sometime daughter.

KENT   ~~former~~   Good my liege—

LEAR

Peace, Kent. ⌊Come not between the dragon and his
    wrath.⌋
I loved her most, and thought to set my rest
On her kind nursery. [*To Cordelia*] Hence, and avoid my
    sight!—   115
So be my grave my peace as here I give
Her father's heart from her. Call France. Who stirs?
Call Burgundy.   [*Exit one or more*]
             Cornwall and Albany,
With my two daughters' dowers digest this third.
Let pride, which she calls plainness, marry her.   120
I do invest you jointly in my power,
Pre-eminence, and all the large effects
That troop with majesty. Ourself by monthly course,
With reservation of an hundred knights
By you to be sustained, shall our abode   125
Make with you by due turns. Only we still retain
The name and all the additions to a king.
The sway, revenue, execution of the rest,

---

119 dowers] F; dower Q

111 **be as** Elided (Cercignani, p. 291).
    neighboured treated in a neighbourly
    fashion
112 **sometime** former
113 **his** its (as often)
114 **set my rest** In gambling, 'stake all that
    remains'; so, figuratively, 'set my final
    hope or trust', though with a sense also
    of 'repose'.
115 **kind nursery** natural care, as from a
    mother
    Hence go away
117 **Who stirs?** 'i.e. Be quick! The courtiers
    are shocked into immobility' (Muir)
119 **digest** assimilate, incorporate
120 **plainness** plain-speaking, bluntness
    marry her win her a husband
121 **in** with (F's word). The Q reading
    makes 'invest' less metaphorical: 'wrap
    you in'.
122 **effects** impressive accompaniments

123 **Ourself** The royal plural, for greater
    effect.
124–5 **With reservation . . . sustained** The
    proviso may come as a shock to Gonoril
    and Regan. Donald Sinden remarks that
    'a hundred knights are not a hundred
    servants, they are a hundred knights *plus*
    their servants . . . The only person who
    gives that clue away is Goneril, when she
    says "Here do you keep a hundred knights
    and squires [4.232]."' ('Playing King
    Lear: Donald Sinden talks to J. W. R.
    Meadowcroft', *SS* 33 (1980), pp. 81–7.)
124 **reservation** In law, the act of 'retaining
    for oneself some right or interest in prop-
    erty which is being conveyed to another'
    (*OED* 2).
127 **additions** titles, honours
128 **sway** power of government
    revenue income; accent on the second
    syllable.

Belovèd sons, be yours; which to confirm,
This crownet part betwixt you.

KENT   Royal Lear,   130
Whom I have ever honoured as my king,
Loved as my father, as my master followed,
As my great patron thought on in my prayers—

LEAR
The bow is bent and drawn; make from the shaft.

KENT
Let it fall rather, though the fork invade   135
The region of my heart. Be Kent unmannerly
When Lear is mad. What wilt thou do, old man?
Think'st thou that duty shall have dread to speak
When power to flattery bows? To plainness honour's
        bound
When majesty stoops to folly. Reverse thy doom,   140
And in thy best consideration check
This hideous rashness. Answer my life my judgement,
Thy youngest daughter does not love thee least,
Nor are those empty-hearted whose low sound
Reverbs no hollowness.

LEAR   Kent, on thy life, no more!   145

130 crownet] Q (Coronet)   133 prayers—] Q (~.)   137 mad] Q2, F; man Q1   145 more!]
Q (~.)

130 **crownet** The coronet carried on at his
      entrance; if it had been intended for
      Cordelia's successful suitor, its division
      between Albany and Cornwall would be
      ironically symbolic of her rejection. (The
      old spelling is retained to preserve the
      metre.)
134–6 **The bow . . . my heart** A difficult pas-
      sage to construe precisely. Some com-
      mentators take Lear to mean that, taut
      with anger, he interrupts Kent to warn
      him to avoid (*make from*—an odd sense)
      the (metaphorical) arrow he is ready to
      shoot; if this is so, Kent's reply must
      mean 'rather let the arrow fly'—though
      fall seems an odd choice of word for this—
      'even if its barbed head [*OED*'s only in-
      stance of this sense of *fork*] pierces me to
      the heart'. Perhaps a more natural inter-
      pretation of Lear's words is that he is
      demonstrating impatience with Kent's
      preamble, in which case *make from the
      shaft* would have to be strained into

meaning 'let the arrow go', i.e. 'say
what you have to say', 'fire away'; then
Kent's words would have to mean 'let the
weapon I have prepared fall back upon
myself rather than be directed at you,
even . . .'. But then *Be Kent unmannerly*
would indicate a sudden change of tactic:
that he will speak plainly—i.e. direct an
arrow at Lear—even at risk to himself.
137 **thou . . . old man** Kent breaches de-
      corum with familiar terms of address.
138–40 The personified abstractions—*duty*,
      power, *flattery*, *plainness*, *honour*,
      majesty, *folly*—suggest a morality play.
140 **doom** sentence (on Cordelia; but could
      also be interpreted as Lear's own *doom*)
142 **Answer . . . judgement** let my life be an-
      swerable for my opinion
145 **Reverbs . . . hollowness** does not rever-
      berate hollowly; proverbial (Dent V36). In
      Henry V the Boy says of Pistol 'I did never
      know so full a voice issue from so empty
      a heart. But the saying is true: "The

KENT

My life I never held but as a pawn
To wage against thy enemies, nor fear to lose it,
Thy safety being the motive.

LEAR   Out of my sight!

KENT

See better, Lear, and let me still remain
The true blank of thine eye.

LEAR   Now, by Apollo—   150

KENT

Now, by Apollo, King, thou swear'st thy gods in vain.

LEAR [*making to strike him*]

Vassal, recreant Villain

KENT   Do, kill thy physician,

And the fee bestow upon the foul disease.
Revoke thy doom, or whilst I can vent clamour
From my throat I'll tell thee thou dost evil.   155

LEAR

Hear me; on thy allegiance hear me!
Since thou hast sought to make us break our vow,
Which we durst never yet, and with strayed pride
To come between our sentence and our power,
Which nor our nature nor our place can bear,   160
Our potency made good take thy reward:

148 sight!] Q (~.)   150 Apollo—] Q2; ~, Q1   152 *making . . . him*] *not in* Q   recreant!]
Q (~.)   156 me!] Q (~?)

empty vessel makes the greatest sound."'
(4.4.64–6.) 'Reverb' is Shakespeare's
coinage.

145 **on . . . more** In *Leir*, when Perillus
stands up for Cordella, Leir says 'Urge
this   no more, and if thou love thy life'
(l. 569).

146–7 **pawn . . . wage** stake to wager (with a
glance at the sense of *pawn* as the piece of
lowest value in the game of chess)

150 **blank** the white at the centre of an
archery target. Kent asks Lear to continue to 'look to' him for guidance.
Apollo Pagan god of the sun, and the
archer god.

151 **swear'st** swearest by

152 **Vassal** servant, menial owing allegiance
to a feudal master

152 **recreant** allegiance-breaker, villain. Lear
makes a threatening gesture, restrained in
F by Albany and Cornwall (or Cordelia)
with the words 'Good sir, forbear!'

154 **vent** utter

156 **on thy allegiance** A solemn adjuration
which may cause Kent to kneel.

157 **us** Again Lear switches to the plural for
greater solemnity.

158 **durst** dared
strayed uncontrolled ('strained', i.e.
forced, unnatural, in F; misreading is
possible)

160 **nor . . . nor** neither . . . nor
place status

161 **made good** Various shades of meaning
are possible: carried into effect; defended;
repaired (after Kent's attacks on it)
(Horsman).

Four days we do allot thee for provision
To shield thee from dis-eases of the world,
And on the fifth to turn thy hated back
Upon our kingdom. If on the next day following   165
Thy banished trunk be found in our dominions,
The moment is thy death. Away! By Jupiter,
This shall not be revoked.

KENT

Why, fare thee well, King; since thus thou wilt appear,
Friendship lives hence, and banishment is here.   170
(*To Cordelia*) The gods to their protection take thee, maid,
That rightly thinks, and hast most justly said.
(*To Gonoril and Regan*)
And your large speeches may your deeds approve,
That good effects may spring from words of love.
Thus Kent, O princes, bids you all adieu;   175
He'll shape his old course in a country new.   *Exit*
        Flourish. Enter the King of France and the Duke of
        Burgundy, with the Earl of Gloucester

GLOUCESTER

Here's France and Burgundy, my noble lord.

---

163 dis-eases] Q (diseases)   165 next] BLAYNEY; tenth QF   167 Away!] Q (~,)   171 thee,] Q
(the͵)   176 Exit] F; not in Q   176.1 Flourish] F; not in Q   176.1–2 Enter . . . Gloucester] Q
(*Enter France and Burgundie with Gloster.*)

163 **dis-eases** discomforts, misfortunes—
    closer in meaning to F's 'disasters' than
    the modern sense of the word, and hy-
    phenated here to signal the difference.
165 **next** Q and F read 'tenth', which seems il-
    logical and was questioned by e.g. Daniel,
    who suggested 'se'nth' (Muir, finding this
    'more logical'). The emendation, by
    Blayney, is accepted by Foakes but not by
    Halio, who however does not attempt to
    defend Q in either of his editions. Sohmer
    overcomes the difficulty by stating that
    Lear 'allows Kent four days to prepare, a
    fifth day to depart, and an additional ten
    days' grace before the decree matures into
    a death-sentence' (paragraph 14).
166 **trunk** body
167 **Jupiter** Chief Roman god, worshipped
    also by the Ancient Britons.
169–76 Kent moves into rhyme. The effect
    may be one of weary detachment.
170 **banishment is here** i.e. I shall experi-

ence banishment if I remain here [?]
173 **approve** prove to be true
175 **adieu** farewell. The word had been an-
    glicized, and rhymes with 'new'.
176 **shape . . . course** pursue his customary
    conduct, i.e. retain his integrity. Kent's
    couplet marks a decisive exit, probably
    from the opposite door to that from which
    Gloucester and the suitors enter.
176.1 The '*Flourish*' is from F. The suitors
    may have worn distinctive costumes, and
    would presumably make some form of
    obeisance to Lear.
    King of France The Gallian—i.e. French
    —King in *Leir*, where he plays a much
    larger role. Burgundy and he are pre-
    sumably thought of as young.
176.1–2 *Duke of Burgundy* Shakespeare's
    invention as a suitor to Cordelia; more
    authentically historical Dukes of Bur-
    gundy also occur in *1 Henry VI* and
    Henry V.

LEAR My lord of Burgundy,
    We first address towards you, who with a king
    Hath rivalled for our daughter: what in the least   180
    Will you require in present dower with her
    Or cease your quest of love?
BURGUNDY   Royal majesty,
    I crave no more than what your highness offered;
    Nor will you tender less.
LEAR   Right noble Burgundy,
    When she was dear to us we did hold her so;   185
    But now her price is fallen. Sir, there she stands.
    If aught within that little seeming substance,
    Or all of it, with our displeasure pieced,
    And nothing else, may fitly like your grace,
    She's there, and she is yours.
BURGUNDY   I know no answer.   190
LEAR   *weaknesses of character*
    Sir, will you with those infirmities she owes,
    Unfriended, new-adopted to our hate,
    Covered with our curse and strangered with our oath,
    Take her or leave her?
BURGUNDY   Pardon me, royal sir.
    Election makes not up on such conditions.   195
LEAR
    Then leave her, sir; for by the power that made me,
    I tell you all her wealth. (*To France*) For you, great King,
    I would not from your love make such a stray

178 lord] Q (L.)   184 less.] Q (~?)

180 **rivalled** competed; the first known use of 'rival' as a verb.
    in the least at the lowest estimate
181 **present dower** immediately available dowry
184 **tender** offer
    less. Q and F follow with a question mark, retained by some editors, but it is not supported by the sentence structure, and could be interpreted as an exclamation mark.
185 **so** Quibbling on *dear* as 'beloved' and 'highly valued'.
187 **little seeming** may be interpreted as 'appearing (physically) small', or 'refusing to put on an act'.

188 **pieced** added
189 **fitly like** reasonably please
191 **infirmities . . . owes** weaknesses of character she possesses
193 **Covered with** concealed by
    strangered with alienated by (*OED*'s first instance of this rare verb)
195 **Election . . . up** choice is not possible (a strained expression; *OED*, *make*, *v.*[1], 96k. (b), citing Schmidt, defines 'make up' as '? To come to a decision', offering no other instances)
197 **tell** give a (financial) account of
198 **stray** 'action of straying or wandering' (*OED sb.* 4)

To match you where I hate, therefore beseech you
To avert your liking a more worthier way   200
Than on a wretch whom nature is ashamed
Almost to acknowledge hers.

FRANCE
This is most strange, that she that even but now
Was your best object, the argument of your praise,
Balm of your age, most best, most dearest,   205
Should in this trice of time commit a thing
So monstrous to dismantle
So many folds of favour. Sure, her offence
Must be of such unnatural degree
That monsters it, or your fore-vouched affections   210
Fall'n into taint; which to believe of her
Must be a faith that reason without miracle
Could never plant in me.

CORDELIA (*to Lear*)
I yet beseech your majesty,
If for I want that glib and oily art   215
To speak and purpose not—since what I well intend,
I'll do 't before I speak—that you acknow
It is no vicious blot, murder, or foulness,
No unclean action or dishonoured step
That hath deprived me of your grace and favour,   220

---

210 your] F; you Q   217 acknow] OXFORD; may know Q; make knowne F

---

199 **To** as to
  beseech (I) beg
200 **a . . . way** on to a more deserving object
204 **object** being within sight (?)
  argument theme
206 **trice** instant
207 **to dismantle** (as) to strip off (*OED*'s first use in this sense)
210 **monsters** makes a monster of (*OED*'s first example of the rare use of the word as a verb)
  your Weis defends Q's 'you', paraphrasing 'or the affections you asserted you felt for her have now discredited you'.
  fore-vouched previously declared
211 **taint** discredit
212 **reason without miracle** 'an obvious allusion to the theological idea that mir-

acles are needed to bring the reason of man to faith in God' (Milward, p. 163).
215 **if . . . want** if (what you say is) because I lack
217 **acknow** acknowledge. Oxford's emendation, comparing *Othello* 3.3.324, 'where Q has "you knowne" for F "acknowne"'. *OED* finds the word 'very rare' after the Old English period except in the past participle. Q reads 'may know', F 'make known', adopted in HalioQ. John Jowett (privately) suggests emendation of Q's 'you' to 'hee', i.e. 'he—France—may know'.
218 **vicious blot** stain of vice
219 **dishonoured** stained with dishonour. *OED*'s first use of the adjective is in *Measure*, 4.4.30.

But even the want of that for which I am rich—
A still-soliciting eye, and such a tongue
As I am glad I have not, though not to have it
Hath lost me in your liking.

LEAR   Go to, go to.

Better thou hadst not been born than not to have pleased
　　　me better.   225

FRANCE

Is it no more but this—a tardiness in nature,
That often leaves the history unspoke
That it intends to do?—My lord of Burgundy,
What say you to the lady? Love is not love
When it is mingled with respects that stands   230
Aloof from the entire point. Will you have her?
She is herself a dower.

BURGUNDY   Royal Lear,
Give but that portion which yourself proposed,
And here I take Cordelia by the hand,
Duchess of Burgundy—

LEAR   Nothing. I have sworn.   235

BURGUNDY (*to Cordelia*)

I am sorry, then, you have so lost a father
That you must lose a husband.

---

221 the] HANMER; for QF   231 point. Will] Q (~‿~)   232 a] F; and Q

221 **the want** Hanmer's emendation of Q's
'for want', defended by Oxford since 'The
syntax requires a noun clause, not a
prepositional phrase, and QF's 'for'
could easily arise from contamination'
(*TC*). HalioQ and Weis follow Q.

222 **still-soliciting** always begging; OED's
first instance of *soliciting* as a participial
adjective.

224 **lost me in** deprived me of

225 A metrically crowded line which becomes an alexandrine if *thou hadst not* is
spoken as 'thou'dst not' and 'to have' as
'to've'.

226 **tardiness in nature** natural hesitation
(OED's first instance of 'tardiness')

227 **history unspoke** tale untold; OED's only
instance of the 'arch[aic] variant' of
'unspoken'.

228 **do** act out

229 **Love . . . love** recalls Sonnet 116: 'Love

is not love | Which alters when it alter-
ation finds'—unpublished when the play
appeared.

230 **respects** considerations
stands The grammar was acceptable.

231 **the entire** (elided) the essential
Will . . . her? France's willingness to
defer to Burgundy may seem less than
complimentary to Cordelia, but sustains
the dramatic tension.

232 **a dower** Ridley and Weis retain and defend Q's 'and dower'.
dower dowry (F's word; the forms were
interchangeable)

233 **portion** dowry

234 **take . . . hand** Alluding to the betrothal
formality of handfasting; presumably
'Burgundy takes her hand, and drops it
again when he hears Lear's reaction,
only for France to *seize* Cordelia's hand at
[242]' (Foakes).

CORDELIA

   Peace be with Burgundy; since that respects

   Of fortune are his love, I shall not be his wife.

FRANCE

   Fairest Cordelia, that art most rich, being poor;   240

   Most choice, forsaken; and most loved, despised:

   Thee and thy virtues here I seize upon.

   Be it lawful, I take up what's cast away.

   Gods, gods! 'Tis strange that from their cold'st neglect

   My love should kindle to inflamed respect.—   245

   Thy dowerless daughter, King, thrown to my chance,

   Is queen of us, of ours, and our fair France.

   Not all the dukes in wat'rish Burgundy

   Shall buy this unprized precious maid of me.—

   Bid them farewell, Cordelia, though unkind.   250

   Thou losest here, a better where to find.

LEAR

   Thou hast her, France. Let her be thine, for we

   Have no such daughter, nor shall ever see

   That face of hers again. Therefore be gone,

   Without our grace, our love, our benison.—   255

   Come, noble Burgundy.

               ⌈*Flourish.*⌉ *Exeunt Lear and Burgundy, then*

               Albany, Cornwall, Gloucester, ⌈Edmund,⌉

               and followers

244 cold'st] Q (couldst)   246 my] F; thy Q   250 Cordelia, . . . unkind.] Q (~, ~ˏ)
255 benison.—] Q (~?)   256 *Flourish*] F; *not in* Q   *Exeunt*] Q (*Exit*)   *then . . . followers*] *not
in* Q   sisters.] Q (~?)

238 **respects** considerations

240 **most . . . poor** The paradox is biblical, e.g. 'Our Lord Jesus Christ, that he being rich, for your sakes became poor' (2 Corinthians 8: 9).

242 **seize upon** take possession of. Probably he takes her by the hand.

244 **their** Either the gods' or Lear's and Burgundy's. The movement into rhyme formalizes the outcome of the episode.

245 **inflamed** fervent (possibly deriving from Geoffrey of Monmouth's reference to France as '*amore virginis inflammatus*': Bullough, vii. 273)

246 **dowerless** without a dowry; *OED*'s first instance.

246 **thrown . . . chance** 'cast (as in throwing dice) to my (good) fortune' (Foakes)

248 **in** of; a hyperbole resulting from France's *inflamed* condition, as Burgundy would have only one duke at a time. **wat'rish** well, or over, watered (derisory, 'wet'); 'the province is full of rivers and streams' (Sugden).

249 **unprized** (a) priceless (*OED*'s only use of this conjectured sense); (b) unvalued

250 **unkind** unnatural

251 **where** place

255 **benison** blessing

256 *Flourish* Not in Q, but this is a ceremonial exit, marked by the sound of trumpets, and such directions are often absent in foul papers.

FRANCE (*to Cordelia*)   Bid farewell to your sisters.

CORDELIA

The jewels of our father, with washed eyes
Cordelia leaves you. I know you what you are,
And like a sister am most loath to call
Your faults as they are named. Use well our father.   260
To your professèd bosoms I commit him.
But yet, alas, stood I within his grace
I would prefer him to a better place.
So farewell to you both.

GONORIL Prescribe not us our duties.   265

REGAN Let your study

Be to content your lord, who hath received you
At fortune's alms. You have obedience scanted,
And well are worth the worst that you have wanted.

CORDELIA

Time shall unfold what pleated cunning hides.   270
Who covers faults, at last shame them derides.
Well may you prosper.

FRANCE   Come, fair Cordelia.

                    Exeunt France and Cordelia

GONORIL Sister, it is not a little I have to say of what most
nearly appertains to us both. I think our father will hence
tonight.   275

257 The] QF; Ye ROWE 1709   264 both.] Q (~?)   265 duties.] Q (~?)   268 At fortune's
alms] QF; at fortune's arms STONE *conj.*; as fortune's alms CAPELL (*subs.*)   269 worst]
OXFORD; worth Q; want F; words STONE *conj.*   272 Cordelia.] Q (~?)   272.1 *Exeunt . . .
Cordelia*] Q (*Exit . . . Cord.*)

257 **The** Oxford adopts Rowe's 'Ye', arguing that QF's 'The' is 'almost certainly
no more than an alternative interpretation of an ambiguous manuscript
"ye/yᵉ"' (*TC*), but the change seems
unnecessary.
washed (with tears)
260 **as . . . named** by their plain names
261 **professèd bosoms** pretended affections
262 **grace** favour
263 **prefer** promote
266 **study** aim
268 **At fortune's alms** as an object of charity
scanted been sparing of (*OED, scant, v.* 5)
269 **well . . . wanted** thoroughly deserve the
ill fate that you have courted
worth the worst Oxford's emendation (not
accepted by HalioQ) of Q's 'worth the

worth': '. . . to say that Cordelia is "worth
the wanted worst" is intelligibly venomous in a way that "worth the wanted
worth" is not' (*TC*). John Jowett (privately) finds 'worth the worth' acceptable
as 'a quibble between *worth* as 'deserving'
and 'quality'. F reads 'worth the want'.
270 **Time . . . hides** Time will unwrap what
cunning hides in folds; a version of the
common saying 'Veritas filia temporis',
'Truth is the daughter of time' (Dent T324).
271 **Who . . . derides** In the end shame
mocks those who seek to cover their
faults. Cordelia makes an oracularly
cryptic exit with a biblical echo: 'He that
hideth his sins shall not prosper'
(Proverbs 28: 13).
274 **nearly** closely

REGAN That's most certain, and with you. Next month
with us.

GONORIL You see how full of changes his age is. The observation we have made of it hath not been little. He always
loved our sister most, and with what poor judgement he   280
hath now cast her off appears too gross.

REGAN 'Tis the infirmity of his age; yet he hath ever but
slenderly known himself.

GONORIL The best and soundest of his time hath been but
rash; then must we look to receive from his age not alone   285
the imperfection of long-engrafted condition, but therewithal unruly waywardness that infirm and choleric
years bring with them.

REGAN Such unconstant starts are we like to have from him
as this of Kent's banishment.   290

GONORIL There is further compliment of leave-taking between Burgundy and him. Pray, let's hit together. If our
father carry authority with such dispositions as he bears,
this last surrender of his will but offend us.

292 Burgundy] HANMER; *France* QF

281 **gross** palpably
284 **The best . . . time** i.e. even when he was
in his prime and at his fittest
285 **look** expect
286 **long-engrafted** long-implanted (*OED*'s
first example of *engrafted* is in Sonnet
37)
286–7 **therewithal** along with that
289 **unconstant starts** unpredictable out-
bursts
291–2 **further . . . him.** If this is supposed to
be taking place off stage it could be
prompted by a sound such as a flourish of
trumpets. QF read 'France', not 'Burgundy' and spell 'complement' but the
forms were not distinct; *OED*, noting that
'the word has since *c*.1655–1725 been
supplanted by the parallel F[rench] word
COMPLIMENT', cites this passage under
'complement' (*sb*. 8b), defining 'obser-
vance of ceremony . . . formal civility, po-
liteness, or courtesy.' Richard Knowles
(in a private communication) favours
''That which completes or makes perfect'
(*OED* 3), remarking 'in addition to the
exile of Kent, what completes the picture

of Lear's "poore iudgement" is his (perhaps predictable) further alienation of
France', taking the phrase to imply that
Lear is finalizing the break between the
two countries. But 'leave-taking') surely
implies courtesy (*Macbeth* 2. 3. 143, 'let
us not be dainty of leave-taking') rather
than dismissal. At 2. 22 we are told that
France parted *in choler*. Duthie and
Wilson's comment that the original is
'Prob[ably] sarcastic' seems like an attempt to save Shakespeare from the
accusation of 'authorial inadvertence'
(Foakes). Hanmer made the change but
has not been followed by modern editors.
The lines have been cut in many productions (e.g. RSC 1953, 1959, 1968, 1976,
1982, 1993) but retained unaltered in
others (e.g. RSC 1950, 1955, 1962, and
1990).
292 **hit** agree (*OED v*. 17; first recorded use
in this sense); perhaps also 'act'.
293 **carry . . . bears** exercises power in his
characteristic way
294 **surrender . . . offend** 'renunciation of
his will do us nothing but harm' (Weis)

REGAN We shall further think on't.   295
GONORIL We must do something, and i'th' heat.   *Exeunt*

Sc.2 *Enter Edmund the bastard*

EDMUND

Thou, nature, art my goddess. To thy law
My services are bound. Wherefore should I
Stand in the plague of custom and permit
The curiosity of nations to deprive me
For that I am some twelve or fourteen moonshines ~~months~~   5
Lag of a brother? Why 'bastard'? Wherefore 'base',
When my dimensions are as well compact,
My mind as generous, and my shape as true
As honest madam's issue?
Why brand they us with 'base, base bastardy',   10
Who in the lusty stealth of nature take
More composition and fierce quality
Than doth within a stale, dull-eyed bed go

2.0.1 *Edmund . . . Bastard*] Q (*Bastard Solus.*)   3 Stand in] QF; Stand on STONE *conj.*
4 curiosity] QF; courtesy THEOBALD   13 dull-eyed] BLAYNEY (*conj.* Stone); dull lyed Q

---

296 **i'th' heat** (of the moment), 'while the
   iron is hot' (Dent I94)
2.1 Edmund probably enters through the
   door opposite that by which the sisters
   have exited. A letter is required (l. 19).
 1 **nature** 'Nature' is a key word and concept of the play, used with varying shades
   of meaning. Though it often relates to
   natural ties of human feeling, here it
   seems most closely related to its use in the
   phrase 'state of nature', defined by *OED*
   as 'the condition of man before the foun-
   dation of an organized society' (*nature*,
   sb. 14 a (*b*)). The phrase '*thy* law' disso-
   ciates Edmund from the world of the
   opening scene; and 'law' is a paradox.
   The speech in general bears interesting
   resemblances to 'A Paradox, in the defence of Bastardy' in Thomas Milles's
   Treasurie of Ancient and Modern Times
   (1613), quoted, along with other paradoxes relevant to the play, in '*King Lear*
   and Renaissance Paradoxes', by Brian
   Vickers, *MLR* 63 (1968), 305–14.
 3 **Stand . . . custom** be subject to pestilen-
   tial custom (by which a bastard could not

inherit his father's property)
 4 **curiosity** faddiness, over-scrupulosity
   deprive *OED*'s only instance of the
   absolute use (*v.* 3b).
 5 **For that** just because
   moonshines months; described by *OED*
   (*sb.* 1d) as a jocular nonce-use.
 6 **Lag of** later than
 7 **dimensions** parts, 'proportions'
   compact (past participle) put together
 8 **generous** magnanimous, appropriate to
   one of high birth
 9 **honest** virtuous
11 **lusty stealth** vigorous but furtive activity
11–12 **take . . . quality** acquire a better constitution and more ardent nature? require greater effort and a fiercer sexuality
   in the engendering?
13 **dull-eyed** Stone's proposed emendation
   (pp. 51–2), accepted by HalioQ and Weis,
   of Q's 'dull lyed' gives, as he says, 'not
   only a vivid image, but one entirely appropriate to the state "'tween asleep and
   wake" which it is meant to suggest'. The
   compound also occurs at *Merchant*
   3.3.14 and *Pericles* Scene 2.2.

To the creating a whole tribe of fops 15
Got 'tween a sleep and wake? Well then,
Legitimate Edgar, I must have your land.
Our father's love is to the bastard Edmund
As to the legitimate. Well, my legitimate, if
This letter speed and my invention thrive,
Edmund the base shall to th' legitimate. 20
I grow, I prosper. Now gods, stand up for bastards!
Enter the Earl of Gloucester. Edmund reads a letter
GLOUCESTER
Kent banished thus, and France in choler parted,
And the King gone tonight, subscribed his power,
Confined to exhibition—all this done
Upon the gad?—Edmund, how now? What news? 25
EDMUND So please your lordship, none.
GLOUCESTER Why so earnestly seek you to put up that
letter?

14 creating] F; creating of Q   15 then,] F; the˄ Q   20 to th'] QF (tooth' Q); top the CAPELL
21.1 *Gloucester . . . letter*] *Gloster.* Q   25 gad?] Q (~;)

14 **creating** Weis (but not HalioQ) retains
Q's 'creating of'; adoption of F is explained in *TC*. This is *OED*'s first instance
of the verbal noun.
fops fools ('dandies' is a later meaning)
15 **Got** begotten
wake the state of wakefulness
18 **As** no less than
19 **letter** It may have been visible earlier.
speed succeed in its purpose
invention scheme
20 **shall to** shall advance to, usurp. This
reading, common to both Q (tooth') and
F (to'th), was long supplanted by 'shall
top the' (Capell). QF are defended by
T. Clayton and M. Pittock in separate
articles in *N & Q* 229 (1964), 207–8,
209–10. *TC* suggests a possible pun on
'tooth' meaning 'bite' (*OED*, *tooth*, *v*. 3).
Hanmer's derided interpretation of QF as
'toe' (see Furness), described by Schmidt
as 'a pretended provincialism' meaning
'to pluck up by the root', may deserve
reconsideration. Though *OED*'s first
recorded verbal use is the golfing term
meaning 'to kick with the toe', first
recorded in 1865, Shakespeare was perfectly capable of using a noun as a verb.
Johnson defended Hanmer: 'To "toe"
him is perhaps to "kick" him "out", a
phrase yet in vulgar use; or, to "toe"
may be literally to "supplant".'
21 **stand up for** champion (*OED*, *stand*,
v. 1030, first recorded use in this sense);
possibly with a hint of 'have an erection',
the 'phallic pun' suggested by Heilman
(p. 274).
21.1 *Edmund reads* Gloucester enters preoccupied with his thoughts, then sees
Edmund reading the letter.
22 **choler** anger (doubtless at Lear's treatment of Cordelia)
23 **subscribed** (having) signed away, yielded
up (*OED*, *subscribe*, *v*. 5, only use in this
sense)
24 **Confined to exhibition** reduced to (accepting) a pension
25 **Upon the gad** as if pricked with a gad, or
spike, suddenly; *OED*'s only example of
the phrase (*gad*, *sb*.[1] 4b).
Edmund . . . news? Gloucester, who has
been preoccupied, notices Edmund and
his letter.
27 **put up** conceal (in his pocket)

EDMUND I know no news, my lord.

GLOUCESTER What paper were you reading?   30

EDMUND Nothing, my lord.

GLOUCESTER No? What needs then that terrible dispatch of
    it into your pocket? The quality of nothing hath not such
    need to hide itself. Let's see. Come, if it be nothing I shall
    not need spectacles.   35

EDMUND I beseech you, sir, pardon me. It is a letter from
    my brother that I have not all o'er-read; for so much as I
    have perused, I find it not fit for your liking.

GLOUCESTER Give me the letter, sir.

EDMUND I shall offend either to detain or give it. The con-   40
    tents, as in part I understand them, are to blame.

GLOUCESTER Let's see, let's see!

EDMUND I hope for my brother's justification he wrote this
    but as an assay or taste of my virtue.

        He gives Gloucester a letter

GLOUCESTER (*reads*) 'This policy of age makes the world   45
    bitter to the best of our times, keeps our fortunes from us
    till our oldness cannot relish them. I begin to find an idle
    and fond bondage in the oppression of aged tyranny,
    who sways not as it hath power but as it is suffered. Come
    to me, that of this I may speak more. If our father would   50
    sleep till I waked him, you should enjoy half his revenue
    for ever and live the beloved of your brother,

                                                Edgar.'

36 EDMUND] Qb (*Ba<stard>*); *not in* Qa   41 to] Q (too)   42 see!] Q (~?)   44.1 *He . . . Gloucester*] *not in* Q

31 **Nothing** The choice of a keyword of the
    play where 'none' might have been ex-
    pected seems deliberate.

32 **terrible** fearful, affrighted (Schmidt; a
    sense not recorded in *OED*)
    dispatch disposal, the act of putting away
    hastily; *OED*'s first use in this sense.

33 **pocket** could refer to a bag or pouch not
    attached to a garment.

34–5 **I . . . spectacles** A proverbial notion
    (Dent S733.1). It is not necessary to sup-
    pose that Gloucester actually uses specta-
    cles (as Teague does, p. 185).

37 **all o'er-read** read right through

41 **to blame** blameworthy (Q's 'too blame'

could be an intensifier followed by an ad-
    jective, i.e. 'too much to blame')

44 **assay** trial (or possibly, as Salingar sug-
    gests, p. 113, 'essay', literary exercise)
    taste trial, test (*OED sb.*[1] 2a)

45 **This** Absence of an antecedent may indi-
    cate that at first Gloucester reads silently.
    policy of age government by the aged?
    cunning of old people? policy of reveren-
    cing age?

46 **best of our times** our prime years

47–8 **idle and fond** absurd and foolish

49 **who sways** which governs
    suffered tolerated

50 **I** (stressed)

Hum, conspiracy! 'Slept till I waked him, you should
enjoy half his revenue'—my son Edgar! Had he a hand to   55
write this, a heart and brain to breed it in? When came
this to you? Who brought it?

EDMUND It was not brought me, my lord, there's the
cunning of it. I found it thrown in at the casement of my
closet. **bedroom window** ~ **handwriting**   60

GLOUCESTER You know the character to be your brother's?

EDMUND If the matter were good, my lord, I durst swear it
were his; but in respect of that, I would fain think it were
not.

GLOUCESTER It is his?   65

EDMUND It is his hand, my lord, but I hope his heart is not
in the contents.

GLOUCESTER Hath he never heretofore sounded you in this
business?

EDMUND Never, my lord; but I have often heard him main-   70
tain it to be fit that, sons at perfect age and fathers declin-
ing, his father should be as ward to the son, and the son
manage the revenue.

GLOUCESTER O villain, villain—his very opinion in the
letter! Abhorred villain, unnatural, detested, brutish vil- 75
lain—worse than brutish! Go, sir, seek him, ay, apprehend him. Abominable villain! Where is he?

EDMUND I do not well know, my lord. If it shall please you
to suspend your indignation against my brother till you
can derive from him better testimony of this intent,   80
act on certainty you should run a certain course; where if you violently
proceed against him, mistaking his purpose, it would
make a great gap in your own honour and shake in pieces

55 Edgar!] Q (~,)   63–4 respect of that, . . . not.] Q2; ~, ~ . . . ~, . . . ~, Q1   65 It is his?]
Q; ~ ~ ~. F (Is it his? Q2)   75–7 letter! . . . villain— . . . brutish! . . . apprehend him. . . . villain!] Q (~, . . . ~, . . . ~, . . . ~~, . . . ~,)   76 ay] Q (I)

59–60 **casement . . . closet** window of my
room. In *Caesar*, a letter is thrown
through the window of Brutus' closet
(2.1.35–8).
61 **character** handwriting
63 **fain** gladly
65 **his?** So Q, but a question mark could indicate an exclamation; either Gloucester's

mind is already made up, or he asks for
confirmation.
68 **sounded** indirectly examined, sounded
out
71 **at perfect age** fully grown, 'of age'
76–7 **apprehend** arrest
81 **run . . . course** act on certainty
where whereas

the heart of his obedience. I dare pawn down my life for
him he hath wrote this to feel my affection to your hon-   85
our, and to no further pretence of danger.

GLOUCESTER Think you so?

EDMUND If your honour judge it meet, I will place you
where you shall hear us confer of this, and by an auricular assurance have your satisfaction, and that without   90
any further delay than this very evening.

GLOUCESTER He cannot be such a monster.

EDMUND Nor is not, sure.

GLOUCESTER To his father, that so tenderly and entirely
loves him—heaven and earth! Edmund, seek him out,   95
wind me into him. I pray you, frame your business after
your own wisdom. I would unstate myself to be in a due
resolution.

EDMUND I shall seek him, sir, presently, convey the business as I shall see means, and acquaint you withal.   100

GLOUCESTER These late eclipses in the sun and moon portend no good to us. Though the wisdom of nature can
nature reason thus and thus, yet nature finds itself scourged by
the sequent effects. Love cools, friendship falls off, broth-

84 **pawn down** stake
85 **wrote** written (an unusual but not
unique form)
feel sound out, put to the test
86 **pretence of danger** dangerous purpose (a
now obsolete sense)
88–91 **If . . . evening** 'But he never does',
writes Granville Barker, who sees this as
a 'slight change of plan'. 'Shakespeare
may have remembered, besides, that he
had lately used this none too fresh device
in *Othello*' (p. 274).
88 **meet** fitting
89–90 **auricular assurance** directly heard
confirmation
90 **satisfaction** (of any doubts you may entertain)
96 **wind me into him** insinuate yourself into
his confidence (*OED*, *wind*, *v.*[1] 13b) for
me
frame . . . after contrive . . . according to
97–8 **unstate . . . resolution** give up my
status and property to be resolved about
the truth of the matter
99 **presently** immediately
convey manage confidentially (*OED*, *convey*, *v.* 12b)

100 **withal** therewith
101 **late** recent
eclipses The possibility of a topical reference is discussed in the Introduction,
pp. 12–13.
102–3 **wisdom . . . yet nature** wisdom of
human nature (as expressed in e.g. philosophy or science) can offer such and
such explanations, nevertheless the natural world
104 **sequent** consequent (*OED* 2, first
recorded in this sense in *All's Well*,
2.2.51)
104–7 **Love . . . father** This passage expresses a common theme—there is a
parallel in, e.g., the play *Gorboduc*, by T.
Norton and T. Sackville (acted 1561),
which has been suggested as a source for
Lear (B. H. C. de Mendonça, 'The Influence of *Gorboduc* on *King Lear*, *SS* 13
(1960), pp. 41–8). It was well known
from the Bible, especially Matthew 10: 21
(echoed in the homily 'Against Disobedi-
ence and Wilful Rebellion'): 'The brother
shall betray the brother to death, and the
father the son, and the children shall rise
against their parents, and shall cause

ers divide; in cities mutinies, in countries discords, 105
palaces treason, the bond cracked between son and *the world*
father. Find out this villain, Edmund; it shall lose thee *is coming*
nothing. Do it carefully. And the noble and true-hearted *apart*
Kent banished, his offence honesty! Strange, strange!

Exit

EDMUND This is the excellent foppery of the world: that 110
supreme folly
when we are sick in fortune—often the surfeit of our own *excess*
behaviour—we make guilty of our disasters the sun, the
moon, and the stars, as if we were villains by necessity,
fools by heavenly compulsion, knaves, thieves, and
treacherers by spherical predominance, drunkards, 115
liars, and adulterers by an enforced obedience of planet-
ary influence, and all that we are evil in by a divine
thrusting on. An admirable evasion of whoremaster
man, to lay his goatish disposition to the charge of stars!
My father compounded with my mother under the 120
Dragon's tail and my nativity was under Ursa Major, so

109 honesty] F (~.); honest Q   115 spherical] F; spirituall Q

them to die' (Shaheen, p. 608). Ovid also
expresses similar ideas (*Metamorphoses*,
translated by Golding, 1.162–7, cited by
Bate, p. 172). Shakespeare sounds the
same theme in e.g. 2.5 of *Richard Duke of
York* (*3 Henry VI*) where we see a soldier
who has killed his son and one who has
killed his father, and in Ulysses' 'degree'
speech (*Troilus* 1.3.74–137, especially
'the rude son should strike his father
dead', l. 115).

104 **falls off** diminishes, dwindles (*OED*'s
first use in this sense, *fall*, *v.*, 92f)

105 **mutinies** discord, contention

110 **excellent** supreme. *OED*'s first instance
of this 'bad or neutral sense' is in *Titus*
2.3.7, 'A very excellent piece of villainy'.
foppery folly

111 **surfeit** (result of) excess, over-
indulgence

115 **treacherers** traitors (a form current in
the later part of the sixteenth century)
by spherical predominance because certain spheres were in a dominant (astrological) position. Q's 'spirituall',
retained by HalioQ and Weis, without
note, seems implausible and is not supported by *OED*. *TC*, interpreting Q as a

misreading, observes that it is 'more un-
derstandable if the copy had the obsolete
"spir" spelling of the noun *sphere*'.

116 **adulterers** In the Elliott–Olivier film, Edmund isolates the word, clearly thinking
of his father.

117–18 **divine thrusting on** heavenly
compulsion

118 **whoremaster** lecherous

119 **goatish** lustful

120–2 **My . . . lecherous** Edmund moves into
a sarcastic parody of what 'whoremaster
man' might say.

120 **compounded** united, copulated

120–1 **the Dragon's tail** 'The descending
node of the moon's orbit with the ecliptic'
(*OED*, *dragon's tail*, 1, recording this as
its first instance, though 'dragon's
head', for the 'ascending node', is
recorded from 1509, and Chaucer refers
to the 'tail of the dragon' as a 'wicked
planete' (*Treatise of the Astrolabe*, in
Works, ed. Robinson, p. 551) (Weis)).
Edmund's astral auspices were ominous.

121 **nativity . . . Major** birth took place
when the constellation of the Great
Bear—which was embraced by *the
Dragon's tail*—was dominant, i.e. at its
point of greatest visibility

that it follows I am rough and lecherous. Fut! I should
have been that I am had the maidenliest star of the firma-
ment twinkled on my bastardy. Edgar . . .

  Enter Edgar

and out he comes, like the catastrophe of the old comedy; 125
my cue is villainous melancholy, with a sigh like them of
Bedlam.—O, these eclipses do portend these divisions.

EDGAR How now, brother Edmund, what serious contemplation are you in?

EDMUND I am thinking, brother, of a prediction I read this 130
other day, what should follow these eclipses.

EDGAR Do you busy yourself about that?

EDMUND I promise you, the effects he writ of succeed unhappily, as of unnaturalness between the child and the
parent, death, dearth, dissolutions of ancient amities, div- 135

---

123 maidenliest] Q (maidenlest) 124.1 *Enter Edgar*] Q2; '*Edgar*' *in left margin* Q1
125 out] Q; Pat F; on's cue out OXFORD 126 my cue] F; mine Q sigh] Q2; sith Q1 them]
Q; Tom F

122 **Fut!** An expression of surprise, recorded
by *OED* only in Marston's *Antonio and
Mellida* (printed 1602).

123 **maidenliest** most chaste, also perhaps
newest. A bright new star, or nova, dis-
covered by Kepler in 1604 'would
have been shining throughout 1605 and
1606' (F. G. Butler, article noted in Introduction, p. 13 n. 1, p. 39). *TC* gives
parallels to Q's spelling.

124.1 **Edgar** Gloucester's elder son, Lear's
godson (6.91), is asked, along with Kent,
to assume rule of the kingdom at the end
of the play; an Edgar was King of England
from 959 to 975, and Edgar Atheling was
leader of the Saxons in the reign of
William the Conqueror. Shakespeare
chose the name for the play. Historical
derivation of this and the other Anglo-
Saxon names in the play is suggested by
T. Perrello in the article cited in the Introduction, p. 34 n. 3.

125 **out** i.e. of the tiring house on to the
stage, continuing the theatrical imagery.
Oxford emends to 'on's cue out' arguing
that 'an earlier use of "cue" has been
omitted. Eyeskip from "ons" to "out"
would be easy enough' (*TC*). HalioQ and
Weis accept Q without emending 'mine'
(l. 126).

catastrophe of the old comedy event or

person which produces the denouement
of a classical, or old-fashioned, comedy;
deus ex machina. B. Spivack, *Shakespeare and the Allegory of Evil* (New York,
1958), compares allegorical figures in
late morality plays who 'come in at the
end to inflict on the sinner his sublunar
suffering' (p. 67).

126 **my cue** my role; *cue* could mean 'The
part assigned one to play at a particular
juncture' (*OED sb.*² 3). Q's 'mine' is a
possible misreading of 'my cue', assuming minim error and consequent mis-
understanding.

126–7 **them of Bedlam** i.e. Bedlam beggars,
mental patients from the Hospital of
St Mary of Bethlehem, in London, who
were licensed to roam the country
begging for alms. Rogues sometimes
feigned madness to gain sympathy. Q's
reading may be an error for F's '*Tom*
o'Bedlam'.

127 **O . . . divisions** He reverts to his father's
theme. In F Edmund hums a few notes of
music, as if in pretended abstraction, a
piece of business that may have been
added in rehearsal.

127 **divisions** disagreements, discords

133–4 **succeed unhappily** turn out badly
(*OED, succeed, v.* 11a)

135 **dearth** famine

isions in state, menaces and maledictions against king
and nobles, needless diffidences, banishment of friends,
dissipation of cohorts, nuptial breaches, and I know not
what.

EDGAR How long have you been a sectary astronomical? 140

EDMUND Come, come, when saw you my father last?

EDGAR Why, the night gone by.

EDMUND Spake you with him?

EDGAR Two hours together.

EDMUND Parted you in good terms? Found you no displeas- 145
ure in him by word or countenance?

EDGAR None at all.

EDMUND Bethink yourself wherein you may have offended
him, and at my entreaty forbear his presence till some
little time hath qualified the heat of his displeasure, 150
which at this instant so rageth in him that with the mischief of your person it would scarce allay.

EDGAR Some villain hath done me wrong.

EDMUND That's my fear, brother. I advise you to the best.
Go armed. I am no honest man if there be any good 155
meaning towards you. I have told you what I have seen
and heard but faintly, nothing like the image and horror
of it. Pray you, away.

EDGAR Shall I hear from you anon?

EDMUND I do serve you in this business. *Exit Edgar* 160
A credulous father, and a brother noble,
Whose nature is so far from doing harms
That he suspects none; on whose foolish honesty
My practices ride easy. I see the business.
Let me, if not by birth, have lands by wit. 165
All with me's meet that I can fashion fit. *Exit*

---

152 person] Q1 (parson), Q2   157 heard‸] Q (~,)   160 I do] QF; Ay, I do OXFORD *conj*.

136 **maledictions** curses
137 **diffidences** mistrust, absence of
  faith
138 **dissipation of cohorts** dispersal of bands
  of soldiers
140 **sectary astronomical** votary (*OED*,
  sectary, sb. 3) of astronomy
150 **qualified** modified, reduced

151–2 **with . . . allay** even physical injury to
  you could scarcely calm it
157 **image and horror** horrific reality; 'the
  horror which an exact description would
  fill you with' (Muir)
159 **anon** soon
164 **practices** machinations
165 **wit** exercise of intelligence

King Lear

Sc. 3 *Enter Gonoril and Oswald, her gentleman*
GONORIL
  Did my father strike my gentleman
  For chiding of his fool?
OSWALD   Yes, madam.
GONORIL
  By day and night he wrongs me. Every hour
  He flashes into one gross crime or other
  That sets us all at odds. I'll not endure it.   5
  His knights grow riotous, and himself upbraids us
  On every trifle. When he returns from hunting
  I will not speak with him. Say I am sick.
  If you come slack of former services
  You shall do well; the fault of it I'll answer.   10
      [*Hunting horns within*]
OSWALD He's coming, madam. I hear him.
GONORIL
  Put on what weary negligence you please,
  You and your fellow servants. I'd have it come in
      question.
  If he dislike it, let him to our sister,
  Whose mind and mine I know in that are one,   15
  Not to be overruled. Idle old man,
  That still would manage those authorities
  That he hath given away! Now, by my life,

3.0.1 *Oswald, her*] *not in* Q   6 upbraids] Q1 (obrayds), Q2   7 trifle.] Q ($\sim_\wedge$)   10.1 *Hunting . . . within*] *not in* Q   18 away!] Q ($\sim$,)

3 The imagined location has moved to the dwelling of Gonoril and Albany.
0.1 ***Oswald*** Like Edgar and Edmund, an Anglo-Saxon name, not used in any surviving earlier play. Shakespeare may have got the name from William Camden's *Remains* (1605), where 'Osvvold' is defined as a 'house-ruler or steward' (S. Musgrove, 'The Nomenclature of *King Lear*', *RES* 7 (1956), 294–8). His age is not indicated, but he is clearly able-bodied. ***gentleman*** retainer, a man, normally of noble birth, attached to a great household. As Albany's Steward, Oswald would have had important responsibilities, discussed in Chapter 5 of *Masters and Servants in English Renaissance Drama* (Basingstoke, 1997), by M. T. Burnett, who however points out that the role was liable to be occupied by upstarts, and that Kent, at least, regards Oswald as an unworthy representative of 'the traditional order of chief officers' (p. 173). He would presumably have worn his master's livery.

9 **services** i.e. to Lear
10 **answer** answer for
10.1 **within** in the tiring house, behind the back wall of the Jacobean stage
12 **Put on** affect
13 **come in question** become an issue
17 **authorities** powers

Old fools are babes again, and must be used
With checks as flatteries, when they are seen abused.   20
Remember what I tell you.

OSWALD   Very well, madam.
GONORIL

And let his knights have colder looks among you.
What grows of it, no matter. Advise your fellows so.
I would breed from hence occasions, and I shall,
That I may speak. I'll write straight to my sister   25
To hold my very course. Go prepare for dinner.

Exeunt severally

Sc. 4 *Enter the Earl of Kent, disguised*
KENT

If but as well I other accents borrow
That can my speech diffuse, my good intent
May carry through itself to that full issue *erased appearance*
For which I razed my likeness. Now, banished Kent,
If thou canst serve where thou dost stand condemned,   5
Thy master, whom thou lov'st, shall find thee full of
      labour.

Enter King Lear and servants from hunting

25 speak.] Q (~,)   26.1 *Exeunt severally*] Q (*Exit.*)
4.0.1 *disguised*] ROWE; *not in* QF   2 diffuse] QF (defuse)   6 lov'st] Q (lovest)   thee] Q (the)
6.1 *Enter . . . hunting*] *Enter Lear.* Q; *Hornes within. Enter Lear and Attendants.* F

19 **Old . . . again** The idea that 'Old men are twice children' was proverbial (Dent M570).
   are i.e. become
19–20 **used . . . abused** treated with rebukes as well as with indulgences when they are seen to make ill use of them or when they (the old men) are seen to be illused. Line 20 may have ten syllables ('flatt'ries', 'they're') or twelve.
23 **grows of** happens as a result of
24–5 **breed . . . speak** generate . . . opportunities . . . speak (my mind)
26 **very** exact, unswerving
4 No change of time or location from the previous scene is imagined. At l. 89, Lear gives Kent money. Lear's Fool wears a coxcomb (l. 90) and may also carry the traditional bauble—a stick with a carved head, or an inflated bladder. Shickman suggests that he also carries a hand mir-

ror, and that 'In so doing, he presents emblems of folly, prudence, and self-knowledge, consonant with the tragic polarities of the play' (p. 76). Lear may carry a whip (l. 104). Taylor, *Moment by Moment*, pp. 162–236, offers a close analysis of 'Shakespeare's control of emphasis and point of view' in this scene.
1 **as well** i.e. as successfully as I have disguised my appearance
2 **diffuse** render confused or indistinct. *OED*'s first use in this sense (but Muir cites earlier parallels).
   good intent benevolent intention
3 **carry . . . issue** work itself through to the perfect outcome
4 **razed my likeness** erased my natural appearance (perhaps by shaving off his beard)
6.1 *servants* Q, which does not mention them in the entry direction, calls them

LEAR Let me not stay a jot for dinner. Go get it ready.

[*Exit one*]

(*To Kent*) How now, what art thou?

KENT A man, sir.

LEAR What dost thou profess? What wouldst thou with us?   10

KENT I do profess to be no less than I seem, to serve him
truly that will put me in trust, to love him that is honest,
to converse with him that is wise and says little, to fear
judgement, to fight when I cannot choose, and to eat no
fish.   15

LEAR What art thou?

KENT A very honest-hearted fellow, and as poor as the
King.

LEAR If thou be as poor for a subject as he is for a king,
thou'rt poor enough. What wouldst thou?   20

KENT Service.

LEAR Who wouldst thou serve?

KENT You.

LEAR Dost thou know me, fellow?

KENT No, sir, but you have that in your countenance   25
which I would fain call master.

LEAR What's that?

KENT Authority.

7.1 *Exit one*] not in Q

'servants' in speech-prefixes; F calls
them 'attendants' in the direction and
'knights' in prefixes, clarifying their relation to Lear, discussed in the note to
1.124–5.

6.1 *from hunting* An editorial deduction
from 3.7, reinforced in F by a direction for
the sounding of horns. As Dessen (*Conventions*, pp. 32–3) shows, directions to
enter from hunting are common in plays
of the period; an illustrative example is
'*Enter* Orion *like a hunter, with a horn
about his neck; all his* Men *after the same
sort hallooing and blowing their horns*'
(*Summer's Last Will and Testament*, in
Thomas Nashe, *Selected Writings*, ed.
S. Wells (1964), p. 106). They often
imply that the character wears hunting
boots.

10 **profess** practise as your trade. Kent
replies as if Lear meant 'claim'.

13 **converse** 'associate' or 'talk'

13 **him . . . little** 'He that hath knowledge
spareth his words . . . Even a fool (when
he holdeth his peace) is counted wise'
(Proverbs 17: 27–8).

14 **judgement** Either earthly or heavenly.

14–15 **eat no fish** Self-deflatingly anticli-
mactic, but possibly also implying that he
is either 'a proper—meat-eating—man',
or a loyal Protestant who does not fast on
Fridays—Craig cited Marston, *The Dutch
Courtesan*, 'Yet I trust I am none of
the wicked that eat fish o' Fridays'
(1.2.18–19)—or even that he does not
consort with prostitutes. Williams (*Glossary*) explains as 'to avoid the ways of
Roman Catholics and of whores'.

16 **What . . . thou** Lear's repetition of the
question he had asked at l. 8 may reflect
revision in the course of composition, but
could simply indicate impatience with
Kent for not giving a straight answer.

25 **countenance** could mean 'bearing' as
well as (facial) appearance.

LEAR What services canst do?

KENT I can keep honest counsel, ride, run, mar a curious   30
tale in telling it, and deliver a plain message bluntly.
That which ordinary men are fit for I am qualified in; and
the best of me is diligence.

LEAR How old art thou?

KENT Not so young to love a woman for singing, nor so old   35
to dote on her for anything. I have years on my back
forty-eight.

LEAR Follow me. Thou shalt serve me, if I like thee
no worse after dinner. I will not part from thee yet.—
Dinner, ho, dinner! Where's my knave, my fool? Go   40
you and call my fool hither.   [*Exit one*]
  Enter Oswald the steward

You, sirrah, where's my daughter?

OSWALD So please you—   thickhead*Exit*

LEAR What says the fellow there? Call the clotpoll back.
  Exeunt Servant [and Kent]

Where's my fool? Ho, I think the world's asleep.   45
  Enter the Earl of Kent [and a Servant]

How now, where's that mongrel?

KENT He says, my lord, your daughter is not well.

LEAR Why came not the slave back to me when I called
him?   bluntest

SERVANT Sir, he answered me in the roundest manner he   50
would not.

39 dinner.] JENNENS; ~, QF 41 Exit one] not in Q 41.1 *Enter . . . steward*] Q ('*Enter Steward.*', *after l.* 42) 43, 74, 77, 80 OSWALD] Q (*Steward*) 43 you—] Q2; ~, QI Exit] not in Q
44.1 *Exeunt Servant and Kent*] OXFORD; *not in* QF; *Exit a Knight* DYCE 45.1 *Enter the Earl of
Kent [and a Servant]*] OXFORD; *not in* QF

30 **keep honest counsel** keep an honourable
  secret (*OED, counsel, sb*. 5d)
30–1 **mar . . . tale** spoil an elaborate tale
  (a paradoxically oblique way of saying
  that he is plain-spoken)
32 **ordinary** The word had a range of meanings including 'methodical' and 'on the
  regular staff' as well as 'unexceptional'.
33 Shakespeare reveals Kent's disguise name
  only in the final scene (Sc. 24.278), and
  then cryptically; some nineteenth-century
  actors had Kent give it here: 'LEAR Thy
  name? | KENT. Caius.' (Bratton).

35 **singing** Possibly sexual; Williams (*Glossary*) glosses 'sing' as 'coit with'.
38 **Follow me** i.e. be my follower
40 **knave** boy, servant; not necessarily
  rogue, though the conjunction of knave
  and fool was commonplace (Dent F506.1).
41.1 *steward* a household official, major-
  domo
43 **So please you** excuse me; I'm busy (an
  example of *weary negligence*, 3.12)
44 **clotpoll** thickhead; judging by *OED*,
  Shakespeare's coinage.
50 **roundest** bluntest

LEAR A would not?

SERVANT My lord, I know not what the matter is, but to my
  judgement your highness is not entertained with that
  ceremonious affection as you were wont. There's a great   55
  abatement appears as well in the general dependants as
  in the Duke himself also, and your daughter.

LEAR Ha, sayst thou so?

SERVANT I beseech you pardon me, my lord, if I be
  mistaken, for my duty cannot be silent when I think your   60
  highness wronged.

LEAR Thou but rememberest me of mine own conception. I
  have perceived a most faint neglect of late, which I have
  rather blamed as mine own jealous curiosity than as a
  very pretence and purport of unkindness. I will look fur-   65
  ther into't. But where's this fool? I have not seen him
  these two days.

SERVANT Since my young lady's going into France, sir, the
  fool hath much pined away.

LEAR No more of that, I have noted it. Go you and tell my   70
  daughter I would speak with her.   [*Exit one*]
  Go you, call hither my fool.   [*Exit one*]
      Enter Oswald the steward [crossing the stage]

      O you, sir, you, sir, come you hither. Who am I, sir?

OSWALD My lady's father.

LEAR My lady's father? My lord's knave, you whoreson   75
  dog, you slave, you cur!

OSWALD I am none of these, my lord, I beseech you pardon
  me.

---

66 this] Q; my F   67 these] QF (this)   71 *Exit one*] *not in* Q   72 *Exit one*] *not in* Q
72.1 *Oswald the*] *not in* Q   *crossing the stage*] OXFORD; *not in* QF

---

52 **A** Unemphatic form of 'he'.

54 **entertained** treated

54–5 **that . . . wont** such . . . as you used to
  be

56 **abatement** F adds 'of kindness', but the
  word could be used absolutely, as in
  Twelfth Night I.I.I3, 'abatement and
  low price'.

56 **dependants** retainers, servants

62 **rememberest** remindest

conception idea, perception

64 **jealous curiosity** suspicious over-
  interpretation, 'sensitiveness'

65 **very pretence** actual intention
  purport expression

72.1 *crossing the stage* i.e. entering at
  one of the doors in the back wall of
  the Jacobean stage and leaving by another

77 **these** F's modernization of Q's 'this'.

LEAR Do you bandy looks with me, you rascal?

> ⌜*Lear strikes him*⌝

OSWALD I'll not be struck, my lord—   80

KENT (*tripping him*) Nor tripped neither, you base football
    player.

LEAR (*to Kent*) I thank thee, fellow. Thou serv'st me, and
    I'll love thee.

KENT (*to Oswald*) Come, sir, I'll teach you differences.   85
    Away, away. If you will measure your lubber's length
    again, tarry; but away if you have wisdom.

> *Exit Oswald*

LEAR Now, friendly knave, I thank thee.

> *Enter Lear's Fool*

There's earnest of thy service.

> *He gives Kent money*

FOOL Let me hire him, too. (*To Kent*) Here's my coxcomb.   90

LEAR How now, my pretty knave, how dost thou?

FOOL (*to Kent*) Sirrah, you were best take my coxcomb.

KENT Why, fool?

FOOL Why, for taking one's part that's out of favour. Nay,
    an thou canst not smile as the wind sits, thou'lt catch   95
    cold shortly. There, take my coxcomb. Why, this fellow
    hath banished two on's daughters and done the third a
    blessing against his will. If thou follow him, thou must
    needs wear my coxcomb. (*To Lear*) How now, nuncle?
    Would I had two coxcombs and two daughters.   100

79.1 *Lear . . . him*] *not in* Q   81 *tripping him*] *not in* Q   87 if you have] BLAYNEY; you haue Q
88.1 *Enter . . . Fool*] Q ('*Enter Foole.*', *after l.* 89)   89.1 *He . . . money*] *not in* Q   94 one's] Q1
(on's), Q2   99 nuncle?] Q (~,)

79 **bandy looks** exchange (insolent) glances

81 **football** Regarded as a game 'wherein is
    nothing but beastly fury and extreme vio-
    lence' and 'to be utterly abjected of all
    noblemen' (Sir Thomas Elyot, *Book of the
    Governor*, 1531; Everyman edn. (1907),
    p. 113).

85 **differences** i.e. how to recognize your
    betters

86 **lubber** lout

87 **if you** HalioQ (but not Weis) retains Q's
    'you': 'away, you'. The ellipsis may
    have been acceptable.

88.1 **Enter . . . Fool** 'it makes sense if the
    Fool enters in time to see Kent's *service* in
    tripping Oswald' (Foakes). The role of the

    Fool is discussed on pp. 39–43.

89 **earnest of** token payment to secure

90 **coxcomb** Traditional fool's cap; Craig
    compares J. Minsheu, *Ductor in Linguas*,
    1617: 'Natural idiots and fools have, and
    still do accustom themselves to wear in
    their caps cocks' feathers or a hat with a
    neck and head of a cock on the top, and a
    bell thereon, and think themselves finely
    fitted and proudly attired therewith'.

92 **were best** had better

95 **an . . . sits** i.e. if you cannot adapt your
    mood to that of those in power

95–6 **catch cold** i.e. be in trouble

97 **on** of

99 **nuncle** A variant of 'uncle'.

LEAR Why, my boy?

FOOL If I gave them my living I'd keep my coxcombs myself. There's mine; beg another off thy daughters.

LEAR Take heed, sirrah—the whip.

FOOL Truth is a dog that must to kennel. He must be   105
whipped out when Lady the brach may stand by the fire
and stink.

LEAR A pestilent gall to me!

FOOL [*to Kent*] Sirrah, I'll teach thee a speech.

LEAR Do.   110

FOOL Mark it, uncle.

> Have more than thou showest,
> Speak less than thou knowest,
> Lend less than thou owest,
> Ride more than thou goest,   115
> Learn more than thou trowest,
> Set less than thou throwest,
> Leave thy drink and thy whore,
> And keep in-a-door,
> And thou shalt have more   120
> Than two tens to a score.

102 my] OXFORD; any Q; all my F   103 off] QF (of)   106 Lady the brach] STEEVENS; Ladie
oth'e brach Q; theLady [*sic*] Brach F   108 gall] F; gull Q   119 in-a-door] Q (in a doore)

102 **my living** Q's 'any liuing' is accepted by
HalioQ and defended by Weis 'since it ren-
ders the Fool's remark particularly
barbed: even the slightest gift to his daughters makes Lear a fool, let alone parting
with everything for their sakes'. Weis, but
not HalioQ, also accepts 'any' at l. 250,
where F, more plausibly, has 'my'.

104 **whip** A common instrument of punishment of dogs (l. 106)—in *Two Gentlemen*,
Lance speaks of 'the fellow that whips the
dogs', 4.4.23–4—as well as of people.
Lear may threaten the Fool with a whip.

105 **to kennel** be forced into the doghouse

106 **Lady the brach** the bitch called Lady
(oblique reference to Regan or Gonoril,
just as 'Truth' may suggest the Fool,
Cordelia, or Kent); *brach* (pronounced
'bratch') was used as 'a term of abuse'
(*OED* b, first rec. 1610).

108 **prestilent gall** poisonous cause of distress

109 **Sirrah . . . speech** Direction of the speech
to Kent rather than to Lear is suggested by
Taylor, *Moment by Moment*, p. 196, not-

ing that the Fool 'nowhere else calls Lear
"sirrah", but he does so address Kent'.

112–21 There are earlier parallels to this
proverbial-sounding jingle, e.g. Sir
Richard Barckley, *Discourse of the Felicity
of Man* (1598), v. 535: 'believe not all thou
hearest; do not all thou maist; nor speak
all that thou knowest' (cited by Dent
A202) and Florio's *Second Fruits* (1591),
'The bottom of your purse or heart | To
any man do not impart. | Do not give
yourself to play | Unless you purpose to
decay . . . | Shun wine, dice, and lechery,
| Else will you come to beggary'
(pp. 101–5, cited Muir). In Q, the repeated
word *than* is spelt 'then'; Taylor, *Moment
by Moment*, pp. 198–204, discusses potential ambiguities resulting from this.

114 **owest** ownest

115 **goest** walkest

116 **trowest** believest

117 **Set . . . throwest** stake less than you
stand to win

119 **in-a-door** indoors

LEAR   This is nothing, fool.

FOOL   Then, like the breath of an unfee'd lawyer, you gave
    me nothing for't. Can you make no use of nothing,
    uncle?   125

LEAR   Why no, boy. Nothing can be made out of nothing.

FOOL   (*to Kent*) Prithee, tell him so much the rent of his land
    comes to. He will not believe a fool.

LEAR   A bitter fool.

FOOL   Dost know the difference, my boy, between a bitter   130
    fool and a sweet fool?

LEAR   No, lad. Teach me.

FOOL [*sings*]   That lord that counselled thee
                To give away thy land,
            Come, place him here by me;   135
                Do thou for him stand.
            The sweet and bitter fool
                Will presently appear,
            The one in motley here,
                The other found out there.   140

LEAR   Dost thou call me fool, boy?

133, 157, 166, 188, 207, 216 *sings*] *not in* Q

123 **Then** F, perhaps correctly, reads 'Then
    'tis'.
    breath . . . lawyer i.e. nothing, as
    lawyers proverbially 'will not plead but
    for a fee' (Dent L125)
127 **Prithee** I pray you, please
    rent of income from
132 **lad** man of low birth (not necessarily
    young)
133 *sings* The direction is editorial, sup-
    ported by l. 162.
133–48 **That . . . snatching** These lines,
    which might have seemed critical of King
    James, are omitted from F, possibly as the
    result of theatrical censorship (discussed
    by G. Taylor, 'Monopolies, Show Trials,
    Disaster, and Invasion: *King Lear* and
    Censorship', *Division*, pp. 75–119).
133–4 **That . . . land** There is no such lord in
    this play, but the Fool's remark may hark
    back to the second speech in *Leir* in which
    Skalliger advises the King to make each of
    his daughters a jointure of part of the
    kingdom.
136 **thou** Wiles (p. 191) suggests that this is
    the Fool's bauble, or *marotte*, 'who can

swivel his gaze from the sweet fool in
Motley (Armin) to the bitter fool (Lear)'.
139 **motley** The variegated costume of the
    professional fool.
140 **The other** the *bitter fool*, i.e. Lear himself
    there The Fool indicates Lear, who may
    have joined in the game by standing by
    him. Shickman suggests, however, that
    the Fool gives a mirror to Lear before de-
    claring himself the *sweet* fool, 'and then
    points, not at King Lear, but *into the mir-
    ror*. The "bitter fool" will presently ap-
    pear *within the looking-glass*. The old man
    credulously looks where the Fool points,
    and sees—himself. "Dost thou call me
    fool, boy?" he demands, perhaps still
    uncertain of the Fool's intent' (p. 80).
    This ingenious interpretation, suitable
    enough for film, might seem difficult to
    project on stage, but in a production by
    Max Stafford-Clark at the Royal Court
    Theatre, London, a gay fool 'powdered
    his nose and then, movingly, showed
    Lear his own reflection in the mirror in
    the lid of his powder-compact' (Peter Hol-
    land, *English Shakespeares*, p. 156).

FOOL All thy other titles thou hast given away. That thou
    wast born with.

KENT (*to Lear*) This is not altogether fool, my lord.

FOOL No, faith; lords and great men will not let me. If I had   145
    a monopoly out, they would have part on't, and ladies
    too, they will not let me have all the fool to myself—
    they'll be snatching. Give me an egg, nuncle, and I'll
    give thee two crowns.

LEAR What two crowns shall they be?   150

FOOL Why, after I have cut the egg in the middle and eat up
    the meat, the two crowns of the egg. When thou clovest
    thy crown i'th' middle and gavest away both parts, thou
    borest thy ass o'th' back o'er the dirt. Thou hadst little
    wit in thy bald crown when thou gavest thy golden one   155
    away. If I speak like myself in this, let him be whipped
    that first finds it so.

    [*Sings*]

            Fools had ne'er less wit in a year,
                For wise men are grown foppish.
            They know not how their wits do wear,   160
                Their manners are so apish.

146 ladies] Qb; lodes Qa

144 **altogether fool** completely foolish

145 **will . . . me** 'The Fool catches up "al-
    together", substituting the sense "the
    only" for "entirely"' (Duthie and
    Wilson).

146 **out** i.e. granted to me. Monopolies,
    granted by the sovereign, privileged their
    holders to exclusive trading in a commod-
    ity, or with a particular country. The
    Fool may glance critically at King
    James's abuse of the system by his
    'wholesale granting of monopolies to
    royal favorites' (Marcus, p. 149).
    on't of it

147 **fool** (a) a dessert made of eggs and
    cream, leading to *egg*, l. 148; (b) possibly
    bawdy—'The natural fool was thought
    to be generously endowed genitally'
    (Williams, *Dictionary*, p. 523).

148 **egg** Physically present in some
    twentieth-century productions (Bratton).

151 **eat** eaten

152–3 **clovest . . . middle** i.e. divided your
    kingdom

154 **borest . . . dirt** Alluding to a fable attrib-

uted to Aesop in which an old man,
accused of overloading his ass, carries it
to market.

155 **wit** intelligence
    bald crown At 8.6 Lear is white-haired;
    bald may be metaphorical (Wiles, p. 190)
    or refer to the top of his head.

156 **If . . . myself** i.e. if I am thought to speak
    foolishly
    whipped . . . so i.e. punished as a fool
    who first thinks so

158–61 **Fools . . . apish** One of the Fool's
    more enigmatic utterances; possibly to be
    sung, perhaps 'echoing some popular
    song or rhyme of the day' (Seng, p. 201).
    Presumably the first two lines mean that
    there was never a time when fools were
    less witty than now, because they have
    been supplanted by *wise men* who (like
    Lear) have grown *foppish* and are even
    more foolish than the fools. In the second
    two lines, *They* presumably refers to the
    wise men who behave in such an *apish*
    (foolish) manner that they don't realize
    how threadbare their wits have become.

LEAR When were you wont to be so full of songs, sirrah?

FOOL I have used it, nuncle, ever since thou madest thy
daughters thy mother; for when thou gavest them the
rod and puttest down thine own breeches,   165

[*Sings*] Then they for sudden joy did weep,
And I for sorrow sung,
That such a king should play bo-peep
And go the fools among.

Prithee, nuncle, keep a schoolmaster that can teach thy   170
fool to lie. I would fain learn to lie.

LEAR An you lie, we'll have you whipped.

FOOL I marvel what kin thou and thy daughters are.
They'll have me whipped for speaking true, thou wilt
have me whipped for lying, and sometime I am whipped   175
for holding my peace. I had rather be any kind of thing
than a fool; and yet I would not be thee, nuncle. Thou
hast pared thy wit o' both sides and left nothing in the
middle.

Enter Gonoril

Here comes one of the parings.   180

171 learn to] Qb (learneto); learne Qa   179.1 *Enter Gonoril*] Q (*after l.* 180)

Dent (F535) regards the first line as
proverbial on the basis of an earlier occurrence in Lyly's *Mother Bombie* (1594).
The passage is slightly clarified in F,
which reads 'grace' for *wit*, 'And' for
They, and 'to' for *do*. Johnson para-
phrased F's first two lines as 'There never
was a time when fools were less in favour,
and the reason is, that they were never so
little wanted, for wise men now supply
their place.'

159 **foppish** foolish; *OED*'s first instance of
the adjective.

163 **used it** made a habit of it

164–5 **thou . . . breeches** 'He has made a rod
for his own tail' was proverbial (Dent
R153).

166–7 **Then . . . sung** Adapting the first line
of a ballad by John Careless first printed in
1564 (Seng, pp. 203–4); Steevens found
another version in Thomas Heywood's
play *The Rape of Lucrece*, 1608, and Seng
demonstrates that it was very well
known. Sternfeld prints an early setting,
pp. 175–7, with a correction in his *Songs
from Shakespeare's Tragedies* (1964,

pp. 20 ff.). The paradoxes of weeping for
joy and singing for sorrow are characteristic of Lear's Fool.

168 **play bo-peep** 'The implication is that
Lear has blinded himself, hidden himself
(i.e. abdicated), or played silly pranks'
(Muir, adding that 'the game seems to
have been more like hide-and-seek than
the modern [peep-bo]').

171 **would . . . lie** would dearly like to learn
to lie (presumably because the truth is so
painful). Ken Tynan, reviewing Paul
Daneman's Fool in Douglas Seale's Old
Vic production of 1958, wrote that the
words were 'uttered with the sincere re-
gret of one to whom candour will always
be sacred' (*Observer*, 22 Feb. 1958), cited
M. Clarke, *Shakespeare at the Old Vic*,
vol. 5 (1958), entry for *Lear*.

172 **An** if

173 **what kin** how alike

176 **peace** Perhaps playing on 'piece', i.e.
genitals (Foakes); Williams, *Glossary*,
finds this sense only outside Shakespeare.

178 **pared** shaved away
wit intelligence

180 **parings** shavings

LEAR

How now, daughter, what makes that frontlet on?
Methinks you are too much o' late i'th' frown.

FOOL   Thou wast a pretty fellow when thou hadst no need to
care for her frown. Now thou art an O without a figure. I
am better than thou art, now. I am a fool; thou art noth-   185
ing. ⌈*To Gonoril*⌉ Yes, forsooth, I will hold my tongue; so
your face bids me, though you say nothing.
⌈*Sings*⌉ Mum, mum.
                He that keeps neither crust nor crumb,
                Weary of all, shall want some.   190
That's a shelled peascod.

GONORIL (*to Lear*)

Not only, sir, this your all-licensed fool,
But other of your insolent retinue
Do hourly carp and quarrel, breaking forth
In rank and not-to-be-endurèd riots.   195
Sir, I had thought by making this well known unto you
To have found a safe redress, but now grow fearful,
By what yourself too late have spoke and done,
That you protect this course, and put it on
By your allowance; which if you should, the fault   200
Would not scape censure, nor the redress sleep
Which in the tender of a wholesome weal

185 now.] Qb (~ ‸); thou Qa   199 it] F; *not in* Q

181 **frontlet** headband, frown (*OED* records
      as its first instance of the figurative use)
182 **Methinks** it seems to me
      frown *OED*'s first use of the word as 'A
      wrinkled aspect of the brow' (but Shake-
      speare often uses it earlier, e.g. *Titus*,
      2.1.11).
183 **pretty** fine
184 **O . . . figure** a zero with no figure before
      it to give it value; a cipher, nothing
186 **forsooth** truly
188 **Mum, mum** softly, softly
189 **keeps . . . crumb** i.e. gives everything
      away
190 **want some** experience need
191 **shelled peascod** empty peapod, nothing
      (perhaps indicating Lear). Foakes sug-
      gests 'overtones of sexual impotence, re-
      inforced by the echo of "codpiece"'.
192 **all-licensed** privileged, completely
      tolerated

193–5 **insolent . . . riots** The degree to which
      Lear's followers conform to this descrip-
      tion, along with that at ll. 232–7, signifi-
      cantly affects the balance of sympathies
      in the play; Brook made them riotous
      (Introduction, p. 00).
194 **carp** could mean 'contend, fight' (*OED*
      v.[1] 8) as well as 'find fault'.
197 **safe redress** certain amendment, im-
      provement (*OED*, *redress*, *sb.* 3a)
198 **too late** all too recently
199 **put it on** urge it on, encourage it (sense
      first recorded in *Hamlet* 5.2.351; *OED*,
      put, v.[1] 47h).
200 **allowance** approval
201–3 **redress . . . their** The plural ending
      was often omitted after 's' (Abbott 471);
      F reads 'redresses'.
202 **tender of** tender consideration, care, con-
      cern for (*OED*, *tender*, *sb.*[2] 3; *obsolete, rare*)
      wholesome weal healthy society

Might in their working do you that offence,

That else were shame, that then necessity

Must call discreet proceedings.   205

FOOL (*to Lear*) For, you trow, nuncle,

⌈*Sings*⌉

      The hedge-sparrow fed the cuckoo so long

      That it had it head bit off by it young;

so out went the candle, and we were left darkling.

LEAR (*to Gonoril*) Are you our daughter?   210

GONORIL

Come, sir, I would you would make use of that good

    wisdom

Whereof I know you are fraught, and put away

These dispositions that of late transform you

From what you rightly are.

FOOL May not an ass know when the cart draws the horse?   215

⌈*Sings*⌉ 'Whoop, jug, I love thee!'

LEAR

Doth any here know me? Why, this is not Lear.

Doth Lear walk thus, speak thus? Where are his eyes?

Either his notion weakens, or his discernings

---

208 by it] Q (beit)   219 notion‸ weakens] F; ~, weaknes Q

203–5 **Might . . . proceedings** (The actions
   needed to bring about the redress) might
   in their workings cause you such hurt as
   would be shameful were it not that the
   need for them must cause them to be regarded as judicious.
206 **trow** know (which F prints)
207–8 **hedge-sparrow . . . young** Cuckoos
   lay their eggs in the nests of other birds,
   including sparrows, which feed the
   young. The host is faced with the task of
   inserting food into the mouth of a bird
   which rapidly grows much bigger than
   itself, and so appears to be in danger of
   having its head bitten off. The Fool is
   obliquely warning Lear against his
   daughter.
208 **it head . . . it** its head . . . its. 'Its' was
   only just beginning to supplant 'his' as
   the genitive neuter pronoun at this time;
   it is not used, for example in the 1611
   Bible (*OED*). The uninflected genitive 'it'

was common; it does not necessarily signify baby-talk, but Shakespeare tends to
use it in juvenile contexts.
209 **darkling** in the dark
210 **our** Lear reverts to the royal pronoun.
212 **fraught** supplied
213 **dispositions** moods
215 **May . . . horse** i.e. even a fool can tell
   when the natural behaviour of daughter
   to father is inverted (putting the cart before the horse was proverbial: Dent C103)
216 **'Whoop . . . thee'** Perhaps, as HalioF
   suggests, Gonoril 'makes a threatening
   gesture that elicits this mock protestation
   of love'. *Whoop* is an interjection of vari-
   able significance; *jug* was a pet name for
   Joan, sometimes used derogatorily. The
   words may be the refrain of a lost song
   (Steevens).
219 **notion** understanding, intellect; *OED*'s
   first instance of this obsolete sense (5a).
   discernings powers of perception

Are lethargied. Sleeping or waking, ha? 220
Sure, 'tis not so.
Who is it that can tell me who I am?
Lear's shadow? I would learn that, for by the marks
Of sovereignty, knowledge, and reason
I should be false persuaded I had daughters. 225
FOOL Which they will make an obedient father.
LEAR (*to Gonoril*)
Your name, fair gentlewoman?
GONORIL   Come, sir,
This admiration is much of the savour
Of other your new pranks. I do beseech
You understand my purposes aright, 230
As you are old and reverend, should be wise.
Here do you keep a hundred knights and squires,
Men so disordered, so debauched and bold
That this our court, infected with their manners,
Shows like a riotous inn, epicurism 235
And lust make more like to a tavern, or brothel,
Than a great palace. The shame itself doth speak
For instant remedy. Be thou desired,

---

220 lethargied] F; lethergie Q; lethargic OXFORD *conj.*   230 understand] Q; To vnderstand F
233 debauched] Q (deboyst)   236 more like to] OXFORD; more like Q; it more like F, BL2
tavern, or] tauerne‸ or Q; Tauerne, or a F

220 **lethargied** affected with lethargy;
OED's first instance of this rare form.
220–1 **Sleeping . . . so** Possibly, as HalioF
suggests, Lear 'pinches or shakes himself
to be sure he is not asleep or dreaming'.
In any case the moment looks forward
to Lear's uncertainty of his condition as
he wakes into reunion with Cordelia
(21.53–5).
221 **Sure . . . so** Presumably an expression of
incredulity at what seems to be.
223–5 **Lear's shadow . . . daughters** F as-
signs *Lear's shadow* to the Fool and omits
the difficult remainder of the speech and
the Fool's response. *I would learn that . . .*
may mean 'I wish I knew who I am,
(I can't be Lear) because . . . everything
tells me I can't be the father of my supposed daughters.' Or perhaps he means
'I should like to be persuaded I am merely
Lear's shadow, not Lear himself, because
everything tells me that I, Lear, cannot

really be the father of these daughters.'
223–4 **marks . . . reason** all indications of
kingship, the faculty of knowledge, and
my reasoning power
226 **Which** whom (i.e. Lear)
228 **admiration** (pretended) surprise
savour same character
229 **other . . . pranks** your other new tricks
231 **reverend** (therefore) deserving of respect
233 **disordered** riotous
bold impudent
235 **epicurism** the pursuit of pleasure
236 **make more like** i.e. make it (the court)
more like
237 **great** Possibly an error for F's 'graced',
i.e. well-conducted, dignified.
shame disgrace (to me)
speak call
238 **Be . . . desired** i.e. 'let me entreat you'
(an awkward phrase, perhaps con-
sciously pompous)
thou HalioQ follows F's 'then', without

By her that else will take the thing she begs,

A little to disquantity your train,   240

And the remainder that shall still depend

To be such men as may besort your age,

That know themselves and you.

LEAR   Darkness and devils!

Saddle my horses, call my train together!—

[Exit one or more]

Degenerate bastard, I'll not trouble thee.   245

Yet have I left a daughter.

GONORIL

You strike my people, and your disordered rabble

Make servants of their betters.

Enter the Duke of Albany

LEAR

We that too late repent's—O sir, are you come?

Is it your will that we—prepare my horses.   250

[Exit one or more]

Ingratitude, thou marble-hearted fiend,

More hideous when thou show'st thee in a child

244.1 *Exit one or more*] BLAYNEY (*Exeunt some*); *not in* QF   248.1 *the* . . . *Albany*] Q (*Enter Duke.*)   250 will that we—prepare my] OXFORD; will that wee ‸ prepare any Q; will, speake Sir? Prepare my F   250.1 *Exit one or more*] OXFORD; *Exit a Knight* FOAKES; *not in* QF

comment; this may be right since elsewhere in this scene Gonoril regularly uses the plural form to Lear.

239 **else** otherwise

240 **disquantity** diminish; *OED*'s first instance of this rare word. The threat in the preceding line may ironize Gonoril's seeming wish not to cause offence.

241 **depend** be dependent on you. *OED* has only one instance of this absolute sense, from 1673.

242 **besort** befit; *OED*'s only instance of this verb. Shakespeare had used the word, also uniquely, as a noun at *Othello* 1.3.237.

244 *Exit* . . . *more* We assume here and at l. 250 that Lear is obeyed, but he still seems to be attended at ll. 263 and 280. HalioF says 'Lear's servants seem frozen here; thus, he must order them again at [253] and [283]'. Either interpretation is possible; Shakespeare may have left the precise action to be determined in rehearsal.

246 **a** could mean 'one' (i.e. Regan), implying that he disowns both Cordelia and Gonoril.

247 **disordered** disorderly

248 **Make** . . . **betters** i.e. treat their betters as servants

249 **We** . . . **repent's—** So Q except for a comma instead of a stop. We interpret as an interrupted sentence: 'We'—royal plural—'who repent us of our actions too late'. F has 'Woe that too late repents:'.

250 **Is** . . . **horses** After starting to address Albany he turns to his followers. Q reads 'is it your will that we prepare any horses,'. F, which revises the lines, has 'Prepare my Horses.' Weis reads 'Is it your will that we—prepare any horses!' No certain interpretation of either text is possible, but it is clear that Lear is speaking distractedly.

250.1 *Exit* . . . *more* The direction assumes that Lear is obeyed; Foakes directs '*Exit a knight*'.

Than the sea-monster—(*to Gonoril*) detested kite, thou ~BIRD OF PREY~
    liest.

My train are men of choice and rarest parts,

That all particulars of duty know,   255

And in the most exact regard support

The worships of their name. O most small fault,

How ugly didst thou in Cordelia show,

That, like an engine, wrenched my frame of nature

From the fixed place, drew from my heart all love,   260

And added to the gall! O Lear, Lear!

Beat at this gate that let thy folly in

And thy dear judgement out.—Go, go, my people!

ALBANY

My lord, I am guiltless as I am ignorant.

LEAR

It may be so, my lord. Hark, nature, hear: 265

Dear goddess, suspend thy purpose if   ~Revenge?~

Thou didst intend to make this creature fruitful.

Into her womb convey sterility.

Dry up in her the organs of increase,

253–4 liest. | My train are] F; list‸ my traine, and Q   263 people!] Q (~?)   264, 281, 286, 303, 326, 329 ALBANY] Q (*Duke*)   267 fruitful.] Q (~‸)

253 **the sea-monster** i.e. any fabulous monster of the sea; but Bate, p. 193, suggests that the passage derives from Ovid's *Metamorphoses*: 'the image conflates two of the monsters slain by Perseus: "marble-hearted" and "hideous" come from the grotesque Gorgon's head which turns to stone, and the sea-monster itself is that from which Perseus saves Andromeda.'
    kite The bird of prey symbolic to Shakespeare 'of cowardice, meanness, cruelty and death' (Armstrong, p. 12).

254 **choice** i.e. 'choicest', by association with *rarest*

255 **particulars** details

256 **in the most exact regard** 'with the greatest care' (Schmidt)

257 **worships . . . name** dignity (*OED, worship, sb.* 3b) . . . reputation

259 **engine** *OED* (*sb.* 5b) defines as 'an engine of torture', but J. C. Maxwell suggested that 'the picture called up . . . is rather of Lear's frame being prised apart, once a lever has been introduced far enough to get purchase' (in Muir).

259 **frame of nature** i.e. physical fabric

260 **fixed** established, normal

261 **gall** bitterness

262 **gate** i.e. his head

263 **Go . . . people** The instruction is repeated at l. 280, just as Lear twice calls for his horses to be readied (ll. 244, 250). Foakes writes 'Perhaps Lear's remaining attendants, including Kent, leave the stage here; Lear and the Fool must remain on stage'; that would fit the Folio text, which has 'Away, away' instead of 'Go . . . people' at the end of l. 280, but Q's 'my people' there implies more than Lear and the Fool.

266 **Dear . . . if** The line would be more regular if *goddess* were followed by another 'hear', as in F; on the other hand, the irregularity in Q gives weight to the invocation.

And from her derogate body never spring   270
A babe to honour her. If she must teem,
Create her child of spleen, that it may live
And be a thwart disnatured torment to her.
Let it stamp wrinkles in her brow of youth,
With cadent tears fret channels in her cheeks,   275
Turn all her mother's pains and benefits
To laughter and contempt, that she may feel—
That she may feel
How sharper than a serpent's tooth it is
To have a thankless child.—Go, go, my people!   280
                    Exeunt Lear, [Kent, Fool, and servants]

ALBANY

Now, gods that we adore, whereof comes this?

GONORIL

Never afflict yourself to know the cause,
But let his disposition have that scope
That dotage gives it.
            Enter King Lear [and his Fool]

LEAR

What, fifty of my followers at a clap?   285
Within a fortnight?
ALBANY   What is the matter, sir?

273 thwart] Q (thourt)   disnatured] F; disuetur'd Q   275 cadent] F; accent Q   278 That she may feel] Q1; *not in* Q2, F   280.1 *Exeunt Lear, [Kent, Fool, and servants]*] OXFORD; *not in* Q; *Exit*. F; *Exit Lear, Kent, and Foole* BLAYNEY   284.1 *Enter . . . Fool*] *not in* Q   285 clap?] Q (~,)

270 **derogate** deteriorated, debased; *OED*'s first use in this rare sense, but Muir, p. 236, notes its occurrence in Florio's *Montaigne*.

271 **teem** give birth

272 **spleen** foul temper

273 **thwart** perverse
    disnatured rendered unnatural (a rare word, used in Florio's *Montaigne*; Muir, p. 236)

275 **cadent** falling (*OED*'s first instance of the literal use of an astrological term)

276 **Turn . . . benefits** turn all her maternal cares and rewards to a source of derision and contempt

278 **That . . . feel** The repetition, not in F, and possibly accidental here, may nevertheless indicate difficulty in finding the right words.

279 **sharper . . . tooth** 'They have sharpened their tongues like a serpent' (Psalm 140: 3).

284 **dotage** senility, second childhood

285–6 **fifty . . . fortnight** The natural interpretation is that Lear's train has been halved within the past two weeks. Realistically, however, Lear has not had the chance to learn this, and directors have occasionally introduced business to get round this (Rosenberg, 133). Knowles, however (p. 39, following an edition of 1792 by Ambrose Eccles), considers that 'Lear may equally well mean "Goneril has just given orders that my train must be cut in half within the *next* fortnight".' Knowles discusses the implications for the play's time scheme.

285 **at a clap** at one stroke

LEAR

I'll tell thee. (*To Gonoril*) Life and death! I am ashamed
That thou hast power to shake my manhood thus,
That these hot tears, that break from me perforce
And should make thee—worst blasts and fogs upon
    thee!   290
Untented woundings of a father's curse
Pierce every sense about thee! Old fond eyes,
Beweep this cause again I'll pluck you out
And cast you, with the waters that you make,
To temper clay. Yea,   295
Is't come to this? Yet have I left a daughter
Whom, I am sure, is kind and comfortable.
When she shall hear this of thee, with her nails
She'll flay thy wolvish visage. Thou shalt find
That I'll resume the shape which thou dost think   300
I have cast off for ever; thou shalt, I warrant thee.

                                      Exit

GONORIL Do you mark that, my lord?

ALBANY

I cannot be so partial, Gonoril,
To the great love I bear you—

GONORIL   Come, sir, no more.—
You, more knave than fool, after your master!   305

---

290 And should make thee—worst blasts] OXFORD; should make the͜worst blasts Q; Should make thee ͜ worth them. | Blastes F; Should make the worse: blasts BLAYNEY   thee!] OXFORD; the ͜ Q; ~: | Th' F   291 Untented] Qb (vntented); vntender Qa   292 Pierce] Qb (pierce); peruse Qa   thee!] F (~.); ~ ͜ Q   294 cast you] F; you cast Q   301 *Exit*] F; *not in* Q   304 you—] Q (~,)   305 master!] Q (~?)

290 **make thee—worst** This is our interpretation of Q's 'make the worst'. HalioQ interprets 'make.—The worst', but 'the' is a common spelling of 'thee' in Q and elsewhere. 'The conjecture adopted here presumes that Lear breaks off before finishing his sentence, *thee* distracting his attention from his own tears back to Gonoril, whom he then curses' (*TC*).

291 **Untented** unprobed, not dressed (i.e. breeding infection?). *OED*'s first example of a rare sense.

292–4 **Old . . . cast you** 'Wherefore if thy right eye cause thee to offend, pluck it out

and cast it from thee' (Matthew 5: 29).

292 **fond** foolish

293 **Beweep** if you weep for

295 **temper clay** mix with, or soften, clay; presumably as a sign of contempt for his own emotion

297 **Whom** Ungrammatical but not uncommon (*OED*, *whom*, *pron.* 11); 'Who' in F.
    comfortable comforting

300 **shape** of kingliness; in theatrical use, a role or stage costume (*OED sb.*[1] 8a, b)

303–4 **partial . . . To** biased because of (Hunter; an unusual construction)

FOOL Nuncle Lear, nuncle Lear, tarry, and take the fool
   with thee.
                    A fox when one has caught her,
                    And such a daughter,
                    Should sure to the slaughter,   310
                    If my cap would buy a halter.
                    So, the fool follows after.   *Exit*
GONORIL What, Oswald, ho!
         Enter Oswald
OSWALD Here, madam.
GONORIL
   What, have you writ this letter to my sister?   315
OSWALD Yes, madam.
GONORIL
   Take you some company, and away to horse.
   Inform her full of my particular fears,
   And thereto add such reasons of your own
   As may compact it more. Get you gone,   320
   And after, your retinue.   *Exit Oswald*
                    Now, my lord,
   This milky gentleness and course of yours,
   Though I dislike not, yet under pardon
   You're much more attasked for want of wisdom
   Than praised for harmful mildness.   325
ALBANY
   How far your eyes may pierce I cannot tell.
   Striving to better aught, we mar what's well.

[handwritten note: "improve anything"]

307 with thee. | A] F; with ͜ a Q (*prose*)   312 *Exit*] Q4; *not in* Q1   313.1 *Enter Oswald*]
not in Q   321 And after] Qa; & hasten Qb   retinue.] OXFORD; returne ͜ QF   *Exit Oswald*] *not
in* Q   322 milky] Qa; mildie Qb   324 attasked] Qb (attaskt), DUTHIE (*conj.* Greg) (ataxt);
alapt Qa; at task F   for want] Qb; want Qa; for harmless want BLAYNEY *conj.*   325 praised]
F; praise Q   327 aught, we] Q (ought, we); oft we F

308–12 The line-endings may have made
   better rhymes than now but the original
   pronunciation is uncertain (Cercignani,
   p. 325, etc.).
311 **halter** 'both a rope to lead her like a
   beast, and a hangman's noose' (Foakes)
318 **full** fully
320 **compact** confirm, give consistency to;
   OED's only instance of this sense (*v.*¹3).
321 **And after, your retinue** and afterwards,
   let your retinue (those under the
   Steward's command) follow you. The

uncorrected Q reads '& after your returne'; corrected, '& hasten your
   returne'. Our emendation (not accepted
   by HalioQ or Weis) of QF's 'returne', and
   adoption of the uncorrected Q reading, is
   explained and defended in *TC*.
322 **milky** tender-hearted
   course (of action)
324 **attasked** taken to task, blamed; *OED*'s
   only instance of this word.
327 **better aught** improve anything (F's
   'better, oft' makes easier sense, but

GONORIL Nay, then—
ALBANY Well, well, the event.   *Exeunt*

Sc. 5 *Enter King Lear, the Earl of Kent disguised, and*
            Lear's Fool

LEAR [*to Kent*] Go you before to Gloucester with these let-
    ters. Acquaint my daughter no further with anything
    you know than comes from her demand out of the letter.
    If your diligence be not speedy, I shall be there before you.

KENT I will not sleep, my lord, till I have delivered your   5
    letter.   *Exit*

FOOL If a man's brains were in his heels, were't not in
    danger of kibes?

LEAR Ay, boy.

FOOL Then, I prithee, be merry: thy wit shall ne'er go   10
    slipshod.

LEAR Ha, ha, ha!

FOOL Shalt see thy other daughter will use thee kindly, for

---

328 then—] Q (~.)
    5.0.1–2 Enter . . . Fool] Q2 (subs.); Enter Lear. Q   7 were] Q2; where Q1   were't] Q (wert)

'ought' (Q) is not recorded as a spelling of
'oft'). The expression 'let well alone' was
proverbial (Dent W260).

329 **the event** the outcome, i.e. we must see
    what happens
  5 The scene follows rapidly on the previous
    one—Lear still awaits his horses. He
    enters with a letter.
  1 **Gloucester** Either the Earl or the city. In
    the following scene the Earl gives no sign
    of having received a letter. Conceivably,
    then, Lear is asking Kent to take a letter
    addressed to his daughters to the place,
    Gloucester; or 'Shakespeare anticipated
    here the arrival of Cornwall and Regan at
    Gloucester's house in the next scene, as if
    Lear could already know they would be
    there' (Foakes). Duthie and Wilson (but
    not Oxford, *pace* Foakes), following
    Granville Barker and Greg, *Collected
    Papers*, p. 325, emended to Cornwall
    'since the letter is for Corn[wall]'s wife
    Reg[an].' Some Stratford productions

(like the Elliott–Olivier film) have followed Duthie and Wilson, others (including Gielgud in 1950) have altered to
Regan, and one (Glen Byam Shaw, in
1959) even to Gloucestershire.

 1–2 **letters** The plural form could be used
    with singular meaning: *OED*, *letter*, *sb.*[1]
    4b).
  3 **demand out of** questions arising from
  7 **brains . . . heels** The idea that a fool's
    brains were in his heels was proverbial
    (Dent H386.1, citing de Serres, *Godlie and
    Learned Commentarie upon . . . Ecclesiastes*
    (1585), 113f.: 'So the Greeks do speak of
    a fool that he hath his mind in his heels').
  8 **kibes** chilblains
10–11 **thy . . . slipshod** 'You will never have
    to wear slippers because of chilblains, for
    you show you have no wit, even in your
    heels, in undertaking your journey to
    Regan' (Muir).
 13 **Shalt** thou shalt
    kindly could mean 'according to her na-
    ture' as well as 'affectionately'.

though she's as like this as a crab is like an apple, yet I
con what I can tell. 15

LEAR Why, what canst thou tell, my boy?

FOOL She'll taste as like this as a crab doth to a crab. Thou
canst not tell why one's nose stands in the middle of his
face?

LEAR No. 20

FOOL Why, to keep his eyes on either side 's nose, that
what a man cannot smell out, a may spy into.

LEAR I did her wrong.

FOOL Canst tell how an oyster makes his shell?

LEAR No. 25

FOOL Nor I neither; but I can tell why a snail has a house.

LEAR Why?

FOOL Why, to put his head in, not to give it away to his
daughters and leave his horns without a case.

LEAR

I will forget my nature. So kind a father! 30
Be my horses ready?

FOOL Thy asses are gone about them. The reason why the
seven stars are no more than seven is a pretty reason.

LEAR Because they are not eight.

FOOL Yes. Thou wouldst make a good fool. 35

LEAR take it back by force
To take't again perforce — monster ingratitude!

FOOL If thou wert my fool, nuncle, I'd have thee beaten for
being old before thy time.

18 stands] Q2; stande Q1   29 daughters] F; daughter Q

14 **she . . . this** Regan . . . Gonoril
like this . . . apple Proverbial (Dent
A290.1).
crab crab-apple (much smaller and
sourer than a normal apple)
14–15 **I con . . . tell** Based on the proverb
'I know what I know' (Dent K173); a
cryptic way of saying 'I am in on a secret'.
15 **con** know
18 **stands** Q1's 'stande' is an easy
misreading.
22 **a may** he may
23 **her** Cordelia (though D. G. James,
The Dream of Learning (1951), 94–6,
suggests Gonoril)
26–9 **snail . . . case** The idea that a snail

'keeps his house on his back (head)' was
proverbial (Dent S580).
29 **daughters** Q's singular is probably a simple error; omission of final 's' also occurs
at e.g. 7.270 and 9.44.
case cover, shelter
32 **asses** servants (perhaps implying the
Fool's opinion of them)
33 **seven stars** i.e. the Seven Sisters, chief
stars in the constellation of the Pleiades,
or the seven stars forming the Plough, or
Great Bear, mentioned by Edmund at
2.121.
36 **take't . . . perforce** (for them to) take it
(the kingdom, power, or crown) back by
force

LEAR How's that?

FOOL Thou shouldst not have been old before thou hadst   40
been wise.

LEAR

O, let me not be mad, sweet heaven!

I would not be mad.

Keep me in temper. I would not be mad.

> *Enter a Servant*

Are the horses ready?

SERVANT   Ready, my lord.   45

LEAR (*to Fool*) Come, boy.   *Exeunt Lear and Servant*

FOOL

She that is maid now, and laughs at my departure,

Shall not be a maid long, except things be cut shorter.

Exit

Sc. 6 *Enter Edmund the bastard, and Curan, meeting*

EDMUND Save thee, Curan.

CURAN And you, sir. I have been with your father, and
given him notice that the Duke of Cornwall and his
duchess will be here with him tonight.

EDMUND How comes that?   5

CURAN Nay, I know not. You have heard of the news
abroad?—I mean the whispered ones, for there are yet
but ear-bussing arguments.

Rumour

43–4 I would not be mad . . . I would not be mad] Q; not mad . . . I would not be mad BLAYNEY
44.1 *Enter a Servant*] *not in* Q   46 *Exeunt . . . Servant* | *Exit.* Q
  6.0.1 *Edmund the bastard*] Q (*Bast.*)   7 abroad?] Q (~,)

---

44 **in temper** in proper (mental) condition
47–8 **She . . . shorter** 'The maid who sees only
the funny side of the Fool's gibes, and does
not realize that Lear is going on a tragic
journey is such a simpleton that she won't
know how to preserve her virginity' (Muir).
The Fool addresses the audience, suggesting a break in the play's time scheme.
'Things . . . shorter' plays on *thing* as penis;
a pun on departure/deporter, French for
'bauble' has been suggested. 'Departure'/'shorter' would have rhymed.
6 The action takes place at Gloucester's
dwelling. This is the only scene to require
an upper level. It probably requires

torches for Gloucester's entrance (l. 36),
and Edmund and Edgar need swords
(ll. 29–30).
0.1 **Curan** Though the word was a common
form of 'currant', its use as a name is unusual, appearing in no other play of the
period. Foakes suggests it may be a version of the Irish 'Ciaran'. He appears only
in Scene 6. His age is not indicated.
meeting implies entrance by separate
doors.
1 **Save thee** A greeting: God protect you!
8 **ear-bussing arguments** ear-kissing (so F)
topics, i.e. communications made only
close to the ear, rumours

EDMUND Not. I pray you, what are they?

CURAN Have you heard of no likely wars towards twixt the   10
  two Dukes of Cornwall and Albany?

EDMUND Not a word.

CURAN You may then in time. Fare you well, sir.   *Exit*

EDMUND

  The Duke be here tonight! The better, best.

  This weaves itself perforce into my business.   15

      ⌐Enter Edgar at a window above⌐

  My father hath set guard to take my brother,

  And I have one thing of a queasy question

  Which must ask briefness. Wit and fortune help!—

  Brother, a word. Descend, brother, I say.

      ⌐Edgar climbs down⌐

  My father watches. O, fly this place.   20

  Intelligence is given where you are hid.

---

9 Not. I‸] Q (~, ~); Not‸ I: F   13 *Exit*] Q2; *not in* Q1   15.1 *Enter Edgar at a window above*] OXFORD; *Enter Edgar* Q1 (*in the left margin, before* 'it selfe', *the first word of a line set as prose*); *Enter Edgar* Q2 (*after* '*Which*' *in l.* 18, *before the prose line in which* 'Brother, a word' *occurs*); *Enter Edgar.* F (*before* 'Brother, a word')   18 briefness. Wit and] OXFORD; breefnes and Q   19.1 *Edgar climbs down*] OXFORD; *not in* QF

9 **Not.** A common idiom (as illustrated in
  TC), though HalioQ follows F and Weis
  emends without note to 'Not I.'

10–11 **Have . . . Albany** This is a loose end,
  though there is another hint of it at Sc. 8,
  18–20. Granville Barker finds in it 'some
  signs that the emphasis of the play's
  whole scheme was altered . . . Edmund,
  with admirable promptitude, turns the
  notion to the further confusing of the
  so easily confused Edgar, but the wars
  themselves come to nothing. . . . It looks
  a little as if Shakespeare had thought of
  making the hypocrite inheritors of
  Cordelia's portion fall out over it (an obvious nemesis) and had changed his
  mind' (p. 273).

10 **towards** impending

14 **The . . . best** so much the better—the best
  that could happen!

15 **perforce** inevitably

15.1 **Enter . . . above** Q1 has *Enter Edgar* in
  the margin before the line starting *itself*,
  whereas Q2 and F place the entry closer
  to the point at which he is addressed.
  Edgar appears as his brother starts to
  speak of him.

16 **My . . . brother** The line 'explains to an

audience why Edgar is peering nervously
from an upstairs window' (*TC*), or from
the balcony above the stage.

16 **take** capture

17 **thing . . . question** deed of hazardous uncertainty (*queasy*, uncertain, hazardous
  (*OED* 1b, citing this passage))

18 **must . . . help!** Q reads 'must aske
  breefnes and fortune helpe'. The Folio
  variant ('Which I must act, Briefnesse,
  and Fortune worke') is too far removed to
  be plausible as the source of this. HalioQ
  accepts Q without note; Ridley, unmetrically and without note, reads 'must ask
  briefness and fortune's help'. Weis
  emends by adding 'to' before *help*—
  scarcely, as he claims, a metrical im-
  provement—regarding our reading,
  explained in *TC*, as 'an ingenious and unnecessary emendation'.

  must . . . briefness requires speed

19.1 **Edgar . . . down** As he is addressed
  in the next line Edgar probably jumps
  or climbs down in view of the
  audience rather than by an inner stair-
  case.

20 **watches** is on the lookout

21 **Intelligence** information

You have now the good advantage of the night.
Have you not spoken 'gainst the Duke of Cornwall
    aught?
He's coming hither now, in the night, i'th' haste,
And Regan with him. Have you nothing said   25
Upon his party against the Duke of Albany?
Advise you—

EDGAR   I am sure on't, not a word.

EDMUND

I hear my father coming. Pardon me.
In cunning I must draw my sword upon you.
Seem to defend yourself. Now, quit you well.   30
(*Calling*) Yield, come before my father. Light here, here!
(*To Edgar*) Fly, brother, fly! (*Calling*) Torches, torches!
    (*To Edgar*) So, farewell.   *Exit Edgar*
Some blood drawn on me would beget opinion
Of my more fierce endeavour.
    He wounds his arm

                    I have seen
Drunkards do more than this in sport. (*Calling*) Father,
    father!   35
Stop, stop! Ho, help!

---

27 you] BLAYNEY; your—Q; your selfe F   28–9 me. | In cunning] F; me in crauing Q
32, 35 *Calling*] *not in* Q   32 *Exit Edgar*] F; *not in* Q   34 *He . . . arm*] ROWE; *not in* Q   36 Ho,
help!] OXFORD (*conj.* Stone); no, helpe? Q1; no͵ helpe? Q2, F   *the Earl of Gloucester*] Q (*Glost.*)
and others] BLAYNEY; *not in* Q; *and Seruants with Torches* F

---

23 **'gainst . . . aught** anything against
24 **i'th' haste** An unusual construction,
though *OED a.* 3d records 'the' as 'Formerly sometimes used before abstract
nouns'.
26 **Upon his party** If, as seems likely, this
means 'on his side', Edmund must be deliberately confusing Edgar by suggesting
first that he may have spoken for, then
against, Cornwall.
27 **Advise you** think about it. Q reads 'advise
your---', accepted by HalioQ as a broken
word or sentence.
28 **I . . . coming** Greg suggested that this is
spoken 'only to frighten Edgar' (*Collected
Papers*, p. 324), implying that Gloucester's entry is motivated purely by
Edmund's calls for help.
29 **In cunning** as a device. In fact his cun-

ning is used against, not for, Edgar. Weis
accepts Q's 'crauing' (an easy misreading of 'cunning'), glossing 'accusation'
while admitting that this is a Middle English sense (recorded only once, and dated
1300).
30 **quit** 'acquit', and 'leave'
33–4 **beget . . . endeavour** create an impression that I have fought even more fiercely
35 **in sport** for fun (perhaps to impress their
mistresses: Kittredge cites Witgood's renunciation of youthful follies such as
'Stabbing of arms for a common mistress'
in Middleton's *A Trick to Catch the Old One*
(*c.*1605), 5.2.178–91)
36 **Stop, stop!** (to the retreating Edgar)
Ho, help! Addressed to Gloucester as he
enters. Weis and HalioQ adapt Q's 'no,
helpe?', ignoring its comma.

Enter the Earl of Gloucester [and others]

GLOUCESTER   Now, Edmund, where is the villain?

EDMUND

Here stood he in the dark, his sharp sword out,
Warbling of wicked charms, conjuring the moon
To stand 's auspicious mistress.

GLOUCESTER   But where is he?

EDMUND

Look, sir, I bleed.

GLOUCESTER   Where is the villain, Edmund?   40

EDMUND

Fled this way, sir, when by no means he could—

GLOUCESTER

Pursue him, go after.   *Exeunt others*

                 By no means what?

EDMUND

Persuade me to the murder of your lordship,
But that I told him the revengive gods
'Gainst parricides did all their thunders bend,   45
Spoke with how manifold and strong a bond
The child was bound to the father. Sir, in fine,
Seeing how loathly opposite I stood

---

42 *Exeunt others*] DYCE (*subs.*); *not in* Q   46 manifold] Q (many fould)   47 fine] F; a fine Q

---

36 *Enter . . . others* F (calling the *others* servants) adds 'with torches', which 'probably represents the original intention'
(*TC*). Urkowitz, p. 27, argues that the
extras are not needed. Gurr and
Ichikawa (p. 89) remark that 'Gloucester
and his servants do not enter just after the
bastard's first call ([6.]31), but do so
three and a half lines after Edgar begins to
exit ([6].36). The exit and the entrance
are presumably made through different
doors. This three-and-a-half-line gap en-
sures that the entrance of Gloucester and
his servants does not overlap with
Edgar's exit, though Edgar probably does
not need all three and a half lines since he
exits running. Neither Edgar's exit nor
Gloucester's entrance could be clothed in
darkness . . . It seems likely, therefore,
that the three-and-a-half-line gap reflects
Shakespeare's wish to prevent Gloucester's entrance overlapping with Edgar's
exit.'

38 **Warbling of** singing, chanting (F changes
to 'mumbling of')
conjuring calling solemnly on
39 **stand's** act as
auspicious mistress propitious patroness
(Shakespeare uses the same phrase of
Fortune in *All's Well*, 3.3.8). The *moon* is
probably thought of as Hecate (see 1.102).
41 **this way** It would be natural for Edmund to
point in the wrong direction, so as to gain
time; but this would be difficult if there
were only two stage doors as Gloucester
must have entered by a different one from
that by which Edgar departed.
44 **revengive** revenging, vindictive; *OED*'s
only instance. F alters to 'revenging',
possibly a compositorial reversion to a
more familiar form; there is no reason to
question Q as Shakespeare's coinage.
45 **thunders bend** aim their thunderbolts
46 **manifold** many-sided
47 **in fine** to sum up
48 **loathly opposite** abhorrently opposed

To his unnatural purpose, with fell motion,
With his preparèd sword he charges home   50
My unprovided body, lanced mine arm;
But when he saw my best alarumed spirits
Bold in the quarrel's rights, roused to the encounter,
Or whether gasted by the noise I made
Or ⌈   ⌉ I know not,   55
But suddenly he fled.
GLOUCESTER   Let him fly far,
Not in this land shall he remain uncaught,
And found, dispatch. The noble Duke my master,
My worthy arch and patron, comes tonight.
By his authority I will proclaim it   60
That he which finds him shall deserve our thanks,
Bringing the murderous caitiff to the stake;
He that conceals him, death.

EDMUND
When I dissuaded him from his intent
And found him pitched to do it, with curst speech   65

---

51 lanced] Q (lancht)   55 Or . . . not] OXFORD; *not in* QF   65 pitched] QF (pight)

49 **fell motion** fierce thrust (in fencing, 'motion' was a regulated movement)
50 **preparèd** readied, unsheathed
51 **unprovided** unarmed
lanced wounded (*OED, launch, v.* 1a; obsolete). Q reads 'lancht', F 'latched'. Editors (e.g. Foakes) regard Theobald's 'lanced' as an emendation but it is more properly a modernization.
52–6 **But . . . fled** This is a difficult passage. Q prints (as prose): 'but when he saw my best alarumd spirits, bould in the quarrels, rights, [*sic*] rousd to the encounter, or whether gasted by the noyse I made, but sodainely he fled.' F prints as verse: 'And when he saw my best alarum'd spirits | Bold in the quarrels right, rouzd to th'encounter, | Or whether gasted by the noyse I made, | Full sodainely he fled.' 'Full' improves on Q's 'but', which seems to lack a contradicting previous statement, but still provides no 'or . . .' to balance 'Or whether . . .'. Duthie thought the irregularity a conscious indication of 'Edmund's perturbation', but 'this difficulty is itself the only syntactical evidence of any such "perturbation"' (*TC*). We

suppose that Q has accidentally omitted a verse line ending 'I know not', with an unrecoverable alternative following the 'Or'. R. Proudfoot (reported in Foakes) attractively conjectures that 'when' in l. 52 misrepresents 'whe'er', i.e. 'whether', but although this supplies the missing alternative, and makes good sense with F's 'Full . . .', it still provides no alternative justifying Q's 'but', which seems unlikely to be a misreading of 'full'.
52 **best . . . spirits** energies best called to arms, roused to action (*OED*'s first instance of 'alar[u]med' as ppl. a.)
53 **Bold . . . rights** emboldened by the justice of my cause
54 **gasted** frightened (as in 'aghast')
56 **Let . . . far** i.e. however far he may fly
58 **found, dispatch** when he is found—death!
59 **arch** chief (*OED, arch, a.* B, *quasi-n*[*oun*].; one of its only two instances, both dated to 1605)
62 **caitiff** miserable wretch
64 **dissuaded** i.e. tried to dissuade
65 **pitched** determined
curst angry

I threatened to discover him. He replied,
'Thou unpossessing bastard, dost thou think
If I would stand against thee, could the reposure
Of any trust, virtue, or worth in thee
Make thy words faithed? No, what I should deny—   70
As this I would, ay, though thou didst produce
My very character—I'd turn it all
To thy suggestion, plot, and damned pretence,
And thou must make a dullard of the world
If they not thought the profits of my death   75
Were very pregnant and potential spurs
To make thee seek it.'

GLOUCESTER   Strong and fastened villain!
Would he deny his letter? I never got him.
    Trumpets within
Hark, the Duke's trumpets. I know not why he comes.
All ports I'll bar. The villain shall not scape.   80
The Duke must grant me that; besides, his picture
I will send far and near, that all the kingdom
May have note of him—and of my land,
Loyal and natural boy, I'll work the means
To make thee capable.   85
    Enter the Duke of Cornwall and Regan

CORNWALL
How now, my noble friend? Since I came hither,

---

70 No, what] F; no. what Q; nowhat STONE *conj.*   77 villain!] Q (~,)   78.1 *Trumpets
within*] ROWE; *not in* Q; *Tucket within*. F (*after* '*it*', *l*. 77)   83 have] Q; haue due F   85.1 *and
Regan*] *not in* Q

66 **discover** betray
67 **unpossessing** Bastards could not inherit
   property. *OED*'s first use of a rare form.
68 **reposure** reposal, placing. Both this and
   F's 'reposal' are *OED*'s first instances of
   rarely recorded words.
70 **faithed** believed
72 **character** handwriting (as evidence)
   turn twist
73 **suggestion** prompting (to evil)
   pretence intention
74 **must . . . world** would have to suppose
   everybody to be stupid
75 **not thought** did not think
   profits of benefits resulting from

76 **Were . . . spurs** would be very compelling
   and powerful incentives
77 **fastened** confirmed
78 **got** begot—an accusation of bastardy
   ('And this to Edmund his bastard!':
   Granville Barker, p. 316, describing this
   as a stroke of irony 'only to be fully appre-
   ciated perhaps by the shade of Lady
   Gloucester'.)
80 **ports** seaports, or gates of walled towns
81 **picture** could mean simply 'description'.
85 **capable** qualified to inherit (*OED*'s first
   instance of this sense)
86 **How now** i.e. how is it now? (a common
   form of greeting)

Which I can call but now, I have heard strange news.

REGAN

If it be true, all vengeance comes too short

Which can pursue the offender. How dost, my lord?

GLOUCESTER

Madam, my old heart is cracked, is cracked.   90

REGAN

What, did my father's godson seek your life?

He whom my father named, your Edgar?

GLOUCESTER

Ay, lady, lady; shame would have it hid.

REGAN

Was he not companion with the riotous knights

That tend upon my father?   95

GLOUCESTER

I know not, madam. 'Tis too bad, too bad.

EDMUND Yes, madam, he was.

REGAN

No marvel, then, though he were ill affected.

'Tis they have put him on the old man's death,

To have the spoil and waste of his revenues.   100

I have this present evening from my sister

Been well informed of them, and with such cautions

That if they come to sojourn at my house

I'll not be there.

CORNWALL   Nor I, assure thee, Regan.

Edmund, I heard that you have shown your father   105

A childlike office.

89 dost] Q, F1; does F2   95 tend] THEOBALD; tends Q; tended F   100 the spoil and waste]
BLAYNEY; these---and wast Qa, Q2; the wast and spoyle Qb; th'expence and wast F   his] Qb;
this his Qa   105 heard] Q; heare F

87 **but** just
91 **godson** A Christian term in spite of the
   pagan setting.
95 **tend** Q's 'tends', retained in HalioQ and
   Weis, may be right (Abbott 333), but
   could equally be a misprint for 'tende'.
98 **though . . . affected** if he was ill disposed,
   disloyal
99 **put . . . on** incited him to. *OED*'s first instance of this construction (*put*, *v*.¹ 27a (b)).
100 **the spoil and waste of his** BlayneyQ's
   reading, accepted by HalioQ and Weis,

for uncorrected Q's 'these—and waste of
this his' and corrected Q's 'the wast
and spoyle of his'. The reading assumes
'that Qb inadvertently transposed
the two nouns, in correcting the first'
(*TC*).
100 **revenues** (accent on the second syllable)
105 **heard** This is Q's reading, retained
   by Oxford, Weis, and HalioQ, but
   misreading in Q of F's 'heare' would be
   easy, as conversely at 7.166.
106 **childlike office** service proper to a son

EDMUND   'Twas my duty, sir.

GLOUCESTER (*to Cornwall*)

He did betray his practice, and received

This hurt you see striving to apprehend him.

CORNWALL

Is he pursued?

GLOUCESTER   Ay, my good lord.

CORNWALL

If he be taken, he shall never more   110

Be feared of doing harm. Make your own purpose

How in my strength you please. For you, Edmund,

Whose virtue and obedience doth this instant

So much commend itself, you shall be ours.

Natures of such deep trust we shall much need.   115

You we first seize on.

EDMUND   I shall serve you truly,

However else.

GLOUCESTER (*to Cornwall*) For him I thank your grace.

CORNWALL

You know not why we came to visit you—

REGAN

This out-of-season threat'ning dark-eyed night—

Occasions, noble Gloucester, of some poise,   120

Wherein we must have use of your advice.

Our father he hath writ, so hath our sister,

Of differences which I least thought it fit

To answer from our home. The several messengers

115–16 need. | You�‸] Q1 (need you,), Q2, F   118 you—] Q (you?)   119 This] OXFORD (*conj*. Stone); Thus QF   120 poise] Qb; prise Qa, Q2, F   123 differences] Qb (diferences); defences Qa   least] Qb (lest); best Qa, Q2, F   124 home] Qb, F; hand Qa, Q2

107 **betray . . . practice** reveal Edgar's plot
111 **Be . . . doing** arouse fear that he will do
111–12 **Make . . . please** i.e. pursue your intents making whatever use you please of my power and authority
117 **However else** to whatever extent
119 **This** Our reading (suggested by Stone and accepted by HalioQ) is based on the belief that 'It is much easier to suppose that "This" was misread "Thus" than that F's "threadding" was taken for Q's "threatning"' (*TC*).

120 **poise** weight, gravity. Weis (but not HalioQ) accepts the uncorrected and Folio reading, but the case for the corrected 'poyse' is made in *Division*, pp. 362–3.
123 **differences** disagreements
123–4 **which . . . home** which I thought it unfitting to respond to from our home (presumably so that Lear cannot descend on her; in F's reading, accepted by Weis and HalioQ, 'best thought', *from* has to mean 'away from')

From hence attend dispatch. Our good old friend,   125
Lay comforts to your bosom, and bestow
Your needful counsel to our business,
Which craves the instant use.

GLOUCESTER I serve you, madam.
Your graces are right welcome.   *Exeunt*   130

Sc. 7   *Enter the Earl of Kent, disguised, at one door, and*
          Oswald the steward, at another door

OSWALD Good even to thee, friend. Art of the house?

KENT Ay.

OSWALD Where may we set our horses?

KENT I'th' mire.

OSWALD Prithee, if thou love me, tell me.

KENT I love thee not.

OSWALD Why then, I care not for thee.

KENT If I had thee in Lipsbury pinfold I would make thee
care for me.

---

130 *Exeunt*] *not in* Q; *Exeunt. Flourish*. F

7.0.1–2 *Enter . . . door*] *Enter Kent, and Steward*. Q   1 OSWALD] Q ('*Steward*' *subs. throughout
the scene*)   even] Qb (euen), Q2; deuen Qa; dawning F

125 **attend dispatch** wait to be sent off
128 **craves . . . use** demands immediate
    attention
  7 The opening line locates the action outside
    Gloucester's dwelling soon after that of
    the previous scene. (Line 26 pins it down
    to *two days* after that of Sc. 4.) Edgar's so-
    liloquy (ll. 166–86), however, is unlocal-
    ized. Stocks (l. 130.1) and a letter
    (l. 155.1) are needed. Dessen (*Recovering*,
    107–8) considers that in this simultaneous
    staging 'The stocks would signal not a
    courtyard or other specific locale but
    rather a general sense of imprisonment or
    bondage . . . just as Edgar would be as-
    sumed to be in flight, anywhere'. Both
    Kent and Oswald are armed.
  1 **even** This modernization of the uncor-
    rected Q reading, 'deuen', is identical
    with the corrected Q reading, 'euen'. F
    reads 'dawning', and a number of edi-
    tors, including Weis and Foakes (in his
    note), follow Greg in thinking that uncor-
    rected Q's 'deuen' means 'dawn', and
    that Qb's 'euen' is a miscorrection. *OED*
    however does not record 'deven' or any
    similar spelling for 'dawn', and indeed
    the word 'dawn' is first recorded in

Romeo (the previous equivalent is
'dawing' or 'dawning'). According to
HalioF 'deuen' is colloquial. HalioF naturally accepts 'dawning' and argues that 'it
is night-time before dawn' on the basis of
l. 28 (substantively identical in Q and F),
though HalioQ accepts 'even' without
comment. Following Stone he regards
F's 'Good dawning' as a neologism, but
though *OED* does not record the greeting,
the noun 'dawning' is standard for dawn
and occurs several times in Shakespeare.
It is difficult to argue from the time of
day since 'Good even' might not seem
inappropriate in darkness, and anyhow
consistency even from one part of a scene
to another cannot be assumed. There
seems no reason not to accept Q.

  2 **Ay** (Not true—but Kent is in disguise.)
  8 **in Lipsbury pinfold** A pinfold is a pound
    for stray animals. *Lipsbury*, not a known
    place-name, means 'liptown'. R. Nares
    conjectured that the phrase means 'If I
    had you in my teeth', i.e. in my clutches,
    while adding that 'it remains for some
    more fortunate inquirer to discover what
    is really meant' (*Glossary of Words . . .*,
    1822, etc.).

152

OSWALD Why dost thou use me thus? I know thee not.   10
KENT Fellow, I know thee.

OSWALD What dost thou know me for?

KENT A knave, a rascal, an eater of broken meats, a base,
proud, shallow, beggarly, three-suited, hundred-pound,
filthy worsted-stocking knave; a lily-livered, action-   15
taking knave; a whoreson, glass-gazing, superfinical
rogue; one-trunk-inheriting slave; one that wouldst be a
bawd in way of good service, and art nothing but the
composition of a knave, beggar, coward, pander, and
the son and heir of a mongrel bitch, whom I will beat into   20
clamorous whining if thou deny the least syllable of the
addition.

OSWALD What a monstrous fellow art thou, thus to rail on
one that's neither known of thee nor knows thee!

KENT What a brazen-faced varlet art thou, to deny thou   25
knowest me! Is it two days ago since I beat thee and
tripped up thy heels before the King? Draw, you rogue;
for though it be night, the moon shines.

　　　[He draws his sword]

---

14 suited] Q (shewted)   15 stocking] Q (stocken)   28.1 *He . . . sword*] ROWE (*subs.*);   *not in* Q

10 **use** treat
12 **for** i.e. as, to be
13 **broken meats** left-overs
14 **three-suited** Serving men appear to have
been allowed three suits of clothes a year;
at 11.121 Edgar (as Tom o'Bedlam) boasts
of having had *three suits to his back*. This
use of *suited* as a participial adjective antedates *OED*'s first instance (2), from 1632.
hundred-pound This would be a large in-
come. Steevens and later editors have
seen it as a jibe at James I's creation of
knights in return for this sum, but the
joke is not easily evident. Kent seems to
veer between accusing Oswald of behaving like a despised menial and, on the
other hand, a pampered favourite.
15 **worsted-stocking** Worsted stockings were
cheaper than the silk ones worn by the
wealthy.
lily-livered i.e. cowardly, as having no
blood in the liver. Falstaff speaks of cold
blood which has 'left the liver white and
pale, which is the badge of pusillanimity

and cowardice' (*2 Henry IV*, 4.2.101–2).
15–16 **action-taking** litigious, taking legal in
preference to physical action
16 **glass-gazing** always looking into mirrors,
vain
superfinical over-fussy (not exclusively in
dress). The compound is not in *OED*
(F has 'superserviceable, finical').
17 **one-trunk-inheriting** possessing, or in-
heriting, no more than would go into one
trunk. (Johnson took the phrase to mean
'a wearer of old cast-off cloaths, an inher-
itor of torn breeches', but *OED* records
this meaning of 'trunk' only in the
plural.)
17–18 **wouldst . . . service** would be willing
to do anything, however contemptible,
and count it good service
19 **composition** combination
22 **addition** style of address
27 **Draw** i.e. draw your sword (implying
that Kent does so). Oswald appears not to
accept the challenge, but there is clearly
some sort of scuffle.

I'll make a sop of the moonshine o' you. Draw, you
whoreson, cullionly barber-monger, draw!   30
OSWALD Away. I have nothing to do with thee.
KENT Draw, you rascal. You bring letters against the King,
    and take Vanity the puppet's part against the royalty of
    her father. Draw, you rogue, or I'll so carbonado your
    shanks—draw, you rascal, come your ways!   35
OSWALD Help, ho, murder, help!
KENT Strike, you slave! Stand, rogue! Stand, you neat
    slave, strike!
OSWALD Help, ho, murder, help!
        Enter Edmund the bastard with his rapier drawn,
        [then] the Earl of Gloucester, [then] the Duke of
        Cornwall and Regan the Duchess
EDMUND *[parting them]* How now, whats the matter?   40
KENT With you, goodman boy. An you please come, I'll
    flesh you. Come on, young master.
GLOUCESTER Weapons? Arms? What's the matter here?
CORNWALL Keep peace, upon your lives. He dies that
    strikes again. What's the matter?   45

39.1 *the bastard*] *not in* Q   39.2 *[then] the Earl of Gloucester, [then]* OXFORD; *Gloster* Q   39.2–3
of Cornwall] *not in* Q   39.3 *Regan the*] *not in* Q   40 *parting them*] *not in* Q   44 CORNWALL] Q
('*Duke*' *throughout the scene*)

29 **sop . . . moonshine** Could mean 'I'll turn
    you into a sop (piece of soggy bread) by
    the light of the moon'; or 'I'll render you
    no more substantial than moonlight'
    (*OED*, *sop*, *sb.*¹ 2b); or 'I'll turn you into
    moonshine', which could be either a dish
    made of eggs (*OED sb.* 3a) or a dessert of
    blancmange or custard (the sky) decor-
    ated with moon and stars in jelly (*OED
    sb.* 3b). Duthie and Wilson's paraphrase
    'make mincemeat of you' catches the
    sense.
30 **cullionly** base; 'cullion', meaning 'test-
    icle', was also used as a general term of
    contempt. This is *OED*'s first instance of
    cullionly.
    barber-monger 'a constant frequenter of
    the barber's shop, a fop' (*OED*, *barber*,
    sb. 2)
33 **Vanity the puppet** Editors usually follow
    Johnson in explaining that Gonoril is seen
    as a personified character in an allegor-

ical play, or in a puppet play, but
J. C. Meagher, noting that 'Lady Vanity
does not appear in the extant old moral-
ities at all', points out that 'puppet' was
used for 'a vain and "dolled-up"
woman', and glosses 'the epitome of the
vain woman, the personification of
Vanity' ('Vanity, Lear's Feather, and the
Pathology of Editorial Annotation', in
Shakespeare 1971, cited in the Introduction, p. 52 n. 4).
34 **carbonado** slash, like meat to be grilled
35 **come . . . ways** come on, now!
37 **Stand** defend yourself (*OED*, *stand*, *v.* 10)
    neat trim (scornful)
39.1 *rapier* a small sword
41 **With you** i.e. the quarrel is with you
    goodman boy A scornful way of address-
    ing a cocky young man.
    An if
42 **flesh** initiate (into tasting blood, implying
    that Edmund has not fought before)

REGAN The messengers from our sister and the King.

CORNWALL (*to Kent and Oswald*) What's your difference?
Speak.

OSWALD I am scarce in breath, my lord.

KENT No marvel, you have so bestirred your valour, you   50
cowardly rascal. Nature disclaims in thee; a tailor made
thee.

CORNWALL Thou art a strange fellow—a tailor make a
man?

KENT Ay, a tailor, sir. A stone-cutter or a painter could not   55
have made him so ill though he had been but two hours
at the trade.

GLOUCESTER Speak yet; how grew your quarrel?

OSWALD This ancient ruffian, sir, whose life I have spared
at suit of his grey beard—   60

KENT Thou whoreson Z, thou unnecessary letter—
(*to Cornwall*) my lord, if you'll give me leave I will tread
this unboulted villain into mortar and daub the walls of a
jakes with him. (*To Oswald*) Spare my grey beard, you
wagtail?   65

CORNWALL

Peace, sir. You beastly knave, have you no reverence?

KENT

Yes, sir, but anger has a privilege.

CORNWALL Why art thou angry?

KENT

That such a slave as this should wear a sword,
That wears no honesty. Such smiling rogues   70
As these, like rats, oft bite those cords in twain

54 man?] Q (~.)   61 Z] QF (Zedd)   66 have you] RIDLEY; you haue Q; know you F

47 **difference** quarrel
51 **disclaims in** renounces all part in
51–2 **tailor . . . thee** Proverbial (Dent A283,
T17), meaning that he is no more than
his clothes.
60 **at suit of** at the request of
61 **unnecessary** (because it can always be re-
placed by s)
63 **unboulted** normally means unsifted (as of
the lime from which *mortar* is made), but
'bolt' could mean 'penis' (Williams,
Glossary)—Kent is calling him a eunuch.

64 **jakes** privy
65 **wagtail** Contemptuous form of address;
OED's first instance; womanizer (Williams,
Glossary).
66 **have you** Weis accepts Q's 'you haue'
without comment. F reads 'know you'.
Accidental inversion seems likely.
67 **anger . . . privilege** i.e. the right to speak
out; possibly proverbial (Dent P595.1).
69 **sword** Thought of as a gentleman's
weapon, though most men appear to
have carried arms in Shakespeare's time.

Which are too entrenched to unloose, smooth every
    passion
That in the natures of their lords rebel,
Bring oil to fire, snow to their colder moods,
Renege, affirm, and turn their halcyon beaks   75
With every gale and vary of their masters,
Knowing naught, like dogs, but following.
(*To Oswald*) A plague upon your epileptic visage!
Smile you my speeches as I were a fool?
Goose, an I had you upon Sarum Plain   80
I'd send you cackling home to Camelot.

CORNWALL

What, art thou mad, old fellow?

GLOUCESTER [*to Kent*]   How fell you out? Say that.

KENT

No contraries hold more antipathy
Than I and such a knave.

---

72 too entrenched] OXFORD (*conj.* Stone); to intrench Q; t'intrince F   unloose,] F (~:); in-
loose‸ Q   74 fire] F; stir Q   77 dogs] F; dayes Q   79 Smile] Q (smoyle), F   81 Camelot.] F;
Camulet., Q1; Camulet. Q2

---

72 **entrenched** embedded. Stone suggests
that 'A somewhat loose reference is apparently intended to the mouse in the
fable [of Aesop] who, out of gratitude to a
lion for once saving his life, released him
from the net in which he lay entrapped by
gnawing through the ropes.' HalioQ and
Weis accept Stone's proposal, adopted
here, for Q's 'intrench'. The fable is
clearly alluded to in *Leir* (Bullough,
ll. 642–3).
    smooth *OED* (*v.* 6a) glosses as 'allay, as-
suage', but Onions's 'flatter, humour'
seems equally apt.
73 **rebel** against reason
74 **Bring . . . fire** i.e. feed the flame (of their
lords' passions); proverbial (Dent O30).
75 **Renege** deny
75–6 **turn . . . gale** Proverbial (Dent W439).
    halcyon the kingfisher. A dried corpse
was supposed, when suspended, to act as
a weathervane (*OED*, *kingfisher*).
76 **gale and vary** varying wind (hendiadys),
whim
78 **epileptic** *OED*'s first use of the adjective;
epilepsy is first recorded in 1578 as a technical term replacing 'falling sickness', so

the word may well have sounded unfami-
liar. Perhaps one of Kent's exaggerated
insults—epileptic fits were 'often
attributed to possession by devilish
spirits, from which the unfortunate
victims needed to be exorcised, after
appropriate repentance' (Hoeniger,
p. 199)—or Oswald may be smiling
twitchily.
79 **Smile** deride, laugh at (*OED v.* 7, citing
this as its only instance)
80–1 **an . . . Camelot** Picturesque but ob-
scure. Sarum is the old name for
Salisbury, the cathedral city in Wiltshire.
The plain, which has Stonehenge at its
centre, was notorious for highwaymen,
and geese 'are plentifully pastured' there
(Sugden). *Camelot* (chosen partly for allit-
erative, partly for historical effect), the
legendary capital of King Arthur, is
sometimes identified with Winchester, in
Hampshire, not very far from Salisbury.
Kent calls Oswald a goose because his
smiles remind him of cackling, and says
that if he had him at his mercy he would
chase him a long way. There may be sexual overtones: 'goose' could mean both

CORNWALL   Why dost thou call him knave?
  What's his offence?
KENT   His countenance likes me not.   85
CORNWALL
  No more perchance does mine, or his, or hers.
KENT
  Sir, 'tis my occupation to be plain: *[candid]*
  I have seen better faces in my time   *[Blunt]*
  Than stands on any shoulder that I see
  Before me at this instant.
CORNWALL   This is a fellow   90
  Who, having been praised for bluntness, doth affect
  A saucy roughness, and constrains the garb
  Quite from his nature. He cannot flatter, he.   *[calls Kent*
  He must be plain, he must speak truth.   *on his*
  An they will take't, so; if not, he's plain.   *speech]*   95
  These kind of knaves I know, which in this plainness
  Harbour more craft and more corrupter ends
  Than twenty silly-ducking observants
  That stretch their duties nicely.
KENT
  Sir, in good sooth, or in sincere verity,   100
  Under the allowance of your grand aspect,

89 Than] Q2, F; That Q1   92 roughness] F (roughnes); ruffines Q   94 He must be plain] Q;
An honest mind and plaine F; Honest he must be, plain OXFORD *conj.*

'whore' and 'a whore's client' (Williams, *Dictionary*), and Winchester House in London was adjacent to brothels.

85 **likes** pleases
87 **plain** candid
91 **bluntness** curtness, rudeness. *OED*'s first instance of this sense.
92 **saucy** insolent
  roughness rudeness. *OED*'s first instance of this sense.
  constrains forces, wrenches the style (of speaking) completely away from its true nature (to express sincerity)
95 **he's plain** i.e. that's how he is—plain-spoken
96 **These kind** A common construction (*OED*, *kind*, *sb*. 14b).

97 **Harbour** conceal
  craft craftiness
  more corrupter i.e. even more corrupt
98 **silly-ducking** foolishly bowing, obsequious
  observants obsequious attendants. *OED*'s first instance of this sense.
99 **stretch . . . nicely** strain (themselves to carry out) their duties punctiliously
100–3 **Sir . . . front** Kent parodies a courtly style.
100 **sooth** truth
  verity A latinate word, grander than the Anglo-Saxon 'sooth'.
101 **allowance . . . aspect** approval of your mighty way of looking (aspect, accented on the second syllable, was an astrological term)

Whose influence, like the wreath of radiant fire
In flickering Phoebus' front—

CORNWALL   What mean'st thou by this?

KENT   To go out of my dialect, which you discommend so
much. I know, sir, I am no flatterer. He that beguiled
you in a plain accent was a plain knave, which for my
part I will not be, though I should win your displeasure to
entreat me to't.

CORNWALL (*to Oswald*)

What's the offence you gave him?

OSWALD   I never gave him any.

It pleased the King his master very late   110
To strike at me upon his misconstruction,
When he, conjunct, and flattering his displeasure,
Tripped me behind; being down, insulted, railed,
And put upon him such a deal of man that
That worthied him, got praises of the King   115
For him attempting who was self-subdued,
And in the fleshment of this dread exploit
Drew on me here again.

KENT   None of these rogues and cowards
But Ajax is their fool.

---

103 flickering] POPE; flitkering Q; flicking F   104 dialect] F; dialogue Q   105 I know] QF;
know OXFORD *conj.*   114–15 man that | That] Q1 (man, that, | That); man, that | That
Q2; Man, | That F; man, | That' [i.e. 'That it'] FURNESS   117 fleshment] F (flechment);
flechuent Q

---

102 **influence** Another astrological term.
103 **flickering** illuminated by an unsteady
light (*OED*'s first instance of this sense);
fickle
Phoebus' front brow of Phoebus Apollo,
the sun god
104 **dialect** normal way of speaking. Q's
'dialogue' is generally rejected.
discommend find fault with
105 **I know** 'Know, sir' may seem a more
natural locution from Kent, and the anticipation of 'I' from later in the line
would be easy.
105–6 **He . . . you** i.e. whoever deceived you
in the way you have described
107–8 **though . . . to't** Probably an awkward way of saying 'even if I should overcome (*OED*, win, v.¹2) your displeasure
so far that you would beg me to be'.

112 **conjunct** in league (with Lear)
flattering his playing up to Lear's
113 **insulted** could mean 'exulted'.
114 **put . . . man** assumed such a large quan-
tity of manliness
115 **That . . . worthied** that deed begot
a good opinion for him. Conceivably
'That' should be 'It' (*TC*).
116 **attempting** attacking
was self-subdued i.e. had already surren-
dered
117 **fleshment** i.e. excitement of his first success. *OED*'s only instance of this word.
Kent uses the verb at l. 42.
dread (sarcastic)
119 **Ajax . . . fool** can mean 'rogues and
cowards like these inflate their importance to make a warrior like Ajax sound
like a fool' (but Ajax was notoriously

CORNWALL [*calling*]   Bring forth the stocks, ho!—

You stubborn, ancient knave, you reverend braggart,   120

We'll teach you.

KENT   I am too old to learn.

Call not your stocks for me. I serve the King,

On whose employments I was sent to you.

You should do small respect, show too bold malice

Against the grace and person of my master,   125

Stocking his messenger.

CORNWALL [*calling*]   Fetch forth the stocks!—

As I have life and honour, there shall he sit till noon.

REGAN

Till noon?—till night, my lord, and all night too.

KENT

Why, madam, if I were your father's dog

You could not use me so.

REGAN   Sir, being his knave, I will.   130

          [*Stocks brought out*]

CORNWALL

This is a fellow of the selfsame nature

Our sister speaks of.—Come, bring away the stocks.

GLOUCESTER

Let me beseech your grace not to do so.

His fault is much, and the good King his master

Will check him for't. Your purposed low correction   135

119, 126 *calling*] *not in* Q   120 ancient] F; ausrent Qa; miscreant Qb   126 Stocking] F;
Stobing Qa; Stopping Qb   stocks!] Q (~?)   130.1 *Stocks brought out*] F; *not in* Q; *after l.* 132
DYCE   132 speaks] Q2, F; speake Q1

stupid, as in *Troilus*); 'rogues and
cowards like these make fools of (deceive)
great men like Ajax (and Cornwall)'.
There may be a submerged pun on
'jakes', a privy. Presumably it is the
implied comparison with Ajax that finally
strains Cornwall's patience beyond the
breaking point.

120 **reverend** venerable (sarcastic)
125 **grace . . . person** kingly and human
     status
126 **stocks!** Either he calls off stage, or on-
     stage servants obey.
130 **being . . . knave** (you) being his servant

132 **sister** sister-in-law, Gonoril
 - **speaks** Q's 'speake' may represent a mis-
     reading of either 'speaks' or 'spake' (*TC*),
     or could be an (unrecorded) spelling of
     'spake'.
     bring away Presumably an order to
     bring the stocks to the place where they
     are to be put to use (as Foakes notes,
     'in some part of the stage that makes it
     practicable for Edgar to deliver his solilo-
     quy at [166—186] and exit without
     noticing Kent'), or to prepare them for
     use.
135 **check** rebuke
     low correction ignoble punishment

159

Is such as basest and contemnèd wretches
For pilf'rings and most common trespasses
Are punished with. The King must take it ill
That he's so slightly valued in his messenger,
Should have him thus restrained.

CORNWALL   I'll answer that.   140

REGAN

My sister may receive it much more worse
To have her gentlemen abused, assaulted,
For following her affairs. Put in his legs.

 They put Kent in the stocks

Come, my good lord, away!

      Exeunt all but Gloucester and Kent

GLOUCESTER

I am sorry for thee, friend. 'Tis the Duke's pleasure,   145
Whose disposition, all the world well knows,
Will not be rubbed nor stopped. I'll entreat for thee.

KENT

Pray you, do not, sir. I have watched and travelled
 hard.
Some time I shall sleep out; the rest I'll whistle.
A good man's fortune may grow out at heels.   150
Give you good morrow.

GLOUCESTER

The Duke's to blame in this; 'twill be ill took.   *Exit*

KENT

Good King, that must approve the common say:

---

136 contemnèd] BLAYNEY; contaned Qa; temnest Qb; contemned'st CAPELL   143.1 *They . . . stocks*] POPE (*conj.* Rowe); *not in* Q   144.1 *Exeunt . . . Kent*] F (*Exit.*); *not in* Q   148 travelled] Q (trauaild)   149 out] Q2, F; ont Q1   152 *Exit*] Q2, F; *not in* Q1   153 say] Qa; saw Qb, Q2, F

136 **contemnèd** despised. Weis and HalioQ both adopt Capell's 'contemned'st' even though Weis says that 'contemned' is 'brilliantly extrapolated by Blayney' (*Texts*, pp. 247–8) 'from the layout of the Q proofsheet'. The superlative in *basest* probably carries itself over to *contemnèd*.
140 **restrained** confined
 answer answer for
141 **more worse** worse (an acceptable construction)
143 **following . . . affairs** pursuing her business

147 **rubbed** impeded, hindered (the only instance of this sense in *OED*, *rub*, *v.*[1] 3b)
150 **A good** i.e. even a good (?)
 out at heels A commonplace (Dent H389), appropriate to one whose heels are in the stocks.
152 **took** taken
153 **approve** confirm
 say saying. Well attested, though HalioQ (but not Weis) adopts corrected Q and F's 'saw', the usual Shakespearian form.

Thou out of heaven's benediction com'st
To the warm sun.   155
        [*He takes out a letter*]
Approach, thou beacon to this under globe,
That by thy comfortable beams I may
Peruse this letter. Nothing almost sees miracles
But misery. I know 'tis from Cordelia,
Who hath now fortunately been informed   160
Of my obscurèd course, and shall find time
For this enormous state, seeking to give
Losses their remedies. All weary and overwatched,
Take vantage, heavy eyes, not to behold
This shameful lodging. Fortune, good night;   165
Smile; once more turn thy wheel.   *He sleeps*
        Enter Edgar

[margin handwritten: irregular]

---

154 com'st] Q (comest)   155.1 *He . . . letter*] OXFORD; *not in* Q   158 miracles] F (myrackles); my rackles Qa; my wracke Qb   160 now] OXFORD; not Qa; most Qb, Q2, F   162 For] ROWE; From QF   163 their] Qb; and Qa   overwatched] Q2, F; ouerwatch Q1   164 Take] Qb; Late Qa   166 *He sleeps* | *Enter Edgar*] OXFORD; *new scene* (2.3) STEEVENS *etc*.   He] *not in* Q   heard] F; heare Q

154–5 **out . . . sun** Proverbial (Dent G272. 'Out of God's blessing into the warm sun'), meaning 'from good to bad' (the heat of the sun being regarded as a misfortune).

156 **beacon** i.e. the sun, just rising
   under globe the earth

157 **comfortable** bringing comfort

158–9 **Nothing . . . misery** A cryptically abstract way of saying 'hardly anyone witnesses miracles except the afflicted' ('because to the desperate any relief seems miraculous' (Foakes)). Kent's 'miracle' is the letter from Cordelia.

160 **now** This emendation of uncorrected Q's 'not' is defended in Taylor, 'Four New Readings'. Weis and HalioQ follow corrected Q's 'most' without comment. Realistically, only Kent could have informed Cordelia of his disguise (Knowles, p. 35).

161 **obscurèd** darkened, disguised

161–3 **and . . . remedies** This is a much disputed passage. We assume that *Cordelia*, not *I*, is the subject of *shall*, and that Kent is saying that she will find the time to act on behalf of England—*this enormous state*—or more generally of the current terrible state of affairs, trying to find

remedies for what has been lost. Q's 'From' (l. 162), retained by Weis but not HalioQ, who also adopts Rowe's 'For'—might just be explicable as 'Away from', i.e. in France, but 'For' would be an easy misreading and seems preferable. Editors have sometimes tried to make sense of the original by assuming that Kent reads one or more disjointed phrases from Cordelia's letter. The passage is discussed at greater length in *TC*.

162 **enormous state** excessively disordered, wildly irregular state of things, or country. A parallel occurs in *Kinsmen* when Arcite prays to Mars as the 'great corrector of enormous times' (5.1.61).

163 **overwatched** exhausted for lack of sleep

164 **vantage** advantage of the opportunity (by going to sleep)

166 **wheel** 'Fortune's wheel is ever turning' was proverbial (Dent F617). Charles Nicholl discusses recurrent wheel imagery in the course of an alchemical interpretation of the play in *The Chemical Theatre* (1980), pp. 145–7, etc., remarking 'The Wheel is the "journey" undertaken by all the central characters . . . in short, the pattern of *King Lear*' (p. 147).

EDGAR   I heard myself proclaimed,
  And by the happy hollow of a tree
  Escaped the hunt. No port is free, no place
  That guard and most unusual vigilance
  Does not attend my taking. While I may scape   170
  I will preserve myself, and am bethought
  To take the basest and most poorest shape
  That ever penury in contempt of man *despise mankind*
  Brought near to beast. My face I'll grime with filth,
  Blanket my loins, elf all my hair with knots,   175
  And with presented nakedness outface
  The wind and persecution of the sky.
  The country gives me proof and precedent
  Of Bedlam beggars who with roaring voices
  Strike in their numbed and mortified bare arms   180
  Pins, wooden pricks, nails, sprigs of rosemary,
  And with this horrible object from low farms,
  Poor pelting villages, sheep-cotes and mills
Unimportant

170 Does] F; Dost Q; doth *or* do OXFORD *conj*.   taking. While] Q (~ ~)   175 elf] F; else Q
180 and] Qb; *not in* Qa   181 Pins] Qb; Pies Qa   182 from] Qb; frame Qa   farms] F (fermes);
seruice Q

166 *Enter Edgar* Shakespeare's audience would have accepted the convention by which Edgar shows no awareness of Kent's presence and appears to be in a different place. Juxtaposition of the two men is emblematically fitting. Editors have often marked a new scene here and at l. 186.1, but the stage is not cleared.

166 **proclaimed** (as an outlaw)
167 **happy** luckily available
168 **port** seaport, gate (as at 6.80)
  free unguarded, i.e. safe
168–9 **no . . . That** i.e. there is no place where
169 **guard** watchfulness
170 **attend my taking** apply itself to my capture, is in waiting for me
  scape escape
171 **bethought** resolved
172 **most poorest** An acceptable double superlative (Abbott 11).
  shape disguise
173 **in . . . man** despising mankind
174–86 **My face . . . am** Actors sometimes alter their appearance as they speak these lines. Rosenberg (p. 151) remarks: 'The process of stripping before the audience is central, will anticipate Lear's action;

particularly so if Edgar too must throw off conspicuously rich clothes to become nothing.'
175 **Blanket** cover with a blanket (*OED*'s first use of the verb)
  elf tangle as an elf might do. *OED*'s first instance of a rare verb.
176 **presented** displayed
178 **proof** evidence
179 **Bedlam beggars** Explained at 2.126–7n. In *The Bellman of London*, Thomas Dekker writes of 'Tom of Bedlam's band of madcaps, otherwise called "Poor Tom's flock of wild geese", whom here thou seest by his black and blue naked arms to be a man beaten to the world' (1608, sig. C1ᵛ).
180 **mortified** numbed, insensible (presumably as the result of long misuse)
181 **pricks** skewers
182 **object** spectacle, sight
  farms F's reading. Both HalioQ and Weis retain Q's 'seruice', Weis glossing as 'lowly, poor servants, perhaps tenant farmers in the countryside'. This seems strained especially as the next line mentions only places, not people.
183 **pelting** unimportant, paltry

Sometime with lunatic ~~bans~~ *curses*, sometime with prayers
Enforce their charity. 'Poor Tuelygod, Poor Tom!'   185
That's something yet. Edgar I nothing am.   *Exit*
    Enter King Lear, his Fool, and a Knight

LEAR
  'Tis strange that they should so depart from home
  And not send back my messenger.
KNIGHT   As I learned,
  The night before there was no purpose
  Of his remove.
KENT (*waking*)   Hail to thee, noble master.   190
LEAR
  How! Mak'st thou this shame thy pastime?
FOOL Ha, ha, look, he wears cruel garters! Horses are tied
  by the heads, dogs and bears by th' neck, monkeys by th'
  loins, and men by th' legs. When a man's over-lusty at
  legs, then he wears wooden nether-stocks.   195
LEAR (*to Kent*)
  What's he that hath so much thy place mistook
  To set thee here?
KENT   It is both he and she:
  Your son and daughter.
LEAR   No.
KENT   Yes.

---

185 Tuelygod] Qa; Turly god Qb, Q2, F; tirlery-gaud STONE *conj.*   186–186.1 *Exit | Enter*]
OXFORD; *new scene* (2.4) STEEVENS   186.1 *Lear . . . Knight*] *not in* Q   187 home] F; hence Q
189 purpose] Q; purpose in them F   190 *waking*] STAUNTON; *not in* Q   193 heads] F; heeles Q

184 **bans** curses
185 **Tuelygod** The word is otherwise un-
    known; editors usually adopt Qb's alter-
    native 'Turlygod', but as neither word
    has meaning, the choice is immaterial.
    Schmidt suggests 'seemingly a name
    given to bedlam-beggars'. The matter is
    discussed at length in *TC*.
186 **That's . . . yet** i.e. at least I shall have
    some identity
    nothing in no way
186.1 Editors often mark a new scene, but
    there is no change in place or time.
    they Cornwall and Regan
189–90 **purpose . . . remove** intention that
    he should leave
192 **cruel** (a) harsh; (b) made of crewel, a

worsted yarn used to make stockings
193 **heads** HalioQ retains Q's 'heeles'; Weis
    follows F, as here. Q is not nonsense, but
    F seems closer to normal practice.
194–5 **over-lusty at legs** Dekker uses the
    phrase to mean simply 'hyper-active':
    'tradesmen, as if they were dancing gal-
    liards, are lusty at legs, and never stand
    still' (*The Seven Deadly Sins of London*
    (1606), quoted Smith, p. 54); here it may
    signify 'too much of a vagabond', or
    'over-active sexually'.
195 **nether-stocks** stockings. *OED*'s only in-
    stance of the transferred sense.
196 **place** position, office
197 **To** as to
198 **son** son-in-law

LEAR   No, I say.

KENT

I say yea.

LEAR   No, no, they would not.

KENT   Yes, they have.

LEAR

By Jupiter, I swear no. They durst not do't,   200

They would not, could not do't. 'Tis worse than murder,

To do upon respect such violent outrage.

Resolve me with all modest haste which way

Thou mayst deserve or they propose this usage,

Coming from us.

KENT   My lord, when at their home   205

I did commend your highness' letters to them,

Ere I was risen from the place that showed

My duty kneeling, came there a reeking post

Stewed in his haste, half breathless, panting forth

From Gonoril, his mistress, salutations,   210

Delivered letters spite of intermission,

Which presently they read, on whose contents

They summoned up their meiny, straight took horse,

Commanded me to follow and attend

The leisure of their answer, gave me cold looks;   215

And meeting here the other messenger,

Whose welcome I perceived had poisoned mine—

---

204 propose] OXFORD; purpose Q; impose F   213 meiny] F; men Q

---

200 **Jupiter** King of the gods in Roman mythology.

202 **upon respect** to one who should be respected (cf. *OED*, *respect*, *sb*. 16c); or upon consideration

203 **Resolve** inform
modest reasonable

204 **propose** Our emendation from Q's 'purpose' improves the metre and, arguably, the sense. It is not accepted by HalioQ or Weis.

205 **Coming** seeing that you came
us The royal plural, used by Lear for the last time (Foakes).

206 **commend** deliver
letters could mean 'a letter'.

208 **duty** respect

208 **reeking** steaming (with sweat); *OED*'s first instance of the adjective used of a person.
post messenger

211 **spite of intermission** although he was interrupting me (or 'in spite of the gasps and pauses that his breathless condition required'—Hunter)

212 **presently** immediately
on i.e. as a result of

213 **meiny** retinue. Q's 'men', accepted by HalioQ and Weis, makes sense, 'but the presence of *meiny* in related contexts in Harsnet, the ease of misreading the rare "meinie" for commonplace "menne", and the metrical irregularity combine to support the emendation' (*TC*).

Being the very fellow that of late
Displayed so saucily against your highness—
Having more man than wit about me, drew.   220
He raised the house with loud and coward cries.
Your son and daughter found this trespass worth
This shame which here it suffers.

LEAR

O, how this mother swells up toward my heart!
Histerica passio, down, thou climbing sorrow;   225
Thy element's below.—Where is this daughter?

KENT

With the Earl, sir, within.

LEAR   Follow me not; stay there.

Exit

KNIGHT (*to Kent*)

Made you no more offence than what you speak of?

KENT

No. How chance the King comes with so small a train?

FOOL   An thou hadst been set in the stocks for that question,   230
thou hadst well deserved it.

KENT   Why, fool?

FOOL   We'll set thee to school to an ant, to teach thee
there's no labouring in the winter. All that follow their

---

220 Having] QF; I, having OXFORD *conj.*   225 *Histerica*] F4; *Historica* QF   227 there.] Q (~?)
227.1 *Exit*] F; *not in* Q

219 **Displayed so saucily** acted ostenta-
    tiously in so insolent a manner (*OED*'s
    only instance of this use of 'display')
220 **Having . . . wit** (I) having more valour
    than discretion
    drew drew my sword
222 **this trespass** this offence of mine
224–5 **mother . . . *Histerica passio*** 'Mother'
    was the common name for hysteria;
    OED's first instance of 'hysterica [*sic*]
    passio' (Latin, 'suffering of the womb') is
    from Harsnet, where Shakespeare may
    have picked it up. Hoeniger, in an inter-
    esting discussion (pp. 320–4), notes that
    the illness is 'marked by fearful and
    painful (*passio*) sensations rising from
    the lower abdomen to the heart and the
    throat'. Properly, as it originates in the
    womb, it could only afflict women, but
    Harsnet (p. 401) includes the confession

of a man who says that he 'had a spice of
the mother . . . whether I do rightly term
it the mother or no, I know not'. He
names other men who suffered from the
same disease, which 'riseth . . . of a wind
in the bottom of the belly, and, proceed-
ing with a great swelling, causeth a very
painful colic in the stomach and an extraordinary giddiness in the head' and fears
that he, like his brother, will die of it.
225 **sorrow** *OED* (*sb*. 5a) cites the obsolete
    sense 'Physical pain or suffering'; its last
    example is from 1398, but this is clearly
    the meaning here.
226 **element** proper place
233–4 **We'll . . . winter** Ants lay up food in
    the summer for the winter. The Fool im-
    plies that no profit is to be gained from
    serving Lear in the winter of his fortunes.
    The passage may be influenced by

noses are led by their eyes but blind men, and there's not   235
a nose among a hundred but can smell him that's stinking. Let go thy hold when a great wheel runs down a hill,
lest it break thy neck with following it; but the great one
that goes up the hill, let him draw thee after. When a
wise man gives thee better counsel, give me mine again.   240
I would have none but knaves follow it, since a fool
gives it.

⌈*Sings*⌉   That sir that serves for gain
                    And follows but for form,
                Will pack when it begin to rain,   245
                    And leave thee in the storm.

            But I will tarry, the fool will stay,
                    And let the wise man fly.
            The knave turns fool that runs away,
                    The fool no knave, pardie.   250

KENT   Where learnt you this, fool?
FOOL   Not in the stocks.
            Enter King Lear and the Earl of Gloucester

LEAR

Deny to speak with me? They're sick, they're weary?
They travelled hard tonight?—mere insolence,
Ay, the images of revolt and flying off.   255
Fetch me a better answer.

GLOUCESTER   My dear lord,
You know the fiery quality of the Duke,

---

250 pardie] Q (perdy)   252.1 *King*] *not in* Q   *the Earl of*] *not in* Q   254 insolence] BLAYNEY;
Iustice Q; fetches F

Proverbs 6: 6, 8: 'Go to the pismire [ant],
O sluggard; behold her ways and be wise.
. . . Prepareth her meat in the summer,
and gathereth her food in harvest.'

236–7 **stinking** like a corpse. Anyone in
their senses would know that it's best to
avoid Lear.
240 **give . . . again** i.e. return it
243 **sir** man, servant
244 **form** mere show
245 **pack** pack up, leave
    begin Subjunctive (Abbott 368).
249–50 **The knave . . . knave** The Fool plays
with paradoxes about folly and wisdom.

'The fellow that forsakes his master is
(from the point of view of the higher wisdom) a fool, since true wisdom implies fidelity; and the fool who, like me, remains
faithful is, at all events, no knave'
(Kittredge).
250 **pardie** by God
253 **Deny** (do they) refuse
254 **tonight** last night (*OED adv.* 3)
    insolence Q's 'Iustice' is obviously wrong
    and could not represent F's 'fetches'. HalioQ
    also accepts BlayneyQ's emendation.
255 **images** symbols, embodiments
    flying off desertion
257 **quality** disposition

How unremovable and fixed he is
In his own course.

LEAR   Vengeance, death, plague, confusion!
What 'fiery quality'? Why, Gloucester, I'd   260
Speak with the Duke of Cornwall and his wife.

GLOUCESTER Ay, my good lord.

LEAR

The King would speak with Cornwall; the dear father
Would with his daughter speak, commands, tends
    service.
'Fiery'? The Duke?—tell the hot Duke that Lear—   265
No, but not yet. Maybe he is not well.
Infirmity doth still neglect all office
Whereto our health is bound. We are not ourselves
When nature, being oppressed, commands the mind
To suffer with the body. I'll forbear,   270
And am fallen out with my more headier will,
To take the indisposed and sickly fit
For the sound man.—Death on my state,
Wherefore should he sit here? This act persuades me
That this remotion of the Duke and her   275
Is practice only. Give me my servant forth.
Tell the Duke and 's wife I'll speak with them,
Now, presently. Bid them come forth and hear me,
Or at their chamber door I'll beat the drum
Till it cry sleep to death.

GLOUCESTER   I would have all well   280
Betwixt you.   *Exit*

---

263 father] Qb; fate Qa   264 his] Qb; the Qa   commands] Qb; come and Qa   tends] Qa;
her Qb; their ALEXANDER   265 'Fiery'? The] BLAYNEY; The fierie Qa; Fierie Qb; Fiery? The
Fiery? F   266 No] Qb; Mo Qa   269 commands] Q2; Cōmand Q1   276 practice only. Give]
F; ~, ~ Q

264 **tends** awaits
267–8 **Infirmity . . . bound** A generalized
  way of saying 'in illness we always neglect that duty which we are committed to
  in health'.
271 **fallen . . . will** have repudiated my more
  precipitate impulse
272–3 **take . . . For** mistake the irregular
  behaviour of one who is unwell for
  that of. Weis interprets *sickly fit* as

'those who are sick while appearing
well', but this is anachronistic: *OED*,
fit, *a*. 6.
273 **state** Both 'condition' and the 'kingly
  power' that he no longer exerts.
275 **remotion** departure (*OED*, first example
  of this sense); 'act of keeping aloof'
  (Schmidt)
276 **practice only** just a cunning trick
278 **presently** immediately

LEAR   O, my heart, my heart!

FOOL   Cry to it, nuncle, as the cockney did to the eels when
        she put 'em i'th' paste alive. She rapped 'em o'th' cox-
        combs with a stick, and cried 'Down, wantons, down!'
        'Twas her brother that, in pure kindness to his horse,   285
        buttered his hay.

        Enter the Duke of Cornwall and Regan, the Earl of
        Gloucester, and others

LEAR   Good morrow to you both.

CORNWALL   Hail to your grace.

        ⌈*Kent here set at liberty*⌉

REGAN   I am glad to see your highness.

LEAR

        Regan, I think you are. I know what reason   290
        I have to think so. If thou shouldst not be glad
        I would divorce me from thy mother's shrine,
        Sepulchring an adultress. (*To Kent*) Yea, are you free?
        Some other time for that.—Belovèd Regan,
        Thy sister is naught. O, Regan, she hath tied   295
        Sharp-toothed unkindness like a vulture here.
        I can scarce speak to thee. Thou'lt not believe
        Of how deplored a quality—O, Regan!

worthless (margin annotation)

286.1–2 *Enter . . . Gloucester*] Q (*Enter Duke and Regan.*)   286.2 *and others*] BLAYNEY; *not in* Q;
Seruants F   288 CORNWALL] Q ('*Duke*' throughout the scene)   288.1 *Kent here set at liberty*] F;
not in Q   292 divorce] Qb (diuorce); deuose Qa   shrine,] OXFORD; fruit, Qa; tombe
Qb, F   297 Thou'lt] Q (thout)   298 deplored] BLAYNEY (*conj.* Stone); deptoued Qa; depriued
Qb; deprau'd F

---

282 **cockney** 'squeamish [because unwilling
    to kill the eels before cooking them],
    over-nice, wanton, or affected woman'
    (*OED sb.* 2d, first instance), also
    'Londoner'.
    did to the eels No other instance of the
    anecdote is known. It is a parable of
    Lear's fruitless attempt to subdue what in
    F he calls 'my heart, my rising heart'.

283 **paste** pastry (for a pie)

283–4 **coxcombs** heads (jocular)

284 **wantons** 'sportive or roguish animal[s]'
    (*OED B sb.* 2b, first instance)

286 **buttered . . . hay** A misplaced kindness
    exemplary of innocent folly.

292 **mother** This is the play's only reference
    to Lear's wife. The critical implications of
    this are investigated by Coppélia Kahn in
    'The Absent Mother in *King Lear*', in

Rewriting the Renaissance, ed. M.
Ferguson, *et al.* (Chicago and London,
1986), 33–49, where she traces 'Lear's
progress toward acceptance of the
woman in himself'.

292 **shrine** tomb. Taylor's emendation of
    uncorrected Q's 'fruit', defended in 'Four
    New Readings'. Weis and HalioQ accept
    corrected Q's 'tombe'.

293 **Sepulchring** serving as a burial place for
    (*OED*'s first instance of this sense)

295 **naught** worthless, wicked

296 **vulture** Alluding to the legend of
    Prometheus, who, having stolen fire
    from the gods, was punished by being
    chained to a rock where a vulture
    gnawed continually at his liver.

298 **deplored** BlayneyQ's emendation, pro-
    posed by Stone but not accepted by

REGAN

    I pray you, sir, take patience. I have hope

    You less know how to value her desert   300

    Than she to slack her duty.

LEAR My curses on her.

REGAN O sir, you are old.

    Nature in you stands on the very verge

    Of her confine. You should be ruled and led   305

    By some discretion that discerns your state

    Better than you yourself. Therefore I pray

    That to our sister you do make return;

    Say you have wronged her, sir.

LEAR   Ask her forgiveness?

    Do you mark how this becomes the house?   310

    [*Kneeling*] 'Dear daughter, I confess that I am old.

    Age is unnecessary. On my knees I beg

    That you'll vouchsafe me raiment, bed, and food.'

REGAN

    Good sir, no more. These are unsightly tricks.

    Return you to my sister.

LEAR [*rising*]   No, Regan.   315

    She hath abated me of half my train,

    Looked black upon me, struck me with her tongue

    Most serpent-like upon the very heart.

    All the stored vengeances of heaven fall

    On her ungrateful top! Strike her young bones,   320

    You taking airs, with lameness!

---

299 you] F; *not in* Q   304 in] F; on Q   309 sir.] Q2; ~? Q1   forgiveness?] Q (~,)
311 *Kneeling*] HANMER; *not in* Q   315 *rising*] DYCE; *not in* Q   320 top!] Q (~,)   321 lameness!] Q (~.)

HalioQ or Weis, attempts to make sense of the Q readings without recourse to F.

299 **you** Metrically desirable and presumably (like 'in' in l. 304) accidentally omitted from Q.

300–1 **You . . . duty** An awkward way of saying 'you are less able to appreciate her worth than she is of neglecting her duty'.

304–5 **Nature . . . confine** A stilted way of saying 'You're very close to death.'

304 **verge** extreme limit

305 **confine** allocated space

306 **some discretion that** i.e. the good sense of someone who **discerns your state** perceives, understands your condition

310 **becomes the house** befits the (royal) household, family

314 **unsightly** ugly (*OED*'s first use of the word 'Applied to immaterial things')

316 **abated** deprived

317 **struck** wounded (*OED*, *strike*, *v.* 37)

318 **serpent** Used generally of venomous reptiles.

320 **top** head
    young bones Probably 'bones of any

CORNWALL   Fie, fie, sir.

LEAR

You nimble lightnings, dart your blinding flames
Into her scornful eyes. Infect her beauty,
You fen-sucked fogs drawn by the pow'rful sun
To fall and blast her pride.

REGAN   O, the blest gods!   325

So will you wish on me when the rash mood—

LEAR

No, Regan. Thou shalt never have my curse.
Thy tender-hested nature shall not give
Thee o'er to harshness. Her eyes are fierce, but thine
Do comfort and not burn. 'Tis not in thee   330
To grudge my pleasures, to cut off my train,
To bandy hasty words, to scant my sizes,
And, in conclusion, to oppose the bolt
Against my coming in. Thou better know'st
The offices of nature, bond of childhood,   335
Effects of courtesy, dues of gratitude.
Thy half of the kingdom hast thou not forgot,
Wherein I thee endowed.

REGAN   Good sir, to th' purpose.
                              what's the point?

LEAR

Who put my man i'th' stocks?
    [*Trumpets within*]

---

322 LEAR] Q2 (*Lear.*); *not in* Q1 (*which however indents the line as though it were the beginning of a
speech*)   328 Thy] F; The Q   339 *Trumpets within*] ROWE; *not in* Q; *Tucket within.* F (*one line
earlier*)

infant that she may breed', as at *Leir*,
l. 844, 'poor soul, she breeds young
bones, | And that is it that makes her so
touchy, sure'. Lear could imply that she
is already pregnant, but it seems likely
that if this were so, more prominence
would have been given to it.

321 **taking** infectious, 'catching' (*OED
ppl. a.* 3, first use of this rare sense)

324 **fen-sucked fogs** As in *Tempest*, 2.2. 1–2
'All the infections that the sun sucks up |
From bogs, fens, flats, on Prosper fall . . .'.

326 **mood** F completes the sentence with 'is
on', but the ellipsis is marked in Q.

328 **tender-hested** may mean 'tender-

purposed': *OED*, *hest*, *v.* 3, offers one instance of the verbal noun 'hesting' meaning 'purpose, design'. F's 'tender-hefted',
defined by *OED* as 'set in a delicate "haft"
or bodily frame; hence, womanly, gentle'
(*tender*, *a.* [*adv.*] and *n.*, C), adopted by
Halio and Weis, is no less recondite.

332 **scant my sizes** curtail my allowances (of
food and drink)

333 **oppose the bolt** shut the doorbolt as an
obstacle

335 **offices of nature** natural obligations
childhood childship, filial relation (*OED*
5, first recorded use in this obsolete sense)

336 **Effects** manifestations

338 **to th' purpose** come to the point

CORNWALL What trumpet's that?

Enter Oswald the steward

REGAN

I know't, my sister's. This approves her letters 340
That she would soon be here. (*To Oswald*) Is your lady
come?

LEAR

This is a slave whose easy-borrowed pride
Dwells in the fickle grace of her a follows.

[*He strikes Oswald*]

Out, varlet, from my sight!

CORNWALL What means your grace?

Enter Gonoril

GONORIL

Who struck my servant? Regan, I have good hope 345
Thou didst not know on't.

LEAR Who comes here? O heavens,

If you do love old men, if your sweet sway
Allow obedience, if yourselves are old,
Make it your cause! Send down and take my part.
(*To Gonoril*) Art not ashamed to look upon this beard? 350
O Regan, wilt thou take her by the hand?

GONORIL

Why not by the hand, sir? How have I offended?

339.1 *Oswald the*] not in Q   343.1 *He strikes Oswald*] OXFORD; *not in* QF   346 on't] Q (ant)
347 your] F; you Q

---

340 **I know't** implies an identifiable trumpet
call (Steevens), specific to Regan.
approves confirms (the contents of)

342 **easy-borrowed pride** *Pride* could mean
'ostentatious adornment or ornamenta-
tion' (*OED sb.*[1] 7), in which case this
phrase would mean that Oswald's finery
has been readily, or casually, lent by
his mistress. The hyphen is editorial;
some editors interpret *easy* as an adjective
(e.g. Foakes, glossing 'casual or
effortless').

343 **fickle grace** uncertain favour
a he (the unemphatic form)

343.1 **He . . . Oswald** Oxford's direction, assuming that Oswald is visibly reeling on
Gonoril's entrance. But possibly '"Who
struck my servant?" refers to Oswald's
earlier encounter with Kent' (*TC*).

344 **Out . . . sight** Weis instructs Oswald
to leave, yet assumes his presence without re-entry at l. 374. Perhaps his mistress encounters him as he is about to
leave through the door by which she
enters.

344.1 **Enter Gonoril** She takes Regan's
hand at some point between here and
l. 351.

346 **heavens** Here equated with the gods.

347–8 **your . . . obedience** your benevolent
rule approves of obedience. HalioQ, like
this edition, adopts F's *your*; Weis
retains Q's 'you', interpreting 'if
you grant (*Allow*) to humility gentle
government'—a possible but tortured
construction.

350 **beard** 'an emblem of age, and therefore
of authority and deserving' (Hunter)

All's not offence that indiscretion finds
And dotage terms so.

LEAR   O sides, you are too tough!
Will you yet hold?—How came my man i'th' stocks?   355

CORNWALL

I set him there, sir; but his own disorders
Deserved much less advancement.

LEAR   You? Did you?

REGAN

I pray you, father, being weak, seem so.
If till the expiration of your month
You will return and sojourn with my sister,   360
Dismissing half your train, come then to me.
I am now from home, and out of that provision
Which shall be needful for your entertainment.

LEAR

Return to her, and fifty men dismissed?
No, rather I abjure all roofs, and choose   365
To be a comrade with the wolf and owl,
To wage against the enmity of the air
Necessity's sharp pinch. Return with her?
Why, the hot-blood in France that dowerless took
Our youngest born—I could as well be brought   370
To knee his throne and, squire-like, pension beg
To keep base life afoot. Return with her?
Persuade me rather to be slave and sumpter
To this detested groom.

366–7 To be . . . air] THEOBALD; *lines in reverse order* QF   371 beg] Q2, F; bag Q1

353–4 **indiscretion . . . so** poor judgement
  considers and second childishness terms so
356 **disorders** misdemeanours
357 **advancement** promotion (ironical)
365–8 Lear's angry response to Regan's
  sweet reasonableness is not entirely coher-
  ent. Somewhat tentatively, we follow
  Theobald in transposing lines 367 and
  366, taking *wage* to mean wager. This
  change is supported by Blayney (*Texts*,
  p. 215), who posits eyeslip causing omission of line 367 followed by inaccurate replacement. The change is disputed by
  Foakes, who (like e.g. Kittredge and Muir)
  takes *Necessity's sharp pinch* to be 'a phrase
  in apposition with, and summing up,

Lear's angry and incoherent choice in the
previous three lines'. Like HalioQ and *OED*
(*v.* 10c, listing as a nonce-use), he takes
wage to mean 'struggle, do battle'.
369 **hot-blood** impetuous person (not
  recorded in *OED*, but similar to F's 'hot-
  bloodied *France*'); 'hot-blooded' is first
  recorded in *Merry Wives* (5.5.2).
371 **knee** do obeisance to
  squire-like 'In the manner of a squire or
  attendant; humbly, submissively' (*OED*,
  giving this as its only instance of the adverbial usage).
372 **base life afoot** a wretched life in existence
373 **sumpter** packhorse, beast of burden
  groom servant or stableman

GONORIL   At your choice, sir.

LEAR

Now I prithee, daughter, do not make me mad. *Goodbye to 2nd*
                                              daughter?
I will not trouble thee, my child. Farewell.

We'll no more meet, no more see one another.

But yet thou art my flesh, my blood, my daughter—

Or rather a disease that lies within my flesh,

Which I must needs call mine. Thou art a boil,   380

A plague-sore, an embossèd carbuncle

In my corrupted blood. But I'll not chide thee.

Let shame come when it will, I do not call it.

I do not bid the thunder-bearer shoot,

Nor tell tales of thee to high-judging Jove.   385

Mend when thou canst; be better at thy leisure.

I can be patient, I can stay with Regan,

I and my hundred knights.

REGAN   Not altogether so, sir.

I look not for you yet, nor am provided

For your fit welcome. Give ear, sir, to my sister;   390

For those that mingle reason with your passion

Must be content to think you are old, and so—

But she knows what she does.

LEAR   Is this well spoken now?

REGAN

I dare avouch it, sir. What, fifty followers?

---

379 that lies within] Q; that's in F   380 boil] QF (bile)

381 **embossèd** swollen, tumid
    carbuncle a gangrenous ulcer (Schmidt;
    also symptomatic of the plague (Hoeniger,
    p. 216)); stressed on the second syllable.
382 **corrupted blood** diseased lineage. 'Cor-
    ruption of blood' was a legal term refer-
    ring to 'the effect of an attainder upon a
    person attainted, by which his blood was
    held to have become tainted or "cor-
    rupted" by his crime, so that he and his
    descendants lost all rights of rank and
    title . . .' (*OED*, *corruption*, 2b).
383 **call** summon, ask for
384 **thunder-bearer** Jupiter, king of the
    gods; *OED*'s first instance.
    shoot throw a thunderbolt (as he does in
    Cymbeline, 5.5.186.2)

385 **high-judging** judging from on high
    Jove A poetical equivalent of Jupiter. Lear
    either uses both *thunder-bearer* and *Jove* to
    refer to the same deity, or thinks of Jupiter
    and Jove as different gods.
386 **Mend** improve
389 **look . . . for** expect. Probably an ex-
    ample of the 'Indicative simple present for
    complete present with adverbs signifying
    "as yet", etc.' (Abbott 346).
391 **mingle . . . passion** temper your emo-
    tionalism with reason
392 **so—** 'Regan breaks off as if she were
    about to repeat what she said at [303–7]'
    (Foakes)—or perhaps she holds back
    from saying what she really means.
394 **avouch it** vouch for, confirm it

173

Is it not well? What should you need of more,   395
Yea, or so many, sith that both charge and danger
Speaks 'gainst so great a number? How in a house
Should many people under two commands
Hold amity? 'Tis hard, almost impossible.

GONORIL

Why might not you, my lord, receive attendance   400
From those that she calls servants, or from mine?

REGAN

Why not, my lord? If then they chanced to slack you,
We could control them. If you will come to me—
For now I spy a danger—I entreat you
To bring but five-and-twenty; to no more   405
Will I give place or notice.

LEAR I gave you all.

REGAN And in good time you gave it.

LEAR

Made you my guardians, my depositaries,
But kept a reservation to be followed   410
With such a number. What, must I come to you
With five-and-twenty, Regan? Said you so?

REGAN

And speak't again, my lord. No more with me.

LEAR

Those wicked creatures yet do seem well favoured
When others are more wicked. Not being the worst   415
Stands in some rank of praise. (*To Gonoril*) I'll go with
          thee.
Thy fifty yet doth double five-and-twenty,
And thou art twice her love. *She loves him twice as much*

---

395 of] QF; have *conj.* This edition

395 **What . . . more** what need should you
have. Possibly, since Q's 'of' means
'have' at 24.301, this should be modernized to 'What [i.e. why] need have
more'.
396 **sith that** since
  charge . . . danger considerations of expense and danger (of riotous behaviour)
399 **Hold amity** sustain friendly relations
402 **slack you** give you inadequate service
406 **place or notice** room or attention
407 **I . . . all** In *Leir*, the King says to Ragan

'Ah, cruel Ragan, did I give thee all'
(l. 2144).
409 **depositaries** trustees. *OED*'s first instance of the word, but it occurs along
with 'guardian' in Florio's *Montaigne*
(Muir, p. 237).
410 **reservation** reserved right, saving
clause (*OED*'s first instance (3a) of this
sense)
414 **well favoured** good looking, attractive
417–18 **Thy . . . love** Lear still thinks that
love can be quantified.

GONORIL   Hear me, my lord. *Systematically*
    What need you five-and-twenty, ten, or five,   *Reduce him*
    To follow in a house where twice so many   420
    Have a command to tend you?
REGAN   What needs one? *]*

LEAR
    O, reason not the need! Our basest beggars
    Are in the poorest thing superfluous.
    Allow not nature more than nature needs,
    Man's life is cheap as beast's. Thou art a lady.   425
    If only to go warm were gorgeous,   *Rationalizing → it*
    Why, nature needs not what thou, gorgeous, wearest, *to define him*
    Which scarcely keeps thee warm. But for true need—
    You heavens, give me that patience, patience I need.
    You see me here, you gods, a poor old fellow, *cannot continue*   430
    As full of grief as age, wretchèd in both.   *argument*
    If it be you that stirs these daughters' hearts
    Against their father, fool me not so much
    To bear it tamely. Touch me with noble anger.
    O, let not women's weapons, water-drops, *tears; tries to fight*   435
    Stain my man's cheeks! No, you unnatural hags, *them away*
    I will have such revenges on you both
    That all the world shall—I will do such things—   *→ Breaks*
    What they are, yet I know not; but they shall be *language*
    The terrors of the earth. You think I'll weep.   *cannot express*   440
    No, I'll not weep.   *anger*
        [Storm within]

---

422 need] F; deed Q   425 life is] F; life as Q1; life's as Q2   433 so] F; to Q   434 tamely] F;
lamely Q   436 cheeks!] Q (~,)   441.1 *Storm within*] OXFORD; *not in* Q; *Storme and Tempest*. F
(*after* 'weeping')

420 **follow** follow, attend you
423 **superfluous** superabundantly supplied
424 **nature . . . nature** Lear struggles to ex-
    press a distinction between human and
    animal nature.
425 **life is** Q2's 'life's as' (adopted by HalioQ)
    is no less plausible than F's correction of
    Q's 'life as'.
427–8 **gorgeous . . . warm** A hint that
    Gonoril should be 'gorgeously'—colour-
    fully—costumed with more concern for
    appearance than for protection or
    modesty.
433–4 **fool . . . To** do not make me such a

fool as to
435 **women's weapons** Proverbial: 'Tears
    are women's weapons' (Dent T82.2).
    water-drops tears (*OED* 2, first instance of
    this sense of an expression first recorded
    at *Richard II* 4.1.252)
441.1 *Storm within* i.e. storm noises,
    probably produced by drum beats or
    the sound of cannon-balls rolled down a
    trough, are heard from behind the
    tiring-house wall. The storm is also
    within Lear himself: the external tempest
    figures that which rages in Lear's mind
    (11.12).

I have full cause of weeping, but this heart
Shall break into a hundred thousand flaws
Or ere I'll weep.—O fool, I shall go mad!
                    Exeunt Lear, Gloucester, Kent, ⌈Knight,⌉ and Fool

CORNWALL

Let us withdraw. 'Twill be a storm.   445

REGAN

This house is little. The old man and his people
Cannot be well bestowed.

GONORIL   'Tis his own blame;
Hath put himself from rest, and must needs taste his
        folly.

REGAN

For his particular I'll receive him gladly,
But not one follower.   450

CORNWALL

So am I purposed. Where is my lord of Gloucester?

REGAN

Followed the old man forth.
            Enter the Earl of Gloucester

                              He is returned.

GLOUCESTER

The King is in high rage, and will I know not whither.

REGAN

'Tis good to give him way. He leads himself.

GONORIL *(to Gloucester)*

My lord, entreat him by no means to stay.   455

---

443 into] F; in Q   flaws] F; flowes Q   444 mad!] Q (~.)   444.1 *Gloucester*] Q2 (*Glocester*);
Leister Q1   *Knight*] *not in* Q   447 blame;] HANMER; ~ˌ QF   451 purposed] Q (puspos'd)
452 *Enter . . . Gloucester*] Q (*'Enter', printed in right margin after l.* 451)

---

443 **into** Both Weis and HalioQ retain Q's
    unmetrical and unidiomatic 'in'.
    flaws fragments (*OED sb.*[1] 2, first in-
    stance of this sense)
444 **Or ere** before (Abbott 131)
444.1 **Kent** He has not been involved in the
    action since l. 288, when he was set free,
    but Q's explicit direction for him to exit
    here suggests that Shakespeare initially,
    at least, intended him to remain on stage
    until now. Foakes, noting that 'if he goes
    off into the storm with Lear it seems odd
    that he returns shortly . . . asking

"Where's the King?"' (8.2), suggests
that he might leave after being released,
at 7.294—as, indeed, Muir directs.
447 **bestowed** accommodated
    blame fault
448 **Hath . . . rest** he has set himself apart
    from rest (both physical and mental).
    Weis follows Q's 'blame hath', without
    comment.
    taste experience
449 **For . . . particular** so far as he himself is
    concerned
453 **will** will go

GLOUCESTER

Alack, the night comes on, and the bleak winds
Do sorely rustle. For many miles about
There's not a bush.

REGAN   O sir, to wilful men
The injuries that they themselves procure
Must be their schoolmasters. Shut up your doors.   460
He is attended with a desperate train,
And what they may incense him to, being apt
To have his ear abused, wisdom bids fear.

CORNWALL

Shut up your doors, my lord. 'Tis a wild night.
My Regan counsels well. Come out o'th' storm.
Exeunt

[handwritten: What's going to happen?]

Sc. 8   *Storm. Enter the Earl of Kent disguised, and First*
            Gentleman, at several doors

KENT

What's here, beside foul weather?

---

465 Regan.] Q (*Reg*)
  8.0.1 *Storm.*] F (*Storme still.*); *not in* Q   0.1 *the ... First*] Q (*Kent and a*)   0.1–2 *First Gen-*
tleman] OXFORD; *a Gentleman* Q

457 **rustle** Q prints 'russel'; F, 'ruffle'. Weis
adopts F in his Q-based text because 'Q's
text makes awkward sense only' and misreading would have been easy; but
Cooper's definition in his *Thesaurus*
(1565) of *Strepito* as 'to make noise often;
to make a great noise: to rustle' (cited
OED v. 1a) supports Q.
461 **with** by
  desperate reckless, violent
462 **being** i.e. he being
463 **wisdom . . . fear** prudence advises us to
take precautions against
465 The stocks would presumably have been
removed at the end of the scene.
  8 The action is imagined as taking place in
an open space traditionally referred to as
a heath, though the word does not occur
in the play. The sounds of the storm
called for in the opening direction (not in
Q) recur sporadically throughout this and
the following scene, and may have been
accompanied by visual effects, desirably

more impressive than those satirized in
the Induction to the play *A Warning for
Fair Women* (anon., 1599), where at the
appearance of a ghost 'a little rosin
flasheth forth, like smoke out of a tobacco
pipe, or a boy's squib' (ll. 59–60). The
interplay between the external and
the internal storm requires careful or-
chestration. Roger Warren writes
(privately) that in Peter Hall's 1997 Old
Vic production 'although the sound
effects were tremendous, they punctuated the speeches, so that the actors
never had to shout them down'. Kent
needs a purse from which he produces a
ring (37–40).
0.1–2 *First Gentleman* Associated with
Kent and Cordelia, he reappears in
Sc. 17, 20, and 21. He is not the same as
the messenger figure associated with
Regan and Gonoril who appears in Sc. 16
and 24, and is usually given to the actor
who plays the principal servant in Sc. 4.

FIRST GENTLEMAN   One minded like the weather,
  Most unquietly.

KENT   I know you. Where's the King?

FIRST GENTLEMAN

  Contending with the fretful element;
  Bids the wind blow the earth into the sea
  Or swell the curlèd waters 'bove the main,   5
  That things might change or cease; tears his white hair,
  Which the impetuous blasts, with eyeless rage,
  Catch in their fury and make nothing of;
  Strives in his little world of man to outscorn
  The to-and-fro-conflicting wind and rain.   10
  This night, wherein the cub-drawn bear would couch,
  The lion and the belly-pinchèd wolf
  Keep their fur dry, unbonneted he runs,
  And bids what will take all.

---

3 element] Q; Elements F   9 outscorn] Q (outscorne); *not in* F; outstorm MUIR (*conj.* Steevens)

---

3 **fretful** agitated, gusty. This predates *OED*'s first instance (3b) of this sense, from 1613.
  element Possibly a misprint for F's 'elements', but Shakespeare uses the singular with a similar sense at e.g. *Henry V* 4.1.102–3: 'the element shows to him as it doth to me'.

4–5 **wind . . . main** A Renaissance commonplace which Shakespeare often uses, possibly influenced by Psalm 46: 2–3: 'Though the earth be moved, and though the hills be carried into the midst of the sea; though the waters thereof rage and swell'.

5 **swell** cause to rise (*OED v.* 2b, first instance of this sense)
  main could mean 'sea'—i.e. the waves swell above the level of the ocean—but more probably 'mainland'; the confusion of the elements is a characteristic Shakespearian theme, as at *Othello* 2.1.3–17, *Winter's Tale* 3.3.82–92, *Tempest* 1.2.3–5.

6 **things** the world
  cease i.e. fall into chaos, in which the elements are indistinguishable from one another

7 **impetuous** moving violently (related to 'impetus')
  eyeless blind, undiscriminating

8 **Catch** 'seize on' (*OED v.* 13, obsolete) seems the most appropriate sense.

8 **make . . . of** treat contemptuously (*OED, make, v.*[1] 21a)

9 **little world of man** The common concept of man as a microcosm, a figure of the world.
  outscorn Misreading of 'outstorm' (Muir, followed by Oxford) is entirely plausible, but 'out-scorn', listed by *OED* (*out-*, 18c), though with no other example, and meaning 'overcome or defeat by scorn', may well be what Shakespeare wrote.

10 **to-and-fro-conflicting** *OED* first records *conflicting* in a passage of *Timon* that has several points of contact with *Lear*: 'Call the creatures | Whose naked natures live in all the spite | Of wreakful heaven, whose bare unhousèd trunks | To the conflicting elements exposed | Answer mere nature; bid them flatter thee' (4.3.228–32.)

11 **cub-drawn** Either 'led by its cubs', or 'drawn, sucked dry' by them, and so ravenous, or possibly 'robbed of its whelps' (Milward, p. 174), and so fierce.
  couch take shelter (in spite of hunger?)

13 **unbonneted** with uncovered head (first recorded in *Othello* 1.2.23); a stage in Lear's progress to nakedness

14 **bids . . . all** says that whoever wishes to do so may take everything—the cry of the gambler, 'Winner takes all.'

KENT   But who is with him?

FIRST GENTLEMAN

None but the fool, who labours to outjest   15
His heart-struck injuries.

KENT   Sir, I do know you,
And dare upon the warrant of my art
Commend a dear thing to you. There is division,
Although as yet the face of it be covered
With mutual cunning, 'twixt Albany and Cornwall;   20
But true it is. From France there comes a power
Into this scattered kingdom, who already,
Wise in our negligence, have secret feet
In some of our best ports, and are at point *war?*
To show their open banner. Now to you: 25
If on my credit you dare build so far
To make your speed to Dover, you shall find
Some that will thank you, making just report
Of how unnatural and bemadding sorrow *going mad?*
The King hath cause to plain.   30
I am a gentleman of blood and breeding,
And from some knowledge and assurance offer
This office to you.

FIRST GENTLEMAN   I will talk farther with you.

KENT No, do not.   35
For confirmation that I am much more

20–1 Cornwall; | But true it is.] BLAYNEY; $\sim_{\wedge}$ | $\sim\sim\sim\sim$, Q1; $\sim.$ | $\sim\sim\sim\sim$, Q2   36 am] F; *not in* Q

15 **outjest** drive out, console, with jokes
16 **heart-struck** struck to the heart (*OED*'s first instance of the compound)
17 **art** skill (in judging character)
18 **Commend . . . thing** entrust an important matter
    division discord. This relates back to the division of the kingdoms, 1.3–4.
21 **France** Either the country or its king.
    power army
22 **scattered** disunited
23 **Wise . . . negligence** clever enough to take advantage of our carelessness
24–5 **at . . . banner** ready, about to reveal their flags of war
26 **on . . . far** you dare trust me so far as
27 **speed** speedy way

27 **Dover** An ancient port on the south coast of England, in Kent, regarded 'in older times' as 'the key to England' (Sugden), and famous for its white cliffs. This is the first of eleven references; the town's function in the play is discussed in the Introduction, pp. 33–4.
28 **making** i.e. when you make
29 **bemadding** driving mad. *OED*'s first use of the verb.
30 **plain** complain
31 **gentleman . . . breeding** man of high birth and education (*gentleman* itself implies, properly, one entitled to bear arms)
32 **assurance** trustworthy information (Muir)
33 **office** task

Than my out-wall, open this purse, and take
What it contains. If you shall see Cordelia—
As fear not but you shall—show her this ring
And she will tell you who your fellow is,   40
That yet you do not know. Fie on this storm!
I will go seek the King.

FIRST GENTLEMAN   Give me your hand.
Have you no more to say?

KENT   Few words, but to effect
More than all yet: that when we have found the King—
In which endeavour I'll this way, you that—   45
He that first lights on him holla the other.

                                        Exeunt severally

Sc. 9   *Storm. Enter King Lear and his Fool*

LEAR

Blow, wind, and crack your cheeks! Rage, blow,
You cataracts and hurricanoes, spout
Till you have drenched the steeples, drowned the cocks!

---

45 In which endeavour I'll this way, you that—] OXFORD; Ile this way, you that; Q; in which
your pain | That way, you that] F; for whom I'll seek | This way, you that BLAYNEY *conj.*
46–9.0.1 on . . . *Enter*] Q ('On him, hollow the other. *Exeunt.* | *Enter*'; Q *also prints 'Enter' as
a catchword after* 'lights')

9.0.1 *Storm.*] F (*Storme still.*);   *not in* Q   *Enter . . . Fool*] Q (*Enter Lear and Foole.*)
2 cataracts] F (caterackes); caterickes Q   hurricanoes] F (Hyrricano's); Hircanios Q

---

37 **out-wall** appearance (*OED* b, first instance of the figurative use, defining as
   'clothing')
39 **ring** He gives the Gentleman a ring.
40 **fellow** companion
43 **to effect** in importance (Onions)
45 **In . . . that** The first three words are our
   conjectural addition to Q. In *TC* we remark: 'Q can only be defended by interpreting "Ile this way, you that" as
   parenthetically (and unmetrically) interrupting Kent's sentence; F suggests that
   Shakespeare would have found such an
   interpretation as impossibly strained as
   we do. F also suggests the gist of what Q
   appears to omit . . . but can hardly represent what stood in Q's copy.' Both
   HalioQ and Weis accept Q, while admitting the metrical difficulty.
46 **lights on** alights upon, finds
 9 The action is virtually continuous. Lear is
   bare-headed, at least by l. 61.

1–3 **Blow . . . cocks!** 'Invoking the round-
   cheeked wind gods and the water spouts
   banished to the edges of the great Renaissance world maps, Lear calls on them to
   reclaim the center of that ordered world
   and return it to chaos' (Mikalachki,
   p. 89). The lines are usually spoken
   defiantly, but Donald Sinden used a stage
   whisper, describing them in the interview
   noted at 1.124–5 as 'an invocation that a
   storm *should* happen, rather than a comment on one that is already happening.'
   (p. 85). Sinden also notes the natural sequence *wind, rain, lightning, thunder*.
 2 **cataracts and hurricanoes** *cataracts* was
   'applied to water-spouts' (*OED sb.* 1b, citing this passage), 'produced by the action
   of a whirlwind on a portion of the sea and
   the clouds immediately above it' (*OED*,
   water-spout, 3); *OED* first records 'hurricano', an 'early form of hurricane', here
   and in *Troilus*, 'the dreadful spout |

You sulphurous and thought-executing fires,
Vaunt-couriers to oak-cleaving thunderbolts,   5
Singe my white head; and thou all-shaking thunder,
Smite flat the thick rotundity of the world,
Crack nature's mould, all germens spill at once
That make ingrateful man.

FOOL O nuncle, court holy water in a dry house is better   10
than this rain-water out o' door. Good nuncle, in, and
ask thy daughters blessing. Here's a night pities neither
wise man nor fool.

LEAR

Rumble thy bellyful; spit, fire; spout, rain.
Nor rain, wind, thunder, fire are my daughters.   15
I task not you, you elements, with unkindness.
I never gave you kingdom, called you children.
You owe me no subscription. Why then, let fall
Your horrible pleasure. Here I stand your slave,
A poor, infirm, weak and despised old man,   20
But yet I call you servile ministers,
That have with two pernicious daughters joined

8 germens] QF (Germains)   16 task] Q (taske);   taxe F

Which shipmen do the hurricano call'
(5.2.174–5).
3 **cocks** weathercocks (at the top of the
steeples—both anachronistic in a play
about ancient Britain)

4 **thought-executing** Either 'doing execution as swiftly as thought' or 'fatal to
thought'.
5 **Vaunt-couriers** advance guards,
forerunners
6 **thou . . . thunder** Virtually another
apostrophe to Jupiter the *thunder-bearer*
(7.384), directly invoked at 1.167 and
7.200.
7 **Smite** Often used of affliction by God
(*OED*, *smite*, *v*. 4).
 thick rotundity solid roundedness; *thick*
here appears to be used in the sense
'solid, not hollow' (*OED a*. 1d), recorded
only in the early part of the fifteenth
century.
8 **nature's mould** the mould in which nature makes men—here tantamount to
'womb'
 germens seeds. *OED*'s first use of the

Latin-derived word, which antedates
'germ'; Lear seems oddly close to the
modern biological use of 'germ' for 'the
female reproductive element, in opposition to *sperm-*' (*OED*, *germ*, *sb*. 1) as if he
were thinking of the world as a vast
woman from whom all the means of conception could be squeezed out.
8 **spill** could mean 'spoil', which 'has taken
the place of the earlier *spill* (*OED v*. 1) in
the sense 'destroy, ruin' (11a).
10 **court holy water** holy water sprinkled as
a matter of form at court, hence empty
promises, flattery; a proverbial phrase
(Dent H532).
16 **task . . . with** call to account for. Editors,
following F, often read 'tax', but *task* is
still current in this sense. Q reads 'taske';
the forms were interchangeable.
18 **subscription** assent, support; submission,
allegiance (*OED* 6b, citing this as its only
instance)
21 **servile** slavish, meanly submissive (*OED
a*. 3, citing this as its first instance)
 ministers agents (of the gods)
22 **pernicious** wicked, villainous

Your high engendered battle 'gainst a head
So old and white as this. O, 'tis foul!

FOOL He that has a house to put his head in has a good   25
headpiece.

    [*Sings*]   The codpiece that will house
                Before the head has any,
         The head and he shall louse,
             So beggars marry many.   30

         The man that makes his toe
             What he his heart should make
         Shall have a corn cry woe,
             And turn his sleep to wake—

for there was never yet fair woman but she made mouths   35
in a glass.

LEAR

No, I will be the pattern of all patience.
    [*He sits.*] *Enter the Earl of Kent disguised*
I will say nothing.

KENT Who's there?

24 foul!] Q (~.)   27 *Sings*] *not in* Q   35 but] Qb; hut Qa   37.1 *He sits*] OXFORD; *not in* QF
Enter . . . disguised] Q (*Enter Kent.*)

23 **high engendered** originated on high, in
the heavens
   battle Often glossed 'army' or 'battalion',
but 'to join battle' was already a common
expression (*OED*, *join*, *v*.[1] 18a).
25 **house . . . in** A commonplace expression
(Dent H784.1).
27 **codpiece** the protective, often showy
covering of the genitals in breeches; here
implying the penis, as in *Measure*
3.1.378–9, 'for the rebellion of a codpiece to take away the life of a man'—
and, more generally, irrationality.
   house find a home
28 **any** i.e. any housing
29 **louse** be infested with lice (*OED*'s only instance: *louse*, *v*. 2)
30 **So . . . many** so it is that poor men take up
with many women. HalioF suggests that
'"many" may also refer to lice; or the
word order may be inverted for the sake of
rhyme: "many beggars marry after this
fashion" (NS)'.

31–2 **makes . . . make** i.e. displays an inverted sense of values; in *Coriolanus*
Menenius insults 'one o'th' lowest,
basest, poorest | Of this most wise rebel-
lion' by calling him 'the great toe of this
assembly' (1.1.153–6). 'Toe' may be 'a
symbol of the phallus, paralleling "codpiece"' (HalioF, citing Danby), in which
case *corn* might allude to venereal disease, but neither sense is recorded by
Williams (*Glossary* and *Dictionary*). The
expression 'I will not set at my heart what
I should set at my heel' was proverbial
(Dent H317).
35–6 **made . . . glass** practised her expressions in a mirror (whether out of vanity
or hypocrisy)
37.1 *He sits* The action, called for by l. 42, is
not marked in QF, but seems suitably
placed here; sitting is an appropriate pos-
ture for an exemplary figure of patience,
as Viola remarks (*Twelfth Night* 2.4.114).
Lear probably rises at l. 49.

FOOL Marry, here's grace and a codpiece—that's a wise   40
man and a fool.

KENT (*to Lear*)

Alas, sir, sit you here? Things that love night
Love not such nights as these. The wrathful skies
Gallow the very wanderers of the dark
And makes them keep their caves. Since I was man   45
Such sheets of fire, such bursts of horrid thunder,
Such groans of roaring wind and rain I ne'er
Remember to have heard. Man's nature cannot carry
The affliction nor the force.

LEAR   Let the great gods,
That keep this dreadful pother o'er our heads,   50
Find out their enemies now. Tremble, thou wretch
That hast within thee undivulgèd crimes
Unwhipped of justice; hide thee, thou bloody hand,
Thou perjured and thou simular man of virtue
That art incestuous; caitiff, in pieces shake,   55
That under covert and convenient seeming
Hast practised on man's life;
Close pent-up guilts, rive your concealèd centres
And cry these dreadful summoners grace.
I am a man more sinned against than sinning.   60

---

44 wanderers] F; wanderer Q   54 simular man] Q; Simular F   58 concealèd centres] Q;
concealing Continents F   60 than] F; their Q

40 **grace . . . codpiece** On the surface, Lear is *grace* and the Fool the *codpiece* as in l. 27; but ambiguity remains.

44 **Gallow** gally, terrify; *OED*'s first instance (under 'gally', to which it should perhaps be modernized; but the spelling may reflect assimilation to 'gallow'—modern 'gallows'—with its frightening associations).
wanderers In view of *caves* presumably refers to animals, not men.

45 **keep** remain in

46 **fire** lightning
horrid causing horror (stronger than in modern usage)

48 **carry** endure

49 **force** 'violence or "stress" of weather' (*OED sb.*[1] 2d, first recorded 1614).

50 **pother** tumult (not, as now, facetious)

52 **undivulgèd** *OED*'s first use of a word not later recorded until 1854.

53 **Unwhipped** *OED*'s first use.
of by

54 **simular . . . of** i.e. man who simulates, counterfeits

55 **caitiff** villain

56 **seeming** hypocrisy

57 **practised on** plotted against

58 **Close pent-up** narrowly confined, deeply buried
rive . . . centres split open your hidden cores, rend asunder the coverings of the containers (F's 'continents') where you cower concealed; *concealed* is stressed on the first syllable (Cercignani, p. 35).

59 **cry . . . grace** beg for mercy from
summoners officials who summoned offenders before the ecclesiastical courts

KENT Alack, bare-headed?
  Gracious my lord, hard by here is a hovel.
  Some friendship will it lend you 'gainst the tempest.
  Repose you there whilst I to this hard house—
  More hard than is the stone whereof 'tis raised,   65
  Which even but now, demanding after you,
  Denied me to come in—return and force
  Their scanted courtesy.
LEAR   My wit begins to turn.
  (*To Fool*) Come on, my boy. How dost, my boy? Art
     cold?
  I am cold myself.—Where is this straw, my fellow?   70
  The art of our necessities is strange,
  That can make vile things precious. Come, your hovel.—
  Poor fool and knave, I have one part of my heart
  That sorrows yet for thee.
FOOL [*sings*]
     He that has a little tiny wit,   75
       With heigh-ho, the wind and the rain,
     Must make content with his fortunes fit,
       For the rain it raineth every day.

LEAR
  True, my good boy. (*To Kent*) Come, bring us to this
     hovel.   *Exeunt*

---

61 bare-headed?] Q (~,)   66 you] F; me Q   72 your] F; you Q   hovel.— Poor͜] Q
(~͜ ~,), F   75 tiny] Q (tine)   79 hovel.] Q2; ~? Q1   *Exeunt*] *not in* Q

66 **demanding after** (as I was) urgently en-
quiring about
67 **Denied me** refused to let me. Properly,
the subject of the verb is the stone of
which the house is made, but (unless
there has been an accidental omission)
this is made to stand for the house's
inhabitants.
68 **scanted** limited, withheld
71 **art . . . necessities** skill resulting from our
needs (*art*, which could also mean
'magic' (Schmidt), may here suggest
alchemy)
73 **fool . . . knave** The expression 'to be both
fool and knave' was commonplace (Dent
F506.1).
75–8 These lines are a version of the first

stanza of the song sung by Feste, the
jester, at the end of *Twelfth Night*, 'and it
is likely that both were sung to the same
tune' (Sternfeld, p. 171; he reproduces
the music, first found in the eighteenth
century, on pp. 188–92). Possibly they
are based on a popular song. There are
verbal resemblances to Robert Armin's
Quips upon Questions, of 1600, and it has
been conjectured that Armin played both
Feste and the Fool.
77 **make . . . fit** 'Either (1) must make
his happiness fit his fortunes (Kittredge),
or (2) must be content with the fortunes
suitable to such a person' (HalioF);
'fit' as the fitting of garments is a later
use.

Sc. 10 *Enter the Earl of Gloucester and Edmund the bastard,*
    with lights

GLOUCESTER   *naïveltrusting of Edmund*

   Alack, alack, Edmund, I like not this
   Unnatural dealing. When I desired their leave
   That I might pity him, they took from me
   The use of mine own house, charged me on pain
   Of their displeasure neither to speak of him,   5
   Entreat for him, nor any way sustain him.

EDMUND   Most savage and unnatural!   *→ danger's audience*

GLOUCESTER   Go to, say you nothing. There's a division betwixt the Dukes, and a worse matter than that. I have received a letter this night—'tis dangerous to be spoken—I   10
   have locked the letter in my closet. These injuries the
   King now bears will be revenged home. There's part of a
   power already landed. We must incline to the King. I will
   seek him and privily relieve him. Go you and maintain
   talk with the Duke, that my charity be not of him per-   15
   ceived. If he ask for me, I am ill and gone to bed. Though
   I die for't—as no less is threatened me—the King my old
   master must be relieved. There is some strange thing
   toward. Edmund, pray you be careful.   *Exit*

EDMUND
   This courtesy, forbid thee, shall the Duke   20
   Instantly know, and of that letter too.
   This seems a fair deserving, and must draw me   *→ how will he fall?*
   That which my father loses: no less than all.
   The younger rises when the old do fall.   *Foreshadow*   *Exit*
                         daughters taking over

10.0.1 *the Earl . . . Edmund*] Q (*Gloster and*)   3 took] Q2, F; tooke me Q1   7 unnatural!]
Q (~.)   24 The] F; then Q

10.0.2 **with lights** i.e. carrying torches,
   which would indicate a night scene. The
   action appears to be imagined as taking
   place outside Gloucester's dwelling.
3 **pity** take pity on, help
6 **sustain** succour
9 **worse matter** Perhaps the French
   invasion.
11 **closet** private room, or cabinet
12 **home** to the full
13 **power** army

13 **incline to** favour, takes sides with
14 **privily** secretly
19 **toward** about to happen
22 **deserving** merit (which will win Edmund
   a reward)
   draw me draw to me, reward me with
24 **The . . . fall** A variant of the proverbial
   'The rising of one man is the falling of another' (Dent R136).
   The Weis, but not HalioQ, retains Q's
   'then', without comment.

Sc. 11 *Storm. Enter King Lear, The Earl of Kent disguised,
and Lear's Fool*

KENT

Here is the place, my lord. Good my lord, enter.
The tyranny of the open night's too rough
For nature to endure.

LEAR   Let me alone.

KENT

Good my lord, enter.

LEAR   Wilt break my heart?

KENT

I had rather break mine own. Good my lord, enter.   5

LEAR

Thou think'st 'tis much that this contentious storm
Invades us to the skin. So 'tis to thee;
But where the greater malady is fixed,
The lesser is scarce felt. Thou'dst shun a bear,
But if thy flight lay toward the roaring sea   10
Thou'dst meet the bear i'th' mouth. When the mind's
    free,
The body's delicate. This tempest in my mind
Doth from my senses take all feeling else
Save what beats there: filial ingratitude.
Is it not as this mouth should tear this hand   15
For lifting food to't? But I will punish sure.

11.0.1 *Storm.*] CAPELL; *not in* Q; *Storme still* F (*after 'endure'*, l. 3)   0.1–2 *King . . . Lear's*]
Q (*Lear, Kent, and*)   2 The] Qb (the); the | the Qa. *Qa sets this speech as prose.*   4 enter] Q;
enter heere F   6 contentious] F; crulentious Qa; tempestious Qb   10 roaring] Qb, F; raging
Qa, Q2   12 This] Qb; the Qa, Q2, F   14 beats] Qb, F; beares Qa, Q2   there] Q (their)

---

11 The action continues from the end of
Scene 9, suggesting proximity to
Gloucester's dwelling. Gloucester needs
a torch (l. 102). This scene may use a
trap door (see note to l. 22).

1 **place** the hovel (9.62); on Shakespeare's
stage, presumably the central opening
(which may have been curtained); possibly the door other than that through
which the characters entered, or just possibly the trap.

2 **open night** night in the open air

3 HalioQ reasonably adds the direction
'Storm still' from F.

4 **enter.** Oxford and HalioQ, but not Ridley
and Weis, accept F's 'enter heere', but a
missing syllable at the caesura is acceptable (Abbott 508).

6 **contentious** argumentative; *OED*'s first
use of the transferred sense. This is more
likely as the source of Qa's 'crulentious'
than Qb's 'tempestious', a recorded
spelling of 'tempestuous'.

8 **fixed** established

11 **free** unpreoccupied, untroubled

12 **delicate** sensitive (to suffering)

15 **tear** rend

16 **sure** thoroughly

No, I will weep no more.—
In such a night as this! O Regan, Gonoril, *generous*
Your old kind father, whose frank heart gave you all—
O, that way madness lies. Let me shun that.   20
No more of that.

KENT   Good my lord, enter.

LEAR

Prithee, go in thyself. Seek thy own ease.
This tempest will not give me leave to ponder
On things would hurt me more; but I'll go in.

                                    [*Exit Fool*]

Poor naked wretches, wheresoe'er you are,   25
That bide the pelting of this pitiless night,
How shall your houseless heads and unfed sides,
Your looped and windowed raggedness, defend you
From seasons such as these? O, I have ta'en
Too little care of this. Take physic, pomp,   30
Expose thyself to feel what wretches feel,
That thou mayst shake the superflux to them
And show the heavens more just.

    Enter Lear's Fool

---

18 In such a night as this!] Q; in such a night, | To shut me out? Poure on, I will endure: | In
such a night as this? F   22 own] Q1 (one), Q2   24.1 *Exit Fool*] BLAYNEY; *not in* Q
33.1 *Enter . . . Fool*] *not in* Q

18 **this!** This makes sense on its own, but the
    additional words printed in F (recorded in
    the collation) could have been omitted as
    the result of eyeslip.
19 **frank** generous
22 **go in thyself** Presumably addressed to
    Kent as he is the previous speaker; but the
    action is not clear. After l. 24, F adds 'In
    Boy, go first. You houselesse pouertie, |
    Nay get thee in; Ile pray, and then Ile
    sleepe.' These lines (perhaps accidentally
    dropped from Q) make sense of Lear's *I'll
    go in* as a deferred intention. Q as it stands
    provides neither direction nor motivation
    for the Fool's exit, though he has to be *in*
    at l. 34. Nor do they (or F) instruct Kent
    to obey Lear's instruction to leave. It
    seems desirable for Kent at least to stand
    unobtrusively aside while Lear speaks his
    prayer, and for the Fool to enter either at
    l. 24 (as marked here) or later into a stage
    door representing the hovel from which

he re-emerges at l. 33. Alternatively,
the hovel might be represented by a
trapdoor (as for example in Adrian
Noble's 1983 Stratford production),
which, as well as providing a point of
entry for Edgar, would help to explain
why Kent says *Give me thy hand* (l. 36)—
though this could be simply an offer of
consolation.
25 **naked** could mean generally 'unpro-
    tected' as well as 'unclothed'.
26 **pelting** *OED*'s first instance of the (rare)
    verbal noun.
28 **looped** full of holes (Schmidt); *OED*'s only
    instance.
    windowed also means 'full of holes'
    (*OED*'s first use of this sense; later uses
    imitate this).
30 **physic** medicine, specifically a purgative
    (Rosenberg, p. 204)
32 **superflux** excess, superabundance.
    OED's first use.

FOOL Come not in here, nuncle; here's a spirit. Help me,
help me!   35

KENT Give me thy hand. Who's there?

FOOL A spirit. He says his name's Poor Tom.

KENT

What art thou that dost grumble there in the straw?
Come forth.

[Enter Edgar as a Bedlam beggar]

EDGAR Away, the foul fiend follows me. Through the sharp   40
hawthorn blows the cold wind. Go to thy cold bed and
warm thee.

LEAR

Hast thou given all to thy two daughters,
And art thou come to this?

EDGAR Who gives anything to Poor Tom, whom the foul   45
fiend hath led through fire and through ford and whirlypool, o'er bog and quagmire; that has laid knives under
his pillow and halters in his pew, set ratsbane by his
potage, made him proud of heart to ride on a bay trotting-horse over four-inched bridges, to course his own   50

34 here's] Q (her's)   37 spirit] Q; spirite, a spirite F   says₍ₐ₎] Q (~,)   39.1 *Enter . . . beggar*]
THEOBALD; *not in* Q

38 **grumble** mutter, mumble (first recorded
in *Shrew*, 4.1.153)

39.1 **as . . . beggar** Edgar is often presented
as virtually, sometimes (in modern performance) entirely, naked; according to
l. 58 he wears a blanket round his loins.

40–1 **Through . . . wind** Possibly a snatch of
an old ballad; Percy incorporated it into
his 'The Friar of Orders Gray' (*Reliques*,
i. 242–6).

41–2 **Go . . . thee** These words, which also
occur in *Shrew*, Ind. 1.7–8, may have
been proverbial (B 186.1). Edgar is simu-
lating madness by plucking associatively
related quotations from his memory.

46–7 **led . . . quagmire** Tom's words resemble Robin Goodfellow's in *Dream*,
3.1.101–2: 'I'll lead you about a round,
| Through bog, through bush, through
brake, through brier.'

  whirlypool A variant of 'whirlpool'.

47–9 **laid . . . potage** The Devil traditionally
offered means of suicide to those guilty of
the sin of despair.

48 **halters** nooses

  in . . . pew The phrase may imply 'even in

church' (Foakes), but *pew* could mean
any sort of raised seat.

49 **potage** soup

  proud . . . to i.e. so over-confident as
to [?]

49–50 **bay trotting-horse** brown (*bay*) horse
used mainly or entirely for trotting, and
for show: 'A great personage entering
a town in state would exchange his
ambling nag for a trotting horse' (D. H.
Madden, *The Diary of Master William
Silence: A Study of Shakespeare and
Elizabethan Sport* (1897), p. 271). Presumably Edgar as Tom is having illusions
of greatness.

50 **four-inched** four-inches-wide; *OED*'s first
instance of *inched* in this sense. It is difficult to see any logic in this unless Edgar
sees himself as performing an amazing
feat while mounted on a horse. The most
famous performing horse, Morocco,
owned by a showman called Banks, was
a bay gelding, alleged, among more plausible accomplishments, to have climbed
St Paul's steeple.

  course chase, hunt

shadow for a traitor. Bless thy five wits, Tom's a-cold!
Bless thee from whirlwinds, star-blasting, and taking.
Do Poor Tom some charity, whom the foul fiend vexes.
There could I have him, now, and there, and there, and
there again.   55

LEAR

What, has his daughters brought him to this pass?
(*To Edgar*) Couldst thou save nothing? Didst thou give
        them all?

FOOL Nay, he reserved a blanket, else we had been all
shamed.

LEAR (*to Edgar*)

Now all the plagues that in the pendulous air   60
Hang fated o'er men's faults fall on thy daughters!

KENT He hath no daughters, sir.

LEAR

Death, traitor! Nothing could have subdued nature

---

52 star-blasting] F; starre-blasting Q   54–5 and there, and there, and there] HALIOQ; and
there, and there Q2; and there, and | and Q1   56 What, has his] OXFORD; What, his Q; Ha's
F1; Has his F2   61 daughters!] Q (~.)

51 **for** in the belief that it was
   Bless . . . wits The expression, used as a
   jocular blessing in Fletcher's play
   The Wild Goose Chase (in *The Dramatic
   Works in the Beaumont and Fletcher Canon*,
   ed. F. Bowers, vol. 6 (1985), 5.6.96,
   cited Dent W575.1), is related to the
   beggar's cry preserved in Orlando
   Gibbons's *Cries of London*: 'Poor naked
   Bedlam, Tom's a-cold, | A small piece of
   cut of thy bacon | Or a piece of the sow's
   side, good Bess' | God almighty bless thy
   wits'; cited by C. Garton (*TLS* 15 Dec.
   1961, p. 904), who calls Edgar's words
   'a conditional benison'. Edgar uses the
   words *Bless thy five wits* again at 13.52,
   and offers a blessing associated with
   begging at 15.38. *Tom's a-cold* recurs at
   ll. 74, 132 and 157, and 15.50.
   five wits Could mean both the bodily
   senses (hearing, smelling, taste, feeling,
   sight) and the five parallel faculties of the
   mind, defined in Stephen Hawes's
   Pastime of Pleasure (*c*.1506; ed. W. E.
   Mead (1928), pp. 33–5) as common wit,
   imagination, fantasy, estimation, and
   memory; but in Sonnet 141 Shakespeare
   distinguishes between them: 'But my five
   wits nor my five senses can | Dissuade

one foolish heart from serving thee'
(ll. 9–10).
52 **Bless** save
   star-blasting 'the pernicious influence of
   malign stars' (*OED, star, sb.*[1] 20)
   taking disease caused by star-blasting
54–5 **There . . . again** 'Edgar makes grabs at
   different parts of his body as if to catch
   vermin—or devils' (Kittredge)—or perhaps strikes around him. Oxford follows
   Q2, but Halio's emendation, supposing
   accidental omission before Q's repeated
   'and', seems preferable.
55 HalioQ adds the direction '*Storm still*'
   from F.
56 **What, has** Q reads 'What, his', retained
   by Ridley and Weis; HalioQ follows
   Oxford. Q is possible though unmetrical.
   pass predicament
58 **reserved** held back
   blanket In *The Bellman of London* (1608),
   Thomas Dekker writes 'shall we not walk
   up and down in the world like beggars,
   with old blankets pinned about us?'
   (sig. C2ᵛ).
60 **pendulous** overhanging; first recorded
   use
63 **subdued** reduced (accent on the first
   syllable)

To such a lowness but his unkind daughters.
(*To Edgar*) Is it the fashion that discarded fathers   65
Should have thus little mercy on their flesh?
Judicious punishment: 'twas this flesh begot
Those pelican daughters.
EDGAR ⌊Pillicock sat on pillicock's hill; a lo, lo, lo.⌋ What?
FOOL This cold night will turn us all to fools and madmen.   70
EDGAR Take heed o'th' foul fiend; obey thy parents; keep
    thy word justly; swear not; commit not with man's
    sworn spouse: set not thy sweet heart on proud array.
    Tom's a-cold.
LEAR What hast thou been?   75
EDGAR A servingman, proud in heart and mind, that
    curled my hair, wore gloves in my cap, served the lust of
    my mistress' heart, and did the act of darkness with her;
    swore as many oaths as I spake words, and broke them in
    the sweet face of heaven; one that slept in the contriving   80
    of lust, and waked to do it. Wine loved I deeply, dice

72 word] POPE; words Q

64 **unkind** unnatural
68 **pelican** The ancient fable that young
   pelicans feed on their parents' blood was
   a common theme in art and literature
   which came to be applied to Christ's re-
   demption of mankind by his blood (*OED*,
   pelican, *sb.* 1c). In *Leir*, Leir compares him-
   self to 'the pelican, | That kills itself to
   save her young ones' lives' (ll. 512–13).
69 **Pillicock . . . hill** A nursery rhyme, 'Pil-
   licock, pillicock sat on a hill, | If he's not
   gone—he sits there still' is known in a
   version of 1810 but clearly lies behind this
   line (Opie, p. 432). *Pillicock*, which Edgar
   associatively picks up from 'pelican', is
   related to 'pillock' and was slang for the
   penis; it was also used as 'a flattering
   word for a young boy'; *pillicock's hill* is
   presumably the female genitals. Around
   1639–40, one Henry Pillchorne 'did shew
   his privie members' to an audience of men
   and women, and declare he 'did daunce
   Piddecocke bolt vpright, and readie to
   fight' (*Somerset*, ed. J. Stokes and Robert
   Alexander, Records of Early English
   Drama, 2 vols. (Toronto, 1996), i. 60).
   a lo . . . lo An exclamation of uncertain
   meaning.
71–3 **obey . . . array** Imitating some of the
   Ten Commandments: to honour one's

parents; not to bear false witness; not to
take the name of the Lord in vain; not to
commit adultery; and to avoid covetous-
ness. Shaheen, p. 611, cites other biblical
parallels.
72 **word** Ridley, Weis and HalioQ retain Q's
   'words', but this is unidiomatic; Foakes
   accepts Pope's emendation, arguing for
   'misreading of a tail on MS "d"'.
   commit commit adultery (*OED*, 6c)
73 **sweet heart** or 'sweetheart' (hyphenated
   in F)
   proud array flashy clothes
76 **servingman** Perhaps, in this context,
   takes on the meaning of 'lover', 'para-
   mour' (*OED*, *servant*, *n.* 4b).
76–88 **proud . . . book** The traditional notion
   of the Seven Deadly Sins (Pride, Envy,
   Sloth, Intemperance, Avarice, Wrath,
   and Lust) pervades this passage.
77 **curled . . . hair** A symbol of pride in
   Harsnet (p. 410).
   wore . . . cap (like a mistress's favours)
   lust sexual desire (and, more generally,
   'pleasure')
78 **act . . . darkness** fornication (Dent
   D184.1). A similar phrase occurs in
   Pericles, Sc. 19.37: 'If she'd do the deed
   of darkness . . .'.
80 **slept in** i.e. dreamt of

dearly, and in woman out-paramoured the Turk. False
of heart, light of ear, bloody of hand; hog in sloth, fox in
stealth, wolf in greediness, dog in madness, lion in prey.
Let not the creaking of shoes nor the rustlings of silks be-   85
tray thy poor heart to women. Keep thy foot out of
brothel, thy hand out of placket, thy pen from lender's
book, and defy the foul fiend. Still through the hawthorn
blows the cold wind. Heigh no nonny. Dolphin, my boy,
my boy! Cease, let him trot by.   90

LEAR Why, thou wert better in thy grave than to answer
with thy uncovered body this extremity of the skies. Is   *denies*
man no more but this? Consider him well. Thou owest   *Ritual*
the worm no silk, the beast no hide, the sheep no wool,   *and pretense*
the cat no perfume. Here's three on 's are sophisticated;   95
thou art the thing itself. Unaccommodated man is no
more but such a poor, bare, forked animal as thou art.
Off, off, you lendings! Come on, be true.

89 no nonny] F; no on ny Q   90 boy!] Q (~,)   Cease,] Q2; caese⌃ Q1; *Sesey:* F   93 more⌃
. . . Consider] Q2; ~,~~⌃ ~, Q1   95 Here's] Q (her's)   98 lendings] Qb; leadings Qa   on,
be true.] Qa; on⌃ Qb; vn-button heere. F

82 **out-paramoured** had more lovers than
   the Turk the Turkish Sultan, or Great
   Turk, with his many concubines
83 **light of ear** 'credulous of evil, ready to receive malicious reports' (Johnson)
83–4 **hog . . . prey** This figuring forth of some
   of the Deadly Sins (Sloth, Stealth (i.e.
   stealing as well as slyness), Greed,
   perhaps Wrath (*OED*, *madness*, 3, records
   the sense of 'ungovernable rage', but not
   until 1665)) in animal form may be
   indebted to Harsnet, pp. 312, 411,
   though there the only close parallel is
   with gluttony, in the form of a wolf.
85 **creaking . . . silks** Apparently regarded as
   seductive.
87 **placket** An apron or petticoat, or 'the
   opening or slit at the top of a skirt or petticoat, for convenience in putting on or off'
   (*OED*, *placket²*, 3, citing this as its first,
   'doubtful', instance).
   lender's money-lender's
89 **Heigh no nonny** A song refrain, as at
   Much Ado 2.3.68.
   Dolphin A normal English spelling of
   Dauphin, possibly the name of a horse
   ('trot'). Muir suggests that 'as Jonson,
   Bartholomew Fair, V. iv . . . uses the
   phrase 'Hee shall be *Dauphin* my boy' it is
   clear that Edgar was quoting from some

song or ballad, unless Jonson was echo-
ing Edgar'.
90 HalioQ adds the direction '*Storm still*'
   from F.
91 **answer** outface
92 **extremity** violent outburst (*OED* 4)
93–5 **Thou . . . perfume** The idea that man
   borrows from the beasts was proverbial
   (Dent M218.1, citing several close
   parallels).
93 **Thou** Edgar
94 **worm** i.e. silkworm
95 **cat . . . perfume** A perfume is made from
   the secretion of the anal gland of the civet
   cat.
   sophisticated altered, not simply 'the
   thing itself'
96 **Unaccommodated** unprovided (with
   clothes; *OED*'s first instance)
97 **forked** i.e. two-legged, as at *2 Henry IV*
   3.2.305–6: 'When a was naked, he was
   for all the world like a forked radish'. The
   same scene includes an extended pa sage
   of wordplay on 'accommodated' (65–79).
98 **Off. . . lendings** Lear starts to strip down to
   nothing, *the thing itself*, though the Fool's
   be content suggests that he, and perhaps
   Kent, try to restrain him. In modern
   productions actors have sometimes literally stripped (Introduction, pp. 77–8).

FOOL Prithee, nuncle, be content. This is a naughty night
to swim in. Now a little fire in a wild field were like an old   100
lecher's heart—a small spark, all the rest on 's body
cold. Look, here comes a walking fire.

    Enter the Earl of Gloucester with a [*torch*]

EDGAR This is the foul fiend Flibbertigibbet. He begins at
curfew and walks till the first cock. He gives the web and
the pin, squinies the eye, and makes the harelip; mildews   105
the white wheat, and hurts the poor creature of earth.
[*Sings*]

      Swithin footed thrice the wold,
      A met the night mare and her nine foal;

[handwritten marginal note: "sounds cool!"]

101 on 's] F; in Q   102.1 *the . . . Gloucester*] Q (*Gloster.*)   *with a* [*torch*]] F; *not in* Q
103 Flibbertigibbet] F; *Sriberdegibit* Qa; *fliberdegibek* Qb   104 gives] Qb; gins Qa   104–5 and
the] Qb (& the); the Qa   105 pin, squinies] DUTHIE (*conj.* Greg); pin-|queues Qa; pin, |
squemes Qb; Pin, squints F   harelip] Qb (hare lip); harte lip Qa   107 *Sings*] *not in* Q
107 Swithin] OXFORD (*after* Tate); swithald Q; *Swithold* F   wold] QF (old)   108 A] Qa (a); he
Qb (Q *aligns as prose*)   met the] Qb; nellthu Qa   mare] Qb; more Qa   foal] QF (fold)

98 **lendings** clothes lent by *the worm . . .
beast . . . sheep* (95). The idea that a king
differs from a peasant only in his clothes
pervades Shakespeare's history plays,
and is expressed by e.g. Henry V: 'I think
the king is but a man, as I am . . . His cere-
monies laid by, in his nakedness he appears but a man' (*Henry V* 4.1.101–5)
(Mack, 52–3).
    Come . . . true Lear may speak to an imag-
inary attendant (*true*, loyal) or to himself.
We follow uncorrected Q. The corrected
Q appears to represent an unfinished
attempt at correction which cannot be
recovered. HalioQ reads 'Come unbutton—', interpreting 'on bee true' as 'a
garbled version of "unbutton"', and
discusses the crux on p. 16. Weis reads
simply 'come on.'

99 **naughty** nasty, bad (cited at *OED a.* 5)
100 **fire** Presumably suggested by the approaching torch carried by the *old lecher*
Gloucester.
    wild field uncultivated waste-land
101 **on 's** of his. HalioQ and Weis emend Q's
'in' to 'in 's'.
102.1 **torch** First named in F, but clearly
called for by Q.
103 **Flibbertigibbet** The name of a devil in
Harsnet (p. 242).
104 **curfew** Originally the time at which fires
were legally required to be extinguished

(*couvrefeu*), signified by the ringing of a
bell; more generally, an hour from which
movements were forbidden or restricted.
104 **first cock** cockcrow, dawn. Spirits
walked abroad at night: e.g. *Dream*
5.2.9–52, *Hamlet* 1.1.138: 'It faded on
the crowing of the cock.'
    gives causes
104–5 **web . . . pin** A disease of the eye causing filming over the surface (*OED, pin
sb.*[1] 11).
105 **squinies** causes to squint (a rare word
found again at 20.131—*OED*'s first instance of the verb—where it means simply 'squint')
    harelip One of the *blots of nature's hand*
which Oberon hopes to obviate with the
fairies' blessing, *Dream* 5.2.39–41.
    mildews taints with mildew
106 **white wheat** wheat which turns white
or light-coloured in ripening (*OED, white,
a.* 2b), ripe corn
107–11 **Swithin . . . witch, aroint thee**
Edgar's spell against devils and evil spirits.
107 **Swithin** The only known parallel to Q's
'swithald' and F's 'Swithold' is a reference in *The Troublesome Reign of King John*
(1591) to 'Sweete S. Withold' (Bullough
(vol. iv), l. 1184), otherwise unknown to
fame. Q is weirdly corrupt here ('swithald footed thrice the old a nellthu night
more'). Theobald's 'St. Withold' is a
reasonable emendation 'only weakened

> Bid her alight
> And her troth plight,   110
> And aroint thee, witch, aroint thee!

KENT (*to Lear*)

How fares your grace?

LEAR   What's he?

KENT (*to Gloucester*) Who's there? What is't you seek?

GLOUCESTER What are you there? Your names?

EDGAR Poor Tom, that eats the swimming frog, the toad,   115
the tadpole, the wall-newt and the water; that in the fury
of his heart, when the foul fiend rages, eats cowdung for
salads, swallows the old rat and the ditch-dog, drinks the
green mantle of the standing pool; who is whipped from
tithing to tithing, and stock-punished, and imprisoned;   120
who hath had three suits to his back, six shirts to his
body,

---

109 her alight] F (her␠a light); her, O light Q   111 aroint . . . aroint] Q (arint . . . arint);
aroynt . . . aroynt F ˄ witch] Qb; with Qa   116 tadpole] Qb (todpole), F (Tod-pole); tode
pold Qa, Q2 (toade pold)   wall-newt] Qb, F; wall-wort Qa, Q2

---

by the fact that nothing whatever is known of this figure' (*TC*). Swithun, or Swithin, on the other hand, was and remains a well-known English saint, famous for healing and associated with rain. HalioQ and Weis read 'Swithold'.

107 **footed** paced, traversed
    wold a stretch of open country, a 'wild field' (l. 100)

108 **mare** A kind of goblin supposed to cause nightmare by sleeping on its victims' chests, or the nightmare itself (*OED*, *mare*[2], 1), sliding into the sense 'female horse'.
    foal *OED*'s definition of *ninefold* as 'an attendant set of nine' simply tries to make sense of this passage. 'Tyrwhitt's suggestion that *fold* is an alternative form of "foal", influenced by the rhyme, is supported by examples of excrescent final *d* elsewhere in Shakespeare (Cercignani, 318); alternatively, *fold* might refer to coils in a serpent's body (*sb.*[3] 1e), appropriate enough for a devil' (*TC*, notes to *Tragedy of King Lear*).

110 **her troth plight** pledge her loyalty,

promise to do no more harm

111 **aroint thee** begone. *OED*'s only other early instance is from *Macbeth* 1.3.5, but Hulme found the phrase in a Stratford document and discusses its possible origins (pp. 17–18).

116 **wall-newt** Presumably the wall-lizard (*OED*, *wall*, *sb.*[1] 25b); newts often hibernate in walls.
    water i.e. water-newt

118 **ditch-dog** 'dead dog thrown in a ditch' (Delius, cited Furness)

119 **mantle** green scum on stagnant (*standing*) water
    whipped As rogues and vagabonds were, according to a statute of 1596, to be 'openly whipped' and 'forthwith sent from parish to parish' (Chambers, *Elizabethan Stage*, iv. 324).

120 **tithing** A rural district, originally of ten householders (*OED sb.* 3), parish.
    stock-punished punished by being set in the stocks

121 **hath had** i.e. formerly had
    three . . . back Kent calls Oswald *three-suited* at 7.14.

    Horse to ride, and weapon to wear.
    But mice and rats and such small deer
    Hath been Tom's food for seven long year—   125
Beware my follower. Peace, Smolking; peace, thou fiend!

GLOUCESTER (*to Lear*)

    What, hath your grace no better company?

EDGAR

    The Prince of Darkness is a gentleman;
    Modo he's called, and Mahu—   130

GLOUCESTER (*to Lear*)

    Our flesh and blood is grown so vile, my lord,
    That it doth hate what gets it.

EDGAR   Poor Tom's a-cold.

GLOUCESTER (*to Lear*)

    Go in with me. My duty cannot suffer
    To obey in all your daughters' hard commands.
    Though their injunction be to bar my doors   135
    And let this tyrannous night take hold upon you,
    Yet have I ventured to come seek you out
    And bring you where both food and fire is ready.

LEAR

    First let me talk with this philosopher.
    (*To Edgar*) What is the cause of thunder?

KENT   My good lord,   140
    Take his offer; go into the house.

---

126 Smolking] OXFORD; snulbug Q; Smulkin F; Smulking BLAYNEY   130 Mahu] F; ma hu Q

123 **weapon to wear** as a gentleman would wear a sword?
124–5 **rats . . . year** Based on a couplet from the old romance *Sir Bevis of Hampton* published in 1503: 'Rats and mice and such small deer | Was his meat that seven year' (Early English Text Society, Extra Series No. 46, 1895, etc., p. 75).
124 **deer** Used generally of animals.
126 **Smolking** A 'puny spirit' in Harsnet (p. 240), said to have taken the form of a mouse (p. 312).
129 **Prince of Darkness** Satan
130 **Modo . . . Mahu** In Harsnet, generals of the infernal furies, serving under 'the grand Prince of Darkness' (p. 317).

131 **flesh and blood** i.e. children
132 **gets** begets
133 **duty . . . suffer** (sense of) duty will not allow me
134 **in all** in every respect
139 **philosopher** The word had a broad range of meaning: learned man, natural scientist, even magician.
140 **What . . . thunder** 'Whether Jove or else the winds in breaking clouds do thunder' (Ovid, *Metamorphoses*, trans. Golding, Book 15, l. 78) had been a stock philosophical question 'ever since the days of Pythagoras' (Muir, 'Madness', p. 36). Elton, pp. 202–8, discusses the role of thunder in *Lear* and shows that 'attitudes

LEAR

I'll talk a word with this most learnèd Theban.

(*To Edgar*) What is your study?

EDGAR

How to prevent the fiend, and to kill vermin.

LEAR

Let me ask you one word in private. 145

    They converse apart

KENT (*to Gloucester*)

Importune him to go, my lord.

His wits begin to unsettle.

GLOUCESTER   Canst thou blame him?

His daughters seek his death. O, that good Kent,

He said it would be thus, poor banished man!

Thou sayst the King grows mad; I'll tell thee, friend, 150

I am almost mad myself. I had a son,

Now outlawed from my blood; a sought my life

But lately, very late. I loved him, friend;

No father his son dearer. True to tell thee,

The grief hath crazed my wits. What a night's this! 155

(*To Lear*) I do beseech your grace—

LEAR   O, cry you mercy.

(*To Edgar*) Noble philosopher, your company.

EDGAR   Tom's a-cold.

147 him] Q; him once more F   149 man!] Q (~,)   155 this!] Q (~?)   156 mercy.] Q (~ˌ)

to thunder on the Renaissance stage were clues to the religious positions of the characters' (p. 207); in this it parallels the opposing attitudes to the eclipses on the part of the credulous Gloucester and the rationalist Edmund, 2.101–24.

142 **Theban** Thebes was a city state not far from Athens, in Boeotia, whose inhabitants were supposed to be particularly stupid. John Marston, in 'Pygmalion's Image' (1598), refers to a 'dull-spirited, fat Boetian boor' (in Satire 2, l. 4), cited by *OED*, *Boeotian*, A. a, b; also Sugden, 'Thebes'. This may then be a joke; F. G. Butler suggested that the reference is to the 'Theban Crates', cynic philosopher and follower of Diogenes, who lived in

self-chosen poverty (*English Studies*, 67 (1986), 511–14). In any case the point lies in the incongruity of Lear's deference to Mad Tom.

143 **study** area of research, or, more generally, aim

144 **prevent** outwit, forestall

146 **him** F's addition of 'once more' may represent an accidental omission from Q (as HalioQ, following Blayney, argues).

148 **His . . . death** We have been shown no direct evidence for this, though at 13.82 Gloucester says he has heard *a plot of death* upon Lear.

152 **outlawed . . . blood** banished and disinherited

156 **cry . . . mercy** (I) beg your pardon

GLOUCESTER

  In, fellow, there in t'hovel; keep thee warm.

LEAR

  Come, let's in all.

KENT   This way, my lord.

LEAR   With him!

  I will keep still with my philosopher.   160

KENT (*to Gloucester*)

  Good my lord, soothe him; let him take the fellow.

GLOUCESTER   Take him you on.

KENT [*to Edgar*]

  Sirrah, come on. Go along with us.

LEAR (*to Edgar*)

  Come, good Athenian.

GLOUCESTER   No words, no words. Hush.

EDGAR   Child Roland to the dark town come,   165

          His word was still 'Fie, fo, and fum;

          I smell the blood of a British man.'   *Exeunt*

Sc. 12 *Enter the Duke of Cornwall and Edmund the bastard*

CORNWALL   I will have my revenge ere I depart the house.

---

158 there in t'hovel; keep] F (into th'); there, in't houell keepe Q   159–60 him! | . . . still] F (~, | . . . ~ˏ); ~ˏ . . . ~, Q   165 town] Q (towne); Tower F   come] Q; came F   167 *Exeunt*] F; *not in* Q

    12.0.1 *Enter . . . bastard*] Q (*Enter Cornewell and Bastard.*)

160 **keep still** stay all the time
161 **soothe** humour (*OED v.* 4a)
164 **Athenian** Referring to Athens as the seat of learning and philosophy. 'Gielgud . . . offered [Edgar] his arm, yet, like a child, put a finger to his lips, made a hushing sound' (Rosenberg, p. 228).
165–7 **Child . . . man** The long-vowelled first line, which has proved haunting to the imagination (in its Folio form it is the title of a poem by Robert Browning), has been conjectured to be a line from a lost ballad about Roland, relative of Charlemagne, hero of the twelfth-century epic *Le Chanson de Roland*. 'Child' was a title given to young noblemen awaiting knighthood (*OED sb.* 5). The lines that follow are cited by *OED*, *fee-faw-fum*, 1, as its first reference to 'The first line of doggerel spoken by the giant in the nursery tale of

"Jack the giant killer" upon discovering the presence of Jack.'

165 **town** Oxford, Weis and HalioQ adopt F's 'Tower'. Spelt 'towne' and 'towre' the words would be graphically almost interchangeable. If a ballad containing this line were definitely known, that would help to decide the issue, but it is not. Tempting as it is to follow the familiar reading, there is no good reason to emend Q in an edition based on its text. Jowett suggests (privately) that *town* 'connects with *Athenian*, Athens being an enlightened city rather than a *dark* (British) town'.

  come The old form of the past tense, still used in dialect, retained here for the rhyme.
12.0.1 *Edmund* He has a letter which he produces at or before l. 9.
1 **the house** i.e. Gloucester's house (clarified by F's 'his')

EDMUND How, my lord, I may be censured, that nature
  thus gives way to loyalty, something fears me to think of.
CORNWALL I now perceive it was not altogether your
  brother's evil disposition made him seek his death, but a   5
  provoking merit set a-work by a reprovable badness in
  himself.
EDMUND How malicious is my fortune, that I must repent to
  be just! This is the letter he spoke of, which approves him
  an intelligent party to the advantages of France. O heav-   10
  ens, that his treason were not, or not I the detector!
CORNWALL Go with me to the Duchess.
EDMUND If the matter of this paper be certain, you have
  mighty business in hand.
CORNWALL True or false, it hath made thee Earl of Glouces-   15
  ter. Seek out where thy father is, that he may be ready for
  our apprehension.
EDMUND [*aside*] If I find him comforting the King, it will stuff
  his suspicion more fully. (*To Cornwall*) I will persever in
  my course of loyalty, though the conflict be sore between   20
  that and my blood.

9 just!] Q (~?)   11 were not] F; were Q

2 **censured** judged
  nature natural affection
3 **something fears** rather frightens
4–7 **not . . . himself** The sense is doubtful. It
  may be a rather awkward way of saying
  'not simply Edgar's evil disposition
  which made him seek his father's death,
  but also a sense of his own worth which
  provoked (or incited) him, inflamed into
  action by a reprehensible wickedness in
  Gloucester himself'; alternatively, 'not
  only your brother's innate wickedness
  that made him seek Gloucester's death,
  but a provoking quality in Gloucester
  (*merit* could mean "that which is deserved or has been earned, whether good
  or evil" (*OED sb.* 1)) set on by a reprehensible wickedness in Edgar'. Cornwall
  is justifying his determination on *revenge*
  both to himself and to Edmund.
5 **his** Gloucester's
9 **letter** Presumably Edmund has stolen the
  letter that Gloucester locked in his closet
  (10.11); he may give it to Cornwall, who
  appears to have it at 14.2.
9–10 **approves . . . party** confirms that he is
  an intelligence agent. *OED a.* 4 has four

uses of 'intelligent' in the sense, defined
by Schmidt, 'Bearing intelligence, giving
information, communicative', two of the
others from F *Lear* (3.1.16, 3.7.10), the
fourth from *Winter's Tale* (1.2.378).
11 **were not** Weis (but not HalioQ) retains
  Q's 'were' as 'the more difficult reading',
  glossing 'if only his treason, or anything
  rather than myself, were the detector of
  his disloyalty'. This seems strained, especially as Q often omits words.
13 **matter** contents
15–16 **it . . . Gloucester** 'Edmund may kneel
  to the Duke, who, with a sword to his
  shoulder, confers the title' (Rosenberg,
  229); but this would slow the action, and
  the award is likely to be anticipative
  rather than actual.
16–17 **for . . . apprehension** for us to arrest
  him
18 **comforting** Craig, followed by Muir, suggests 'The word is used in its strict legal
  sense, referring to the conduct of an acces-
  sory to a crime, after the fact in the manner of helping a condemned prisoner.'
  stuff bolster
21 **blood** family feelings

CORNWALL I will lay trust upon thee, and thou shalt find a
dearer father in my love.   *Exeunt*

Sc. 13 *Enter the Earl of Gloucester and King Lear, the Earl of*
Kent disguised, Lear's Fool, and Edgar as a Bedlam
beggar

GLOUCESTER Here is better than the open air; take it thank-
fully. I will piece out the comfort with what addition I
can. I will not be long from you.

KENT All the power of his wits have given way to impatience; the gods discern your kindness!   5

[*Exit Gloucester*]

EDGAR Frateretto calls me, and tells me Nero is an angler in
the lake of darkness. Pray, innocent; beware the foul
fiend.

FOOL (*to Lear*) Prithee, nuncle, tell me whether a madman
be a gentleman or a yeoman.   10

LEAR

A king, a king! To have a thousand
With red burning spits come hissing in upon them!

23 *Exeunt*] Q (*Exit.*)

13.1–3 *Enter . . . beggar*] Q (*Enter Gloster and Lear, Kent, Foole, and Tom.*)   5 discern] OXFORD
(*conj.* Stone); deserue Q; reward F   5.1 *Exit Gloucester*] CAPELL; *not in* Q; *after l.* 3 *in* F (*Exit*)
6 Frateretto] F; *Fretereto* Q   11 king!] Q (~,)   12 hissing] Q1 (hiszing), Q2 (hissing), F
(hizzing)

13.1 **Here** The action is imagined to be in
an enclosed space connected with
Gloucester's establishment. Seating is
called for (ll. 17–18, 35), perhaps in the
form of join-stools (l. 47), but could be
provided by the stage itself. At l. 30 Lear
is offered cushions to lie on. The curtains
of l. 77 are probably imaginary.

2 **piece out** supplement

4–5 **impatience** inability to endure (though
Lear had promised to be the 'pattern of all
patience', 9.37)

5 **discern** (may they) acknowledge, recognize. HalioQ accepts the emendation
from Q's 'deserue', but Weis follows Q,
glossing 'requite' (*OED* 6, last recorded
1523–5).

6 **Frateretto** Another devil from Harsnet
(p. 242), associated with a 'fiddler',
which may have suggested Nero. The
name means 'little brother'.
Nero The emperor notorious for fiddling
while Rome burned. The primary sense

of *lake of darkness* is the Stygian lake
(mentioned by Harsnet, p. 238), fed by
the River Styx, by which the classical
dead entered the infernal regions, but the
phrase may also have sexual connota-
tions; *angler* was slang for a thief who
used a rod with a hook attached for pilfer-
ing (*OED, angler*[1], 1b). This passage is
discussed at length by S. Musgrove,
'Thieves' Cant in *King Lear*' (*English Studies*, 62 (1981), 5–13), who concludes that
'Edgar, imagining figures of evil to em-
body darkness and horror, combines
visionary devils with notorious and real
criminals . . . Nero, remembered above
all as a matricide, suggests enough murderous and sexual evil . . . to carry the
significance of night's enormous
menace.'

10 **gentleman . . . yeoman** In the social hierarchy, the yeoman was a property holder
but not an arms-bearing gentleman.

12 **them** Probably Gonoril and Regan.

EDGAR The foul fiend bites my back.

FOOL (*to Lear*) He's mad that trusts in the tameness of a
   wolf, a horse's health, a boy's love, or a whore's oath.   15

LEAR

It shall be done. I will arraign them straight.

[*To Edgar*] Come, sit thou here, most learnèd justicer.

[*To Fool*] Thou sapient sir, sit here.—No, you she-
         foxes—

EDGAR Look where he stands and glares. Want'st thou
   eyes at troll-madam?   20

[*Sings*] Come o'er the burn, Bessy, to me.

FOOL [*sings*]

            Her boat hath a leak,
            And she must not speak
            Why she dares not come over to thee.

---

17 justicer] THEOBALD; Iustice Q   19–20 Want'st thou eyes at troll-madam?] OXFORD; wanst
thou eyes, at tral | madam͜ Q1; wantst thou eies at tri-|all madam, Q2   21 burn] CAPELL
(boorne); broome Q   21, 22 sings] *not in* Q

13 **bites my back** Like *vermin* (11.144).

15 **horse's health, whore's oath** Proverbially linked as untrustworthy (Dent
   H711).

16 **arraign . . . straight** indict them
   immediately

17 **justicer** judge, magistrate. HalioQ accepts
   Q's 'Iustice' while admitting that the
   emendation corrects the metre and may be
   supported by Q's 'Iusticer' at l. 51.

18 **sapient** wise

19 **he** the foul fiend? ('she' in F)

19–20 **Want'st . . . troll-madam** do you lack
   (or desire) eyes with which to play at troll-
   madam. In this game, according to
   J. Jones in *Bathes Buckstone* (1572), cited
   OED, **troll-madam**, 'the ladies, gentlewomen, wives and maids may . . . have
   in the end of a bench eleven holes made,
   into the which to troll pummets or bowls
   of lead . . . or also of copper, tin, wood'. Q
   prints 'wanst thou eyes, at tral madam'.
   Editors (including Weis and HalioQ) usually adopt Q2's 'wantst thou eies at triall
   madam', interpreted with some strain as
   'do you want to be the object of admiring
   glances even at your trial'. The crux is
   discussed in *Division*, 486–8.

21 **Come . . . me** The first line of a popular
   song surviving only in moralized ver-

sions, found in William Wager's play
*The Longer Thou Livest, the More Fool Thou
Art* (?1559–69; ed. R. M. Barber (1968),
ll. 93–5) and adapted as a political ballad
by William Birch (Sternfeld, pp. 168–9;
printed in *The Penguin Book of Renaissance
Verse*, ed. Henry Woudhuysen (1992),
pp. 92–4), where it is associated with the
accession of Queen Elizabeth. Sternfeld,
who prints early settings (pp. 180–8),
notes that the lyric 'seems to have had an
unabated popularity for well over three
centuries' (p. 167). He suggests that although 'only one line of the old song is
given . . . there seems to be good reason
for completing the verbal refrain . . . by
expansion: Come o'er the burn, Bessy, |
[My little pretty Bessy, | Come o'er the
burn, Bessy] to me' (p. 170). Seng
(pp. 209–10) gives additional information
about early musical settings. A burn is a
dialectal word for a stream or brook.
Malone (cited Seng, p. 208) noted that
'*Bessy* and poor *Tom* usually travelled
together'—i.e. that Bessy was a type
name for a vagrant whore.

22 **leak** Possibly referring to menstruation
   (Williams, *Glossary*, 'leaky', cites *Tempest*,
   1.1.45–6, 'as leaky as an unstanched
   wench').

EDGAR The foul fiend haunts Poor Tom in the voice of a   25
nightingale. Hoppedance cries in Tom's belly for two
white herring. Croak not, black angel: I have no food for
thee.

KENT (*to Lear*)

How do you, sir? Stand you not so amazed.

Will you lie down and rest upon the cushions?   30

LEAR

I'll see their trial first. Bring in the evidence.

⌐*To Edgar*⌐ Thou robèd man of justice, take thy place;

⌐*To Fool*⌐ And thou, his yokefellow of equity,

Bench by his side. ⌐*To Kent*⌐ You are o'th' commission,

Sit you, too.   35

EDGAR Let us deal justly.

⌐*Sings*⌐

Sleepest or wakest thou, jolly shepherd?
Thy sheep be in the corn,   ꟸhᴇʀɪʟʟ
And for one blast of thy minikin mouth
Thy sheep shall take no harm.   40

Purr, the cat is grey.

---

30 cushions] Q1 (cushings), Q2   31 the] POPE; their Q   32 robèd] Q (robbed)   34 o'th'] Q;
of the HANMER

25–6 **The . . . nightingale** 'Edgar pretends
that the Fool's singing is that of a fiend
disguised as a nightingale' (Muir).
26 **Hoppedance** In Harsnet (p. 242) a devil,
Hoberdidance, is associated with music.
27 **white** fresh, or salted but not smoked
Croak rumble (*OED v.* 3)
black angel Presumably a fallen angel;
devils were portrayed as black.
31 **in the** Q reads 'in their', possibly by contamination from the preceding use of
'their'; '*OED* shows that use of the pos-
sessive, or of constructions with *of* or
from, indicate the source of testimony,
not its object' (*TC*). HalioQ and Weis follow Q.
32 **robèd** Ironical since Edgar has only a
blanket (11.58).
33 **yokefellow of equity** associate, partner in
fairness. In law, 'equity' refers to 'The
recourse to general principles of justice
. . . to correct or supplement the provi-
sions of the law' (*OED* 3). 'In contemporary England, "yokefellows of equity"

were judges in the Court of Chancery'
(Marcus, p. 151).
34 **Bench** take a seat on the (judges') bench
(*OED*'s first instance of this sense: *v.* 3b)
o'th' commission one of those commis-
sioned as justices
37–40 **Sleepest . . . harm** An allusion to the
rhyme 'Little Boy Blue, | Come blow your
horn, | The Sheep's in the meadow, |
The cow's in the corn; | But where is the
boy who looks after the sheep? | He's
under a haycock, | Fast asleep' (Opie,
pp. 98–9).
37 **jolly** had a wide range of meanings, including brave, amorous, arrogant, finely
dressed, handsome; sometimes used
ironically.
39 **for . . . of** i.e. if you will utter but one
blast from
minikin shrill (*OED a.* B2)
41 **Purr** The name of a devil in Harsnet
(p. 242), but evil spirits were often thought
to appear as cats (such as Grimalkin in
the opening scene of *Macbeth*).

LEAR Arraign her first. 'Tis Gonoril. I here take my oath
before this honourable assembly she kicked the poor King
her father.

FOOL Come hither, mistress. Is your name Gonoril?   45

LEAR She cannot deny it.

FOOL Cry you mercy, I took you for a join-stool.

LEAR

And here's another, whose warped looks proclaim
What store her heart is made on. Stop her there.
Arms, arms, sword, fire, corruption in the place!   50
False justicer, why hast thou let her scape?

EDGAR Bless thy five wits.

KENT (*to Lear*)

O pity! Sir, where is the patience now
That you so oft have boasted to retain?

EDGAR (*aside*)

My tears begin to take his part so much   55
They'll mar my counterfeiting.

LEAR   The little dogs and all,
Tray, Blanch, and Sweetheart—see, they bark at me.

EDGAR Tom will throw his head at them.—Avaunt, you
curs!

43 she] Q2, BL2; *not in* QI   47 join-stool] Q (ioyne stoole)   49 on] Q (an)   50 place!] Q (~,)

47 **Cry . . . join-stool** A proverbial excuse for
overlooking someone (Dent M897). A
join- (or joint-) stool was made by a
joiner, rather than clumsily knocked
together. Probably part of the stage
furnishings representing the bench.

48 **another** Regan

49 **store** Perhaps 'abundance', used ironically (Foakes); but could mean 'the stock
of a tradesman' (*OED sb.* 7b), so perhaps
Lear means that her warped appearance
reflects the distorted material—or even
warped wood, like that of a join-stool—of
which her heart is made, in which case
her would be emphatic—hers too'.
Stop . . . there He imagines she is trying to
flee.

57 **Tray . . . Sweetheart** 'Tray' could mean
'pain, affliction' (*sb.* 1, last recorded
1560). 'Blanch' could be the worn-down
form of *blandish* ('flatter', suiting Shake-

speare's habitual characterization of
dogs) recorded only as a verb (*v.* 3). In
Yukio Ninagawa's RSC production
(1999), the three dogs were represented
as toy figures; Lear (Nigel Hawthorne)
threw the first two into a brazier, but
clutched Sweetheart to himself.

58 **throw his head** Variously interpreted
by both actors and editors. Muir reports
that 'in Gielgud's 1950 production,
Edgar made as though to lift his head
from his shoulders', while also suggesting that Edgar might 'throw his horn'
at the imaginary dogs, on the grounds
that 'head' could mean 'the antlers of a
deer', or that 'Edgar might put his
horn on his head, and pretend he is an
ox attacking the dogs with it'. The
simplest gloss seems to be that Edgar
jerks his head forward and glares
threateningly.

Be thy mouth or black or white,   60
Tooth that poisons if it bite,
Mastiff, greyhound, mongrel grim,
Hound or spaniel, brach or him,
Bobtail tyke or trundle-tail,
Tom will make them weep and wail;   65
For with throwing thus my head,
Dogs leap the hatch, and all are fled.
Loudla, doodla! Come, march to wakes and fairs
And market towns. Poor Tom, thy horn is dry.

LEAR Then let them anatomize Regan; see what breeds   70
about her heart. Is there any cause in nature that makes
this hardness? (*To Edgar*) You, sir, I entertain you for one
of my hundred, only I do not like the fashion of your garments. You'll say they are Persian attire; but let them be
changed.   75

KENT

Now, good my lord, lie here a while.

---

62 mongrel] ROWE; ~, QF   62–3 grim, | Hound] F; grim-hoū d Q (*setting the speech as prose*)
63 him] Q; Hym F; lym HANMER

60 **or . . . or** either . . . or
61 **poisons** 'with rabies' (Weis)
63 **brach** bitch-hound
    him Much discussed. The difficulty is that
    parallelism seems to require an alterna-
    tive to *spaniel*. Hanmer's emendation to
    'lym', supposed to mean a species of
    bloodhound, has been refuted by Blayney
    in unpublished work (noted in HalioF).
    'Edgar could simply point to an imagin-
    ary *him*, or even to the Fool or Kent'
    (Foakes), or 'him' ('Hym' in F) might
    mean simply, and lamely, a male dog.
64 **Bobtail tyke** cur with a bobbed, or
    docked, tail
    trundle-tail a dog, usually low-bred, with
    a curly tail
67 **hatch** closed lower part of a divided door
68 **Loudla, doodla** An exclamation of inde-
    terminate meaning, perhaps imitating
    the sound of a horn (l. 69); Weis suggests
    'a beggar's rallying cry, or a cry to an-
    nounce his presence at village *wakes and
    fairs*'.
    wakes Annual parish festivals frequented
    by beggars and tinkers such as Autocylus
    in *Winter's Tale* (e.g. 4.3.100–1).
69 **Poor . . . dry** Hollowed-out animal

horns could be used as drinking vessels
and as musical instruments. John
Aubrey, in his *Natural History of Wiltshire*
(1651–91), 1847 edn., p. 93, says that
Bedlam beggars 'wore about their necks a
great horn of an ox in a string or baldric
which, when they came to an house for
alms, they did wind, and they did put the
drink given them into this horn whereto
they did put a stopple' (cited by Craig).
The primary sense is that Tom is thirsty,
but Edgar may also be saying that his invention is exhausted (so Steevens).
70–2 **Then . . . hardness** Perhaps simply a
non-sequitur of madness, but Lear may
be reverting to his thoughts on Regan's
heart at l. 49.
70 **anatomize** dissect
72 **entertain you** take you into my service
73 **hundred** his (former) hundred knights
74 **Persian** orientally gorgeous (ironical
since Edgar wears only a blanket), and re-
sistant to change, like the laws of the
Medes and Persians, 'which altereth not'
(Daniel 6: 8).
76 **lie here** Lear lies down, possibly in the
opening at the rear of the stage, as
Gloucester does not immediately see him.

LEAR Make no noise, make no noise. Draw the curtains.
So, so, so. We'll go to supper i'th' morning. So, so, so.
He sleeps. Enter the Earl of Gloucester
GLOUCESTER (*to Kent*)
Come hither, friend. Where is the King my master?
KENT
Here, sir, but trouble him not; his wits are gone.   80
GLOUCESTER
Good friend, I prithee take him in thy arms.
I have o'erheard a plot of death upon him.
There is a litter ready. Lay him in't
And drive towards Dover, friend, where thou shalt meet
Both welcome and protection. Take up thy master.   85
If thou shouldst dally half an hour, his life,
With thine and all that offer to defend him,
Stand in assurèd loss. Take up, take up,
And follow me, that will to some provision
Give thee quick conduct.
KENT (*to Lear*)   Oppressèd nature sleeps.   90
This rest might yet have balmed thy broken sinews ~~Shattered~~
Which, if convenience will not allow,   ~~nerves~~
Stand in hard cure. (*To Fool*) Come, help to bear thy
        master.

78.1 *He sleeps*] OXFORD; *not in* Q   *Enter . . . Gloucester*] Q (*Enter Gloster.*)   88 Take up, take
up] F; Take vp to keepe Qa; Take vp the King Qb

---

77 **curtains** Lear imagines the curtains
   around his bed.
82 **upon** against
83 **litter** 'A vehicle . . . containing a couch
   shut in by curtains, and carried on men's
   shoulders or by beasts of burden' (*OED
   sb*. 2a.) A contemporary illustration,
   showing a litter both closed and open,
   and borne by two mules (?) each with a
   rider, is reproduced in S. Schoenbaum,
   Shakespeare: the Globe and the World (New
   York, etc., 1979), p. 74.
84 **drive** may mean simply 'hasten' (*OED v*.
   25a).
   Dover Where, presumably, the French
   army has landed.
86 **dally** delay
88 **Take up, take up** 'Q corr. makes good
   sense, but F probably restores the original

manuscript reading, which again shows
Gloucester repeating short phrases, as at
[2.42, 6.96] etc.' (HalioQ).
89–90 **to . . . conduct** lead you quickly to
   where you will find necessary supplies
91 **balmed** soothed
   broken sinews shattered nerves
93 **Stand . . . cure** will be hard to cure
   Come . . . master This instruction to the
   Fool marks his departure from the play.
   In F he is given a closing line, 'And I'll go
   to bed at noon', immediately after Lear's
   'We'll go to supper i'th' morning'
   (l. 78). This quip, superficially enter-
   taining, is poignant in retrospect. It might
   conceivably have been omitted here by
   accident, but there is no evidence that
   this happened, and it is equally possible
   that Shakespeare deliberately allowed the

Thou must not stay behind.

GLOUCESTER   Come, come away.

Exeunt all but Edgar

EDGAR

When we our betters see bearing our woes,   95
We scarcely think our miseries our foes.
Who alone suffers, suffers most i'th' mind,
Leaving free things and happy shows behind.
But then the mind much sufferance doth o'erskip
When grief hath mates, and bearing fellowship.   100
How light and portable my pain seems now,
When that which makes me bend, makes the King bow.
He childed as I fathered. Tom, away.
Mark the high noises, and thyself bewray
When false opinion, whose wrong thoughts defile thee,   105
In thy just proof repeals and reconciles thee.
What will hap more tonight, safe scape the King!
Lurk, lurk.   *Exit*

94.1 *Exeunt . . . Edgar*] Q (*Exit.*)   108 *Exit*] THEOBALD; *not in* Q

external critic and representative of Lear's folly to fade quietly from the play as madness finally takes charge of Lear's mind. Occasionally directors have indicated to the audience that the Fool will appear no more, notably Adrian Noble in his 1982 RSC production, in which the Fool, played by Antony Sher, was 'stabbed in a dustbin by the mad Lear, continuingly destructive of his own good' (S. Wells, 'Lear in the Fool's shadow', *TLS*, 16 July 1982).

95-6 **When . . . foes** when we see our superiors suffering our own afflictions, we scarcely regard our misfortunes as inimical, i.e. we endure them more easily. Edgar speaks in his own person, directly to the audience.

97 **Who . . . mind** i.e. he suffers most in mind who suffers alone

98 **free things** carefree actions

99 **sufferance** suffering

100 **bearing** endurance

101 **portable** endurable

102 **makes me . . . bow** weighs heavily on me bows the King down

103 **childed . . . fathered** A compressed way of saying 'his children have treated him as my father has treated me'; also explained as 'He (being made), turned into, a child, as I (being) made, turned into, a father' (Kathleen Wales, 'An Aspect of Shakespeare's Dynamic Language', *English Studies*, 59 (1978), 395–404).

104 **Mark . . . noises** pay attention to what's going on in high places? Johnson glossed 'attend to the great events that are approaching'.

thyself bewray reveal your real self

106 **In . . . thee** in proof of your integrity repeals (the sentence of outlawry) and reconciles you (to your father). In this line, the subject is understood to be true, not 'false', opinion.

107 **What** whatever

safe . . . King may the King escape safely

108 **Lurk, lurk** Keep out of sight! Edgar returns to the persona of Poor Tom.

Sc. 14 *Enter the Duke of Cornwall and Regan, and Gonoril*
and Edmund the bastard, and Servants

CORNWALL (*to Gonoril*)

Post speedily to my lord your husband.

Show him this letter. The army of France is landed.

(*To Servants*) Seek out the villain Gloucester.

Exeunt some

REGAN   Hang him instantly.

GONORIL

Pluck out his eyes.

CORNWALL   Leave him to my displeasure.—

Edmund, keep you our sister company.

The revenges we are bound to take upon your traitorous   5

father are not fit for your beholding. Advise the Duke

where you are going, to a most festinate preparation; we

are bound to the like. Our posts shall be swift, and intelli-

gence betwixt us.—

Farewell, dear sister. Farewell, my lord of Gloucester.   10

Enter Oswald the steward

How now, where's the King?

14.0.1–2 *Enter . . . bastard*] Q (*Enter Cornwall, and Regan, and Gonorill, and Bastard.*)
0.2 *and Servants*] F; *not in* Q   6 revenges] F; reuenge Q   8 festinate] F2; festuant Q; festiu-
ate F1   9 posts] F; post Q   11.1 *Enter . . . steward*] Q ('*Enter Steward.*', *after l.* 12)

---

14 The scene of Gloucester's blinding takes
place in his own house (ll. 29, 38). A letter
(l. 2), bindings (l. 27) and chair (l. 32) are
needed, and perhaps something to represent Gloucester's gouged-out eyes—
Brook used peeled grapes. Cornwall has a
sword (l. 77.1), and l. 78 makes clear
that even the servants wear swords.
1 **Post** travel
2 **letter** The one that Gloucester locked in
his closet (10.11, 21) and which is in Edmund's possession at 12.9. It is not clear
who has it at this point.
army The forces mentioned at 8.21–5,
10.13, and, obliquely, at 13.86–8.
4 **Pluck . . . eyes** HalioF points out that
blinding is seen by psychologically ori-
ented critics as symbolic of castration—
appropriate from the emasculating
Gonoril—and that both castration and
blinding were medieval punishments for
adultery (though this is not the sin with
which Gloucester's tormentors are themselves concerned).

5 **sister** i.e. sister-in-law
6 **traitorous** treacherous (to the new
regime)
7 **Duke** i.e. Albany
8 **to** Perhaps shorthand for 'to expedite'
(Abbott 186).
festinate hurried, hasty. *OED*'s first instance of the rare, latinate word. Shakespeare had used the adverbial form—also
apparently for the first time—in *Love's
Labour's Lost* (3.1.5).
preparation (for war)
9 **posts** messengers. HalioQ and Weis
retain Q's 'post', but 'it seems odd for
Cornwall to imply that they have only
one messenger, who will be kept busy
going back and forth' (*TC*).
9–10 **intelligence** i.e. 'will convey information' (*OED*, *intelligence*, v. 1a).
HalioQ, following F, reads 'intelligent'.
11 **lord of Gloucester** i.e. Edmund (see
12.15–16)—confusingly, especially in
view of Oswald's following words.

OSWALD

    My lord of Gloucester hath conveyed him hence.

    Some five- or six-and-thirty of his knights,

    Hot questants after him, met him at gate,

    Who, with some other of the lord's dependants,   15

    Are gone with him towards Dover, where they boast

    To have well-armèd friends.

CORNWALL   Get horses for your mistress.   *Exit Oswald*

GONORIL Farewell, sweet lord, and sister.

CORNWALL   20

    Edmund, farewell.   *Exeunt Gonoril and Edmund*

    (*To Servants*)   Go seek the traitor Gloucester.

    Pinion him like a thief; bring him before us.

                           Exeunt other Servants

    Though we may not pass upon his life

    Without the form of justice, yet our power

    Shall do a curtsy to our wrath, which men

    May blame but not control. Who's there—the traitor?   25

    Enter the Earl of Gloucester brought in by two or three

REGAN

    Ingrateful fox, 'tis he.

CORNWALL (*to Servants*) Bind fast his corky arms.

GLOUCESTER

    What means your graces? Good my friends, consider

    You are my guests. Do me no foul play, friends.

CORNWALL (*to Servants*)

    Bind him, I say—

REGAN   Hard, hard! O filthy traitor!

GLOUCESTER   30

    Unmerciful lady as you are, I am true.

---

15 questants] OXFORD; questrits Q; Questrists F   19 *Exit Oswald*] STAUNTON; *not in* Q
21 *Exeunt . . . Edmund*] Q ('*Exeunt Gon. And Bast.*', *after l.* 20)   22.1 *Exeunt . . . Servants*]
CAPELL; *not in* QF   23 we] Q; well we F   26.1 *the Earl of*] *not in* Q

15 **questants** seekers. A rare word, but used
    by Shakespeare at *All's Well* 2.1.16. The
    emendation (accepted by HalioQ) is dis-
    cussed in *Division*, p. 488.
22 **Pinion . . . thief** tie his arms to his sides
    like a petty criminal (especially humiliat-
    ing for an earl)
23 **pass . . . life** pass a death sentence
24 **form of justice** formal procedure of a trial

24 **power** legal authority *OED sb.*[1] 5a)
25 **do . . . to** A metaphorical way of saying
    'yield to'.
27 **corky** withered, sapless (this sense first
    recorded in Harsnet, p. 221)
30 **Bind . . . say** The repeated order suggests
    that the servants have held back.
31 **true** loyal (i.e. not a *traitor*; F has
    'none')

CORNWALL (*to Servants*)

    To this chair bind him. (*To Gloucester*) Villain, thou

        shalt find—

        Regan plucks Gloucester's beard

GLOUCESTER

    By the kind gods, 'tis most ignobly done,

    To pluck me by the beard.

REGAN So white, and such a traitor!

GLOUCESTER Naughty lady,   35

    These hairs which thou dost ravish from my chin

    Will quicken and accuse thee. I am your host.

    With robbers' hands my hospitable favours

    You should not ruffle thus. What will you do?

CORNWALL   40

    Come, sir, what letters had you late from France?

REGAN

    Be simple, answerer, for we know the truth.

CORNWALL

    And what confederacy have you with the traitors

    Late footed in the kingdom?

REGAN   To whose hands

    You have sent the lunatic King. Speak.

GLOUCESTER   45

    I have a letter guessingly set down,

32.1 *Regan . . . beard*] JOHNSON; *not in* Q   42 simple,] Q (~‸)   45 King. Speak.] F (~: ~.); ~‸~? Q

34 **pluck . . . beard** A contemptuous insult.

35 **So . . . traitor!** Pretending surprise that Gloucester should be a traitor in spite of the whiteness of his beard, betokening both age and innocence.

36 **Naughty** wicked

37 **ravish** pluck

38 **quicken** come to life

39–40 **favours . . . ruffle** An exact sense is indeterminable. The phrase might mean 'treat my kindnesses with contempt . . .' (*OED*, *ruffle*, *v*.² 4, 'to handle roughly; to set upon with violence'), but, at least on a literal level, it is not easy to see how 'hands' could do this; *OED* gives *ruffle* here as its first instance of the sense 'To take or snatch rudely' (*v*.² 5), which seems to require *favours* to be tangible, as in love favours—as if Gloucester had been wearing symbols of welcome—

which seems strained; 'favour' could also mean 'face', or 'features' (of the face), so the phrase might be understood as 'do violence to my looks of welcome'.

41 **late** recently

42 **simple** honest, straightforward. HalioQ interestingly hyphenates—'simple-answerer'—without note. Q's 'Be simple answerer' could be a misreading of F's 'Be simple answer'd', i.e. answer straightforwardly.

    answerer 'One who replies to a charge, objection, argument or statement' (*OED* 1).

43 **traitors** The *well-armèd friends* of l. 18, regarded as traitors by Cornwall because disloyal to him (Knowles, p. 38 n. 15).

44 **Late footed** recently landed

46 **guessingly set down** written by guesswork; *OED*'s first instance of the adverb.

Which came from one that's of a neutral heart,
And not from one opposed.

CORNWALL   Cunning.

REGAN   And false.

CORNWALL

Where hast thou sent the King?

GLOUCESTER   To Dover.

REGAN

Wherefore to Dover? Wast thou not charged at peril—

CORNWALL   50

Wherefore to Dover? Let him first answer that.

GLOUCESTER *Bear mauling — Something bad is*
⌐I am tied to th' stake, and I must stand the course. *going to happen*

REGAN Wherefore to Dover, sir?

GLOUCESTER

Because I would not see thy cruel nails
Pluck out his poor old eyes, nor thy fierce sister
In his anointed flesh rash boarish fangs.   55
The sea, with such a storm as his bowed head
In hell-black night endured, would have buoyed up
And quenched the stellèd fires. Yet, poor old heart,
He helped the heavens to rage.
If wolves had at thy gate howled that dern time,   60

---

56 anointed] Qb (annoynted), F; aurynted Qa   57 as] F; of Qa; on Qb   bowed] BLAYNEY
(*conj.* Greg); lou'd Qa; lowd Qb   58 buoyed] F; layd Qa; bod Qb   59 stellèd] Qb, F; steeled
Qa, Q2   60 helped] Q (holpt); holpe F   61 howled] F (hould); heard Q

50 **at peril** at risk (of your death)

52 **tied . . . course** Gloucester sees himself as
    a bear who must *stand*—endure—
    the course—successive attacks. Macbeth
    uses the same image: 'They have tied me
    to a stake. I cannot fly, | But bear-like I
    must fight the course' (5.7.1–2).

54–5 **Because . . . eyes** Gloucester virtually
    invites his own torment.

56 **anointed** i.e. sacred. Kings are, and were
    from medieval times, anointed with holy
    oil at the coronation service.
    rash strike (F substitutes 'stick', perhaps
    for euphony)

57 **as** This Folio reading is accepted by
    HalioQ, but Weis reverts to corrected Q's
    'on', which makes (rather difficult) sense.
    bowed bent down (*OED*'s first use of the

literal sense of the participial adjective
dates from 1848, but the verbal sense was
common much earlier). Both HalioQ and
Weis accept the emendation, though as
Weis says, 'If Qa's *loved* were accepted, it
could be seen as evidence of Gloucester's
protective affection for the King.'

58 **buoyed** risen, swelled (*OED*'s first use of
    this sense: *buoy, v.* 1)

59 **stellèd** starry (*OED*'s first use)

61 **dern** sombre, dreary. The word, changed
    to 'stern' in F, is used parodically in the
    anonymous manuscript play *Tom o' Lin-
    coln* (*c*.1611); it may have 'become a dan-
    gerous word to use in a context of serious
    emotion' (G. R. Proudfoot, Introduction
    to *Tom o' Lincoln* (Oxford, Malone Society
    Reprints, 1992), p. xxviii).

Thou shouldst have said 'Good porter, turn the key;
All cruels I'll subscribe.' But I shall see
The wingèd vengeance overtake such children.

CORNWALL
See't shalt thou never.—Fellows, hold the chair.—
Upon those eyes of thine I'll set my foot.   65

GLOUCESTER
He that will think to live till he be old
Give me some help!—O cruel! O ye gods!

> ⌈*Cornwall puts out one of Gloucester's eyes and*
> *stamps on it*⌉

REGAN (*to Cornwall*)
One side will mock another; t'other, too.

CORNWALL (*to Gloucester*)
If you see vengeance—

SERVANT   Hold your hand, my lord.
I have served you ever since I was a child,   70
But better service have I never done you
Than now to bid you hold.

REGAN   How now, you dog!

SERVANT
If you did wear a beard upon your chin
I'd shake it on this quarrel. ⌈*To Cornwall*⌉ What do you
    mean?

CORNWALL My villein!   75

---

63 cruels I'll subscribe] OXFORD (*conj*. Stone); cruels else subscrib'd Q; Cruels else subscribe F;
cruel selfe subscrib'd BLAYNEY   68.1–2 *Cornwall . . . it*] This edition *after* ROWE; *not in* Q
71 you] Q2, F; *not in* Q1   75 *To Cornwall*] OXFORD; *not in* QF   76 villein] Q (villaine)

63 **All cruels I'll subscribe** 'all cruel creatures I'll countenance, accept', or 'all
cruel actions I'll surrender, give up, renounce'. This emends Q's 'All cruels else
subscrib'd' ('subscribe', F), difficult to
explain but accepted by HalioQ and Weis,
and explained by Foakes as 'all cruel
creatures but you yield (to feelings of
sorrow and compassion at a time like
this)'.
64 **wingèd vengeance** vengeance of the gods
66 **Upon . . . foot** It is not clear exactly what
action Shakespeare envisaged; perhaps
foot is used for 'boot' or 'spur'. Dessen
(*Conventions*, p. 120) regards it as sym-
bolically appropriate that 'Gloucester,

bound to a chair, is lowered to the stage
floor so that his head is under Cornwall's
foot.' In Peter Brook's production,
Gloucester's chair was tipped backwards
so that Gloucester's head was on the floor
and Cornwall apparently drove his spur
into it.
70–80 **Hold . . . him** The Servant's action is
described at 16.72–7.
71 **served you ever since** Weis accepts Q's
'seru'd euer since'.
75 **What . . . mean** Furness suggested that
these words should be spoken by Cornwall; Kittredge assigned them to Regan.
76 **villein** serf, peasant (spelt 'villaine' in Q
and F)

SERVANT

Why then, come on, and take the chance of anger.

They draw and fight

REGAN [*to another Servant*]

Give me thy sword. A peasant stand up thus!

She takes a sword and runs at him behind

SERVANT (*to Gloucester*)

O, I am slain, my lord! Yet have you one eye left

To see some mischief on him.

[*Regan stabs him again*]

O!   *He dies*

CORNWALL   80

Lest it see more, prevent it. Out, vile jelly!

He [puts out] Gloucester's other eye

Where is thy lustre now?

GLOUCESTER

All dark and comfortless. Where's my son Edmund?

Edmund, enkindle all the sparks of nature

To quite this horrid act.

REGAN   Out, villain!

Thou call'st on him that hates thee. It was he   85

That made the overture of thy treasons to us,

Who is too good to pity thee.

GLOUCESTER

O, my follies! Then Edgar was abused.

Kind gods, forgive me that, and prosper him!

REGAN (*to Servants*)   90

Go thrust him out at gates, and let him smell

His way to Dover. (*To Cornwall*) How is't, my lord?

How look you?

77.1 *They . . . fight*] Q ('*draw and fight.*', *after l.* 76)   80 *Regan . . . again*] OXFORD;   *not in* QF
He dies] Q2; *not in* Q1, F   81.1 *He . . . eye*] This edition *after* ROWE;   *Dashing Gloster's other Eye
to the Ground* CAPELL   84 enkindle] F; vnbridle Q   85 quite] Q (quit)

77 **take . . . anger** accept the risk that (my)
  anger creates
78 **stand up** i.e. confront me (*OED, stand,
  v.* 103n.)
80 **mischief on him** harm done to him
84 **enkindle** F's replacement for Q's
  'vnbridle'. 'Shakespeare elsewhere only

uses the adjective *unbridled*, and one does
not easily "unbridle" sparks' (*Division*,
p. 456). HalioQ, but not Weis, accepts F.
85 **quite** requite, avenge
  horrid horrific
87 **overture** revelation
89 **abused** wronged

210

CORNWALL

I have received a hurt. Follow me, lady.

(*To Servants*) Turn out that eyeless villain. Throw this
    slave

Upon the dunghill.   *Exit one or more with Gloucester*
                                        ⌐*and the body*⌐

                 Regan, I bleed apace.   95

Untimely comes this hurt. Give me your arm.

                         Exeunt Cornwall and Regan

SECOND SERVANT

I'll never care what wickedness I do

If this man come to good.

THIRD SERVANT   If she live long

And in the end meet the old course of death,

Women will all turn monsters.   100

SECOND SERVANT

Let's follow the old Earl and get the bedlam

To lead him where he would. His roguish madness

Allows itself to anything.

THIRD SERVANT

Go thou. I'll fetch some flax and whites of eggs

To apply to his bleeding face. Now heaven help him!   105

                           Exeunt severally

95 *Exit . . . Gloucester*] BLAYNEY (*Exit a seruant . . .*); *not in* Q; *Exit with Glouster.* F (*after* 'Dover', *l.* 92)   *and the body*] OXFORD; *not in* QF   96.1 *Exeunt . . . Regan*] F (*Exeunt.*); *not in* Q   97 SECOND] CAPELL; *not in* Q   98, 104 THIRD] CAPELL; 2 Q   101 SECOND] CAPELL; 1 Q   102 roguish] Qa; *not in* Qb   105.1 *Exeunt severally*] Q (*Exit.*)

94–5 **Throw . . . dunghill** A humiliation visited, oddly enough, on the corpse of John Careless (mentioned in the note to 4.166–7), who, imprisoned for his religious convictions, died and 'was thrown out and buried most ignominiously upon a dunghill, by the adversaries of God's word' (cited Seng, p. 203).

95 *Exit . . . body* F directs '*Exit* [i.e. *Exit the Servant*] *with Gloster*' after 'Dover', l. 92. It may well be that, as Gurr and Ichikawa write (p. 116), 'one of the onstage servants had the task of mutely unbinding Gloucester and leading him away just after Regan's command'. They suggest that 'in the Q1 version, when Cornwall repeats Regan's command' the servant may be 'still untying Gloucester. An alternative possibility is that the servants

are so shocked and intimidated by what they have seen that none of them can even begin to unbind Gloucester until Cornwall gives the order a second time.'

95 **apace** profusely

96.1 *Exeunt . . . Regan* Q's direction is *Exit*, but the absence of a subsequent direction for Regan to leave implies that Regan gives Cornwall the help he seeks. In some productions, however, she has refused (Bratton).

99 **meet . . . death** i.e. die a natural death

101 **bedlam** Edgar as Poor Tom (note to 2.126–7)

102 **roguish** characteristic of vagrants

103 **Allows . . . anything** will agree to whatever we ask

104 **flax . . . eggs** White of egg was a traditional remedy to soothe hurt eyes and to

Sc. 15 *Enter Edgar as a Bedlam beggar*
EDGAR

Yet better thus and known to be contemned
Than still contemned and flattered. To be worst,
The low'st and most dejected thing of fortune,
Stands still in esperance, lives not in fear.
The lamentable change is from the best;
The worst returns to laughter.
    Enter the Earl of Gloucester led by an Old Man
Who's here? My father, parti-eyed? World, world, O
    world!
But that thy strange mutations make us hate thee,
Life would not yield to age.
    [*Edgar stands aside*]
OLD MAN (*to Gloucester*)   O my good lord,

15.0.1 *as . . . beggar*] *not in* Q   2 flattered. To be worst] POPE (*subs.*); ~ ͵ ~ Q   4 esperance]
F; experience Q   6.1 *Enter . . . Man*] Q (*after* 'age', *l.* 9, *and omitting* '*the Earl of*')   7 parti-
eyed] Qb (parti,eyd); poorlie, leed Qa; poorely ͵led Q2, F   8 hate] QF; hold A. WALKER *conj.*
(*see* Muir)   9 *Edgar stands aside*] OXFORD; *not in* QF

staunch bleeding from them, used e.g. by Shakespeare's son-in-law, Dr John Hall, to treat a patient suffering from 'rheum in the eyes' (Hall, pp. 8–10); Hoeniger (p. 258) notes that Dr Walter Bailey, in his *Briefe treatise touching the preservation of the eiesight* (1586, etc.), recommends 'a plaster of flax and the white of egg' for a hurt or bloodshot eye. 'Flax' could mean either linen (woven from flax) or raw flax fibres (tow) which 'could be pressed into pads for application to a wound'. The fibres 'would encourage the formation of blood clots' (Dr Melvin Earles, privately communicated).

15 The presence of Gloucester's old tenant suggests that the action is imagined as taking place not far from Gloucester's dwelling. Gloucester produces a purse at l. 62.

1–2 Yet . . . flattered A somewhat cryptic way of saying 'It's better for me to be like this and know myself to be despised (contemned) than still to be despised yet flattered to my face (as at court)'.

  3 most . . . fortune thing most cast down by fortune

  4 esperance hope (the French word, used in

English in Shakespeare's time). Weis retains Q's 'experience', explaining 'the absence of fear results from being numb and arrested (*Stands still*) in the experience of utter desolation'.

  6 The . . . laughter Related to the proverb 'When things are at the worst they will mend' (Dent T216), varied also at *Macbeth* 4.2.24–5.

  7 parti-eyed with eyesockets of varied colours—bruised and bloody. Both Weis and HalioQ accept this interpretation of Qb's 'parti,eyd' over Qa's 'poorlie, leed', picked up by Q2 and F as 'poorely led'. Slight support for 'led' may be indicated by the fact that in *Arcadia*, the old king is led by his son (Introduction, p. 00). Qb's reading is important because it indicates that Edgar realizes that his father is blind, whereas in the other texts this revelation might be prompted by Gloucester's *I'd say I had eyes again* (l. 22).

  8–9 But . . . age were it not that the strange vicissitudes of life cause us to reject the world, our life would not willingly give way to old age (and death)

  9 Edgar . . . aside The Old Man does not see Edgar until l. 22. It is not clear whether Edgar hears the intervening dialogue.

I have been your tenant and your father's tenant   10
This fourscore—

GLOUCESTER

Away, get thee away, good friend, be gone.
Thy comforts can do me no good at all;
Thee they may hurt.

OLD MAN

Alack, sir, you cannot see your way.   15

GLOUCESTER

I have no way, and therefore want no eyes.
I stumbled when I saw. Full oft 'tis seen
Our means secure us, and our mere defects
Prove our commodities. Ah dear son Edgar,
The food of thy abusèd father's wrath—   20
Might I but live to see thee in my touch
I'd say I had eyes again.

OLD MAN   How now? Who's there?

EDGAR (*aside*)

O gods! Who is't can say 'I am at the worst'?
I am worse than e'er I was.

OLD MAN   'Tis poor mad Tom.

EDGAR (*aside*)

And worse I may be yet. The worst is not   25
As long as we can say 'This is the worst.'

OLD MAN (*to Edgar*) Fellow, where goest?

GLOUCESTER Is it a beggarman?

OLD MAN Madman and beggar too.

GLOUCESTER

A has some reason, else he could not beg.   30
In the last night's storm I such a fellow saw,
Which made me think a man a worm. My son
Came then into my mind, and yet my mind

---

11 **fourscore** F adds 'years.'

18–19 **Our . . . commodities** our assets give
us a false sense of security, and our sheer
defects turn out to our advantage

20 **food of** i.e. victim of, or food for
abusèd deceived, misled

21 **see . . . touch** recognize you by touching
you

22 **How . . . there** Presumably a response to
some movement or sound from Edgar.

30 **A . . . reason** i.e. he is not entirely mad

32 **worm** i.e. mean and defenceless; a biblical theme: Psalm 22: 6, 'I am a worm,
and no man', and Job 25: 6: 'How much
more man a worm, even the son of man,
which is but a worm'.

Was then scarce friends with him. I have heard more
    since.
As flies to wanton boys are we to th' gods;   35
They kill us for their sport.
EDGAR (*aside*)   How should this be?
Bad is the trade that must play fool to sorrow,
Ang'ring itself and others.
    [*He comes forward*]
                  Bless thee, master.
GLOUCESTER
Is that the naked fellow?
OLD MAN   Ay, my lord.
GLOUCESTER
Then prithee, get thee gone. If for my sake   40
Thou wilt o'ertake us hence a mile or twain
I'th' way toward Dover, do it for ancient love,
And bring some covering for this naked soul,
Who I'll entreat to lead me.
OLD MAN   Alack, sir, he is mad.
GLOUCESTER
'Tis the time's plague when madmen lead the blind.   45
Do as I bid thee; or rather do thy pleasure.
Above the rest, be gone.

---

35 flies to] F; flies are toth' Q   36 kill] F; bitt Q   37 that must play fool] F; that must play the | foole Q; must play the fool POPE   38 *He comes forward*] OXFORD; *not in* Q F   41 hence] F; here Q

34 **I . . . since** Indeed he has.

35 **flies to** Weis, but not HalioQ, accepts Q's unmetrical and unidiomatic 'flies are toth''.
wanton cruelly mischievous, like Coriolanus' son who chased a butterfly to 'mammock' it (*Coriolanus* 1.3.62–7).

37 **trade** course of action, manner of life (*OED sb.* 3a)
fool Weis, but not HalioQ, accepts Q's 'the foole'.

38 **Ang'ring** Perhaps in the sense of 'distressing', 'wounding' (though *OED*, *anger*, *v.*[1], does not record this beyond *c*.1440) rather than 'enraging'.
Bless . . . master Probably a begging cry, as noted at 11.51.

41 **hence** Conceivably Q's 'here' may mean 'hence', but I have found no authority for this use of the word.

42 **ancient love** former affection, 'old time's sake'

43 **bring . . . covering** 'Edgar must change his appearance, and the audience must be warned of the change, because as the naked Poor Tom he could not have killed Oswald, and Albany would not have listened to his request to arrange a trial by combat with Edmund.' (W. P. Ringler Jr., 'Shakespeare and his Actors: Some Remarks on *King Lear*' (1981), repr. in Ogden and Scouten, 123–34; p. 131.)

45 **time's plague** disease of our time

47 **the rest** all

OLD MAN

  I'll bring him the best 'parel that I have,

  Come on't what will.   *Exit*

GLOUCESTER   Sirrah, naked fellow!

EDGAR

  Poor Tom's a-cold. I cannot dance it farther.   50

GLOUCESTER Come hither, fellow.

EDGAR Bless thy sweet eyes, they bleed.

GLOUCESTER Know'st thou the way to Dover?

EDGAR Both stile and gate, horseway and footpath. Poor

  Tom hath been scared out of his good wits. Bless thee,   55

  goodman, from the foul fiend. Five fiends have been in

  Poor Tom at once, as of lust Obidicut, Hobbididence

  prince of dumbness, Mahu of stealing, Modo of murder,

  Flibbertigibbet of mocking and mowing, who since pos-

  sesses chambermaids and waiting-women. So bless thee,   60

  master.

GLOUCESTER

  Here, take this purse, thou whom the heavens' plagues

  Have humbled to all strokes. That I am wretched

  Makes thee the happier. Heavens deal so still.

  Let the superfluous and lust-dieted man   65

---

49 *Exit*] F; *not in* Q   55 thee] Q (the)   57 of . . . Obidicut] Q; as Obidicut, of lust HUDSON (*conj.* W. S. Walker)   Hobbididence] Q; hobbididdance CAPELL   59 Flibbertigibbet] POPE; *Stiberdigebit* Q   mocking_∧] DUTHIE–WILSON; Mobing, Q (*arranging as verse*); mopping_∧ THEOBALD   mowing] THEOBALD; *Mohing* Q; mouthing BLAYNEY *conj.*

48 'parel apparel

50 **Poor . . . a-cold** Edgar uses the same words at 11.74, 132, and 157. They seem to have formed a conventional begging phrase which Edgar starts on here, then breaks down into personal emotion as he looks into his father's mutilated face (S. Wells, 'Tom O'Bedlam's Song and *King Lear*, *SQ* 12 (1961), 311–15). The traditional song of Tom O'Bedlam has interesting though enigmatic links with the play; it is reprinted and studied in *Loving Mad Tom: Bedlamite Verses of the XVIth and XVII Centuries*, ed. J. Lindsay (1927, repr. 1969).

  dance it i.e. play the fool. F has 'daub it'. The sentence may be spoken aside.

54 **horseway** bridle-path

56 **goodman** (a title of respect)

  Five fiends Their names are from Harsnet: Obidicut, p. 295, Hobbididence and Flibbertigibbet, p. 242, and Maho and Modu, pp. 241, 243.

57 **of . . . Obidicut** Hudson's re-ordering, accepted by Oxford, seems unnecessary.

59 **mocking** Weis reads 'moping' with no gloss or explanation of the change from Q's 'mobing'. HalioQ accepts Theobald's 'mopping'. Both 'mock and mow' and 'mop and mow' were common expressions, the former the older, meaning 'to make a grimace' (*OED*, *mop*, *v.*¹).

  mowing grimacing mockingly

60 **chambermaids . . . waiting-women** Presumably thought of as mocking their mistresses behind their backs.

63 **humbled . . . strokes** reduced to bear all kinds of humiliation

64 **Heavens** may the heavens

65 **superfluous** superabundantly supplied (as at 7.424, also recalling *superflux* in the similar passage at 11.32)

That stands your ordinance, that will not see
Because he does not feel, feel your power quickly.
So distribution should undo excess,
And each man have enough. Dost thou know Dover?
EDGAR Ay, master.   70
GLOUCESTER

There is a cliff whose high and bending head
Looks saucily in the confinèd deep.
Bring me but to the very brim of it
And I'll repair the misery thou dost bear
With something rich about me. From that place   75
I shall no leading need.
EDGAR Give me thy arm.

Poor Tom shall lead thee.

Exit Edgar guiding Gloucester

Sc. 16 *Enter [at one door] Gonoril and Edmund the bastard*
GONORIL

Welcome, my lord. I marvel our mild husband
Not met us on the way.

Enter [at another door] Oswald the steward
                              Now, where's your master?

---

68 undo] F; vnder Q   72 saucily] OXFORD; firmely Q; fearfully F   78.1 *Exit . . . Gloucester*]
OXFORD; *Exeunt.* F; *not in* Q
  16.0.1 *at one door*] CAPELL (*Enter Goneril and Edmund, Steward meeting them.*)   0.1 *Edmund
the*] *not in* Q   2 *Enter . . . steward*] Q (*Enter Steward.*)

65 **lust-dieted** fed full with pleasure, including the sexual

66 **stands . . . ordinance** stands against,
defies your decrees

67 **feel, feel** feel compassion, sympathize . . .
experience

68 **undo** eliminate, abolish

71 **bending** curving

72 **saucily** insolently. Weis retains Q's
'firmely' but HalioQ emends independently to 'sternly' while admitting that it
'does not correct the metre'. The emendation is defended in *Division*, p. 457.
confinèd deep deep sea bounded (by the
straits of Dover)

74 **repair** remedy, set right again (cited at
*OED v.*² 5)

16 Gonoril, Edmund and Oswald have ar-
rived at Albany's dwelling as planned
(14.1–21).

0.1 *at . . . door* The exact staging is uncertain. It would be possible for Gonoril and
Edmund to enter separately, but they are
imagined as having travelled together
and her enquiry about her husband implies that she has not yet encountered
him. In the opening line she welcomes
Edmund to her home; although Oswald
left with them, the report of his conversation with Albany suggests that he has ar-
rived in advance. At l. 21 Gonoril gives
Edmund some kind of love token, and at
l. 81 the Gentleman produces a letter.

1, 2, 14 **our . . . us . . . Our** Gonoril appears
to be adopting the royal plural.

OSWALD

    Madam, within; but never man so changed.
    I told him of the army that was landed;
    He smiled at it. I told him you were coming;   5
    His answer was 'The worse.' Of Gloucester's treachery
    And of the loyal service of his son
    When I informed him, then he called me sot,
    And told me I had turned the wrong side out.
    What he should most defy seems pleasant to him;   10
    What like, offensive.

GONORIL (*to Edmund*)   Then shall you go no further.
    It is the cowish terror of his spirit
    That dares not undertake. He'll not feel wrongs
    Which tie him to an answer. Our wishes on the way
    May prove effects. Back, Edmund, to my brother.   15
    Hasten his musters and conduct his powers.
    I must change arms at home, and give the distaff
    Into my husband's hands. This trusty servant
    Shall pass between us. Ere long you are like to hear,
    If you dare venture in your own behalf,   20
    A mistress's command. Wear this. Spare speech.
    Decline your head. This kiss, if it durst speak,

---

10 defy] OXFORD (*conj.* Stone); desire Q; dislike F   12 cowish] QF; currish BLAYNEY   terror] Qb, F; curre Qa, Q2; tenor STONE *conj.*   15 Edmund] Q2, F; *Edgar* Q1   21 command] Qb, F; coward Qa, Q2

4 **army** i.e. the French invading forces
8 **sot** fool
9 **turned . . . out** got things the wrong way round (i.e. Gloucester is loyal, Edmund treacherous)
10 **defy** set at nought, reject (*OED v.*[1] 5). HalioQ accepts our emendation; Weis adopts F's 'dislike', but 'Substitution of antonyms is a rare compositorial error, and "desire" is not the most obvious antonym to "dislike"' (*TC*).
12 **cowish** cowardly (a rare sense)
13 **undertake** enter into a commitment (*OED v.*[1] 8)
13–14 **He'll . . . answer** he refuses to acknowledge injuries which require retaliation
14 **wishes . . . way** Presumably 'the wishes we have expressed on our journey'—a

cryptic remark which could allude to their developing sexual relationship, or to their desire to eliminate Albany, or to both.
15 **prove effects** be accomplished
    brother brother-in-law (Cornwall)
16 **musters** assembling of troops
    conduct guide, escort
17 **change arms** exchange the insignia of our sexes, i.e. the sword and distaff
    distaff staff on which wool or flax was wound for spinning, traditionally emblematic of womanhood
19 **like** likely
21 **mistress** Combining the senses of ruler and lover.
    Wear this She gives him a love token, perhaps a chain of office (which would require him to decline his head) or a favour for his hat.

217

Would stretch thy spirits up into the air.

　　[*She kisses him*]

Conceive, and fare you well.

EDMUND Yours in the ranks of death.   25

GONORIL My most dear Gloucester.   [*Exit Edmund*]

　　To thee a woman's services are due;

　　My foot usurps my body.

OSWALD   Madam, here comes my lord.

　　　　　　　　　　　　　　　　　　　　　　　　　Exit

　　　Enter the Duke of Albany

GONORIL

I have been worth the whistling.

ALBANY   O Gonoril,

　　You are not worth the dust which the rude wind   30

　　Blows in your face. I fear your disposition.

　　That nature which contemns it origin

　　Cannot be bordered certain in itself.

　　She that herself will sliver and disbranch

23.1 *She . . . him*] OXFORD; *not in* Q   26 *Exit Edmund*] ROWE; *not in* Q; *Exit*. F (*after preceding line*)   27 a] Qb; *not in* Qa   28 My foot usurps my body] Qa; A foole vsurps my bed Qb; My Foole vsurpes my body F; My foote vsurpes my head Q2   28.1 *Exit*] Q (*Exit Stew.*) 28.2 *Enter . . . Albany*] Q2; *not in* Q1   29 whistling] Qb; whistle Qa, Q2, F   32 it] Qa; ith Qb; its Q3

---

23 **stretch . . . air** raise your spirits to a great height (with the possibility of sexual innuendo; 'spirit' could mean 'penis' (Williams, *Glossary*))

　　thy She moves into the more familiar form of address.

24 **Conceive** imagine, take my meaning

26 **Gloucester** She anticipates his inheritance of his father's title.

27 **services** Again with the possibility of innuendo.

28 **foot . . . body** A difficult line whether we accept Qa (as here, and HalioQ) or Qb (Weis). 'Thomas Clayton has defended Qa by reference to two commonplaces of Renaissance thought: the husband as his wife's "head", and the notion of a "body politic": Albany, who should be Gonoril's head, is no more than a foot, and usurps a place of which he is unworthy ("Old Light on the Text of *King Lear*", *Modern Philology*, 78 (1981), 347–67). One might add that the line has an ironic secondary meaning of which Gonoril is unaware: in its slang sexual sense *foot*

(= French *foutre*, "*to fuck*") suggests that Gonoril has allowed her sexual organs to dominate her body entirely (and unnaturally)' (*TC*).

29 **I . . . whistling** i.e. at one time you would have dearly wanted to see me; varying the proverb 'It is an ill (poor) dog that is not worth the whistling' (Dent D488).

30 **rude** rough, ill-mannered

32 **contemns it origin** despises its maker

　　it its ('an early provincial form of the genitive' (Abbott 228)). HalioQ adopts F's 'its' (and, oddly, reads 'condemns' for Q's 'contemnes').

33 **Cannot . . . itself** An awkward way of saying 'certainly cannot be relied on to control itself'.

　　bordered kept within bounds, limited (*OED v.* 2b, only instance of this sense)

34–6 **She . . . use** This passage appears to be influenced by John 15: 6: 'If a man abide not in me, he is cast forth as a branch, and withereth, and men gather them, and cast them into the fire, and they

From her material sap perforce must wither,   35
And come to deadly use.

GONORIL   No more. The text is foolish.

ALBANY

Wisdom and goodness to the vile seem vile;
Filths savour but themselves. What have you done?
Tigers, not daughters, what have you performed?
A father, and a gracious, agèd man,   40
Whose reverence even the head-lugged bear would lick,
Most barbarous, most degenerate, have you madded.
Could my good-brother suffer you to do it—
A man, a prince by him so benefacted?   *so evil - if ppl*
If that the heavens do not their visible spirits   *like you can*
Send quickly down to tame these vile offences,   *win, the world*
It will come,   *of humanity is*
Humanity must perforce prey on itself,   *bleek*
Like monsters of the deep.

GONORIL   Milk-livered man,
That bear'st a cheek for blows, a head for wrongs;   50

---

43 good-brother] Q (good brother)   44 benefacted] OXFORD; beniflicted Qa; benifited Qb
46 these] Qb (this); the Qa   48 Humanity] Qb; Humanly Qa

burn.' There is also a parallel in *King Leir* (ll. 1242–6) which Shakespeare may have 'transformed . . . into a more explicit biblical reference' (Shaheen, pp. 614–15).

34 **sliver** slice off; *OED*'s first instance of the verb.
   disbranch sever like a branch (*OED* 2, first instance of this sense)

35 **material** 'Forming the material or substance of a thing' (*OED sb.* 3b, only instance of this 'rare' sense), 'which gave her her (moral and physical) substance' (Hunter).

36 **come . . . use** '*i.e.* come, be used as a faggot for the burning' (Craig, comparing Hebrews 6: 8: 'But that which beareth thorns and briars is rejected and is nigh unto cursing; whose end is to be burned').
   The . . . foolish i.e. 'you're preaching on a foolish theme'

38 **savour but themselves** are aware only of their own stink

41 **head-lugged** worried, or baited, by having its head pulled—or, as Hunter plausibly suggests, 'pulled along by the ring in

its nose (and therefore in no good temper)'; possibly influenced by Harsnet's 'as men lead bears by the nose' (p. 285).

42 **madded** driven mad

43 **good-brother** brother-in-law

44 **benefacted** done good to. This rare back-formation from 'benefactor' is first recorded in 1594. It emends uncorrected Q's 'beneflicted', altered to 'benefited' in the corrected state accepted by Weis and HalioQ. The emendation is defended in Taylor, 'Four New Readings'.

45 **visible spirits** 'manifest avenging angels' (Weis)

48–9 **Humanity . . . deep** The idea was proverbial ('The great fish eat the small', Dent F311), and occurs vividly in the Shakespeare part of *Sir Thomas More*: 'men like ravenous fishes | Would feed on one another' (ll. 95–6).

49 **Milk-livered** cowardly, having milk (associated with maternal gentleness) instead of blood in the liver, thought of as the seat of the passions; *OED*'s first use of the compound.

50 **bear'st . . . wrongs** Perhaps elliptically 'passively hold your cheek to endure

Who hast not in thy brows an eye discerning
Thine honour from thy suffering; that not know'st
Fools do those villains pity who are punished
Ere they have done their mischief: where's thy drum?
France spreads his banners in our noiseless land,   55
With plumèd helm thy flaxen biggin threats,
Whiles thou, a moral fool, sits still and cries
'Alack, why does he so?'

ALBANY   See thyself, devil.
Proper deformity shows not in the fiend
So horrid as in woman.

GONORIL   O vain fool!   60

ALBANY
Thou changèd and self-covered thing, for shame
Bemonster not thy feature. Were't my fitness

---

51 discerning] F; deseruing Q   55 noiseless] Qb (noyseles); noystles Qa   56 flaxen biggin threats] OXFORD; thy slayer begin threats Qa; thy state begins thereat Qb; thy state begins to threat JENNENS; thy slyre biggin threats STONE *conj.*   56 biggin] Qa (begin)   57 Whiles] Qa (Whil's); Whil'st Qb; While CAPELL   59 shows] Qb; seemes Qa

blows and your head to submit to wrongful attack'; but conceivably *bear'st* is to be heard as 'bar'st', i.e. 'deliberately make defenceless', as in *Caesar*: 'Have bared my bosom to the thunder-stone' (1.3.49). The idea is biblical: 'Whosoever shall smite thee on thy right cheek' turn to him the other also' (Matthew 5: 39; Shaheen, p. 615).

51–2 **discerning . . . suffering** able to distinguish between what does you honour and what hurts your reputation

53–4 **Fools . . . mischief** A cryptic way of saying 'it is foolish to pity ill-doers even if they have not yet committed the crimes for which they are being punished'—a justification for ill treatment of e.g. Lear, Gloucester, and Cordelia.

55 **noiseless** i.e. with none of the sounds of preparation for war, peaceful (first recorded in *All's Well* 5.3.42)

56 **flaxen biggin threats** threatens your linen nightcap. This is a difficult crux. Most editors accept Jennens's 'state begins to threat' though Muir, while doing so, admits that 'Shakespeare is unlikely to have written it' since 'Greg, *Variants*, p. 174, points out that there would certainly appear to have been no "to" in the copy.' Our emendation, defended in *TC* and *Div-*

ision, p. 488, adopts Stone's 'biggin' (of which Q's 'begin' is a recognized spelling) and emends Qa's 'slayer' to 'flaxen'. Foakes rejects this on the grounds that it 'invents a "flaxen biggin" or nightcap, an implausible association with an aristocrat like Albany', but HalioF, accepting it, remarks that 'The comparison between the King of France with his plumèd helm and Albany in his nightcap is deliberately ludicrous' (p. 303). Shakespeare employs a similar contrast in *2 Henry IV*, where Prince Harry compares the King in his crown with the peasant 'whose brow with homely biggen [*sic*] bound | Snores out the watch of night' (4.3.158–9).

57 **moral** moralizing, sententious

59–60 **Proper . . . woman** deformity (of appearance or character) does not seem as repulsive in the devil, to whom it is appropriate (*Proper*), as in a woman

61 **self-covered thing** An elliptical way of saying that Gonoril has concealed her natural self and so become a thing rather than a person.

62 **Bemonster** deform, make hideous; *OED*'s first instance of the word.
feature 'Good form or shape; comeliness' (*OED sb.* 1b)
Were't . . . fitness if it befitted me

To let these hands obey my blood,
They are apt enough to dislocate and tear
Thy flesh and bones. Howe'er thou art a fiend,   65
A woman's shape doth shield thee.

GONORIL Marry your manhood, mew—
        Enter [Second] Gentleman

ALBANY What news?

[SECOND] GENTLEMAN
O my good lord, the Duke of Cornwall's dead,
Slain by his servant going to put out   70
The other eye of Gloucester.

ALBANY   Gloucester's eyes?

[SECOND] GENTLEMAN
A servant that he bred, thralled with remorse,
Opposed against the act, bending his sword
To his great master, who thereat enraged
Flew on him, and amongst them felled him dead,   75
But not without that harmful stroke which since
Hath plucked him after.

ALBANY   This shows you are above,
You justicers, that these our nether crimes
So speedily can venge. But O, poor Gloucester!
Lost he his other eye?

---

64 dislocate] Q3; dislecate Q1   67 mew] Qb; now Qa   67.1 *Enter . . . Gentleman*] Q ('*Enter a Gentleman.*', *after l.* 68)   69, *etc.* [SECOND GENTLEMAN]] OXFORD; *Gen.* Q (*see* 8.0.1–2 *n.*)
78 You] Qb (you); your Qa   justicers] Qb; Iustices Qa, Q2, F

---

64 **dislocate** *OED*'s earliest use of the finite verb (which was used as a past participle much earlier).

65 **Howe'er** although

67 **Marry** An expression of contempt, as it were 'pooh to'.
mew the cry of a cat, 'used as a derisive exclamation' (*OED int.* and *sb.*³ 2, first recorded 1606).

72 **bred** brought, or trained, up
thralled with in subjection to, governed by ? HalioQ accepts F's 'thrilled', as does Weis, who nevertheless remarks that Q's 'thrald' 'may be intended', but that if so, the punctuation would have to be altered to 'that he bred thralled [i.e. in bondage to him], with remorse'. But it seems possible for someone to be in thrall to the passion of pity, as Macbeth's servants were 'slaves of drink, and thralls of sleep' (3.6.13).

72 **remorse** pity, compassion

73 **Opposed against** acted in opposition to (the intransitive use, now obsolete, *OED*, *oppose*, *v.* 7b)

73–4 **bending . . . To** aiming . . . at

75 **amongst them** between them (i.e. Cornwall and Regan together); or among them all, all present

77 **plucked** i.e. to death

77–9 **This . . . venge** The idea is biblical: 'Shall not God avenge his elect? . . . I tell you he will avenge them quickly' (Luke 18: 7–8). Shaheen, p. 615, cites *Leir*, ll. 1909–10: 'The heavens are just, and hate impiety, | And will no doubt reveal such heinous crimes.'

78 **justicers** ministers of justice, gods
nether belonging to the nether, earthly, regions

79 **venge** avenge

[SECOND] GENTLEMAN   Both, both, my lord.   80
   (*To Gonoril*) This letter, madam, craves a speedy
      answer.
   'Tis from your sister.
GONORIL (*aside*)   One way I like this well;
   But being widow, and my Gloucester with her,
   May all the building on my fancy pluck
   Upon my hateful life. Another way   85
   The news is not so took.—I'll read and answer.
                                   Exit

ALBANY
   Where was his son when they did take his eyes?
[SECOND] GENTLEMAN
   Come with my lady hither.
ALBANY   He is not here.
[SECOND] GENTLEMAN
   No, my good lord; I met him back again.
ALBANY Knows he the wickedness?   90
[SECOND] GENTLEMAN
   Ay, my good lord; 'twas he informed against him,
   And quit the house on purpose that their punishment
   Might have the freer course.
ALBANY   Gloucester, I live
   To thank thee for the love thou showed'st the King,
   And to revenge thy eyes.—Come hither, friend.   95
   Tell me what more thou knowest.   *Exeunt*

Sc. 17 *Enter the Earl of Kent disguised, and* [First] *Gentleman*
KENT Why the King of France is so suddenly gone back
   know you no reason?

92 their] Q (there)   96 *Exeunt*] Q (*Exit*.)
   17.0.1 *Enter . . . Gentleman*] Q ('*Enter Kent and a Gentleman*.')

82 **One way** i.e. in so far as Cornwall's
   death will reduce Regan's power
83 **being** (Regan) being
   Gloucester i.e. Edmund
84–5 **May . . . life** A contorted way of saying
   'may pluck down the entire edifice that
   my amorously inspired imagination has
   constructed on to a life that will have become hateful to me'.
84 **on** HalioQ adopts F's 'in', without comment, whereas Weis considers that it

'weakens the kinetic structure of the
phrase through coalescing *building* and
fancy into a single syntactic unit in relation to *pluck*'.
86 **took** perceived, interpreted (F reads 'tart')
89 **back** on his way back
17 The action takes place near or in Dover,
   to which Lear has been brought. The
   whole of this scene is absent from F; it
   could have been omitted in performances
   based on Q.

[FIRST] GENTLEMAN
  Something he left imperfect in the state
  Which, since his coming forth, is thought of; which
  Imports to the kingdom so much fear and danger   5
  That his personal return was most required
  And necessary.
KENT
  Who hath he left behind him general?
[FIRST] GENTLEMAN
  The Maréchal of France, Monsieur la Far.
KENT Did your letters pierce the Queen to any   10
  demonstration of grief?
[FIRST] GENTLEMAN
  Ay, sir. She took them, read them in my presence,
  And now and then an ample tear trilled down
  Her delicate cheek. It seemed she was a queen
  Over her passion who, most rebel-like,   15
  Sought to be king o'er her.
KENT   O, then it moved her.
[FIRST] GENTLEMAN
  Not to a rage. Patience and sorrow strove
  Who should express her goodliest. You have seen
  Sunshine and rain at once; her smiles and tears
  Were like, a better way. Those happy smilets   20
  That played on her ripe lip seemed not to know

---

9 Maréchal] Q (Marshall), POPE (Mareschal)   12 sir] THEOBALD; say Q   17 strove] BL2, POPE;
streme Q   21 seemed] POPE; seeme Q

1–7 **Why . . . necessary** Granville Barker
  (p. 273) considered these 'the clumsiest
  few lines in the play', suggesting that
  Shakespeare may have thought of having
  Cordelia 'restore her father to his throne
  as in the old play', but changed plan because a French victory in England would
  'not have done'.
1 **gone back** i.e. to France

3 **imperfect** unfinished
5 **imports** portends
9 **Maréchal** 'The French word for "marshal" or "field-marshal" used occas. in
  English' (*OED*, first instance 1699 but
  clearly appropriate here, though not ac-

cepted by HalioQ or Weis).
9 **la Far** The name resembles that of the
  French Soldier, Monsieur le Fer, in *Henry
  V* (4.4.25).
10 **pierce** touch, move deeply
13 **trilled** flowed, rolled
15 **passion who** emotion which
18 **goodliest** most fittingly
20 **a better way** 'but after a better fashion' (Muir). The line has been much
  emended, and some editors drop the
  comma.
  smilets little smiles; a rare word
21 **seemed** Q's 'seeme' may be acceptable as
  the historic present (Weis), but misreading is easy.

What guests were in her eyes, which parted thence
As pearls from diamonds dropped. In brief,
Sorrow would be a rarity most beloved
If all could so become it.

KENT   Made she no verbal question?   25

[FIRST] GENTLEMAN

Faith, once or twice she heaved the name of 'father'
Pantingly forth as if it pressed her heart,
Cried 'Sisters, sisters, shame of ladies, sisters,
Kent, father, sisters, what, i'th' storm, i'th' night,
Let piety not be believed!' There she shook   30
The holy water from her heavenly eyes
And clamour mastered, then away she started
To deal with grief alone.

KENT   It is the stars,
The stars above us govern our conditions,
Else one self mate and make could not beget   35
Such different issues. You spoke not with her since?

[FIRST] GENTLEMAN No.

KENT

Was this before the King returned?

[FIRST] GENTLEMAN   No, since.

KENT

Well, sir, the poor distressèd Lear's i'th' town,
Who sometime in his better tune remembers   40
What we are come about, and by no means
Will yield to see his daughter.

[FIRST] GENTLEMAN   Why, good sir?

KENT

A sovereign shame so elbows him: his own unkindness,

---

23 dropped. In] Q2 (dropt; in); ~ ͵ ~ Q1   29 night,] Q1; ~? Q2   30 Let piety not be believed]
OXFORD; Let pitie not be beleeft Q; Let pity ne'er believe it POPE   32 mastered] OXFORD (*conj.*
Stone); moystened her Q   43 him: his] Q2 (him, his); ~ ͵ ~ Q1

27 **Pantingly** *OED*'s first instance of the
   adverb.
30 **Let . . . believed!** i.e. do not believe that
   filial piety exists (if this be true); *piety* is
   Oxford's emendation of Q's 'pitie', followed by HalioQ and Weis, and discussed
   in *TC*.
32 **clamour mastered** i.e. stopped her tears.
   Most editors emend Q's 'clamour moystened her' by dropping the metrically

irregular 'her' (so HalioQ, Weis); like
us, Foakes accepts Stone's suggestion
'mastered' but keeps 'her' (mistakenly
attributing 'mastered her' to Oxford).
The case is argued at length in *TC*.
35 **one . . . make** one and the same husband
   and wife (*make* could be used of either sex)
38 **returned** went back (to France)
40 **tune** frame of mind
43 **sovereign** overwhelming

That stripped her from his benediction, turned her
To foreign casualties, gave her dear rights   45
To his dog-hearted daughters—these things sting
His mind so venomously that burning shame
Detains him from Cordelia.

[FIRST] GENTLEMAN   Alack, poor gentleman!

KENT

Of Albany's and Cornwall's powers you heard not?

[FIRST] GENTLEMAN 'Tis so; they are afoot.   50

KENT

Well, sir, I'll bring you to our master Lear,
And leave you to attend him. Some dear cause
Will in concealment wrap me up a while.
When I am known aright you shall not grieve
Lending me this acquaintance. I pray you go   55
Along with me.   *Exeunt*

Sc. 18 *Enter Queen Cordelia, a Doctor, and others*

CORDELIA

Alack, 'tis he! Why, he was met even now,
As mad as the racked sea, singing aloud,
Crowned with rank fumitor and furrow-weeds,

---

56 *Exeunt*] Q (Exit.)
    18.0.1 *a*] *not in* Q   2 racked] OXFORD; vent Q; vext F   3 fumitor] Q (femiter)

45 **foreign casualties** the vicissitudes of life overseas

52 **dear cause** important business. 'The real reason is Shakespeare's desire to keep the revelation of Kent's identity till the last scene' (Hunter).

18 This scene too takes place somewhere in or near Dover. As Sohmer observes, there is an 'abrupt shift' from 'wintry night' to 'high summer' (paragraph 13). This has sometimes been reflected in the staging, with ironical effect.

0.1 F adds '*with Drum* [i.e. drummer] *and Colours*', and replaces Q's '*and others*' with '*and Souldiours*', which may well have been used in the original staging to signal Cordelia's role as leader of the French army. Costume has sometimes signalled her changed circumstances (Bratton).

2 **racked** tormented (by winds). HalioQ and Weis accept F's 'vext', but 'Q is unlikely as an error for F' (*TC*), and '*ract* (= racked) presumes an easy misreading in Q, makes good sense, and is supported by one of the play's most sustained patterns of imagery (tortured bodies)' (*Division*, p. 458).

3–5 **Crowned . . . weeds** Possibly influenced by the Homily 'Of the Misery of all Mankind': 'We . . . bring forth but weeds, nettles, brambles, briers, cockle, and darnel' (Shaheen, pp. 615–16).

3 **rank fumitor** 'Rank' means 'Vigorous or luxuriant in growth' (*OED a.* 5), true of fumitory, a weed which 'often forms dense tufts, staying green and lush throughout the winter' (Rydén, p. 26).
furrow-weeds weeds that grow on the furrows of ploughed land

With burdocks, hemlock, nettles, cuckoo-flowers,
Darnel, and all the idle weeds that grow   5
In our sustaining corn. The centuries send forth.
Search every acre in the high-grown field,
And bring him to our eye.   [*Exit one or more*]
                         What can man's wisdom
In the restoring his bereavèd sense,
He that can help him   10
Take all my outward worth.
DOCTOR There is means, madam.
Our foster-nurse of nature is repose,
The which he lacks. That to provoke in him
Are many simples operative, whose power   15
Will close the eye of anguish.
CORDELIA   All blest secrets,
All you unpublished virtues of the earth,
Spring with my tears, be aidant and remediate

---

4 burdocks] HANMER; hor-docks Q; Hardokes F   6 The centuries] OXFORD; a centurie is Q; A
Centery F; Centuries BLAYNEY   send] F; sent Q   8 *Exit one or more*] *not in* QF   14 lacks.
That] Q2 (~, ~); ~ ˌ ~ Q1

4 **burdocks** The burdock is a common weed
which produces burrs. Hanmer's once-
popular emendation, accepted by HalioQ
and Foakes, is discussed in *TC*.
  hemlock A poisonous weed, used medicin-
ally as a sedative.
  cuckoo-flowers A name given to various
plants which flower in spring, when the
cuckoo is heard.
5 **Darnel** Used 'vaguely of any harmful
weed', but possibly specific here to wild
rye grass (*Lolium tenentum*), 'a noxious
plant, with narcotic powers, and hence
appropriate to the demented Lear'
(Rydén, p. 47).
  idle useless
6 **sustaining** life-sustaining (opposed to
'idle'); *OED*'s first instance of *sustaining*
as a participial adjective.
  The . . . forth send out the divisions of the
army (a *century* was made up of 100
men). Weis retains Q's 'a centurie is sent
forth', without comment, but HalioQ follows F's 'A Centery send', arguing that Q
'does not agree, as F does, with the im-
peratives of the next two lines'. Our reading, defended in *TC*, assumes that
'centurie is' results from a misreading of

'centurie' and that, as often, 'a' was substituted for 'the'. John Jowett suggests
(privately) 'A century is sent for', assuming that 'forth' was printed for 'for'. In
mid seventeenth century, 'century' is
recorded as a spelling of 'sentry' (*OED
sb.*[1]), but whereas a hundred may seem a
lot, one does not seem enough.
8 *Exit . . . more* Possibly, in view of 'Seek,
seek for him' at l. 19, no one leaves here.
8-9 **What . . . restoring** whatever human
knowledge can do to restore the sense
which has been driven out of him (often
repunctuated as a question)
10 **He that** let whoever
11 **outward worth** worldly wealth
15 **Are . . . operative** many medicines
(*simples*, medicines made from single
herbs, or the herbs themselves) are
efficacious
17 **unpublished** not divulged or disclosed
(*OED* 2, first recorded use), secret
  virtues (medicinal) powers
18 **with** i.e. germinated by
  aidant helpful
  remediate remedial (*OED*'s first use, suggesting it may be an error for 'remedial'
or 'remediant')

In the good man's distress!—Seek, seek for him,
Lest his ungoverned rage dissolve the life   20
That wants the means to lead it.
          Enter a Messenger
MESSENGER   News, madam.
    The British powers are marching hitherward.
CORDELIA
    'Tis known before; our preparation stands
    In expectation of them.—O dear father,
    It is thy business that I go about;   25
    Therefore great France
    My mourning and important tears hath pitied.
    No blown ambition doth our arms incite,
    But love, dear love, and our aged father's right.
    Soon may I hear and see him!   *Exeunt*   30

Sc. 19 *Enter Regan and Oswald, Gonoril's steward*
REGAN
    But are my brother's powers set forth?
OSWALD   Ay, madam.
REGAN
    Himself in person?
OSWALD   Madam, with much ado.
    Your sister is the better soldier.
REGAN
    Lord Edmund spake not with your lord at home?

---

21 *a*] *not in* Q   28 incite] Q2 (insite), F; in sight Q1   30 *Exeunt*] Q (*Exit.*)
  19.0.1 *Oswald, Gonoril's*] *not in* Q   1 OSWALD] Q ('*Stew.*' subs. *throughout the scene*)
4 Lord] F; Lady Q   home?] Q2; ~. Q1

20 **rage** madness
21 **wants . . . means** i.e. lacks the sanity
23 **preparation** task force
24–5 **O . . . about** The 'clear reference' (Shaheen, p. 616) to words spoken by Christ ('I must go about my father's business', Luke 2: 49) means that *father* may suggest God the Father as well as Lear.
26 **France** the King of France
27 **mourning** grieving, lamenting
   important importunate, urgent
28 **blown** inflated
19 This scene could be thought to take place at either Regan's or Gloucester's dwelling. Oswald has brought Regan a

reply to the letter she sent to Gonoril (16. 81–6) and also carries (but does not necessarily produce) letters from Gonoril to Edmund. Regan gives Oswald a letter or token at l. 33.
2 **with . . . ado** i.e. only after a lot of fuss and worrying
4 **lord** Weis keeps Q's 'lady', arguing that 'Oswald tells Regan a straight lie, because in [16. 18–28] he was present during Goneril's (*the lady*) declaration of "love" to Edmund and the launching of their conspiracy against Albany' and that 'F's change . . . produces a blander text . . . missing the strand of sexual innuendo

OSWALD No, madam.   5
REGAN
What might import my sister's letters to him?
OSWALD I know not, lady.
REGAN
Faith, he is posted hence on serious matter.
It was great ignorance, Gloucester's eyes being out,
To let him live. Where he arrives he moves   10
All hearts against us. Edmund, I think, is gone,
In pity of his misery, to dispatch
His 'nighted life, moreover to descry
The strength o'th' army.
OSWALD
I must needs after with my letters, madam.   15
REGAN
Our troop sets forth tomorrow. Stay with us.
The ways are dangerous.
OSWALD   I may not, madam.
My lady charged my duty in this business.
REGAN
Why should she write to Edmund? Might not you
Transport her purposes by word? Belike—   20
Something, I know not what. I'll love thee much:
Let me unseal the letter.
OSWALD   Madam, I'd rather—
REGAN
I know your lady does not love her husband.
I am sure of that, and at her late being here

11 Edmund] F; and now Q   15 after] OXFORD; after him Q; after him, Madam, F   letters,
madam.] BLAYNEY; letters ₍ QI; Letters. Q2, F   16 tomorrow. Stay] Q2, F (~, ~); ~ ₍ ~ QI

which runs throughout the play between
Goneril and her *trusty servant*'. HalioQ,
like us, regards Q's 'lady' as the mistaken
expansion of the abbreviation 'l'.

6 **import** signify
8 **is . . . hence** has ridden away
9 **ignorance** i.e. of the likely consequence
11 **Edmund** Weis accepts Q's 'and now' following Blayney in interpreting it as a con-
tinuation of l. 9. HalioQ, like us, accepts F.
13 **'nighted** Cited by *OED* ('nighted') as a
first usage meaning 'made dark or black

as night', but here treated as a shortened
form of 'benighted'.
descry discover
15 **after** Both HalioQ and Weis accept Q's
unmetrical 'after him'; we assume accidental interpolation.
madam Neither HalioQ nor Weis accepts
the addition.
18 **charged my duty** commanded my
obedience
20 **word** i.e. word of mouth
Belike probably
24 **late** recent

She gave strange oeillades and most speaking looks   25
To noble Edmund. I know you are of her bosom.

OSWALD I, madam?

REGAN

I speak in understanding, for I know't.
Therefore I do advise you take this note.
My lord is dead. Edmund and I have talked,   30
And more convenient is he for my hand
Than for your lady's. You may gather more.
If you do find him, pray you give him this,
And when your mistress hears thus much from you,
I pray desire her call her wisdom to her.   35
So, farewell.
If you do chance to hear of that blind traitor,
Preferment falls on him that cuts him off.

OSWALD

Would I could meet him, madam. I would show
What lady I do follow.

REGAN   Fare thee well.   40

Exeunt severally

Sc. 20 *Enter Edgar disguised as a peasant, with a staff,*
         guiding the blind Earl of Gloucester

GLOUCESTER

When shall we come to th' top of that same hill?

25 oeillades] Q (aliads)   27 I, madam?] F; Q (I Madam.)   40 *Exeunt severally*] Q (*Exit.*)
   20.0.1–2 *Enter . . . Gloucester*] OXFORD; *Enter Gloster and Edmund.* Q; *Enter Gloucester, and Edgar.* F   0.1 *with a staff*] OXFORD; *not in* QF

25 **oeillades** oglings (the word, originally French, had become naturalized in Shakespeare's time)

26 **of her bosom** in her confidence

29 **take this note** take note of this

31 **convenient** suitable

32 **gather more** i.e. make your own inferences. Weis punctuates 'gather; more', saying 'she is being curt here and is at pains to stress her superior claim to Edmund', but the cryptic quality suggested by the original pointing is in keeping with the rest of the speech.

33 **this** a token or a letter (though Edgar reads only one letter after going through Edmund's pockets at 20.248–62)

34 **thus much** what I have told you

40 **lady** F reads 'party'. Foakes objects to *lady* on the grounds that it is 'incongruous in relation to Oswald's steadfast loyalty to Gonoril shown earlier'; Weis defends Q on the grounds that 'Oswald may mean that although two ladies compete for his loyalty, they are both made of the same steely metal of which he approves.' It seems clear that Shakespeare originally wrote 'lady': Oswald may simply be saying that in this particular matter he supports Regan.

20 As planned, Edgar, wearing the Old Man's *best 'parel* and no longer speaking like Poor Tom (ll. 7–8), has led his father towards Dover. Their opening lines are spoken as they move forward. Edgar

EDGAR

You do climb up it now. Look how we labour.

GLOUCESTER

Methinks the ground is even.

EDGAR   Horrible steep.

Hark, do you hear the sea?

GLOUCESTER   No, truly.

EDGAR

Why, then your other senses grow imperfect   5

By your eyes' anguish.

GLOUCESTER   So may it be indeed.

Methinks thy voice is altered, and thou speak'st

With better phrase and matter than thou didst.

EDGAR

You're much deceived. In nothing am I changed

But in my garments.

GLOUCESTER   Methinks you're better spoken.   10

EDGAR

Come on, sir, here's the place. Stand still. How fearful

And dizzy 'tis to cast one's eyes so low!

The crows and choughs that wing the midway air

Show scarce so gross as beetles. Halfway down

Hangs one that gathers samphire, dreadful trade!   15

Methinks he seems no bigger than his head.

---

2 up it now] F; it vpnow Q   7 speak'st] Q (speakest)   11 here's] Q1 (her's), Q2

needs a staff for his fight with Oswald.
The action is imagined as taking place in
an open space; at l. 265 Edgar mentions
sands. But the unlocalized nature of the
Shakespearian stage is particularly important here in Edgar's deception of
Gloucester at ll. 11–41. Gloucester has a
purse (l. 28), as does Oswald (l. 238),
who also has letters (l. 240). Certain objects mentioned by Lear, such as the challenge (l. 134), may be real or imaginary.

1 **hill** Dover Cliff, to which he had said he
would go at 15.69–76.

2 **up it** Weis, but not HalioQ, follows Q's 'it
vpnow', idiomatically possible but unmetrical. 'In Brook's version, Edgar led
Gloucester with a long pole, suddenly
yanking it up at moments like this to con-

vey the impression, for Gloucester, of
climbing' (R. Warren, privately).

3 **Horrible** horribly, excessively

8 **phrase . . . matter** style and content.
Edgar now speaks verse.

13 **choughs** (pronounced 'chuffs') jackdaws,
or perhaps Cornish choughs, now rare
and restricted in geographical range to
western coasts of the British isles.
wing fly across; *OED*'s first use in this
sense.

14 **Show** appear
gross large

15 **samphire** A plant eaten in salads, and
often pickled, which grows on rocks and
cliffs. John Gerard, in his *Herbal* (1597,
p. 428), says that it 'groweth on the
rocky cliffs at Dover' and elsewhere.
dreadful frightening

The fishermen that walk upon the beach
Appear like mice, and yon tall anchoring barque
Diminished to her cock, her cock a buoy
Almost too small for sight. The murmuring surge   20
That on the unnumbered idle pebble chafes
Cannot be heard, it's so high. I'll look no more,
Let my brain turn and the deficient sight
Topple down headlong.
GLOUCESTER   Set me where you stand.

EDGAR

Give me your hand. You are now within a foot   25
Of th'extreme verge. For all beneath the moon
Would I not leap upright.

GLOUCESTER   Let go my hand.
Here, friend, 's another purse; in it a jewel
Well worth a poor man's taking. Fairies and gods
Prosper it with thee! Go thou farther off.   30
Bid me farewell, and let me hear thee going.

EDGAR

Now fare you well, good sir.
          He stands aside

GLOUCESTER   With all my heart.

EDGAR (*aside*)

Why I do trifle thus with his despair
Is done to cure it.

22 heard, . . . high.] OXFORD; heard, its so hie ͜ Q; heard; it's so high ͜ RIDLEY   24 stand.]
Q2; ~? Q1   32 *He . . . aside*] OXFORD, *after* ROWE (*Seems to go.*)

18 **anchoring** coming to, or lying at, an-
    chor; *OED*'s only use of the adjectival
    form in this sense.
    barque small sailing ship
19 **cock** small ship's boat, dinghy
20 **surge** swell of the sea
21 **unnumbered** uncounted (because un-
    countable)
    idle pebble barren heap or deposit of
    pebble
22 **heard, it's so high.** Ridley reads 'heard:
    it's so high ͜ ', a reasonable alternative in-
    terpretation (also substantively adopted
    in HalioQ) of Q's 'heard, its so hie ͜ '.
23–4 **deficient . . . headlong** An elliptical
    way of saying 'my sight, made faulty by
    my dizziness, causes me to fall headlong

down the cliff'.
25–6 **You . . . verge** It seems important that
    these words are *not* spoken close to the
    edge of the stage.
27 **upright** vertically upwards (*OED adv.* 2),
    because of the danger of landing even a
    fraction too far forward
28 **jewel** Used of any precious personal
    adornment.
29 **Fairies** Alluding to the superstition that
    'hidden treasure is guarded by fairies and
    that they make it multiply miraculously in
    the presence of the discoverer' (Kittredge).
33–4 **Why . . . it** These lines both remind
    the audience of Edgar's true identity and
    draw attention to the artifice of the
    action.

GLOUCESTER O you mighty gods,

> *He kneels*

This world I do renounce, and in your sights 35
Shake patiently my great affliction off!
If I could bear it longer, and not fall
To quarrel with your great opposeless wills,
My snuff and loathèd part of nature should
Burn itself out. If Edgar live, O bless him!— 40
Now, fellow, fare thee well.

EDGAR Gone, sir. Farewell.

> *Gloucester falls forward*

(*Aside*) And yet I know not how conceit may rob
The treasury of life, when life itself
Yields to the theft. Had he been where he thought,
By this had thought been past.—Alive or dead? 45
(*To Gloucester*) Ho you, sir; hear you, sir? Speak.
(*Aside*) Thus might he pass indeed. Yet he revives.
(*To Gloucester*) What are you, sir?

GLOUCESTER Away, and let me die.

EDGAR

Hadst thou been aught but goss'mer, feathers, air,
So many fathom down precipitating 50

---

39 snuff] Q2; snurff Q1 40 bless him!] F (~~:); blesse Q 41.1 *Gloucester . . . forward*] Q
('*He fals.*', *after* 'well.') 42 may] Q2, F; my Q1

37–8 **fall . . . with** descend to challenging
38 **opposeless** irresistible; *OED*'s first
   instance.
39 **My snuff** the last flickerings of life in me.
   Literally, the smouldering wick of a candle; the expression 'to go out like a candle
   in a snuff' was proverbial (Dent C49).
   loathèd . . . nature hated remnants of life
41 **Gone . . . Farewell** Edgar moves or modu-
   lates his voice so as to create the illusion
   that he is departing.
41.1 *Gloucester . . . forward* From Gloucester's perspective, this is a desperately serious action, but the fact that he has no
   distance to fall creates a potential absurdity which has been mitigated in some
   productions; 'Edmund Kean had his
   Edgar advance and catch Gloucester as
   he prepared to fall, and this became the
   accepted practice', but 'The usual twen-
   tieth-century practice has been to require
   Gloucester to make the jump' (Bratton),

so accepting and even stressing the dis-
crepancy between Gloucester's and the
audience's point of view.
42–4 **how . . . Yields** how imagination may
   steal life away, when (the owner of that)
   life himself submits. Probably *how* has
   the force of 'to what degree' (Schmidt 4),
   shading into 'whether' (i.e. the wish to
   commit suicide may have been enough to
   kill him).
45 **this** this moment
   Alive or dead? Edgar may speak these
   words either to himself (in his own voice)
   or to Gloucester (in his feigned voice).
46 **Ho . . . Speak** Edgar puts on a different
   voice.
50 **fathom** The singular form for the plural,
   as often.
   precipitating falling headlong (*OED*'s first
   instance of this obsolete sense); according
   to Muir (p. 236) the word occurs in
   Florio's *Montaigne*.

Thou hadst shivered like an egg. But thou dost breathe,
Hast heavy substance, bleed'st not, speak'st, art
          sound.
Ten masts a-length make not the altitude
Which thou hast perpendicularly fell.
Thy life's a miracle. Speak yet again.   55

GLOUCESTER But have I fallen, or no?

EDGAR

From the dread summit of this chalky bourn.
Look up a-height. The shrill-gorged lark so far
Cannot be seen or heard. Do but look up.

GLOUCESTER Alack, I have no eyes.   60
Is wretchedness deprived that benefit
To end itself by death? 'Twas yet some comfort
When misery could beguile the tyrant's rage
And frustrate his proud will.

EDGAR   Give me your arm.
Up. So, how now? Feel you your legs? You stand.   65

GLOUCESTER

Too well, too well.

EDGAR   This is above all strangeness.
Upon the crown of the cliff what thing was that
Which parted from you?

GLOUCESTER   A poor unfortunate beggar.

EDGAR

As I stood here below, methoughts his eyes

52 speak'st] Q (speakest)   53 a-length] OXFORD (*conj*. Stone); at each QF   57 summit] F (som-
net); sommons Q; somnets STONE *conj*.   59 up.] Q2; ~? Q1   64 arm.] Q2; ~? Q1   65 how
now?] OXFORD; how‸ Q; How is't? F   68 beggar] Q2, F; bagger Q1

51 **shivered** flown into pieces
53 **Ten . . . altitude** i.e. ten ship's masts laid
     end to end would not measure the height
     a-length length-wise (*OED*). The emend-
     ation assumes misreading in Q, followed
     by F. HalioQ, Weis and Foakes accept
     'at each' though Foakes, glossing 'end to
     end', admits that 'no parallel has been
     noticed for this phrase'.
54 **fell** fallen
57 **bourn** boundary (between land and sea),
     i.e. cliff
58 **a-height** aloft (*OED*'s first instance)
     shrill-gorged shrill-throated, shrill-voiced
     (larks sing high in the air)

63–4 **When . . . will** Gloucester appears to
     have in mind noble suicides such as the
     noble act by which Cleopatra avoids being
     led in triumph by Octavius Caesar
     (*Antony*, esp. 5.2.203–22, 280).
63 **beguile** cheat
65 **how now** HalioQ and Weis follow F's
     'How is't?', but 'There is no reason why
     "is't" should have been omitted here;
     "now", on the other hand, is a word fre-
     quently omitted' and 'The emendation
     produces better metre and sense' (*TC*).
69 **methoughts** it seemed to me (a 'curious
     form' by analogy with 'methinks' (*OED*,
     methinks, *v.*, headnote))

Were two full moons. A had a thousand noses,   70
Horns whelked and wavèd like the enridgèd sea.
It was some fiend. Therefore, thou happy father,
Think that the clearest gods, who made their honours
Of men's impossibilities, have preserved thee.

GLOUCESTER

I do remember now. Henceforth I'll bear   75
Affliction till it do cry out itself
'Enough, enough,' and die. That thing you speak of,
I took it for a man. Often would it say
'The fiend, the fiend!' He led me to that place.

EDGAR

Bear free and patient thoughts.

    Enter King Lear mad, ⌈crowned with weeds and
    flowers⌉

                       But who comes here?   80
The safer sense will ne'er accommodate
His master thus.

LEAR No, they cannot touch me for coining. I am the King
himself.

EDGAR O thou side-piercing sight!   85

---

79 'The fiend, the fiend!'] Q (The fiend the fiend,) 80 Bear] Q1 (Bare‸), F; Bare, Q2
Enter . . . flowers] THEOBALD ('*Enter Lear, drest madly with Flowers*'); *Enter Lear mad.* Q, *after
l. 82* 81 ne'er] Q (neare)

71 **whelked** twisted and ridged like a
  whelk's shell
  enridgèd thrown into ridges, ridged;
  OED's only example (F has 'enraged').
72 **fiend** Devils were supposed to tempt
  people to suicide, as Horatio warns
  Hamlet (*Hamlet* 1.4.50–5).
  father Often used respectfully to an old
  man.
73 **clearest** most illustrious (*OED*, *clear*, *a*. 5,
  last example)
73–4 **made . . . impossibilities** gained honour
  by doing things impossible to men. This appears to be influenced by Matthew
  19: 26: 'With men this is unpossible, but
  with God all things are possible', or Luke
  18: 27: 'The things which are unpossible
  with men are possible with God' (Shaheen,
  p. 616). HalioQ, following F, emends *made*
  to 'make', without comment, whereas
  Weis remarks that Q 'seems to refer to the
  gods' mythic deeds in the past, as related
  e.g. in Ovid's *Metamorphoses*'.

77 **thing** i.e. the disguised Edgar
80 **free** happy, untroubled
81–2 **The . . . thus** the saner (*OED*, *safe*, *a*. 4)
  intelligence will not equip (*OED*, *accommodate*, *v*. 11) its master in this way; a
  cryptic way of saying 'no sane man
  would get himself up like this'. Hulme
  (pp. 275–7), however, suggests that
  accommodate means 'to maintain itself
  when confronted by', and that the overall
  sense is 'Gloucester's newly-recovered
  and precarious mental balance—his resolution to endure affliction until death—
  will never be able to maintain itself
  against the shock and horror of encoun-
  tering Lear as he now is'.
83 **touch** censure
  coining making coins (a royal preroga-
  tive)
85 **side-piercing** heart-rending (inevitably
  recalling to a Christian audience the
  piercing of Christ's side by a soldier when
  on the cross; John 19: 34)

LEAR Nature is above art in that respect. There's your
press-money. That fellow handles his bow like a crow-
keeper. Draw me a clothier's yard. Look, look, a mouse!
Peace, peace, this toasted cheese will do it. There's my
gauntlet. I'll prove it on a giant. Bring up the brown   90
bills. O, well flown, bird, in the air. Ha! Give the word.

EDGAR Sweet marjoram.

LEAR Pass.

GLOUCESTER I know that voice.

LEAR Ha, Gonoril! Ha, Regan! They flattered me like a dog,   95
and told me I had white hairs in my beard ere the black
ones were there. To say 'ay' and 'no' to everything I said
'ay' and 'no' to was no good divinity. When the rain

---

91 Ha!] Q (hagh)   word.] Q2; ~? QI   97 said⌃] BLAYNEY; ~, QI; ~: Q2, F   97, 101 to] QI
(toe), Q2 (too)

86 **Nature . . . respect** The relation between
nature and art was a stock theme of the
period, often drawn on by Shakespeare.
Lear's mind is wandering: here, as elsewhere in the scene, it is not possible to define clearly what he means; shafts of
acute perception mingle with nonsense.

87 **press-money** payment given in advance,
especially to a sailor or soldier on enlist-
ment. Presumably Lear hands out real or
imaginary coins.

87–8 **crow-keeper** Person employed to
guard crops against crows, who 'would
squat down clumsily' (Henn, p. 80).

88 **Draw . . . yard** i.e. draw the bow back as
far as it will go; a cloth-yard was the rod
for measuring cloth, which became established at 36 inches; 'only an archer of
exceptional physique would be able to
draw an arrow of a "clothier's yard"'
(Henn, pp. 80–1). It is applied to the
arrow of the long bow in the old ballad of
Chevy Chase: 'An arrow that a cloth
yard was long | To th' hard steel halèd
he' (*OED, cloth-yard*; modernized from
Percy's *Reliques*, i. 31).

89 **do it** Presumably lure the (imaginary?)
mouse.

90 **gauntlet** an armed glove; to throw one
down is to offer a challenge.
prove . . . giant make good my claim even
against a giant (let alone a mouse?)

90–1 **brown bills** (soldiers carrying)
'weapons somewhat shorter than the
pike; its head being a hooked blade with
projecting spikes of various patterns and

painted to prevent rust . . . We may suppose that Lear imagines a special small
squad of the "brown bills"; they would
require more training of rustic recruits
than the relatively simple pike, for their
drill motions were more complicated'
(Henn, p. 81).

91 **O . . . air** Imagining a hawk swooping on
its prey, Lear utters 'applause' for its
'brilliant stoop' (Henn, p. 81).
word password

92 **marjoram** It may be significant that,
according to John Gerard in his *Herbal* of
1597, the herb was 'a remedy against
cold diseases of the brain and head'
(p. 540, cited by Foakes).

95 **like a dog** i.e. as if they were dogs; Shakespeare often associates dogs with flattery
(Spurgeon, p. 195).

96–7 **I had . . . there** i.e. I was wise before I
even began to grow a beard

97–8 **To . . . divinity** to agree with everything I said was not wise. Perhaps influenced by 2 Corinthians 1: 18–19: 'Our
word toward you was not yea and nay,
for . . . Jesus Christ . . . was not yea and
nay, but in him it was yea', or e.g.
Matthew 5: 37: 'Let your communication be "Yea, yea, nay, nay", for what-
soever is more than these cometh of evil'
(Shaheen, p. 617).

98 **divinity** theology

98–101 **When . . . out** Lear recognizes that
suffering has brought insight, seeing
more clearly in his madness than when
sane, as Gloucester does in his blindness.

came to wet me once, and the wind to make me chatter,
when the thunder would not peace at my bidding, there I   100
found them, there I smelt them out. Go to, they are not
men of their words. They told me I was everything; 'tis a
lie, I am not ague-proof.
GLOUCESTER
  The trick of that voice I do well remember.
  Is't not the King?
LEAR   Ay, every inch a king.   105
    ⌈*Gloucester kneels*⌉
  When I do stare, see how the subject quakes!
  I pardon that man's life. What was thy cause?
  Adultery? Thou shalt not die for adultery.
  No, the wren goes to't, and the small gilded fly
  Does lecher in my sight.   110
  Let copulation thrive, for Gloucester's bastard son
  Was kinder to his father than my daughters
  Got 'tween the lawful sheets. To't, luxury, pell-mell,
  For I lack soldiers. Behold yon simp'ring dame,
  Whose face between her forks presageth snow,   115
  That minces virtue, and does shake the head
  To hear of pleasure's name:
  The fitchew nor the soilèd horse goes to't

---

103 ague-proof] F; argue-proofe Q   105 every] Q2, F; euer Q1   105.1 *Gloucester kneels*]
OXFORD; *not in* Q   108 die] Q; dye: dye F   110 Does] F (Do's); doe Q   116 does] F (do's);
do Q   117 To] F; *not in* Q   118 The] F; to Q

99 **me** i.e. my teeth
100 **peace** be silent
103 **ague-proof** immune to fever or shivering
  (*ague* is pronounced 'eh-gyoo')
104 **trick** distinctive tone
105 **every . . . king** The expression 'He is a
  man, every inch of him' was proverbial
  (Dent M161).
107 **cause** case you had to defend
108 **Adultery . . . adultery** Shaheen (p. 617)
  refers to several biblical injunctions
  against adultery (which Lear reverses).
109 **goes to't** copulates (Williams, *Glossary*)
  (in spite of being one of the smallest of
  birds)
  gilded having a gold-coloured sheen (like
  the bluebottle)
110 **lecher** fornicate
113 **Got** begotten
  luxury lust, lechery

pell-mell promiscuously. Q (probably following the manuscript) prints in italics,
suggesting that the expression, deriving
from French and first recorded by *OED* in
1579, was still not fully anglicized.
114 **lack soldiers** i.e. need more subjects to
serve in my army
115 **face . . . snow** facial expression predicts
snow (chastity, frigidity) between her
thighs
  forks legs, thighs (*OED sb.* 12b, first instance of this sense)
116 **minces virtue** feigns virtue by her
affected gait (*minces*, 'perform[s] or
enact[s] mincingly', *OED v.* 6b)
117 **pleasure's name** the very name of
(sexual) pleasure
118 **fitchew** polecat, used for a prostitute
(Williams, *Glossary*)
  soilèd 'fed with fresh-cut green fodder'

With a more riotous appetite. Down from the waist
They're centaurs, though women all above.   120
But to the girdle do the gods inherit;
Beneath is all the fiend's. There's hell, there's
     darkness,
There's the sulphury pit, burning, scalding,
Stench, consummation. Fie, fie, fie; pah, pah!
Give me an ounce of civet, good apothecary,   125
To sweeten my imagination.
There's money for thee.

GLOUCESTER   O, let me kiss that hand!

LEAR   Here, wipe it first; it smells of mortality.

GLOUCESTER

O ruined piece of nature! This great world
Should so wear out to naught. Do you know me?   130

LEAR   I remember thy eyes well enough. Dost thou squiny
on me?
No, do thy worst, blind Cupid, I'll not love.
Read thou that challenge. Mark the penning of't.

GLOUCESTER

Were all the letters suns, I could not see one.   135

---

122 fiend's] Q (fiends)   130 Should] Q (should); Shall F   134 of't] Q (oft)

(*OED*, first instance) to encourage breeding, hence 'randy'

118 **horse** Used for a woman (Williams, *Glossary*).

120 **centaurs** In mythology, monsters, man above and beast below, notorious for lechery.

121 **But . . . girdle** only as far as the waist
inherit have as their portion

122 **hell** Used of the vagina (Williams, *Glossary*), as in Sonnets 129 and 144.

123 **sulphury** sulphurous

124 **consummation** destruction, death

125 **civet** A substance obtained from the anal glands of the muskcat used in perfumery (see 11.95), and also to alleviate melancholy (Hoeniger, p. 257); hence perfume, but with an ironic tinge since civet is 'the very uncleanly flux of a cat' (*As You Like It* 3.2.66).

125 **apothecary** druggist (from whom perfume could be bought)

128 **Here, wipe** Q prints without punctuation; conceivably Lear offers his hand on *Here*, then withdraws it. He may offer Gloucester a piece of cloth, perhaps part of what he is wearing.

129 **piece** could mean 'masterpiece', particularly in parallel with *great world*, i.e. universe.

130 **Should** Oxford adopts F's 'Shall', but both HalioQ and Weis retain Q's 'should'.

131 **squiny** (the rare word used also at 11.106)

133 **Cupid** The god of love, traditionally represented as blind, and according to Benedick (*Much Ado*, 1.1.236–7) portrayed in brothel signs.

134 **Read . . . challenge** Lear hands Gloucester a real or imaginary paper.
penning style (Schmidt), or penmanship

EDGAR (*aside*)
  I would not take this from report; it is,
  And my heart breaks at it.

LEAR (*to Gloucester*) Read.

GLOUCESTER What—with the case of eyes?

LEAR O ho, are you there with me? No eyes in your head,   140
  nor no money in your purse? Your eyes are in a heavy
  case, your purse in a light; yet you see how this world
  goes.

GLOUCESTER I see it feelingly.

LEAR What, art mad? A man may see how the world goes   145
  with no eyes; look with thy ears. See how yon justice
  rails upon yon simple thief. Hark in thy ear: handy-
  dandy, which is the thief, which is the justice? Thou hast
  seen a farmer's dog bark at a beggar?

GLOUCESTER Ay, sir.   150

LEAR An the creature run from the cur, there thou mightst
  behold the great image of authority. A dog's obeyed in
  office.
  Thou rascal beadle, hold thy bloody hand.
  Why dost thou lash that whore? Strip thine own back.   155
  Thy blood as hotly lusts to use her in that kind

---

139 What—with] Q (~!~)   eyes?] Q (~ˏ)   141 purse?] Q2; ~, Q1   151 An] Q (And)   cur,]
Q1; ~? Q2; ~: F   152 dog's obeyed] F (Dogg'sˏ obey'd); dogge, so bade Q   156 Thy blood
as] OXFORD; thy bloud Q; thou F

---

136 **take . . . report** believe this if it were
  reported to me
139 **case of eyes** eyesockets only
140 **are . . . me?** Open to interpretation: 'so
  that's your excuse?' (Foakes); 'is that
  the point you are making?' (Hunter),
  perhaps even 'a match for me'.
141–2 **heavy case** bad way
144 **feelingly** 'by feeling or touch; with
  strong emotion, passionately' (Foakes)
147 **simple** humble, wretched (the word had
  a wide range of meanings)
147–8 **handy-dandy** 'choose which you
  please'; from a children's guessing game
  in which an object is hidden in one of two
  closed hands.
151 **An . . . there** if the beggar runs away
  from the dog. Most editors follow
  Theobald in interpreting 'And . . . cur?

There' (so HalioQ and Weis).
151 **creature** human being (but often used of
  an animal)
152 **A dog** i.e. even a dog
154 **beadle** parish constable, who had the
  duty of whipping offenders
  hold restrain
  bloody bloodstained (from the lashing)
156 **Thy blood as** HalioQ and Weis retain Q's
  unmetrical 'Thy bloud' without comment. '*As*' is often omitted in Shakespeare texts; 'The resulting line is a
  regular hexameter, of which Q *Lear* contains dozens of examples' (*TC*).
  blood 'the fleshly nature of man' (*OED* 6,
  with only two citations, both from
  Shakespeare)
  kind manner

For which thou whip'st her. The usurer hangs the
    cozener.
Through tattered rags small vices do appear;
Robes and furred gowns hides all. Get thee glass eyes,
And, like a scurvy politician, seem   160
To see the things thou dost not. No tears, now.
Pull off my boots. Harder, harder! So.

EDGAR (*aside*)

O, matter and impertinency mixed—
Reason in madness!

LEAR

If thou wilt weep my fortune, take my eyes.   165
I know thee well enough: thy name is Gloucester.
Thou must be patient. We came crying hither.
Thou know'st the first time that we smell the air
We wail and cry. I will preach to thee. Mark me.

GLOUCESTER   Alack, alack, the day!   170

LEAR [*removing his crown of weeds*]

When we are born, we cry that we are come
To this great stage of fools. This' a good block.

158 tattered] Q (tottered)   161 No tears, now] OXFORD (*conj*. Blayney); no now Q; Now, now,
now, now. F   164 madness!] Q (~.)   168 know'st] Q (knowest)   171 *removing . . . weeds*]
OXFORD; *not in* Q   172 This'] Q (this͜)

157 **usurer . . . cozener** moneylender condemns the trickster. An aphoristic way of
saying 'one crook judges another', and
related to the proverb 'The great thieves
hang the little ones' (Dent T119). Usury
had been illegal until 1571, and continued to meet disapproval, as is apparent
in *Merchant*.

159 **Robes . . . gowns** As worn by e.g.
judges and apparently usurers (*Measure*
3.1.275–7: 'of two usuries, the merriest
was put down, and the worser allowed by
order of law, a furred gown to keep him
warm').
    glass eyes spectacles (artificial eyes are of
later invention)

160 **scurvy politician** worthless, contemptible intriguer (perhaps recalling Edmund's pretence of reading a letter from
Edgar, 2.25ff., when Gloucester had
said 'if it be nothing I shall not need
spectacles')

161 **No . . . now** HalioQ and Weis follow Q,
printing 'No; now,' and 'No. [*Sits*]

Now,' respectively. This produces a metrically defective line; we, following
Blayney, suspect omission; the case for
no tears is argued in *TC*.

163 **matter and impertinency** sense and
nonsense (*OED*'s first instance of *impertinency* (and predating 'impertinence'))

165 **weep** beweep, shed tears over

166 **I . . . enough** Titus Andronicus, sus-
pected of madness, utters the same words
(*Titus* 5.2.21).

167–9 **We . . . cry** Varying the proverbial
'We weeping come into the world and
weeping hence we go' (Dent W889), itself
biblical in origin (Wisdom 7: 3).

171 Garrick took off his headgear on the
grounds that Lear would not preach with
his hat on (Rosenberg, p. 279).

172 **stage** The image of the world as a stage
was commonplace (Dent W882).
    block Properly a mould for a hat, here
apparently used either for Lear's crown
of weeds or for a real or imaginary hat
on Gloucester's or Edgar's head—

239

It were a delicate stratagem to shoe
A troop of horse with fell; and when I have stole upon
These son-in-laws, then kill, kill, kill, kill, kill, kill!   175
    Enter three Gentlemen

[FIRST] GENTLEMAN

O, here he is. Lay hands upon him, sirs.
(*To Lear*) Your most dear—

LEAR

No rescue? What, a prisoner? I am e'en
The natural fool of fortune. Use me well.
You shall have ransom. Let me have a surgeon;   180
I am cut to the brains.

[FIRST] GENTLEMAN You shall have anything.

LEAR No seconds? All myself?
Why, this would make a man a man of salt,
To use his eyes for garden water-pots,   185
Ay, and laying autumn's dust.

[FIRST] GENTLEMAN   Good sir—

LEAR

I will die bravely, like a bridegroom.
What, I will be jovial. Come, come,

---

173 shoe] F; shoot Q   174 fell] Q; felt F   176, 182, 186, 190, 193, 198, 200, 204, 206 [FIRST]
GENTLEMAN] OXFORD; *Gent.* QF (*see* 8.0.1–2 *n.*)   177 dear—] Q (~); deere Daughter— F
178 rescue?] Q (~,)   prisoner?] Q2; ~, Q1   183 seconds?] Q (~,)   myself?] Q (~,)   184 a
man a man] F; a man Q   186 [FIRST] GENTLEMAN Good sir—] Q2 (*Gent.*); *not in* Q1
188 What, I] Q2; ~? ~ Q1

though 'The block could also be a mount-
ing-block, by association with horses, or
simply an imaginary tree-stump'
(Foakes).

173 **delicate stratagem** ingenious trick
174 **fell** animal skin, hide, as at 24.24. Oxford and HalioQ adopt F's 'felt', which
was moulded on *blocks* in making hats
and could be thought of as muffling the
sound of horses' hooves in a surprise
attack, but Q (retained by Weis) makes
good sense.
177 **dear—** F adds 'daughter', possibly accidentally omitted in Q. The Gentlemen
restrain Lear.
179 **natural . . . fortune** born to be the dupe
of fortune (like Romeo: 'O, I am fortune's
fool!', *Romeo* 3.1.136)
183 **seconds** supporters (as in a duel)

184 **make . . . salt** turn a man into a man of
tears. Weis retains Q's 'make a man of
salt'.
185 **use . . . for** i.e. to provide the water to fill
water-pots Earthenware vessels with per-
forated bases used to water plants and to
lay dust.
186 **laying** causing (the dust) to settle
Good sir— The case for adding these
words from Q2 is made in *Division*,
pp. 363–4.
187 **bravely** could mean 'handsomely', 'in fine
clothes' as well as 'courageously'; in this
context, *die* may acquire the sense of 'reach
sexual climax' (Williams, *Glossary*).
188 **jovial** majestic (*OED* 1, first recorded in
this sense 1604), merry (*OED* 6), and perhaps, in the context of *die* and *bridegroom*, glancing at Jove's many sexual
conquests.

I am a king, my masters, know you that?

[FIRST] GENTLEMAN

  You are a royal one, and we obey you.   190

LEAR Then there's life in't. Nay, an you get it, you shall
  get it with running.

                Exit running, pursued by two Gentlemen

[FIRST] GENTLEMAN

  A sight most pitiful in the meanest wretch,

  Past speaking in a king. Thou hast one daughter

  Who redeems nature from the general curse   195

  Which twain hath brought her to.

EDGAR Hail, gentle sir.

[FIRST] GENTLEMAN Sir, speed you. What's your will?

EDGAR

  Do you hear aught of a battle toward?

[FIRST] GENTLEMAN

  Most sure and vulgar, everyone hears that   200

  That can distinguish sense.

EDGAR But, by your favour,

  How near's the other army?

[FIRST] GENTLEMAN

  Near and on speedy foot, the main; descriers

  Stands on the hourly thoughts.

EDGAR   I thank you, sir. That's all.   205

---

189 that?] Q2; ~. Q1   192.1 *Exit . . . Gentlemen*] CAPELL (*subs.*); *Exit King running.* Q
194 speaking] OXFORD; speaking of QF   199 aught] Q; ought (Sir) F   200 hears] Q (here's)
204 speedy foot] F; speed fort Q1; speed for't Q2   204 foot, the main; descriers] OXFORD;
fort˳ the maine˳ descryes, Q1; for't, the maine˳ descries, Q2; foot: the maine˳ descry˳ F
205 Stands] F; Standst Q

190 **You . . . you** Their deference may be the
  cue for them to bow or kneel, dropping
  their guard in a way that makes it easier
  for Lear to escape.
191 **there's . . . in't** i.e. I needn't die yet!
  (proverbial: Dent L265)
193 **meanest** humblest
194 **speaking** speaking of (Q, F), describing
  (Schmidt 6); emended for the sake of the
  metre. HalioQ and Weis retain QF 'speaking of'.
195–6 **general . . . to** (a) general curse which
  two individuals—Gonoril and Regan—
  have brought upon her; (b) universal
  curse (of original sin) which Adam and

  Eve brought upon mankind
197 **gentle** noble
198 **speed you** (God) prosper you
199 **toward** in the offing
200 **vulgar** common knowledge
203 **other army** British forces
204–5 **Near . . . thoughts** 'the main part
  (of their army) is nearby and rapidly
  approaching; (their) scouts and spies
  already demand our hourly attention'
  (*TC*). HalioQ follows F, Weis adopts
  Q's 'speed', Q2's 'for't', Q's 'main descries' and F's 'stands' in this textually
  garbled passage, discussed at length in
  TC.

[FIRST] GENTLEMAN

> Though that the Queen on special cause is here,
> Her army is moved on.

EDGAR　　　　　　　　　　　I thank you, sir.

Exit Gentleman

GLOUCESTER

> You ever gentle gods, take my breath from me.
> Let not my worser spirit tempt me again
> To die before you please.　　　　　　　　　　　　210

EDGAR　Well pray you, father.

GLOUCESTER　Now, good sir, what are you?

EDGAR

> A most poor man, made lame by fortune's blows,
> Who by the art of known and feeling sorrows
> Am pregnant to good pity. Give me your hand,　　　215
> I'll lead you to some biding.

GLOUCESTER [*rising*]　　　　　　Hearty thanks.

> The bounty and the benison of heaven
> To send thee boot to boot.

Enter Oswald the steward

OSWALD　　　　　　　A proclaimed prize! Most happy!

> That eyeless head of thine was first framed flesh
> To raise my fortunes. Thou most unhappy traitor,　　　220
> Briefly thyself remember. The sword is out
> That must destroy thee.

---

207 *Exit Gentleman*] Q (*Exit.*)　　211 Well pray] Q2, F; ~, ~ Q1　　216 *rising*] OXFORD; *not in* Q
217 bounty] Qb, Q2, F; bornet Qa　　the benison] Qb, Q2, F; beniz Qa　　218 send thee ͵]
BLAYNEY; saue thee. Qa; *not in* Qb, Q2, F　　boot to boot] Qb, Q2; *not in* Qa; boot, and boot F
Oswald the] *not in* Q　　OSWALD] Q ('*Stew.*' *throughout the scene*)　　219 first] Qb, Q2, F; *not in* Qa

206 **on . . . cause** for a special purpose, i.e.
　to succour Lear
209 **worser spirit** evil angel (as in Sonnet
　144: 'Two loves I have, of comfort and
　despair, | Which like two spirits do sug-
　gest me still. | The better angel is a man
　right fair, | The worser spirit a woman
　coloured ill.')
211 **father** old man (as at l. 72)
214–15 **art . . . pregnant** skill acquired by ex-
　periencing and suffering sorrows am re-
　ceptive (*OED, pregnant, a.*² 3d, 'chiefly in
　Shaks.').
216 **biding** habitation

217–18 **The . . . to boot** (I call upon) the
　generosity and the blessing (*benison*)
　of heaven to send you reward, in
　addition (to my thanks). Blayney (*Texts*,
　pp. 250–2) argues the emendation (not
　adopted by HalioQ, Weis) at length.
218 *Oswald* He wears a sword (l. 221).
　proclaimed prize outlaw for whose cap-
　ture a reward is offered (as it has been at
　19.37–8)
　happy opportune
219 **framed flesh** created
221 **Briefly . . . remember** 'say thy last
　prayer, and make it short' (Hunter)

GLOUCESTER   Now let thy friendly hand
    Put strength enough to't.
OSWALD (*to Edgar*)   Wherefore, bold peasant,
    Durst thou support a published traitor? Hence,
    Lest the infection of his fortune take   225
    Like hold on thee. Let go his arm.
EDGAR 'Chill not let go, sir, without 'cagion.
OSWALD Let go, slave, or thou diest.
EDGAR Good gentleman, go your gate. Let poor volk pass.
    An 'chud have been swaggered out of my life, it would   230
    not have been so long by a vortnight. Nay, come not
    near the old man. Keep out, 'che vor' ye, or I'll try
    whether your costard or my baton be the harder; I'll be
    plain with you.
OSWALD Out, dunghill!   235
       They fight

---

226 arm.] Q2; ~? Q1   231 vortnight] Qb, Q2, F; fortnight Qa   233 costard] Qb, Q2, F;
coster Qa   baton] BLAYNEY (*conj.* Furnivall); bat-|tero Qa; bat Qb, Q2; Ballow F

224 **published** proclaimed; *OED*'s first in-
    stance. 'Ironically, of course, Edgar is al-
    ready himself *proclaimed* on Gloucester's
    orders' (Weis).
227–37 **'Chill . . . foins** Edgar assumes the
    persona of a West Country yokel; Kit-
    tredge lists numerous plays with similar
    spellings indicative of dialectal pronunci-
    ation.
227 **'cagion** occasion, reason
229 **go . . . gate** be on your way
    volk people
230 **An . . . life** if I could have been killed by
    blustering talk
230–1 **it . . . vortnight** it (my life) would have
    been shortened by a fortnight (Halio, ap-
    proved by Foakes, interprets 'I would not
    have lasted a fortnight')
232 **'che vor'** I warn you (Johnson);
    Kökeritz ('Elizabethan *che vore ye*,
    "I warrant you"', *MLN* 57 (1942),
    98–102) showed that elsewhere it means
    'I warrant you', and *OED*, *warrant*, *v.* 10,
    gives one instance from 1631 of the
    meaning 'command'. Even the more
    usual sense, 'guarantee', could be justi-
    fied as an elliptical way of saying 'I guar-
    antee that you had better keep out'.
233 **costard** Literally, a large kind of apple;

often used derisively or jocularly of the
head.
233 **baton** club, cudgel. HalioQ adopts the
    emendation; Weis follows Qb while ad-
    mitting that it may be 'a mere guess'. The
    club, or staff, was a traditional English
    weapon; using it, Edgar 'becomes a
    "popular champion . . . pitting his
    English techniques against the aristo-
    cratic rapier and the Italian technique
    of Oswald"' (Edelman, p. 159, citing
    A. L. Soens, 'Cudgels and rapiers: the
    staging of the Edgar–Oswald fight in
    Lear', *S.St.* 5 (1969), pp. 149–58. This
    article is informative about fencing tech-
    niques.)
235.1 **They fight** Presumably Edgar fights
    with his staff, Oswald with his sword or
    rapier and dagger. George Silver, in his
    Paradoxes of Defence (1599; Shakespeare
    Association Facsimiles 6, 1933, p. 38),
    notes that in such a fight 'the staff-man
    never striketh but at the head, and
    thrusteth presently under at the body;
    and if a blow be first made, a thrust fol-
    loweth'; the aim that is, is to cause the
    opponent to protect his head and then
    swiftly to attack his body before he can
    bring his arms down.

EDGAR   'Chill pick your teeth, sir. Come, no matter for your
foins.

⌈*Edgar knocks him down*⌉

OSWALD

Slave, thou hast slain me. Villain, take my purse.
If ever thou wilt thrive, bury my body,
And give the letters which thou find'st about me   240
To Edmund, Earl of Gloucester. Seek him out
Upon the British party. O untimely death! Death!

He dies

EDGAR

I know thee well—a serviceable villain,
As duteous to the vices of thy mistress
As badness would desire.   245

GLOUCESTER What, is he dead?

EDGAR Sit you down, father. Rest you.

Gloucester sits

Let's see his pockets. These letters that he speaks of
May be my friends. He's dead; I am only sorrow
He had no other deathsman. Let us see.   250
Leave, gentle wax; and manners, blame us not.
To know our enemies' minds we'd rip their hearts;
Their papers is more lawful.

He reads a letter

'Let your reciprocal vows be remembered. You have
many opportunities to cut him off. If your will want not,   255
time and place will be fruitfully offered. There is nothing

237.1 *Edgar . . . down*] ROWE; *not in* Q   247.1 *Gloucester sits*] CAPELL (*seating him at a distance*);
not in Q   249 sorrow] Q1; sorry Q2, F   253.1 *He reads*] *not in* Q

236 **'Chill . . . teeth** i.e. I'll thrash you; Dent
   (T424.1) lists as a proverbial threat.
237 **foins** thrusts with your sword
243 **serviceable** diligent
248 **letters** The plural form could be used
   with singular meaning, as also at 5.1–2.
249 **sorrow** sorry. The idiom (inadequately
   treated in *OED*) occurs in *Cymbeline*
   (5.6.298), Webster's *The White Devil*
   (5.1.45), etc.
250 **deathsman** executioner
251 **Leave, gentle wax** by your leave, wax
   seal, permit me to tear you—'gentle' per-

haps because 'sealed with a noble crest or
coat of arms' (Weis). Malvolio says 'By
your leave, wax' (Twelfth Night,
2.5.90–1).
252 **rip** could mean 'open up', 'lay bare'
   (*OED v.*² 4a).
254 **vows** Exchanged at 16.19–25.
255 **him** Albany
   will want not intention, desire (for me) be
   not lacking
256–7 **There . . . conqueror** nothing will
   have been accomplished if Albany comes
   back as a winner (or at all)

done if he return the conqueror; then am I the prisoner,
and his bed my jail, from the loathed warmth whereof,
deliver me, and supply the place for your labour.
    Your—wife, so I would say—your affectionate   260
      servant, and for you her own for venture,
                        Gonoril.'

O indistinguished space of woman's wit—
A plot upon her virtuous husband's life,
And the exchange my brother!—Here in the sands   265
Thee I'll rake up, the post unsanctified
Of murderous lechers, and in the mature time
With this ungracious paper strike the sight
Of the death-practised Duke. For him 'tis well
That of thy death and business I can tell.   270
                    [Exit with the body]

GLOUCESTER

The King is mad. How stiff is my vile sense,
That I stand up and have ingenious feeling
Of my huge sorrows! Better I were distraught;
So should my thoughts be fencèd from my griefs,
And woes by wrong imaginations lose   275
The knowledge of themselves.
    A drum afar off. [Enter Edgar]

---

257 conqueror;] POPE (*subs.*); ~, Q   262 venture] RIDLEY; *Venter* Q1; *not in* Q2, F
265 brother!—Here] Q2 (*subs.*); ~ ~ Q1   270.1 *Exit . . . body*] CAPELL (*subs.*); *not in* Q
273 distraught] Q (distract)   276 *Enter Edgar*] CAPELL (*subs.*); *not in* Q

259 **for . . . labour** in return for your trouble; for your amorous work
261 **and . . . venture** Not in Q2 or F, and often omitted as inexplicable; perhaps 'and for you (to be) her own whatever the risk (or venture)' (Foakes, admitting that 'the repeated "for" is confusing'). R. Proudfoot (in Foakes) suggests emending to 'for you her own to venture', meaning 'ready to take responsibility for herself in the venture of love for you'. Q italicizes *Venter* as if it were a proper (or foreign) noun.
263 **indistinguished** (*OED*'s first instance); 'implies extent beyond the range of sight' (Kittredge), i.e. unfathomable, imponderable.
    space . . . wit depths of female cunning

265 **Here** i.e. hereby, near here
    sands Perhaps for his father's sake Edgar continues to pretend that they are on a beach; 'or Shakespeare forgot' (Muir).
266 **rake up** bury
    post messenger
267 **in . . . time** when the time is ripe
268 **ungracious** disgraceful
269 **death-practised** whose death has been plotted
271 **stiff** unyielding, stubborn
    vile sense 'Gloucester calls his senses vile because they still allow him to be fully conscious of his sorrows, and do not give him the relief of insanity' (Muir).
272 **ingenious** intelligent, sensitive
274 **fencèd** kept apart, protected
275 **wrong imaginations** false delusions

EDGAR   Give me your hand.

Far off methinks I hear the beaten drum.

Come, father, I'll bestow you with a friend.

Exit Edgar guiding Gloucester

Sc. 21 *[Soft music.] Enter Queen Cordelia, and the Earl of*
Kent, disguised

CORDELIA O thou good Kent,

How shall I live and work to match thy goodness?

My life will be too short, and every measure fail me.

KENT

To be acknowledged, madam, is o'erpaid.

All my reports go with the modest truth,   5

Nor more, nor clipped, but so.

CORDELIA   Be better suited.

These weeds are memories of those worser hours.

I prithee put them off.

KENT   Pardon me, dear madam.

Yet to be known shortens my made intent.

278.1 *Exit . . . Gloucester*] CAPELL (*subs.*); *Exit.* Q

21.0.1 *Soft music*] DYCE (*conj.* Capell); *not in* Q   0.1–2 *and . . . disguised*] BLAYNEY; *Kent and Doctor* Q; *Kent, Gentleman* Fa; *Kent, and Gentleman* Fb; *Kent, Doctor, and Gentleman* CRAIG

---

278 **bestow** lodge

21 This scene derives from *Leir*, ll. 2297–2355, though the tone is very different (Introduction, p. 00). The action is essentially unlocalized. A chair or couch is needed for Lear's appearance.

0.1 **Soft music** *Louder the music there!* (l. 23) implies that it has already sounded; HalioQ also places the direction here, Weis before l. 23.

0.1–2 **Enter . . . disguised** It would be awkward for the Doctor to stand silently by during the opening dialogue; 'Q's entrance direction thus looks like an authorial anticipation of the format of a scene, rather than a precise instruction for the character to enter now' (*TC*). HalioQ rather vaguely instructs '*and after them, a* [GENTLEMAN] *and* DOCTOR', partly because 'the dialogue between Kent and the Gentleman at the end of the scene suggests that the Gentleman does not hear Cordelia identify Kent at the start of the scene but follows after them with the Doctor'. Weis adopts our arrangement, suggesting (somewhat novelistically) that the Gentleman is the same one 'who liaised between Kent and Cordelia, and who has now become a confidant of the royal pair to the extent that he is allowed to witness Cordelia's pitiful encounter with Lear'.

3 **My life** i.e. my entire life
every . . . me all I can do will be inadequate (*measure* here seems to mean 'plan or course of action' (*OED sb.* 21, not recorded before 1698)

5–6 **All . . . so** all my reports (of Lear) accord with the unexaggerated truth, neither overstated nor diminished, but accurate ('go' could be subjunctive, i.e. 'May all . . .')

6 **suited** clothed

7 **weeds** clothes (in which he is disguised)
memories reminders

9 **Yet . . . intent** to be revealed now would spoil the plan I have made (and the dramatic impact of Lear's reunion with Cordelia)

My boon I make it that you know me not   10
Till time and I think meet.

CORDELIA   Then be't so, my good lord.
[Enter the Doctor and First Gentleman]

How does the King?

DOCTOR   Madam, sleeps still.

CORDELIA   O you kind gods,
Cure this great breach in his abusèd nature;
The untuned and hurrying senses O wind up
Of this child-changèd father!

DOCTOR   So please your majesty   15
That we may wake the King? He hath slept long.

CORDELIA
Be governed by your knowledge, and proceed
I'th' sway of your own will. Is he arrayed?

[FIRST GENTLEMAN]
Ay, madam. In the heaviness of his sleep
We put fresh garments on him.   20

[DOCTOR]
Good madam, be by when we do awake him.
I doubt not of his temperance.

CORDELIA   Very well.

DOCTOR

Please you draw near. Louder the music there!
King Lear is [discovered] asleep

11.1 *Enter . . . Gentleman]* BLAYNEY; *not in* QF   17–18 knowledge, . . . will.] Q2 (*subs.*); ~,
. . . ~, QI   19–21 FIRST GENTLEMAN . . . DOCTOR] CAPELL; *Doct . . . Gent.* Q   21 him.] Q2
(~,); ~, QI   23.1 *King . . . asleep*] OXFORD; *not in* Q

10 **My . . . it** I ask this favour:

11 **meet** fit

13 **breach** wound

14 **untuned** slackened, like the string of a
musical instrument
hurrying confused? Weis emends to F's
'jarring', which makes easier sense but is
difficult to explain as a reading of whatever lay behind Q.
wind up tighten, tune up (the strings)

15 **child-changèd** changed into a child *or*
changed by the conduct of his children
(*OED, child, sb.* 22)

18 **I'th' . . . will** according to the dictates of
your desire, as you see fit
arrayed (properly) clothed

19–22 HalioQ, but not Weis, accepts Q's al-
location of these speeches. The Gentleman may be an afterthought—he is not
named in Q's opening direction—but
ll. 19–20 read like a reply to the Doctor's
question and ll. 21–2 come more fittingly
from the Doctor.

22 **temperance** self-control

23.1 *King Lear . . . asleep* It seems likely that
Lear is revealed, seated, behind a curtained opening in the tiring-house wall. F
has him brought on in a chair but omits
Q's 'Please you draw neere'. Granville
Barker (p. 298) suggests that the chair
deliberately recalls the throne of the
opening scene.

247

CORDELIA

  O my dear father, restoration hang
  Thy medicine on my lips, and let this kiss   25
  Repair those violent harms that my two sisters
  Have in thy reverence made!

KENT   Kind and dear princess!

CORDELIA

  Had you not been their father, these white flakes
  Had challenged pity of them. Was this a face
  To be exposed against the warring winds,   30
  To stand against the deep dread-bolted thunder
  In the most terrible and nimble stroke
  Of quick cross-lightning, to watch—poor *perdu*—
  With this thin helm? Mine injurer's mean'st dog,
  Though he had bit me, should have stood that night   35
  Against my fire. And wast thou fain, poor father,
  To hovel thee with swine and rogues forlorn
  In short and musty straw? Alack, alack,
  'Tis wonder that thy life and wits at once

---

33 *perdu*] THEOBALD; *Per du* Q   34 injurer's] CAPELL; iniurious Q; Enemies F   mean'st] OXFORD; *not in* Q

---

24 **restoration** 'Perhaps personified as a goddess' (HalioF).
    hang An odd choice of word; Schmidt defines 'attach, tie, adhere'.

25 **Thy medicine** 'the medicine which will cure you (Lear)'; or possibly 'restoration' is apostrophized: 'the medicine which you provide'.

27 **reverence** venerable condition

28 **flakes** locks of hair (*OED sb.*² 8), with perhaps a hint of 'snowflakes'

29 **challenged** . . . **of** claimed . . . from

30 **warring** *OED*'s first instance of the participial adjective.

31 **dread-bolted** hurling dreadful thunderbolts

32 **nimble** rapid

33 **cross-lightning** forked lightning
    watch stand on guard
    perdu sentinel (placed in mortal danger; *OED a. and sb.*, B2, first use in this sense); Q prints in italics, indicating that the word, first recorded in 1591, could still be thought of as French.

34 **helm** covering (of hair)

34 **injurer's mean'st** Both HalioQ and Weis accept Q's 'iniurious', which is both metrically awkward and 'adds nothing to the following line ("Though he had bit me")'. (*TC*). F reads 'Enemies' which 'confirms one's conviction that Q is inadequate' but 'is unlikely to be what stood in Q's copy'. Capell's emendation assumes an easy misreading and 'seems more appropriate' in that 'it emphasized the injury done to Cordelia herself, rather than presupposing a state of mutual hostility.' (*TC*). Our addition of 'mean'st' is defended in *TC*.

36 **fain** obliged

37–8 **hovel . . . straw** Possibly influenced by the parable of the Prodigal Son, who was sent 'to feed swine; and he would fain have filled his belly with the husks that the swine ate' (Luke 15: 15–16).

37 **hovel** shelter as in a hovel
    rogues forlorn wretched outcasts

38 **short** broken up, over-used
    musty damp and decaying

39 **at once** at one and the same time

Had not concluded all! (*To the Doctor*) He wakes. Speak
   to him. 40

DOCTOR Madam, do you; 'tis fittest.

CORDELIA (*to Lear*)
   How does my royal lord? How fares your majesty?

LEAR
   You do me wrong to take me out o'th' grave.
   Thou art a soul in bliss, but I am bound
   Upon a wheel of fire, that mine own tears 45
   Do scald like molten lead.

CORDELIA   Sir, know me.

LEAR
   You're a spirit, I know. Where did you die?

CORDELIA (*to the Doctor*) Still, still far wide!

DOCTOR
   He's scarce awake. Let him alone a while.

[handwritten margin note: Lear thinks she has died, does not believe what he sees]

LEAR
   Where have I been? Where am I? Fair daylight? 50
   I am mightily abused. I should e'en die with pity
   To see another thus. I know not what to say.
   I will not swear these are my hands. Let's see:
   I feel this pin prick. Would I were assured
   Of my condition.

CORDELIA (*kneeling*) O look upon me, sir, 55
   And hold your hands in benediction o'er me.
   No, sir, you must not kneel.

LEAR   Pray do not mock.
   I am a very foolish, fond old man,

---

40 all!] Q (~,)   46 know] Q1; know ye Q2; do you know F   50 daylight?] Q (~,)   55 *kneeling*] OXFORD; *not in* Q

40 **all** altogether
  He wakes Lear's awakening may be preceded by a long silence. 'Rossi took a full minute . . . to open his eyes, and begin to focus them' (Rosenberg, p. 284).

44 **bliss** heaven

44–5 **bound . . . fire** A complex image, recalling the classical figure of Ixion, condemned by Jove to be bound on an ever-whirling wheel. The relevance of Ixion to the play is discussed by Bate (pp. 194–6). See fig. 7.

45–6 **that . . . scald** with the result that my

tears (heated by the fire) scald (what they fall on)

48 **wide** wide of the mark, delirious

51 **abused** The word had a range of meanings, including ill-treated and deluded.

54 **pin** Perhaps part of a jewel or fastening on Lear's or Cordelia's garments.

56 **benediction** blessing

57 **No . . . kneel** Foakes precedes this with the direction '*She restrains him as he tries to kneel*'.

58 **fond** had a range of meanings from 'foolish', 'doting', to 'mad'.

Fourscore and upward, and to deal plainly,
I fear I am not in my perfect mind.   60
Methinks I should know you, and know this man;
Yet I am doubtful, for I am mainly ignorant
What place this is; and all the skill I have
Remembers not these garments; nor I know not
Where I did lodge last night. Do not laugh at me,   65
For as I am a man, I think this lady
To be my child, Cordelia.
CORDELIA   And so I am.
LEAR
Be your tears wet? Yes, faith. I pray, weep not.
If you have poison for me, I will drink it.
I know you do not love me; for your sisters
Have, as I do remember, done me wrong.
You have some cause; they have not.
CORDELIA   No cause, no cause.
LEAR Am I in France?
KENT In your own kingdom, sir.
LEAR Do not abuse me.   75
DOCTOR
Be comforted, good madam. The great rage
You see is cured in him, and yet it is danger
To make him even o'er the time he has lost.
Desire him to go in; trouble him no more
Till further settling.   80
CORDELIA (*to Lear*) Will't please your highness walk?
LEAR You must bear with me.
Pray now, forget and forgive. I am old
And foolish.
                Exeunt all but Kent and [First] Gentleman

75 me.] Q2; ~? Q1   84 *all . . . Gentleman*] Q (*Manet Kent and Gent.*)

61 **this man** Presumably Kent.
62 **mainly** entirely, absolutely
63 **skill** knowledge, brain power
73 **France** i.e. Cordelia's kingdom
75 **abuse me** (by suggesting that I still have a kingdom)
76 **rage** madness
78 **even o'er** fill up the gap in, go over in his mind

79 **Desire** ask
80 **settling** 'becoming quiet or composed' (*OED vbl. sb.* 5a, first instance of this sense)
81 **Will't . . . walk** Peggy Ashcroft spoke these words with 'feigned courtliness' (T. C. Worsley, *The Fugitive Art* (1952), p. 154).

[FIRST] GENTLEMAN Holds it true, sir, that the Duke
  Of Cornwall was so slain?
KENT   Most certain, sir.   85
[FIRST] GENTLEMAN
  Who is conductor of his people?
KENT   As 'tis said,
  The bastard son of Gloucester.
[FIRST] GENTLEMAN   They say Edgar,
  His banished son, is with the Earl of Kent
  In Germany.
KENT   Report is changeable.
  'Tis time to look about. The powers of the kingdom   90
  Approach apace.
[FIRST] GENTLEMAN The arbitrament is
  Like to be bloody. Fare you well, sir.   *Exit*
KENT
  My point and period will be throughly wrought,
  Or well or ill, as this day's battle's fought.   *Exit*

Sc. 22 *Enter Edmund, Regan, and their powers*
EDMUND
  Know of the Duke if his last purpose hold,
  Or whether since he is advised by aught
  To change the course. He's full of abdication
  And self-reproving. Bring his constant pleasure.

                              Exit one or more

92 *Exit*] THEOBALD; *not in* Q
    22.1 EDMUND] Q ('*Bast.*' *throughout the scene*)   3 abdication] Qa; alteration Qb   4.1 *Exit*
. . . *more*] *not in* QF

86 **conductor** leader, commander (*OED* 4)
87–9 **They . . . Germany** It is obviously iron-
    ical that these words are spoken to Kent,
    whose laconic response may be con-
    sciously, even humorously, evasive. No
    more is heard of the suggestion.
90 **look about** be wary (as at *Romeo* 3.5.40:
    'be wary, look about')
91 **arbitrament** deciding of the dispute,
    decisive encounter
93 **My . . . wrought** the full stop and round-
    ing off of my life will be wholly brought
    about, for better or for worse, by the out-
    come of today's battle. In style and
    rhyme, a highly formal, gnomic way of

    rounding off the scene, emphasizing to
    the audience the importance of Kent's
    concern with what is happening.
22 The remainder of the action is imagined
    as taking place somewhere near Dover.
    Edgar carries a letter (l. 42) and Edmund
    a paper (l. 54).
1   **Duke** i.e. Albany
    last purpose hold most recent intention
    (i.e. to fight) still obtains
2   **since . . . aught** in the meantime any-
    thing has warned him
3   **full of abdication** filled with, or ob-
    sessed by, desire to renounce his position.
    Both HalioQ and Weis accept Qb's

REGAN

Our sister's man is certainly miscarried.   5

EDMUND

'Tis to be doubted, madam.

REGAN   Now, sweet lord,

You know the goodness I intend upon you.

Tell me but truly—but then speak the truth—

Do you not love my sister?

EDMUND   Ay: honoured love.

REGAN

But have you never found my brother's way   10

To the forfended place?

EDMUND That thought abuses you.

REGAN I am doubtful

That you have been conjunct and bosomed with her,

As far as we call hers.

EDMUND   No, by mine honour, madam.   15

REGAN

I never shall endure her. Dear my lord,

Be not familiar with her.

EDMUND Fear me not.

She and the Duke her husband.

Enter the Duke of Albany and Gonoril with troops

GONORIL (*aside*)

I had rather lose the battle than that sister   20

Should loosen him and me.

---

19 husband.] QF; ~—ROWE   19.1 *the Duke of*] *not in* Q

'alteration' without comment, though as
Stone says (p. 251), this is less pointed
than the original.

4 **constant pleasure** (information about) his
fixed intentions, final decision

5 **sister's man** Oswald, killed by Edgar at
20.242.
miscarried come to harm

6 **doubted** feared

7 **intend upon** mean to bestow upon

9 **honoured** honourable

10 **brother's** brother-in-law's (Albany's)

11 **forfended** forbidden (by the command-
ment against adultery)

12 **abuses** discredits, disgraces

13 **doubtful** apprehensive

14 **conjunct** united
bosomed . . . her received into her bosom,
intimate with her (*OED*'s first instance of
this sense)

15 **As . . . hers** An odd way of saying 'in the
fullest sense of the word'.

17 **familiar** unduly intimate (*OED a.* 2c)

19 **She . . . husband.** Oxford treats as an interrupted sentence, but it seems more
likely that Edmund is simply drawing
attention to the arrival of Albany and
Gonoril, perhaps as a warning to Regan.

21 **loosen** loosen the ties, make a breach
between (*OED* 3b, only instance of this
sense)

ALBANY (*to Regan*)

  Our very loving sister, well bemet,

  For this I hear: the King is come to his daughter,

  With others whom the rigour of our state

  Forced to cry out. Where I could not be honest   25

  I never yet was valiant. For this business,

  It touches us as France invades our land;

  Yet bold's the King, with others whom I fear.

  Most just and heavy causes make oppose.

EDMUND

  Sir, you speak nobly.

REGAN   Why is this reasoned?   30

GONORIL

  Combine together 'gainst the enemy;

  For these domestic poor particulars

  Are not to question here.

ALBANY

  Let us then determine with the ensign of war

  On our proceedings.

EDMUND   I shall attend you   35

  Presently at your tent.   [*Exit with his powers*]

REGAN   Sister, you'll go with us?

GONORIL No.

REGAN

  'Tis most convenient. Pray you go with us.

---

28 Yet] BLAYNEY; Not Q   bold's] Q (bolds)   32 poor] OXFORD (*conj.* Collier); dore Q; deare
MALONE *conj.*   34 ensign] Q (auntient)   36 *Exit . . . powers*] OXFORD; *not in* QF

22 **bemet** met

23 **King** Albany acknowledges Lear's rank.

24 **rigour of our state** harshness of our government

25 **Forced . . . out** impelled to complain (*OED, cry, v.* 21b)
  honest in admitting *the rigour of our state*?

27 **touches us as** concerns us (the royal plural?) in so far as

28 **bold's . . . fear** Lear, along with supporters whom I fear, is bold (in claiming his kingdom). HalioQ and Weis accept Q's 'Not bolds' (i.e. does not embolden).

29 **Most . . . oppose** 'Fair and serious causes are driven into opposition' (Norton). The syntax is difficult. Though *OED* does not record *oppose* as a noun, it seems to act as one here.

30 **Sir . . . nobly** (possibly ironical)

30 **reasoned** discussed (*OED, reason, v.* 5a), brought up now

32–3 **poor . . . here** insignificant details are not worth discussing here. We assume foul case or a turned letter in emending 'dore' to 'pore' (*poor*). HalioQ and Weis accept Q's 'domestique dore', Halio concurring with Steevens's gloss 'particulars at our very doors, close to us, and consequently fitted to be settled at home'.

34 **ensign** standard-bearer (thought of by Shakespeare as a general's third-in-command: *Shakespeare's England* (Oxford, 1916), i. 117, adding that Shakespeare's use of the term indicates 'no very profound acquaintance with the art of war')

35–6 **attend . . . Presently** wait upon you immediately

38 **convenient** proper

GONORIL *[aside]*

O ho, I know the riddle! *(To Regan)* I will go.
　　Enter Edgar disguised as a peasant

EDGAR *(to Albany)*

If e'er your grace had speech with man so poor,　　　　40
Hear me one word.

ALBANY *(to the others)* I'll overtake you.
　　　　　　　　Exeunt all but Albany and Edgar
　　　　　　　　　　　Speak.

EDGAR

Before you fight the battle, ope this letter.
If you have victory, let the trumpet sound
For him that brought it. Wretched though I seem,
I can produce a champion that will prove　　　　　45
What is avouchèd there. If you miscarry,
Your business of the world hath so an end.
Fortune love you—

ALBANY　Stay till I have read the letter.

EDGAR　I was forbid it.　　　　　　　　50
When time shall serve, let but the herald cry,
And I'll appear again.

ALBANY　Why, fare thee well.
I will o'erlook the paper.　　　　　　*Exit Edgar*
　　Enter Edmund

EDMUND

The enemy's in view; draw up your powers.　　　55
　　He [offers] Albany a paper

39.1 *disguised . . . peasant*] THEOBALD (*subs.*); *not in* Q　　41 *all . . . Edgar*] Q ('*Exeunt.*' *after*
'word')　　54 *Exit Edgar*] Q (*after l.* 52)　　55.1 *He . . . paper*] OXFORD; *not in* QF

39 **know the riddle** can see through your lit-
　　tle plan (to keep an eye on me)
42–6 **Before . . . there** 'When Edgar ap-
　　proaches Albany . . . he sets in motion a
　　complex legal procedure, and Shake-
　　speare, with allowances for condensing a
　　long process into one dramatic scene, fol-
　　lows with surprising fidelity the tenets of
　　the High Court of Chivalry, an Anglo-
　　French institution established in the reign
　　of Edward III as part of the neo-chivalric
　　revival . . . The use of the word "cham-
　　pion", and . . . the instruction to "let the
　　trumpet sound", indicate that Edgar will
　　do more than produce a witness; he as-

sumes that his accusation will have to be
proved in trial by battle' (Edelman,
p. 146).

42 **letter** (found on Oswald: 20.248–63)
46 **avouchèd** asserted (borne witness to?)
　　miscarry lose
47 **Your . . . end** it will put an end to your
　　traffic with the world, i.e. you will die
51 **cry** make his proclamation (*OED v.* 5,
　　only instance of the absolute use)
54 **o'erlook** read through. It is not clear
　　whether he does.
55.1 *He . . . paper* Here (l. 56) seems to imply
　　that he supplies the evidence (though
　　Weis accepts Q's 'Hard', presumably

Here is the guess of their great strength and forces
By diligent discovery; but your haste
Is now urged on you.

ALBANY   We will greet the time.   *Exit*

EDMUND

To both these sisters have I sworn my love,
Each jealous of the other as the stung   60
Are of the adder. Which of them shall I take?—
Both?—one?—or neither? Neither can be enjoyed
If both remain alive. To take the widow
Exasperates, makes mad, her sister Gonoril,
And hardly shall I carry out my side,   65
Her husband being alive. Now then, we'll use
His countenance for the battle, which being done,
Let her that would be rid of him devise
His speedy taking off. As for his mercy
Which he intends to Lear and to Cordelia,   70
The battle done, and they within our power,
Shall never see his pardon; for my state
Stands on me to defend, not to debate.   *Exit*

Sc. 23 *Alarum. The powers of France pass over the stage*
           [led by] Queen Cordelia with her father in her hand.
           Then enter Edgar disguised as a peasant, guiding the
           blind Earl of Gloucester

56 Here] F; Hard Q   the guess] Q2; thequesse Q1   59 sisters] Q2, F; sister Q1   60 stung] F;
sting Q   62 Both . . . neither?] F (SUBS.); ~ʌ ~ʌ ~ʌ ~, Q
23.0.1–2 *The . . . hand*] Q (*Enter the powers of France ouer the stage, Cordelia with her father in
her hand.*)   0.2 *led by*] OXFORD; *not in* Q   0.3–4 *Then . . . Gloucester*] Q (*Enter Edgar and
Gloster.*)

interpreting 'even diligent (efforts at) discovery experience difficulty in guessing',
which seems strained.) Albany does not
necessarily take the paper. As an alternative to the emendation, we conjecture that
a line may have been omitted after *forces*.

57 **discovery** investigation, reconnaissance
   (*OED* 3b, first instance of this sense)
58 **greet the time** embrace the occasion, take
   advantage of our opportunities
60 **jealous** suspicious
65 **hardly . . . side** it will be difficult for me to
   fulfil my side of the agreement (to satisfy
   Gonoril); or perhaps 'to become king'

67 **countenance** authority, support
69 **taking off** dispatch, murder
72 **Shall** i.e. they shall
   state condition, success
73 **Stands on** requires
23 Edelman (pp. 153–8) has a helpful discussion of the background to the combat
   between Edgar and Edmund, and of its
   practical requirements.
0.1 *Alarum* a trumpet summons to battle
   pass over the stage Probably entering
   from the door at one side, processing
   round the stage, and leaving by the door
   at the other side, perhaps before Edgar
   and his father enter, or possibly after l. 4,

EDGAR

Here, father, take the shadow of this bush
For your good host; pray that the right may thrive.
If ever I return to you again
I'll bring you comfort.   *Exit*

GLOUCESTER   Grace go with you, sir.
        Alarum and retreat. Enter Edgar

EDGAR

Away, old man. Give me thy hand. Away.   5
King Lear hath lost, he and his daughter ta'en.
Give me thy hand. Come on.

GLOUCESTER

No farther, sir. A man may rot even here.

EDGAR

What, in ill thoughts again? Men must endure
Their going hence even as their coming hither.   10
Ripeness is all. Come on.   *Exit Edgar guiding*
                                              Gloucester

Sc. 24 *Enter Edmund with King Lear and Queen Cordelia*
        prisoners, a Captain, and soldiers

EDMUND

Some officers take them away. Good guard

4.1 *Enter Edgar*] Q2; *not in* Q1   9 again? Men] Q2; ~ ˄ ~ ˄ Q1
   24.1–2 *Enter . . . soldiers*] F (*subs.*); *Enter Edmund, with Lear and Cordelia prisoners.* Q
1 EDMUND] Q ('*Bast.*' *subs. throughout the scene*)

if their dialogue is presented as an inter-
lude in the stylized battle.

0.2 **with . . . hand** holding her father by the
hand

1 **bush** Probably represented by one of the
pillars supporting the canopy over the
Jacobean stage.

2 **For . . . host** i.e. as shelter

4.1 *retreat* A different trumpet call. The battle is represented in stylized form merely
by sound effects.

6 **King . . . lost** Knowles (p. 46) takes this
as evidence that Cordelia has ceded 'even
her titular leadership of the army to
Lear', but it would be natural to refer to
the cause as Lear's without thinking of
him as the active leader.

9–11 **Men . . . all** Recalling Hamlet's 'If it
be now, 'tis not to come. If it be not to
come, it will be now. If it be not now, yet
it will come. The readiness is all'
(5.2.166–8).

11 **Ripeness** One of *OED*'s definitions is
'maturity'.

24 Edmund gives the Captain a note at l. 27,
Albany and Edmund throw down gloves
at ll. 89 and 95, Albany reveals a paper
at l. 151, a Gentleman enters with a
bloodstained knife at l. 218; biers might
be used for the bodies of Gonoril and
Regan at 233 (though they might simply
be carried by actors); someone should
presumably hand Lear a looking-glass at
l. 257 and he probably needs a feather at
l. 261.

Until their greater pleasures best be known
That are to censure them.
CORDELIA (*to Lear*)   We are not the first
Who with best meaning have incurred the worst.
For thee, oppressèd King, am I cast down,   5
Myself could else outfrown false fortune's frown.
Shall we not see these daughters and these sisters?

LEAR
No, no⌈ Come, let's away to prison.
We two alone will sing like birds i'th' cage.   *father/daughter*
When thou dost ask me blessing, I'll kneel down   *image for*   10
And ask of thee forgiveness; so we'll live,   *a short moment*
And pray, and sing, and tell old tales, and laugh
At gilded butterflies, and hear poor rogues
Talk of court news, and we'll talk with them too—
Who loses and who wins, who's in, who's out,   15
And take upon 's the mystery of things
As if we were God's spies; and we'll wear out
In a walled prison packs and sects of great ones
That ebb and flow by th' moon.⌉
EDMUND (*to soldiers*)   Take them away.

LEAR (*to Cordelia*)
Upon such sacrifices, my Cordelia,   20

2–3 **their . . . them** i.e. the wishes are best
known of the greater personages who are
to pass judgement on them

4 **meaning** intentions

6 **outfrown** outdo in frowning, frown
down; *OED*'s first instance (of two).

9 **birds . . . cage** birds (even when they are)
caged (*cage* could also mean 'prison').
The paradoxical image was proverbial
(Dent B387.1).

10–11 **When . . . forgiveness** Recalling
Sc. 21. 55–7 (and 'That scene in the
old play' which 'haunted Shakespeare'
(Granville Barker, p. 298)).

13 **butterflies** foppish courtiers (like Osric, in
Hamlet, described as a 'waterfly'); *OED*'s
first instance of the figurative sense
(*sb.* 2a), though Craig cites an example in
Marston's *Antonio and Mellida*, *c.* 1600.

16 **take upon 's** take upon ourselves, assume
understanding of. Schmidt defines *take
upon* here as 'to pretend to a quality or to
a knowledge, to profess'.

16 **mystery** theologically, religious truth
known only through divine revelation;
also used for 'a matter unexplained or inexplicable; something beyond human
knowledge or comprehension' (*OED
sb.*[1] 5a).

17 **God's** Printed without an apostrophe in
early editions; could mean 'of the
gods'—otherwise, the play's only direct
reference to a Christian god.
wear out outlast, outlive

18 **packs and sects** parties and cliques

19 **by th' moon** as the moon governs the
tides. Sohmer finds Lear, 'who imposes
himself on his daughters "by monthly
course"' (1.123) 'evocatively self-
referential' here (paragraph 1).

20 **sacrifices** may allude to the sacrifices
Cordelia has made for Lear, or to their
joint loss of freedom (Foakes); draws on
the biblical tradition of sacrifice as a tribute to the gods, as in the story of Abra-
ham and Isaac (Genesis 22: 1–19).

The gods themselves throw incense. Have I caught
    thee?
He that parts us shall bring a brand from heaven
And fire us hence like foxes. Wipe thine eyes.
The goodyear shall devour 'em, flesh and fell,
Ere they shall make us weep. We'll see 'em starve first.
    Come.   *Exeunt all but Edmund and the Captain*   25
EDMUND Come hither, captain. Hark.
Take thou this note. Go follow them to prison.
One step I have advanced thee; if thou dost
As this instructs thee, thou dost make thy way
To noble fortunes. Know thou this: that men   30
Are as the time is. To be tender-minded
Does not become a sword. Thy great employment
Will not bear question. Either say thou'lt do't,
Or thrive by other means.
CAPTAIN   I'll do't, my lord.

---

24 goodyear] OXFORD; good Q; good yeares F; gore crows STONE *conj.*   25 *Exeunt . . . Captain*] Q2, F (*Exit.*); *not in* Q1   28 One] Q (*text*); And (*catchword*)

21 **throw incense** (like priests performing a ritual)
Have . . . thee Philip Brockbank suggests that Lear 'takes Cordelia in his arms . . . there is an advantage in having Lear leave the stage with Cordelia live but relaxed in his arms, later to return with her dead' ('*Upon Such Sacrifices*', British Academy Annual Shakespeare Lecture, 1976, p. 16).

22 **shall bring** i.e. will have to do something as drastic as bringing
brand burning torch

23 **like foxes** Explained, and perhaps influenced, by Harsnet: 'as men smoke out a fox out of his burrow' (p. 278). There may also be biblical influence: 'Samson went out and took three hundred foxes, and took firebrands, and turned them tail to tail, and put a firebrand in the midst between the two tails. And when he had set the brands on fire he sent them out into the standing corn' (Judges 15: 4–5).

24 **goodyear** From its use in the phrase 'What the goodyear?', 'goodyear' (or 'good year') came to be used for 'devil', or more generally for any inimical forces (*OED*). This reading is explained in *Div-*

ision, p. 489. An alternative explanation is offered by Shaheen, p. 619, who remarks that 'Lear's words appear to allude to Pharaoh's dream of seven "good" years of plenty followed by seven years of famine' (Genesis 41: 1–36). 'Lear tells Cordelia that although their enemies have won the day, even in their "good yeeres" (Gen. 41. 35), her sisters will not enjoy their victory, but will starve and be "deuoured" (Gen. 41. 7, 24) as if living in the seven years of famine.' Q's unmetrical 'good' is accepted by Weis; HalioQ follows F.

24 **flesh and fell** 'the whole substance of the body' (*OED*, *flesh*, *sb.* 1c), entirely (*fell*, skin)

25 **starve** die (not necessarily of hunger)

27 **note** It turns out to be the death warrant for Lear and Cordelia: see ll. 248–51.

29–30 **dost . . . fortunes** will be nobly advanced (perhaps 'to the ranks of the nobility')

31 **Are . . . is** reflect the issues of the time, fluctuate according to circumstances. 'Times change and we with them' was proverbial (Dent T343).

32 **a sword** i.e. a sword-bearer, soldier

33 **bear question** admit argument

EDMUND

About it, and write 'happy' when thou hast done.   35

Mark, I say, instantly, and carry it so

As I have set it down.

CAPTAIN   I cannot draw a cart,

Nor eat dried oats. If it be man's work, I'll do't.   *Exit*

Enter the Duke of Albany, the two ladies Gonoril

and Regan, ⌈another Captain,⌉ and others

ALBANY (*to Edmund*)

Sir, you have showed today your valiant strain,

And fortune led you well. You have the captives   40

That were the opposites of this day's strife.

We do require then of you, so to use them

As we shall find their merits and our safety

May equally determine.

EDMUND   Sir, I thought it fit

To send the old and miserable King   45

To some retention and appointed guard,

Whose age has charms in it, whose title more,

To pluck the common bosom on his side

And turn our impressed lances in our eyes

Which do command them. With him I sent the Queen,   50

---

38 *Exit*] F (*subs.*); *not in* Q   38.1–2 *Enter . . . others*] Q (*Enter Duke, the two Ladies, and others.*)
38.2 *another Captain*] OXFORD; *not in* QF   42 then] Q; them F   45 send] Qb, Q2, F; saue Qa
46 and appointed guard,] Qb, Q2; *not in* Qa, F   48 common] Qb; coren Qa   on] F; of Q

35 **write 'happy'** write yourself down a
  happy (fortunate) man
36 **Mark** attend
  carry it so manage it in such a way (to
  look as if Cordelia has hanged herself:
  ll. 250–1)
37–8 **I . . . do't** A cryptic utterance. Muir
  interprets 'I'm not a horse. I don't want
  to be driven by necessity after the war to
  be an agricultural labourer.' This may be
  over-specific. There is a vague resemblance to a speech by the villainous messenger in *Leir*: 'if I fail in anything, tie me
  to a dung cart, and make a scavenger's
  horse of me, and whip me, so long as I
  have any skin on my back' (ll. 1015–17).
38.2 **another Captain** He could alternatively
  come on with the Herald at l. 106. The
  trumpeter also might enter here, but is a
  natural attendant for a herald.

39 **strain** lineage. 'Albany implies that
  Edmund has shown himself worthy
  of being a legitimate son of Gloucester'
  (Kittredge).
41 **opposites** opponents
42 **then** next, besides (*OED* 3b), in those circumstances (4a). HalioQ (but not Weis)
  adopts F's 'them', without comment.
43 **merits** deserts
44 **equally** equitably, justly
46 **retention** detention (*OED* 4a)
47 **Whose** i.e. the King's
48 **pluck . . . on** draw the sympathy of the
  common people on to
49–50 **turn . . . them** turn the weapons
  of our conscripted soldiers into the eyes
  of us who command them. *OED*'s first
  instance of *impressed* as a participial
  adjective.

My reason all the same, and they are ready
Tomorrow, or at further space, to appear
Where you shall hold your session. At this time
We sweat and bleed. The friend hath lost his friend,
And the best quarrels in the heat are cursed   55
By those that feel their sharpness.
The question of Cordelia and her father
Requires a fitter place.
ALBANY   Sir, by your patience,
I hold you but a subject of this war,
Not as a brother.
REGAN   That's as we list to grace him.
Methinks our pleasure should have been demanded   60
Ere you had spoke so far. He led our powers,
Bore the commission of my place and person,
The which immediate may well stand up
And call itself your brother.
GONORIL   Not so hot.   65
In his own grace he doth exalt himself
More than in your advancement.
REGAN   In my right
By me invested, he compeers the best.
GONORIL
That were the most if he should husband you.
REGAN
Jesters do oft prove prophets.
GONORIL   Holla, holla—   70
That eye that told you so looked but asquint.

---

53 session. At] THEOBALD; Q (~ ~)   54 We] Qb (wee); mee Qa   56 sharpness] Qb (sharp-
nes); sharpes Qa

53 **session** sitting of your court of justice
55–6 **And . . . sharpness** Perhaps because he
is playing for time, Edmund starts to pon-
tificate in vague generalization. Hunter
paraphrases 'even good arguments [*quarrels*] are hateful at this moment of pas-
sionate involvement, when we are all
suffering the pains and losses of battle'.
59 **subject of** subordinate in
60 **we list** (royal plural) I please
63 **commission . . . place** authority of my
rank
64–5 **The . . . brother** The language is contorted; she seems to be saying that the im-

mediacy (F's word; *OED* does not support
the substantive use of 'immediate' in this
sense) of Edmund's relationship to her
may well confer on him the right to call
himself Albany's brother.
68 **invested** endowed
compeers equals. *OED*'s first instance of
a rare word (but Muir (p. 236) says that it
occurs in Florio's *Montaigne*).
69 **were the most** would be most true
70 **Jesters . . . prophets** Proverbial (Dent
W772: 'There is many a true word
spoken in jest').
Holla often meant 'stop', 'cease', i.e.

REGAN

    Lady, I am not well, else I should answer

    From a full-flowing stomach. (*To Edmund*) General,

    Take thou my soldiers, prisoners, patrimony.

    Witness the world that I create thee here   75

    My lord and master.

GONORIL   Mean you to enjoy him, then?

ALBANY

    The let-alone lies not in your good will.

EDMUND

    Nor in thine, lord.

ALBANY   Half-blooded fellow, yes.

EDMUND

    Let the drum strike and prove my title good.

ALBANY

    Stay yet, hear reason. Edmund, I arrest thee   80

    On capital treason, and in thine attaint

    This gilded serpent. (*To Regan*) For your claim, fair

        sister,

    I bar it in the interest of my wife.

    'Tis she is subcontracted to this lord,

    And I, her husband, contradict the banns.   85

    If you will marry, make your love to me.

    My lady is bespoke.—Thou art armed, Gloucester.

    If none appear to prove upon thy head

    Thy heinous, manifest, and many treasons,

       [*He throws down a glove*]

    There is my pledge. I'll prove it on thy heart,   90

finally someone's going to fight Edmund

79 EDMUND . . . good] Q (*Bast*. . . .); *Reg<an>*. . . . thine F   83 bar] QF (bare)   85 banns] QF
(banes)   89.1 *He . . . glove*] MALONE (*subs., after* 'pledge', *l*. 90; *not in* Q

    'Whoa there!', or 'mind what you're
saying!'

71 **asquint** awry

73 **full-flowing stomach** heart full of anger
('stomach' was used for 'the inward seat
of passion, emotion . . . feelings' (*OED
sb*. 6a))

77 **let-alone** power to say yea or nay

78 **Half-blooded** 'of superior blood . . . by one
parent only' (*OED*, first of two instances
cited)

79 **Let . . . strike** i.e. prepare for battle

(Edelman, p. 155)

80 **thee** The change to the second person singular indicates Albany's contempt.

81 **in thine attaint** in, i.e. along with, your
impeachment, accusation of treason

84 **subcontracted** betrothed for a second
time (*OED*; first use of the verb, and only
instance in this sense; no other uses
recorded before 1842)

87 **bespoke** already spoken for

89 **heinous** wicked, atrocious

90 **pledge** gage, glove thrown down as a
challenge. Albany offers 'proof in the

Ere I taste bread, thou art in nothing less
Than I have here proclaimed thee.

REGAN Sick, O sick!

GONORIL (*aside*) If not, I'll ne'er trust poison.

EDMUND (*to Albany,* [*throwing down a glove*])
  There's my exchange. What in the world he is   95
  That names me traitor, villain-like he lies.
  Call by thy trumpet. He that dares, approach;
  On him, on you—who not?—I will maintain
  My truth and honour firmly.

ALBANY A herald, ho!   100

EDMUND A herald, ho, a herald!

ALBANY
  Trust to thy single virtue, for thy soldiers,
  All levied in my name, have in my name
  Took their discharge.

REGAN   This sickness grows upon me.

ALBANY
  She is not well. Convey her to my tent.   105

                       Exit one or more with Regan

    [*Enter a Herald and a trumpeter*]

  Come hither, herald. Let the trumpet sound,
  And read out this.

SECOND CAPTAIN Sound, trumpet!

    Trumpeter sounds

HERALD (*reads*) 'If any man of quality or degree in the host
  of the army will maintain upon Edmund, supposed Earl   110
  of Gloucester, that he's a manifold traitor, let him appear
  at the third sound of the trumpet. He is bold in his
  defence.'

---

95 *throwing . . . glove*] MALONE (*subs.*); *not in* Q   105.1 *Exit . . . Regan*] THEOBALD (*subs.*); *not in* Q   105.2 *Enter . . . trumpeter*] OXFORD; *not in* Q; *Enter a Herald* HANMER   108.1, 114 *Trumpeter sounds*] OXFORD; *not in* Q

appropriate manner should no other
appellant appear' (Edelman, p. 146).

91 **in nothing** in no way less guilty
95 **exchange** i.e. my glove in return for
    yours
    What whoever
97 **Call** summon
102 **single virtue** unaided valour

105.2 **Herald** 'The heralds wore tabards
    emblazoned on back and front, and on
    the elbow-length sleeves, with their
    Sovereign's arms. They were thus
    clearly recognizable' (C. W. Scott-Giles,
    Shakespeare's Heraldry (1950), p. 120).
109 **quality or degree** high birth or rank
112 **third . . . trumpet** Edelman, p. 153,
    quotes Thomas of Woodstock's account

EDMUND Sound! (*Trumpeter sounds*) Again! *melodramatic*
      Enter Edgar, armed, at the third sound, a trumpeter Edgar
      before him   *appears at the
                                                              last moment.*
ALBANY (*to the Herald*)
    Ask him his purposes, why he appears   115
    Upon this call o'th' trumpet.
HERALD (*to Edgar*)   What are you?
    Your name and quality, and why you answer
    This present summons?
EDGAR   O, know my name is lost,
    By treason's tooth bare-gnawn and canker-bit.
    Yet ere I move't, where is the adversary   120
    I come to cope withal?
ALBANY   Which is that adversary?
EDGAR
    What's he that speaks for Edmund, Earl of Gloucester?
EDMUND
    Himself. What sayst thou to him?
EDGAR   Draw thy sword,
    That if my speech offend a noble heart
    Thy arm may do thee justice. Here is mine.   125
          He draws his sword
    Behold, it is the privilege of my tongue,
    My oath, and my profession. I protest,

---

114 Sound!] Q (~?)   Again!] Q (~?)   114.1 *armed*] F; *not in* Q   *trumpeter*] Q (*trumpet*)
119 tooth‸] THEOBALD; ~. Q1; ~: Q2, F   120 ere] Q (are)   125.1 *He . . . sword*] HUNTER; *not
in* Q   127 profession.] Q2; ~, Q1

of how the marshal was required to call at
the four corners of the lists 'Oyez, oyez,
oyez, defendant [here, appellant] come to
your journey'; if he did not appear at the
third call, it was assumed he would not
honour his pledge to appear.

114.1 *armed* Edgar needs to wear a helmet
'as "closed" as is practical to allow
speech while hiding his identity'; his
'armour, at best, would have to be
without a covering gown or other
colourful insignia, and would therefore
look drab compared with that of the Duke
of Gloucester' (Edelman, pp. 147, 154).
119 **canker-bit** eaten by canker-worms,
ruined

120 **ere I move't** before I state my case.
HalioQ, following Duthie, oddly adopts
and adapts F to read 'am I noble'; 'are' is
a well-attested spelling of 'ere'.
121 **cope withal** encounter, enter into combat with (*OED, cope, v.*[2] 2; now obsolete
sense)
126 **tongue** Foakes says that *tongue* ('honours' in F) 'seems unrelated to Edgar's
act of drawing his sword'. Perhaps it
means 'my native tongue'; Weis suggests
'report', 'reputation', or 'well-bred
accent'.
127 **oath . . . profession** oath sworn on becoming a knight, and the profession of
knighthood itself

263

Maugre thy strength, youth, place, and eminence,
Despite thy victor-sword and fire-new fortune,
Thy valour and thy heart, thou art a traitor,   130
False to thy gods, thy brother, and thy father,
Conspirant 'gainst this high illustrious prince,
And from th'extremest upward of thy head
To the descent and dust beneath thy feet
A most toad-spotted traitor. Say thou no,   135
This sword, this arm, and my best spirits are bent
To prove upon thy heart, whereto I speak,
Thou liest.

EDMUND   In wisdom I should ask thy name,
But since thy outside looks so fair and warlike,
And that thy tongue some say of breeding breathes,   140
My right of knighthood I disdain and spurn.
Here do I toss those treasons to thy head,
With the hell-hated lie o'erturn thy heart,
Which, for they yet glance by and scarcely bruise,
This sword of mine shall give them instant way   145

---

129 victor-sword] Q (~, ~)   fortune] F; fortun'd Q   132 Conspirant] F; Conspicuate Q;
Conspirate CAPELL   136 are] F; As Q1 (*as first word of verse line*); Is Q2   140 tongue] F; being
Q   141 My] OXFORD (*conj.* BL2); By Q   143 hell-hated lie] F; hell hatedly Q   o'erturn] OX-
FORD; oreturnd Q; oer-whelme F; returnd BLAYNEY

128 **Maugre** in spite of
   place . . . eminence high rank and status
129 **victor-sword** victorious sword
   fire-new fresh from the fire or furnace,
   brand-new (first recorded in *Richard III*,
   1.3.254)
   fortune i.e. success in victory, and
   promotion
132 **Conspirant** conspiring, or a conspirator
   (*OED*'s only two instances before 1880
   are from Harsnet and here)
133 **upward** top part, crown (*OED*'s only
   instance)
134 **descent** lowest part (recorded by *OED* as
   a nonce-use)
135 **toad-spotted** spotted with evil as a toad
   (regarded as especially obnoxious) bears
   spots believed to be poisonous
   Say . . . no if you deny it
138 **In wisdom** (because according to the
   laws of chivalry he could refuse to fight a
   man of lower rank, as Gonoril says at
   ll. 148–9)

140 **tongue** Weis (but not HalioQ) retains
   Q's 'being' while admitting that *tongue*
   may be the stronger reading.
   say assay, i.e. evidence, taste
141 **My** Weis retains Q's 'By' without comment. HalioQ accepts the emendation,
   regarded as 'obvious' by Stone
   (pp. 69–70), commenting 'Edmund is
   saying that he waives his right, by the
   rules of trial by combat, to know the identity of his appellant (Edgar)'.
143 **With** Perhaps 'at the same time as'
   rather than 'by means of' (*TC*).
   hell-hated hated as much as hell
   o'erturn HalioQ accepts our emendation,
   explained in *TC*.
144 **Which** i.e. Edgar's alleged treasons
   and lie
   by off
145–6 **give . . . ever** make an immediate passage for them to the place where they
   shall find their eternal home (i.e. in your
   dead body)

Where they shall rest for ever. Trumpets, speak!
⌈*Flourish.*⌉ *They fight. Edmund is vanquished*
⌈ALL⌉
Save him, save him!
GONORIL   This is mere practice, Gloucester.
By the law of arms thou art not bound to answer
An unknown opposite. Thou art not vanquished,
But cozened and beguiled.
ALBANY   Stop your mouth, dame,   150
Or with this paper shall I stopple it.
Thou worse than anything, read thine own evil.
Nay, no tearing, lady. I perceive you know't.
GONORIL
Say if I do, the laws are mine, not thine.
Who shall arraign me for't?
ALBANY   Most monstrous!   155
Know'st thou this paper?
GONORIL   Ask me not what I know.
                                                                        Exit

ALBANY
Go after her. She's desperate. Govern her.
                                                            Exit one or more

EDMUND
What you have charged me with, that have I done,
And more, much more. The time will bring it out.
'Tis past, and so am I. (*To Edgar*) But what art thou,   160
That hast this fortune on me? If thou beest noble,
I do forgive thee.

146.1 *Flourish*] OXFORD; *not in* Q; *Alarums*. F (*after the following speech*)   *They fight*] F
('Fights.', *after* 'him!', *l*. 147; *not in* Q   *Edmund is vanquished*] OXFORD; *not in* QF; *Edmund
falls* HANMER   147 ALL] BLAYNEY (*conj*. Van Dam); *Alb*. QF   155 monstrous!] Q (~ₐ)
156.1 *Exit*] Q (*Exit. Gonorill*.)   157.1 *Exit* . . . *more*] CAPELL (*subs*.); *not in* Q

147 ALL HalioQ and Weis retain Q's
  '*Alb*[*any*]', though HalioF admits that
  '*Alb*.' could be a 'misreading of *All*,
  which could also make sense dramatically'. Edelman (pp. 156–7), pointing out
  that interference with a battle of chivalry
  was strictly forbidden, is 'led to agree'
  with Theobald's suggestion that 'the
  words are meant to be spoken by' Gonoril
  since it is logical for her 'emotionally to
  beseech her soldiers to step in at a mo-

  ment when Edmund appears to be in
  danger'.
147 **practice** trickery
150 **cozened and beguiled** tricked and
  deceived
151 **stopple** close with a stopper or bung; first
  recorded as a verb *c*.1795.
155 **arraign me** bring me to trial
157 **Govern** control, restrain
161 **fortune on** good fortune, victory, over

EDGAR   Let's exchange charity.
    I am no less in blood than thou art, Edmund.
    If more, the more ignobly thou hast wronged me.
        [*He takes off his helmet*]
    My name is Edgar, and thy father's son.   165
    The gods are just, and of our pleasant vices
    Make instruments to scourge us.
    The dark and vicious place where thee he got
    Cost him his eyes.
EDMUND   Thou hast spoken truth.
    The wheel is come full circled. I am here.   170
ALBANY (*to Edgar*)
    Methought thy very gait did prophesy
    A royal nobleness. I must embrace thee.
    Let sorrow split my heart if I did ever hate
    Thee or thy father.
EDGAR Worthy prince, I know't.   175
ALBANY Where have you hid yourself?
    How have you known the miseries of your father?
EDGAR
    By nursing them, my lord. List a brief tale,
    And when 'tis told, O that my heart would burst!
    The bloody proclamation to escape   180
    That followed me so near—O, our lives' sweetness,
    That with the pain of death would hourly die
    Rather than die at once!—taught me to shift

164 ignobly] OXFORD (*conj.* Blayney); *not in* Q
166 vices‸] F; vertues. Q   170 circled] Q; circle F
Q1   182 with] Q; we F

164.1 *He . . . helmet*] OXFORD; *not in* Q
179–80 burst! | The] Q2 (*subs.*); ~‸ ~)

164 **If more** (in being legitimate)
    more ignobly thou HalioQ and Weis
    retain Q's unmetrical 'more thou'. Our
    addition is defended in *TC*.
166 **pleasant** pleasurable
168 **dark . . . place** Either the vagina or the
    brothel.
    got begot
170 **The wheel . . . circled** the wheel has be-
    come completely rounded, i.e. 'I am
    punished for the events that I set in train'.
    (Or perhaps, as Kittredge annotates F's
    '. . . full circle', 'I began life at the very
    lowest point on Fortune's wheel . . . Now
    its revolution is completed, and here I
    am—at the very bottom, where I was at

the beginning.' The expression 'Fortune's wheel is ever turning' was
proverbial (Dent W 617). Though F's
reading may seem more natural, *come*
may easily mean 'become' (*OED v.* 24a),
and *OED* records *circled* as 'Rounded;
circular'.
171 **gait** bearing, demeanour
172 **royal** regal, befitting royalty (though
    Edgar is not royal, he is Lear's godson)
178 **List** listen to
180 **bloody proclamation** sentence of death
    (7.166–70)
182–3 **with . . . die** i.e. would suffer the
    pains of death hour after hour. Weis also
    follows Q; HalioQ adopts F's 'we . . .'

Into a madman's rags, to assume a semblance
That very dogs disdained; and in this habit   185
Met I my father with his bleeding rings,
The precious stones new-lost; became his guide,
Led him, begged for him, saved him from despair;
Never—O father!—revealed myself unto him
Until some half hour past, when I was armed.   190
Not sure, though hoping, of this good success,
I asked his blessing, and from first to last
Told him my pilgrimage; but his flawed heart—
Alack, too weak the conflict to support—
'Twixt two extremes of passion, joy and grief,   195
Burst smilingly.

EDMUND   This speech of yours hath moved me,
And shall perchance do good. But speak you on—
You look as you had something more to say.

ALBANY
If there be more, more woeful, hold it in,
For I am almost ready to dissolve,   200
Hearing of this.

EDGAR   This would have seemed a period
To such as love not sorrow; but another
To amplify, too much would make much more,
And top extremity.
Whilst I was big in clamour came there in a man   205
Who, having seen me in my worst estate,
Shunned my abhorred society; but then, finding
Who 'twas that so endured, with his strong arms
He fastened on my neck and bellowed out

---

187 new-lost; became] Q2 (*subs.*); (~ ~) Q1   196 smilingly] Q (smillingly)   203 amplify, too much] OXFORD; ~ ~ ~, Q   205 there in] Q; there THEOBALD

184 **semblance** outward appearance
186 **rings** i.e. eye-sockets
191 **success** outcome, victory
193 **pilgrimage** pious journey
    flawed cracked. *OED*'s first instance of a verbal usage.
200 **dissolve** faint away, melt into tears (*OED v.* 15, first instance of the figurative sense)
201 **period** closing point
202–3 **another . . . more** to enlarge upon an-

other sorrow (Kent's fate) would make what is already excessive much greater, and exceed all limits. HalioQ punctuates 'another | To amplify too much would make much more'.
205 **big** loud (*OED a.* 6)
    clamour expression of grief
206 **estate** condition
208 **so endured** i.e. had suffered through the role of Poor Tom

As he'd burst heaven; threw him on my father,   210
Told the most piteous tale of Lear and him
That ever ear received, which in recounting
His grief grew puissant and the strings of life
Began to crack. Twice then the trumpets sounded,
And there I left him tranced.

ALBANY   But who was this?   215

EDGAR

Kent, sir, the banished Kent, who in disguise
Followed his enemy king, and did him service
Improper for a slave.

Enter [Second] Gentleman with a bloody knife CORdelia?

[SECOND] GENTLEMAN   Help, help!

ALBANY   What kind of help?

What means that bloody knife?

[SECOND] GENTLEMAN   It's hot, it smokes.   teasing
It came even from the heart of—

ALBANY   Who, man? Speak.   220

[SECOND] GENTLEMAN

Your lady, sir, your lady; and her sister   suspenseful
By her is poisonèd—she hath confessed it.   trick
                                                  so everything
EDMUND   might be ok,

I was contracted to them both; all three
Now marry in an instant.

ALBANY

Produce their bodies, be they alive or dead.   225
This justice of the heavens, that makes us tremble,
Touches us not with pity.

Enter Kent as himself

---

210 him] THEOBALD; me Q   214 crack. Twice] THEOBALD (*subs*); ~ ⌃ ~ Q   218 [*Second*]
Gentleman] OXFORD; *one* Q   227 *Enter . . . himself*] Q ('*Enter Kent*', *after* l. 228)

210 **As** as if
  my father i.e. Gloucester's body
213 **puissant** overpowering
  strings of life heart strings
215 **tranced** in a trance, unconscious
  (*OED*'s first instance of the past participle
  adjective)
218 **Improper** unfitting
219 **smokes** steams (with the heat of
  blood)

226–7 **This . . . pity** These lines invoke the
  Aristotelian notion of catharsis through
  terror and pity: 'The death of the cruel
  daughters produces fear ("makes us
  tremble") at the spectacle of divine justice, but because it is just . . . it does
  not produce pity. The tragedy has not
  yet reached its "promised end . . ."'
  (L. Danson, *Shakespeare's Dramatic Genres*
  (Oxford, 2000), p. 26).

EDGAR   Here comes Kent, sir.

ALBANY

  O, 'tis he; the time will not allow

  The compliment that very manners urges.

KENT I am come   230

  To bid my king and master aye good night.

  Is he not here?

ALBANY   Great thing of us forgot!—

  Speak, Edmund; where's the King, and where's

      Cordelia?

      The bodies of Gonoril and Regan are brought in

  Seest thou this object, Kent?

KENT Alack, why thus?   235

EDMUND Yet Edmund was beloved.

  The one the other poisoned for my sake,

  And after slew herself.

ALBANY   Even so.—Cover their faces.

EDMUND

  I pant for life. Some good I mean to do,

  Despite of my own nature. Quickly send,   240

  Be brief in't, to th' castle; for my writ

  Is on the life of Lear and on Cordelia.

  Nay, send in time.

ALBANY   Run, run, O run!

EDGAR

  To who, my lord? Who hath the office? Send

  Thy token of reprieve.   245

EDMUND

  Well thought on! Take my sword. The captain,

  Give it the captain.

---

232 ALBANY] Q (*'Duke.'* here and throughout the rest of the scene)   241 brief in't] F; ~, ~ Q

229 **compliment** formal greeting
    very manners urges simple good manners call for
231 **aye** for ever
234 **Seest . . . Kent?** Noting awkwardness in Albany's quick shift of attention from Lear and Cordelia to 'the sight of the dead sisters', D. Senes proposes that these words should be spoken by Edmund ('A Proposed Emendation for *King Lear*, V. iii. 237', *N & Q* 242 (1997), 64–7).

234 **object** spectacle
238 **Cover . . . faces** Presumably attendants should obey.
241 **writ** warrant of execution
244 **office** authority, responsibility
246 **Take my sword** i.e. as the 'token of reprieve'. 'Give it to the captain', along with Albany's instruction 'Bear him hence a while', implies that Edmund is incapacitated.

ALBANY   Haste thee for thy life.

                                    Exit ⌈Second Captain⌉

EDMUND

He hath commission from thy wife and me
To hang Cordelia in the prison, and
To lay the blame upon her own despair,   250
That she fordid herself.

ALBANY

The gods defend her!—Bear him hence a while.

                                    Exeunt some with Edmund
           Enter King Lear with Queen Cordelia in his arms,
           ⌈followed by the Second Captain⌉

LEAR

Becomes pure noise — not meaning anything [handwritten marginal note]

Howl, howl, howl, howl! O, you are men of stones.
Had I your tongues and eyes, I would use them so
That heaven's vault should crack. She's gone for ever.   255
I know when one is dead and when one lives.
She's dead as earth.

           ⌈He lays her down⌉

                        Lend me a looking-glass.
If that her breath will mist or stain the stone,
Why, then she lives.

KENT   Is this the promised end?

247.1 *Exit ⌈Second Captain⌉*] OXFORD; *not in* QF; *Exit Edgar* MALONE   252.1 *Exeunt . . .
Edmund*] THEOBALD (*subs.*); *not in* Q   252.2 *King*] *not in* Q   *Queen*] *not in* Q   252.3 *followed
by the Second Captain*] OXFORD; *not in* QF   257 *He lays her down*] OXFORD; *not in* QF

251 **fordid** killed
253 **Howl . . . howl!** The words are heard as
      both a cry of anguish and a command to
      others to join him in mourning.
      men of stones like statues
255 **heaven's . . . crack** (as if rent by thunder
      from tongues and lightning from eyes)
257 **looking-glass** Possibly an on-stage char-
      acter has a looking-glass ready to hand:
      'in the seventeenth century hand-
      mirrors were worn decoratively at the
      waist or elsewhere by many women and
      even men' (Herbert Grabes, trans. Gor-
      don Collier, *The Mutable Glass: Mirror-
      imagery in titles and texts of the Middle Ages
      and the English Renaissance* (Cambridge,
      1982), p. 71). J. C. Meagher, in the art-
      icle cited at 7.33, reproduces (Plate 1) a
      Hollar engraving of a woman with a pen-

dant mirror, suggesting that this is a
symptom of Gonoril's vanity; in this case
the glass might be brought from her
body. On the other hand, there is nothing to indicate that Lear's request is
granted. (In *Richard II*, attendants are
sent off to bring a looking-glass for the
King (4.1.255–66).)

258 **stone** reflector; more usually 'specular
      stone', a transparent or semi-transparent
      substance such as mica, selenite, or talc,
      which could be used as a reflector (*OED*,
      specular, 1).
259 **promised end** A suggestive phrase
      which Edgar takes to refer to the end of
      the world, the Day of Judgement, and
      which could also refer to the outcome
      of the events set in train by Lear's
      abdication.

EDGAR

  Or image of that horror?

ALBANY   Fall and cease.   260

LEAR

  This feather stirs. She lives. If it be so,

  It is a chance which does redeem all sorrows

  That ever I have felt.

KENT [*kneeling*]   Ah, my good master!

LEAR

  Prithee, away.

EDGAR   'Tis noble Kent, your friend.

LEAR

  A plague upon you, murderous traitors all.   265

  I might have saved her; now she's gone for ever.—

  Cordelia, Cordelia: stay a little. Ha?

  What is't thou sayst?—Her voice was ever soft,

  Gentle, and low, an excellent thing in women.—

  I killed the slave that was a-hanging thee.   270

[SECOND] CAPTAIN

  'Tis true, my lords, he did.

LEAR   Did I not, fellow?

  I have seen the day with my good biting falchion

---

261 stirs. . . . If] Q (stirs she liues, if), F (stirs, she liues:if)   263 *kneeling*] THEOBALD; *not in* Q
265 you] Q2, F; your Q1   267 Ha?] Q (~,)   271 [SECOND] CAPTAIN] OXFORD; *Cap.* Q

260 **image . . . horror** recalls 2.157: 'image and horror'
   image exact likeness, as Macduff calls the dead Duncan 'This great doom's image' (*Macbeth* 2.3.78)
   Fall and cease may be taken as a plea for Lear to be granted the peace of death, or for the world to disintegrate and cease to be. In, e.g., Trevor Nunn's 1968 RSC production, Albany directed these lines, with violence and scorn, to the heavens.

261 **This . . . stirs** Prince Harry uses the same test for death (with an inaccurate result) in *2 Henry IV*, 4.3.162–5: 'By his gates of breath | There lies a downy feather which stirs not. | Did he suspire, that light and weightless down | Perforce must move.' Lear might pick a feather from the ground, from clothing or a hat (Teague, p. 135), or even from an arrowhead; or it might be imagined. Q has no punctuation before *she lives*. F has a comma. Either text might be interpreted as indicating that in his excitement, Lear runs together two positive statements, or as conditional: 'if this feather stirs, she is alive'. Either interpretation is open to the actor.

268 **What . . . sayst?** Halio (in the article cited at 1.35) proposes that Cordelia may give 'some last fleeting indication of life' (p. 106).

272 **I . . . falchion** A formulaic expression (Dent D81.1), varied at e.g. *Merry Wives* 2.1.213–15: 'I have seen the time with my long sword I would have made you four tall fellows skip like rats', and *Othello* 5.2.268–70: 'I have seen the day | That, with this little arm and this good sword, | I have made my way . . .'
   good biting falchion good, keen, or well-cutting, sharp broadsword. A *falchion* was 'a short sword with a curved, sharpened edge, thicker towards the point, a

I would have made them skip. I am old now,
And these same crosses spoil me. (*To Kent*) Who are
    you?
Mine eyes are not o' the best, I'll tell you straight.   275

KENT

If fortune bragged of two she loved or hated,
One of them we behold.

LEAR   Are not you Kent?

KENT

The same, your servant Kent. Where is your servant
    Caius?

LEAR

He's a good fellow, I can tell you that.
He'll strike, and quickly too. He's dead and rotten.   280

KENT

No, my good lord, I am the very man—

LEAR   I'll see that straight.

KENT

That from your first of difference and decay
Have followed your sad steps.

LEAR   You're welcome hither.

KENT

Nor no man else. All's cheerless, dark, and deadly.   285
Your eldest daughters have fordone themselves,

279 you] F; *not in* Q   283 first] F; life Q   286 fordone] F; foredoome Q1; fore-doom'd Q2

cutting rather than a thrusting weapon'
(Edelman, p. 26).

274 **crosses** troubles, frustrations (caused by
his being 'old')
spoil me 'i.e. as a swordsman' (Muir)
275 **Mine . . . best** A sign of approaching
death (Hoeniger, p. 96).
276–7 **If . . . behold** A cryptic utterance.
Perhaps the general meaning is 'if there
were ever two people whom Fortune
might boast that she had supremely
favoured or ill-treated, one of them—
Lear (or Cordelia?), the object of her
hatred—is here.
278 **Caius** We are left to deduce that this
was Kent's disguise name.
282 **see . . . straight** look into that in a moment. 'Lear resists being distracted from
Cordelia' (Foakes).

283 **first . . . decay** from the beginning of
your period of difference and decay.
HalioQ also emends; Weis retains Q, saying it 'is elliptical and requires "the beginning of" to be understood'. Foakes
considers that Q makes good sense. Possibly 'the error lies in Q's preposition:
perhaps "from" was substituted for
"in"' (TC).
difference change of fortune
285 **Nor . . . else** 'This completes his preceding sentence . . . but also begins his reply
to Lear's *welcome* ("I am not welcome,
nor is anyone else . . .")' (Hunter).
286 **fordone** ruined (*OED*, *fordo*, 3; may
mean 'killed', but Regan has not committed suicide). Weis adopts Q2's 'fore-
doom'd' while allowing that Q's
'foredoome' 'may be a misreading of *fore-
done*'.

And desperately are dead.
LEAR   So think I, too.
ALBANY
He knows not what he sees; and vain it is
That we present us to him.
EDGAR   Very bootless.
    Enter another Captain
[THIRD] CAPTAIN (*to Albany*)
Edmund is dead, my lord.
ALBANY   That's but a trifle here.—   290
You lords and noble friends, know our intent.
What comfort to this great decay may come
Shall be applied; for us, we will resign
During the life of this old majesty
To him our absolute power; (*to Edgar and Kent*) you
    to your rights,   295
With boot and such addition as your honours
Have more than merited. All friends shall taste
The wages of their virtue, and all foes
The cup of their deservings.—O see, see!
LEAR
And my poor fool is hanged. No, no life.   300
Why should a dog, a horse, a rat have life,

289.1 *another*] *not in* Q   290 [THIRD] CAPTAIN] OXFORD; *Capt.* Q   292 great] F; *not in* Q
296 honours] Q2, F; honor Q1   301 have] Q2, F; of Q1

287 **desperately** in despair
289 **bootless** useless
291 **our** Albany, now head of state, assumes
    the royal plural.
292 **decay** ruined remains (*OED sb.* 3b), i.e.
    Lear. HalioQ also adopts F's 'great';
    'as an alternative one might suggest
    "dark"' (*TC*).
295 **you to your** i.e. 'our intent' is that you
    should have
296 **boot** advantage, reward
    addition titles, distinctions
    honours honourable deeds (in battle)
299 **cup** painful experience (*OED sb* 9; bib-
    lical in origin; Shaheen, p. 620, cites
    examples)
    O see, see! Something turns his attention
    to Lear.
300 **fool** The word was 'Used as a term of en-
    dearment or pity' (*OED sb.*[1] 1c) and the

primary referent here must be Cordelia,
but inevitably the Fool is recalled (especially if the roles are doubled). He was last
seen helping to carry Lear off stage in
Scene 13, and is not known to have died.
Conceivably the dying Lear conflates the
two characters, both dear to him, but the
effect is confusing. S. Booth, in the article
cited in Introduction, p. 39 n. 3, writes:
'The context that dictates that "fool"
refers to Cordelia—Lear's position over
her body, the pronoun "thou", her death
by hanging, and the echo of two earlier
cycles of grief and hope—coexists with
the context provided by a play in which
one character is a fool, a professional
clown, who has vanished noiselessly
during Act II [*for* III], and by a scene
punctuated with six reports of off-stage
deaths; moreover, the syntactic habit of

[Handwritten marginalia: "Juxtapose animals and human", "why should Cordelia die?"]

And thou no breath at all? O, thou wilt come no more.
Never, never, never.—Pray you, undo
This button. Thank you, sir (O, O, O, O!)

EDGAR He faints. (*To Lear*) My lord, my lord!   305

LEAR Break, heart, I prithee break.

EDGAR Look up, my lord.

KENT

Vex not his ghost. O, let him pass. He hates him
That would upon the rack of this tough world
Stretch him out longer.

      [*Lear dies*]

EDGAR   O, he is gone indeed.   310

KENT

The wonder is he hath endured so long.
He but usurped his life.

ALBANY (*to attendants*)

Bear them from hence. Our present business
Is to general woe. (*To Kent and Edgar*) Friends of my
    soul, you twain
Rule in this kingdom, and the gored state sustain.   315

---

310 *Lear dies*] RIDLEY; *not in* Q

the word "and" is to introduce material relatively extraneous to what precedes it. One sentence, "And my poor fool is hanged," makes—and cannot be reasoned out of making—two distinct and yet inseparable statements' (p. 129).

302 **O, thou . . . more** Shaheen, p. 620, compares Job 7: 9–10: 'He that goeth down to the grave shall come up no more. He shall return no more.'

303–4 **Pray . . . button** It is not clear to whom these words are addressed; Edgar or Kent seems most likely. Lear may be seeking relief from another attack of the *mother* (7.224) or asking for a button on his or Cordelia's costume to be undone. L. Thomson takes *undo* as a starting point for a discussion of this scene, ' "Pray you, undo this button": Implications of "Un-" in *King Lear*', SS 45 (1993), 79–88, and P. C. McGuire examines theatrical options and their interpretational implications in Chapter 5, 'Open Silences and the Ending(s) of *King Lear*', of his *Speech-*

less Dialect: Shakespeare's Open Silences (Berkeley, 1985).

307 **Look up** perhaps 'take courage' (*OED*, *look*, *v.* 45c, all three instances from Shakespeare)

308 **ghost** spirit

309 **rack** The instrument of torture on which victims were fastened by their limbs and stretched at risk of death.

310 **longer** In both time and extent.
   Lear dies Rosenberg, pp. 319–22, records a variety of ways in which actors have portrayed Lear's death.

312 **usurped** stole, clung on to (beyond the normal term)

314 **to . . . woe** An odd construction: 'directed towards the expression of general mourning'. HalioQ, following F, omits 'to'.

315 **Rule** It is not clear whether Albany is inviting Kent and Edgar to share the rule with him (perhaps as members of his council), or to resume their feudal roles.
   gored severely wounded, bloody

KENT

I have a journey, sir, shortly to go:
My master calls, and I must not say no.

ALBANY

The weight of this sad time we must obey,
Speak what we feel, not what we ought to say. PROBLEM with
The oldest have borne most. We that are young failure of
Shall never see so much, nor live so long. language

Exeunt carrying the bodies

321.1 *Exeunt . . . bodies*] OXFORD; *Exeunt with a dead March.* F

318 **obey** submit to
319 **Speak . . . say** (as Cordelia did in the opening scene)
320 **borne** experienced, suffered

THE BALLAD OF KING LEAR AND
HIS THREE DAUGHTERS

A BALLAD about King Lear dating from no later than 1620 has long been known, but is ignored by the play's recent editors. It is worth reprinting here both because it reflects early interest in the story and, more importantly, may be based in part on memories of the play in performance. Ballad versions of plays, 'meant to be sung and sold in the streets',[1] are not uncommon in the period, and specimens relating to *Titus Andronicus*, *The Taming of the Shrew*, and *The Merchant of Venice* as well as to *King Lear* have survived. The first known appearance in print of the Lear ballad is in a volume described on its title-page as 'The Golden Garland of Princely Pleasures and Delicate Delights, wherein is contained the histories of many of the kings, queens, princes, lords, ladies, knights and gentlewomen of this kingdom. Being most pleasant songs and sonnets to sundry new tunes now most in use; the third time imprinted, enlarged and corrected by Rich[ard]. Johnson.' The volume, of which only one copy is known to survive, is dated 1620. Johnson was probably the compiler rather than the author.[2] There is no trace of a first or second edition; equally, there is no reason to believe that they did not exist, so the ballad very probably dates from earlier than 1620. Indeed, it might well have already appeared as a broadsheet.[3]

Richard Johnson (1573–1659?) was a prolific and popular writer, best known for his prose romance *The Seven Champions of Christendom* (1596–7), which went on being reprinted and adapted into the nineteenth century. He had published a collection of ballads, *A Crown Garland of Golden Roses*, in 1612; it was frequently reprinted. Although he is not known to have had any direct association with the theatre, *The Golden Garland* contains other ballads related to plays, including 'Titus Andronicus' Complaint', which may be the one entered on the Stationers' Register along with the play in 1594, and which Bullough (who reprints it as an analogue) and Jonathan Bate (in his Arden 3 edition, p. 83) regard as a derivative from the play. A 'thirteenth edition' of *The Golden Garland* appeared in 1690; intervening editions were presumably read to pieces.

The ballad of King Lear was anthologized in *A Collection of Old Ballads* (3 vols., 1723–5) edited anonymously, conjecturally by Ambrose Phillips (ii. 12–17), with changes probably designed as improvements, of which

[1] Perrett, p. 136.

[2] Allan G. Chester, 'Richard Johnson's *Golden Garland*' (*Modern Language Quarterly*, 10 (1949), 61–7), p. 66.

[3] 'Of the 4,000 ballads likely published before 1600, only about 260 sheets survive, including fragments and duplicates' (Bruce R. Smith, *The Acoustic World of Early Modern England* (Chicago, 1999), p. 170).

the most significant is the alteration of the name 'Cordela' to 'Cordelia'. Mrs Charlotte Lennox, in her *Shakespear Illustrated* (3 vols., 1753–4), reprints the ballad from this collection, quoting its editor as saying 'I cannot be certain directly as to the time when this ballad was written; but that it was some years before the play of Shakespeare appears from several circumstances which to mention would swell my Introduction too far beyond its usual length.' To which Mrs Lennox responds, with pardonable exasperation,

It is to be wished that this writer, since he was resolved not to exceed a certain length in his Introduction, had omitted some part of it in order to introduce those circumstances that were of infinitely more consequence than anything else he has said on the subject of that old ballad: if it was really written before Shakespeare's play, that great poet did not disdain to consult it, but has copied it more closely than either the chronicle or Sidney. From thence—for 'tis mentioned nowhere else—he took the hint of Lear's madness, and the extravagant and wanton cruelty his daughters exercised on him. The death of King Lear is also exactly copied. (iii. 301–2)

Shortly after this, Thomas Percy printed the ballad in his *Reliques of Ancient English Poetry* (3 vols., 1765; i. 211–19) in a section containing 'ballads that illustrate Shakespeare' which also includes the ballads of 'Gernutus the Jew of Venice'—a version (regarded by Bullough as 'probably pre-Shakespearean') of the Shylock story—and of Titus Andronicus. Percy claims to print the ballad from 'an ancient copy in the "Golden Garland"' but gives no date, and seems also to have used Phillips's or, more probably, Lennox's text. In his headnote he concurs with the 'sensible female critic' Mrs Lennox that Shakespeare must have copied the ballad 'if it were certain that it was written before the tragedy' but offers no personal opinion on the subject. In the 1886 reprint (itself reprinted by Dover Books, New York, in 1966) Percy's editor, Henry B. Wheatley, offers no further relevant comment. In stating that 'The Cordella of the [old] play is softened in the ballad to Cordelia' he is misled by the change introduced by Phillips.

During the eighteenth and nineteenth centuries the ballad was extensively discussed as a possible source of the play. In the New Variorum edition of *King Lear* (1880, repr. 1963), H. H. Furness reprints it avowedly from Percy, and discusses the question of priority, concurring with Halliwell-Phillipps that the ballad was probably written 'in consequence of the popularity of the tragedy'. The most rigorous discussion of the ballad and of the scholarship surrounding it, however, comes in Perrett, published in 1904 but written earlier, before Furness's edition appeared. Perrett convincingly argues not merely that the ballad was written after the play, but that its author 'did not read the play' but saw it performed (p. 139). There is no question that the ballad-maker also consulted another source, because he calls the King of France Aganippus, a name that does not occur in Shakespeare but is in Holinshed, whose account Perrett believed the writer consulted. Other variants, such as causing Cordela to die in battle, and reversing the relative ages of the Gonoril and Regan characters, probably arise from the need to simplify and perhaps from faulty memory.[1]

Perrett shows touching affection for the ballad, indicating that it must have retained popular currency well into the nineteenth century:

this ballad made a lasting impression on me before I could read, so that I remember the circumstances when I first heard it. And to thousands of children it tells Cordelia's pathetic story when Shakespeare is a mere name, and conveys some inkling of a different morality from that which is inculcated by the customary materialism of a golden crown to reward the Beautiful. The writer of the ballad, it seems to me, learnt the lesson of *King Lear*, and some credit is due for his reflection of something of that supreme calm of the final scene . . . (p. 141)

In the twentieth century, interest in the ballad dwindled, partly no doubt because it was no longer thought of as a possible source, and also, I suspect, because some authorities did not know, or give, the date of the first edition, with consequent obscuring of the fact that it must have been in existence no later than 1620, may well have been written several years before that date, and probably gives us the only eyewitness account of a performance of the play in Shakespeare's time, albeit both popularized and conflated with memories of Holinshed. So C. J. Sisson, in a passing reference: 'One need not, I think, hesitate to imagine that the writer of the ballad . . . had actually been present at the Globe before he wrote it . . .'[2] The passages most likely to reflect performance are the description of Lear in his madness (ll. 137–44) and the account of his death over Cordela's body (ll. 169–76), in which the play, as Perrett says, 'differs utterly from all other versions' (p. 126). In later productions of the play, Lear has died in many different ways (Rosenberg, pp. 319–22). The ballad may afford a glimpse of how Burbage himself expired over the body of the boy actor playing Cordelia.

An echo in the ballad's account of Lear's madness of lines found only in the Quarto opens up the possibility that the ballad dates from before performances of the Folio revision. In the penultimate stanza, the statement that Cordela 'died indeed for love | Of her dear father, in whose cause | She did this battle move' recalls her words 'O dear father, | It is thy business that I go about' (18. 24–5). The balladeer's use of Holinshed, too, may offer a shred of evidence that the ballad was composed before the Quarto appeared: if, wishing to supplement memories of performance, he had been able to consult the Quarto he might not have felt impelled to resort to the bulky volume of *Chronicles*.

[1] Perrett, p. 139.   [2] *Lost Plays of Shakespeare's Age* (Cambridge, 1936), p. 120.

The tune, identical with that called 'Chevy Chase', is given by William Chappell, *Popular Music of the Olden Time* (2 vols., 1855–9), pp. 198–9, who describes it as one 'to which a large number of ballads have been written'.

The ballad is reprinted here in a text modernized from a microfilm of the 1620 edition.

A Lamentable Song of the Death of King Lear and his Three Daughters

TO THE TUNE OF 'WHEN FLYING FAME'

> King Lear once rulèd in this land
>   With princely power and peace,
> And had all things with heart's content
>   That might his joys increase.
> Amongst those gifts that nature gave   5
>   Three daughters fair had he,
> So princely-seeming beautiful
>   As fairer could not be.
>
> So on a time it pleased the king
>   A question thus to move: 10
> Which of his daughters to his grace
>   Could show the dearest love;
> 'For to my age you bring content,'
>   Quoth he, 'then let me hear
> Which of you three in plighted troth   15
>   The kindest will appear.'
>
> To whom the eldest thus began:
>   'Dear father mine,' quoth she,
> 'Before your face to do you good
>   My blood shall tendered be.   20
> And for your sake my bleeding heart
>   Shall here be cut in twain
> Ere that I see your reverend age
>   The smallest grief sustain.'
>
> 'And so will I,' the second said,   25
>   'Dear father, for your sake
> The worst of all extremities
>   I'll gently undertake,
> And serve your highness night and day

With diligence and love,   30
That sweet content and quietness
    Discomforts may remove.'

'In doing so you glad my soul,'
    The agèd king replied;
'But what sayst thou, my youngest girl,   35
    How is thy love allied?'
'My love,' quoth young Cordela then,
    'Which to your grace I owe,
Shall be the duty of a child,
    And that is all I'll show.'   40

'And wilt thou show no more,' quoth he,
    'Than doth thy duty bind?
I well perceive thy love is small
    Whenas no more I find.
Henceforth I banish thee my court,   45
    Thou art no child of mine,
Nor any part of this my realm
    By favour shall be thine.

'Thy elder sisters' loves are more
    Than well I can demand,   50
To whom I equally bestow
    My kingdom and my land,
My pompal state and all my goods,
    That lovingly I may
With these thy sisters be maintained   55
    Until my dying day.'

Thus flattering speeches won renown
    By these two sisters here;
The third had causeless banishment,
    Yet was her love more dear.   60
For poor Cordela patiently
    Went wand'ring up and down,
Unhelped, unpitied, gentle maid,
    Through many an English town,

Until at last in famous France   65
    She gentler fortunes found,
Though poor and bare, yet was she deemed

44 **Whenas** seeing that   67 **bare** destitute; defenceless
53 **pompal** splendid, showy; first rec. 1650;
    rare

281

The fairest on the ground.
Where when the king her virtues heard,
   And his fair lady seen,   70
With full consent of all his court
   He made his wife and queen.

Her father, old King Lear, this while,
   With his two daughters stayed.
Forgetful of their promised loves,   75
   Full soon the same denayed,
And living in Queen Ragan's court,
   The elder of the twain,
She took from him his chiefest means,
   And most of all, his train.   80

For whereas twenty men were wont
   To wait with bended knee,
She gave allowance but to ten,
   And after scarce to three.
Nay, one she thought too much for him,   85
   So took she all away,
In hope that in her court, good king,
   He would no longer stay.

'Am I rewarded thus?' quoth he,
   'In giving all I have   90
Unto my children, and to beg
   For what I lately gave?
I'll go unto my Gonorel;
   My second child, I know,
Will be more kind and pitiful   95
   And will relieve my woe.'

Full fast he hies then to her court,
   Where when she heard his moan,
Returned him answer that she grieved
   That all his means were gone,   100
But no way could relieve his wants,
   Yet if that he would stay
Within her kitchen, he should have
   What scullions gave away.

When he had heard with bitter tears,   105
   He made his answer then,

---

76 **denayed** renounced   104 **scullions** kitchen-servants, skivvies

'In what I did let me be made
    Example to all men.
I will return again,' quoth he,
    'Unto my Ragan's court,   110
She will not use me thus, I hope,
    But in a kinder sort.'

Where when he came, she gave command
    To drive him thence away.
When he was well within her court   115
    She said he could not stay.
Then back again to Gonorel
    The woeful king did hie,
That in her kitchen he might have
    What scullion boys set by.   120

But there of that he was denied
    Which she had promised late;
For one refusing he should not
    Come after to her gate.
Thus twixt his daughters for relief   125
    He wandered up and down,
Being glad to feed on beggars' food,
    That lately wore a crown.

And calling to remembrance then
    His youngest daughter's words,   130
That said the duty of a child
    Had all that love affords,
But doubting to repair to her
    Whom he had banished so,
Grew frantic mad, for in his mind   135
    He bore the wounds of woe.

Which made him rend his milk-white locks
    And tresses from his head,
And all with blood bestain his cheeks,
    With age and honour spread,   140
To hills and woods and wat'ry founts
    He made his hourly moan,

112 **sort** manner
123 **one** The change to 'once', first found in
    Phillips, may be correct.
133 **doubting** hesitating, fearing
136 Perrett compares 'I am cut to the brains'
    (20.181).

138 This passage recalls lines found only in
    the Quarto text of the play: the
    Gentleman's statement that Lear 'tears
    his white hair, | Which the impetuous
    blasts, with eyeless rage, | Catch in their
    fury and make nothing of' (8.6–8).

Till hills and woods and senseless things
　　Did seem to sigh and groan.

Even thus possessed with discontents　　　　　　　　145
　　He passèd o'er to France,
In hope from fair Cordela there
　　To find some gentler chance.
Most virtuous dame, where when she heard
　　Of this her father's grief,　　　　　　　　　　150
As duty bound, she quickly sent
　　Him comfort and relief.

And by a train of noble peers
　　In brave and gallant sort,
She gave in charge he should be brought　　　　　　155
　　To Aganippus' court,
Her royal king, whose noble mind
　　So freely gave consent
To muster up his knights at arms,
　　To fame and courage bent.　　　　　　　　　　160

And so to England came with speed
　　To repossess King Lear,
And drive his daughters from their thrones
　　By his Cordela dear.
Where she, true-hearted noble queen,　　　　　　　165
　　Was in the battle slain,
Yet he, good king, in his old days
　　Possessed his crown again.

But when he heard Cordela dead,
　　Who died indeed for love　　　　　　　　　　170
Of her dear father, in whose cause
　　She did this battle move,
He swooning fell upon her breast,
　　From whence he never parted,
But on her bosom left his life,　　　　　　　　　175
　　That was so truly-hearted.

The lords and nobles when they saw
　　The end of these events,
The other sisters unto death
　　They doomèd by consents,　　　　　　　　　180

156 The name of the French king in Holin-　　176 **That** i.e. Cordela
　　shed and other versions of the story.　　180 **doomèd . . . consents** condemned by
172 **move** instigate　　　　　　　　　　　　　general agreement

And being dead, their crowns were left
   Unto the next of kin.
Thus have you heard the fall of pride
   And disobedient sin.

[FINIS]

OFFSHOOTS OF *KING LEAR*

THE Introduction mentions a few of the writings and other works of art deriving from the play. It may be helpful here to note works of reference providing additional information, and to supply a brief guide to the criticism and scholarship on the play most likely to be useful to students.

Bibliographies of Criticism and Scholarship

Larry S. Champion, *King Lear: An Annotated Bibliography*, 2 vols. (New York, 1980) covers writings from 1940 to 1978, with some earlier material. All items, which include 'books, chapters, articles, reviews, notices of stage productions of *Lear* itself, and accounts of writers and works directly influenced by the tragedy', are summarized. The Introduction provides a valuable analysis of a wide range of criticism and scholarship.

Harmer, James L., ed., *The World Shakespeare Bibliography on CD-ROM* (Cambridge, 1996; to be updated so that it runs from 1900 to the present)
Muir, Kenneth, '*King Lear*', in *Shakespeare: A Bibliographical Guide*, ed. S. Wells (Oxford, 1990)
Additional information may be sought in the review sections and the annual bibliographies published in *Shakespeare Quarterly*, and in the review articles of *Shakespeare Survey*.

A Selective List of Scholarship and Criticism

Barker, Harley Granville, *Preface* to *King Lear* (1927, revised 1935, variously reprinted)
Bickersteth, G. L., *The Golden World of 'King Lear'* (British Academy Lecture, 1946)
Blayney, Peter W. M., *The Texts of King Lear and their Origins: Vol. 1: Nicholas Okes and the First Quarto* (Cambridge, 1982)
Bonheim, H., *The King Lear Perplex* (San Francisco, 1960)
Booth, Stephen, *King Lear, Macbeth, Indefinition and Tragedy* (New Haven, 1983)
Bradley, A. C., *Shakespearean Tragedy* (1904; often reprinted)
Brooke, Nicholas, 'The Ending of *King Lear*', in *Shakespeare 1564–1964*, ed. E. A. Bloom (Providence, RI, 1964), pp. 71–87
——*Shakespeare: King Lear*, Arnold's Studies in English Literature, 15 (1963)

Brownlow, F. W., *Shakespeare, Harsnett, and the Devils of Denham* (Newark, NJ, 1993)

Bullough, Geoffrey, *Narrative and Dramatic Sources of Shakespeare*, vol. vii, Major Tragedies (1975)

——'*King Lear* and the Annesley Case', in *Festschrift Rudolf Stamm*, ed. E. Kolb and J. Hasler (Bern and Munich, 1969), 43–50

Campbell, Lily B., *Shakespeare's Tragic Heroes* (Cambridge, 1930)

Carroll, William C., *Fat Beggar, Lean King: Representations of Poverty in the Age of Shakespeare* (Ithaca and London, 1996)

Cavell, Stanley, 'The Avoidance of Love', in *Must We Mean What We Say?* (New York, 1969, repr. Cambridge, 1987), pp. 39–23

Chambers, R. W., *King Lear*, W. P. Ker Memorial Lecture (Glasgow, 1940)

Clemen, W. H., *The Development of Shakespeare's Imagery* (1951)

Coleridge, S. T., *Lectures on Literature 1808–19*, ed. R. A. Foakes, in *The Collected Works of Samuel Taylor Coleridge*, vol. v. 2 vols. (Princeton, 1987)

Colie, Rosalie L., and F. T. Flahiff, eds., *Some Facets of 'King Lear': Essays in Prismatic Criticism* (Toronto and London, 1974)

Cox, Brian, *The Lear Diaries: The Story of the Royal National Theatre's Productions of Shakespeare's 'Richard III' and 'King Lear'* (1992)

Danby, J. F., *Shakespeare's Doctrine of Nature* (1949)

Danson, Lawrence, ed., *King Lear* (Princeton, 1981; original essays by Alvin Kernan, Michael Goldman, G. E. Bentley, Theodore Weiss, Thomas McFarland, Lawrence Danson, Thomas P. Roche Jr., and Daniel Seltzer)

Dollimore, Jonathan, *Radical Tragedy: Religion, Ideology and Power in the Drama of Shakespeare and his Contemporaries* (1984; 2nd edn., 1989)

Elton, W. R., *King Lear and the Gods* (San Marino, 1966; repr. Lexington, Ky., 1988)

Empson, W., *The Structure of Complex Words* (1951)

Everett, Barbara, 'The New King Lear', *Critical Quarterly*, 2 (1960), 325–39

Foakes, R. A., *Hamlet versus Lear: Cultural Politics and Shakespeare's Art* (Cambridge, 1993)

Fraser, Russell, *Shakespeare's Poetics in Relation to 'King Lear'* (1962)

Frost, William, 'Shakespeare's Rituals and the Opening of *King Lear*', *Hudson Review*, 10 (1958), 577–85

Gardner, Helen, *King Lear*, John Coffin Memorial Lecture (1967)

Goldberg, S. L., *An Essay on 'King Lear'* (Cambridge, 1974)

Goldsmith, R. H., *Wise Fools in Shakespeare* (East Lansing, Mich., and Liverpool, 1955)

Greenblatt, Stephen, *Shakespearean Negotiations* (Oxford, 1988)

Greenfield, Thelma, 'The Clothing Motif in *King Lear*', *SQ* 5 (1954), 281–6

Greg, W. W., 'The Date of *King Lear* and Shakespeare's Use of Earlier Versions of the Story', *The Library*, 20 (1940), 377–400

Hawkes, Terence, *Shakespeare and the Reason* (1964)

——*King Lear*, Writers and Their Work (1995)

Heilman, R. B., *This Great Stage* (Baton Rouge, La., 1948)

Henderson, W. B. Drayton, 'Montaigne's *Apologie of Raymond Sebonde*, and *King Lear*', *Shakespeare Association Bulletin*, 14 (1939), 209–15, and 15 (1940), 40–54

Holloway, John, *The Story of the Night: Studies in Shakespeare's Major Tragedies* (1961)

James, D. G., *The Dream of Learning: An Essay on 'The Advancement of Learning', 'Hamlet', and 'King Lear'* (Oxford, 1931)

Johnson, Samuel, *Johnson on Shakespeare*, ed. Arthur Sherbo, 2 vols. (New Haven and London, 1968); notes on *King Lear*, ii. 659–705; also *Samuel Johnson on Shakespeare*, ed. Henry Woudhuysen (Harmondsworth, 1989)

Jones, Emrys, *Scenic Form in Shakespeare* (Oxford, 1971)

Jorgensen, Paul, *Lear's Self-Discovery* (Berkeley, 1967)

Kermode, Frank, ed., *Shakespeare: 'King Lear', A Casebook* (1969) (includes selections from early criticism along with essays and selections from books by Maynard Mack, A. C. Bradley, G. Wilson Knight, Enid Welsford, George Orwell, Robert Heilman, Terence Hawkes, Barbara Everett, John Holloway, C. J. Sisson, W. R. Elton, Northrop Frye, and Jan Kott)

Knight, G. Wilson, *The Wheel of Fire: Interpretations of Shakespearian Tragedy* (1930; revised edn., 1949)

Kott, Jan, *Shakespeare our Contemporary* (1964)

Kozintsev, Grigori, *King Lear: The Space of Tragedy* (1977)

Lamb, Charles, 'On the Tragedies of Shakespeare' (1811), in e.g. Jonathan Bate, ed., *The Romantics on Shakespeare*, New Penguin Shakespeare Library (Harmondsworth, 1992)

Leggatt, Alexander, *King Lear*, Harvester New Critical Introductions (Hemel Hempstead, 1988)

——*King Lear*, Shakespeare in Performance series (Manchester, 1991)

Mack, Maynard, *King Lear in Our Time* (Berkeley, 1965; London, 1966)

McGuire, Philip C., *Speechless Dialect: Shakespeare's Open Silences* (Berkeley, 1985)

Marcus, Leah, *Puzzling Shakespeare: Local Reading and its Discontents* (Berkeley, etc., 1988); reprinted in part in Ryan, *New Casebook*, pp. 114–29

Marowitz, Charles, '*Lear Log*', in *Peter Brook: A Theatrical Casebook*, ed. David Williams (1988, revised 1991), 6–22

Mooney, Michael F., '"Edgar I nothing am": *Figurenposition* in *King Lear*', *SS 38* (1985), 153–66

Mueller, Martin, 'From Leir to Lear', *PQ*, 73 (1994), 195–217

Muir, Kenneth, *King Lear: A Critical Study* (Harmondsworth, 1986)

——'Samuel Harsnett and *King Lear*', *RES*, NS 2 (1951), 11–21

Nowottny, Winifred, 'Lear's Questions', *SS 10* (1957), 90–7

——'Some Aspects of the Style of *King Lear*', *SS 13* (1960), 45–57

Ogden, James and Arthur H. Scouten, eds., *'Lear' from Study to Stage: Essays in Criticism* (Madison, 1997)

Ornstein, Robert, *The Moral Vision of Jacobean Tragedy* (Madison, 1960)

Orwell, George, 'Lear, Tolstoy and the Fool', in *Shooting an Elephant and Other Essays* (New York, 1945), 32–52

Perrett, Wilfrid, *The Story of King Lear from Geoffrey of Monmouth to Shakespeare* (Berlin, 1904)

Reibetanz, John, *The 'Lear' World: A Study of 'King Lear' in its Dramatic Context* (Toronto, 1977)

Rosenberg, Marvin, *The Masks of King Lear* (Berkeley, 1982)

Ryan, Kiernan, ed., *New Casebooks: King Lear: Contemporary Critical Essays* (1993) (includes essays and extracts from books by Arnold Kettle, Howard Felperin, Kathleen McLuskie, Leonard Tennenhouse, Kiernan Ryan, Terry Eagleton, Coppélia Kahn, Leah Marcus, Annabel Patterson, Jonathan Goldberg, and Stephen Greenblatt)

Salgādo, G., ed., *King Lear*, Text and Performance series (1984)

Salingar, Leo, '*King Lear*, Montaigne and Harsnett', in his *Dramatic Form in Shakespeare and the Jacobeans* (Cambridge, 1986), pp. 107–39

Shickman, Allan R., 'The Fool's Mirror in *King Lear*', *ELR* 21 (1991), 75–86

Snyder, Susan, *The Comic Matrix of Shakespeare's Tragedies* (Princeton, 1979)

Speaight, Robert, *Nature in Shakespearian Tragedy* (1955)

Spurgeon, Caroline F. E., *Shakespeare's Imagery and What it Tells Us* (Cambridge, 1935)

Stone, P. W. K., *The Textual History of 'King Lear'* (1980)

Taylor, Gary, and Michael Warren, eds., *The Division of the Kingdoms: Shakespeare's Two Versions of 'King Lear'* (Oxford, 1983, 1986)

Taylor, Gary, *Moment by Moment by Shakespeare* (1985)

Thompson, Ann, *King Lear*, The Critics Debate series (1988)

Urkowitz, Steven, *Shakespeare's Revision of 'King Lear'* (Princeton, 1980)

Vickers, Brian, *The Artistry of Shakespeare's Prose* (1968)

——'*King Lear* and Renaissance Paradoxes', *MLR* 63 (1968), 305–14

Wiles, David, *Shakespeare's Clown* (Cambridge, 1987)

Wilson, Richard, 'A constant will to publish; Shakespeare's dead hand', in his *Will Power* (1993), 184–237

Zimmerman, Susan, ed., *Shakespeare's Tragedies*, New Casebooks (1998) (includes 'Perspectives: Dover Cliff and the Conditions of Representation', by Jonathan Goldberg, and 'The Ideology of Superfluous Things: *King Lear* as Period Piece', by Margreta de Grazia)

Film and Television adaptations

Rothwell, Kenneth, and Annabelle Henkin Melzer, *Shakespeare on Screen: An International Filmography* (New York, 1990); 'a guide to the major share of films and videos based on Shakespeare's plays' from 1899 to 1989, with detailed information about each. There are 42 entries for *King Lear*.

Terris, Olwen and Luke McKernan, *Walking Shadows: Shakespeare in the National Film and Television Archive* (1994); includes 14 items related to *King Lear*.

Rothwell, Kenneth S., *A History of Shakespeare on Screen: A Century of Film and Television* (Cambridge, 1999)

Music

A Shakespeare Music Catalogue, by Bryan N. S. Gooch and David Thatcher, 5 vols. (Oxford, 1991), lists over five hundred items relating to *King Lear*, including incidental music (much of it unpublished), operas, non-theatrical vocal music, and non-theatrical instrumental music. Detailed information is provided about each item. Works listed include incidental music by Milii Balakirev (1837–1910), composed 1858–61, revised 1902–5; Dimitri Shostakovitch (1906–75), Opus 58, 1941, for a production by Grigori Kozintsev, and Opus 137, 1970, for Kozintsev's film; and an unpublished score by Virgil Thomson (1896–1989), 1953, for an adaptation directed by Peter Brook with Orson Welles as Lear. The best-known opera based on the play is by Aribert Reimann (b. 1936), first performed in Munich, 1978, with Dietrich Fischer-Dieskau as Lear, recorded by Deutsche Gramophon. In addition, Ernest Bloch (1880–1959), Benjamin Britten (1913–76), Henri Duparc (1848–1933), Edward Elgar (1857–1934), Pietro Mascagni (1863–1945), possibly Giacomo Puccini (1858–1924), and Giuseppe Verdi (1813–1901) all contemplated operas on the theme; a ballet, with music by Vincent Persichetti (1915–87), was performed by the Martha Graham Company in 1949. Probably the best-known orchestral work based on the play is the *Grande Ouverture du Roi Léar*, Opus 4, by Hector Berlioz (1803–69) composed in 1831 and revised *c.*1840; it has been frequently recorded, and was arranged for piano by Franz Liszt (1811–86).

Theatre

Avery, E. L., *et al.* (eds.), *The London Stage: A Calendar of Plays, Entertainments and Afterpieces, 1660–1800*, 11 vols. (Carbondale, 1960–5); a comprehensive catalogue.

Hogan, C. B., *Shakespeare in the Theatre: A Record of Performances in London, 1701–1800* (Oxford, 1952–7); partially superseded by the above, but includes detailed information about versions used, along with cast lists.

Odell, G. C. D., *Shakespeare from Betterton to Irving*, 2 vols. (New York, 1920); a discursive account, outdated in some respects, but still useful.

Rosenberg, M., *The Masks of King Lear* (Berkeley, 1971); an extensive critical study based on the play's theatre history.

Shattuck, C. H., *The Shakespeare Promptbooks: A Descriptive Catalogue* (Urbana, 1965)

Trewin, J. C., *Shakespeare on the English Stage 1900–1964* (1964); critical assessments along with lists of performance dates.

Visual Art

There is no comprehensive catalogue. Artists who have produced distinguished work inspired by the play include James Barry (1741–1806); William Blake (1757–1827); Ford Madox Brown (1821–93); William Dyce (1806–64); Johann Heinrich Fuseli (1741–1825); Sir Joshua Reynolds (1723–92); George Romney (1734–1802); John Runciman (1744–68); Robert Smirke (1752–1845); Peter van Bleeck (1697–1764); Benjamin West (1738–1820), and Benjamin Wilson (1721–88). Useful information and discussion is provided in works on individual artists and by:

Friedman, Winifred H., *Boydell's Shakespeare Gallery* (New York and London, 1976)

Merchant, W. Moelwyn, *Shakespeare and the Artist* (1959; includes information on stage designs)

Pape, Walter, and Frederick Burwick, eds., *The Boydell Shakespeare Gallery* (Bottrop, 1996)

Pressly, William L., *A Catalogue of Paintings in the Folger Shakespeare Library* (New Haven and London, 1993)

Shakespeare in Western Art (exhibition catalogue, Tokyo, 1992)

Literary and Dramatic Texts

Along with those mentioned on pp. 78–80, Foakes discusses literary, dramatic and cinematic offshoots in his Arden edition, pp. 85–9, and others are mentioned in Ruby Cohn's *Modern Shakespeare Offshoots* (Princeton, 1976).

The final section (ii. 309–60) of Larry Champion's *Annotated Bibliography* (listed above) is devoted to 'Adaptations, Influence, and Synopses'.

ALTERATIONS TO LINEATION

Q1 OFTEN sets manifest verse as prose, and sometimes prose as verse. From the printing of Q2 onwards, editors have attempted to regularize the typographical distinction between the two media. It is, however, often difficult to tell which was intended by either the compositors or the author. Inevitably, therefore, any attempt to introduce regularity is governed by personal judgement, and readers seriously concerned with the topic would be well advised to consult facsimiles of the early editions.

The following list aims to record all changes from the lineation of Q1 (referred to here as Q except when Q1 is needed to distinguish it from Q2). Some of these changes were first made in Q2, and many in F, but the issue is complicated by the many verbal differences in F. An attempt has been made to attribute other changes to the edition in which they first appeared.

Quotations to the left of the square bracket are from this edition; words quoted to the right of the bracket are modernized from the text quoted; an upright line (|) indicates a line ending.

1.62–3	Sir . . . is] RIDLEY; *1 line* Q
65–7	I find . . . joys] F; *2 lines* Q: short	
69–70	And . . . love] F; *1 line* Q
70–2	Then . . . tongue] F; *2 lines* Q: sure	
82–4	Unhappy . . . less] F; *prose* Q
90–4	Why . . . sisters] F; all	hand	him	never	Q
135–8	Let . . . speak] F; *5 lines* Q: rather	heart	mad	duty	
139	When . . . bound] *2 lines* QF: bows	
140–2	When . . . judgement] F; *4 lines* Q: folly	consideration	life	
178–82	My . . . love] F; *4 lines* Q: you	daughter	present	
182–4	Royal . . . less] F; *2 lines* Q: what	
184–8	Right . . . pieced] F; *4 lines* Q: us	fallen	little	
194–5	Pardon . . . conditions] F; up	Q
207–9	So . . . degree] F; *2 lines* Q: favour	
224–5	Go . . . better] OXFORD; born	Q
227–30	That often . . . stands] F; *3 lines* Q: do	lady	
232–5	Royal . . . Burgundy] F; *3 lines* Q: portion	Cordelia	
252–4	Thou . . . see] F; thine	Q
255–6	Without . . . Burgundy] F; *1 line* Q
257–60	The . . . father] F; our father	are	faults	Q
266–8	Let . . . scanted] F; lord	alms	Q
273–5	Sister . . . tonight] CAPELL; *verse* QF: say	both	

2.1–8	Thou . . . true] F; *prose* Q
9–10	As . . . bastardy] BLAYNEY; *prose* Q
11–12	Who . . . quality] F; *prose* Q
13–14	Than . . . fops] OXFORD; *prose* Q
15–17	Got . . . Edmund] F; *prose* Q
18–21	As . . . bastards] OXFORD; *prose* Q
22–5	Kent . . . news] F; *prose* Q
3.1–2	Did . . . fool] OXFORD; *prose* QF
3–4	By . . . other] F; me | Q
12–15	Put . . . one] F; *prose* Q
16–20	Not . . . abused] THEOBALD; *prose* Q
21	Remember . . . you] F; *prose* Q
22–3	And . . . so] CAPELL; *prose* QF
24–6	I . . . dinner] HANMER; *prose* QF
4.1–5	If . . . condemned] F; *prose* Q
6	Thy . . . labour] OXFORD; *prose* Q
112–21	Have . . . score] F; *prose* Q
133–40	That . . . there] CAPELL; *4 lines* Q: land | stand | appear |
166	Then . . . weep] THEOBALD; prose QF
167–9	And . . . among] F; *prose* Q
188–9	Mum . . . crumb] CAMBRIDGE; *1 line* QF
190–1	Weary . . . peascod] CAPELL; *1 line* QF
192–4	Not . . . forth] F; *prose* Q
195–6	In . . . you] OXFORD; *prose* Q; Sir | F
197–205	To . . . proceedings] F; *prose* Q
207–8	The hedge-sparrow . . . young] *prose* QF
211–14	Come . . . are] F; *prose* Q
217–19	Doth . . . discernings] F (*4 lines, dividing l.* 217 *at* '*me*'); *prose* Q; *5 lines* BLAYNEY: me | walk | speak thus | notion |
220–1	Are . . . so] OXFORD; *prose* Q
222	Who . . . am] F; *prose* Q
223–5	Lear's . . . daughters] POPE; *prose* Q
227	Come, sir] OXFORD; *prose* Q
228–34	This . . . manners] F; *prose* Q
235–6	Shows . . . brothel] BLAYNEY; *prose* Q; lust | F
247–8	You . . . betters] F (*prose?*); *prose* Q
249–52	We . . . child] F (*subs.*); *prose* Q
253	Than . . . liest] BLAYNEY; *prose* Q
254–63	My train . . . people] F; *prose* Q
265–7	It . . . fruitful] BLAYNEY; *prose* Q; *4 lines* F: lord | goddess [hear] | intend |
268–77	Into . . . feel] F; *prose* Q
278	That she may feel] OXFORD; *prose* Q

279–80	How . . . people] F; *prose* Q
282–4	Never . . . it] F; *prose* Q
285–6	What . . . fortnight] F; *prose* Q
287	I'll . . . ashamed] ROWE; *prose* Q; *2 lines* F: thee |
288–9	That . . . perforce] F; *prose* Q
290	And . . . upon thee] ROWE; *prose* Q; *2 lines* F: | blasts
291–4	Untented . . . make] F; *prose* Q
295–6	To . . . this] OXFORD; *prose* Q
296–301	Yet . . . ever] F; *prose* Q
302–4	Do . . . you—] F; *prose* Q
304–5	Come . . . master] BLAYNEY; *prose* Q
308–12	A . . . after] F; *prose* Q
317–25	Take . . . mildness] F; *prose* Q
326–7	How . . . well] F; *prose* Q
328–9	Nay . . . event] F; *1 type-line* Q
5.30–1	I . . . ready] OXFORD; *prose* QF
42–5	O . . . ready] OXFORD; *prose* QF
6.14–27	The Duke . . . you—] F; *prose* Q
28–9	I . . . you] F; *prose* Q
30	Seem . . . well] CAPELL; *prose* Q; *2 lines* F: [Draw,] seem . . . yourself |
31–3	Yield . . . opinion] F; *prose* Q
34–6	Of . . . help] OXFORD; *prose* Q
37–9	Here . . . mistress] F; *prose* Q
39	GLOUCESTER But . . . he] F; *same type-line as the end of the preceding speech* Q
43–54	Persuade . . . made] F; *prose* Q
56	But . . . fled] F; *prose* Q
56–63	Let . . . death] F; *prose* Q
64–77	When . . . it] F; *prose* Q
77–85	Strong . . . capable] F; *prose* Q
86–7	How . . . news] F; *prose* Q
88–9	If . . . lord] F; *prose* Q
91–2	What . . . Edgar] F; *prose* Q
94–5	Was . . . father] F; *prose* Q
103–4	That . . . there] F; *1 line* Q
104–6	Nor . . . office] F; *prose* Q
110–16	If . . . on] F; *prose* Q
116–17	I . . . else] JENNENS; *1 line* QF
126–8	Lay . . . use] F; *2 lines* Q: counsel |
129–30	I . . . welcome] F; *1 line* Q
7.2–3	KENT . . . horses] F; *1 type-line* Q
4–5	KENT . . . tell me] F; *1 type-line* Q

6–7	KENT . . . for thee] F; *1 type-line* Q
39	OSWALD . . . murder, help] F; *on the same type-line as the end of the preceding speech* Q
70–1	That . . . twain] OXFORD; these	QF
77–9	Knowing . . . fool] Q2, F; *2 lines* Q1: epileptic	
84–5	Why . . . offence] F; *1 line* Q
90–9	This . . . nicely] F; *9 lines* Q: praised	roughness	nature	plain	so	know	craft	silly-ducking	
109–11	I . . . misconstruction] F; *2 lines* Q: master	
118–19	None . . . fool] F; *1 line* Q
121–3	I . . . you] F; *2 lines* Q: me	
126–7	Fetch . . . noon] F; honour	Q
129–30	Why . . . so] F; *prose* Q
136–8	Is . . . with] POPE; *2 lines* Q: pilf' rings	
138–40	The King . . . restrained] F; *2 lines* Q: valued	
188–90	As . . . remove] F; *2 lines* Q: was	
192–5	Ha . . . nether-stocks] F; *verse* Q: garters	bears	men	at legs	
196–7	What's . . . here] ROWE; *prose* Q
197–8	It . . . daughter] F; *1 line* Q
198	LEAR No . . . Yes] OXFORD; *1 type-line* Q
198–9	LEAR No, I . . . yea] OXFORD; *1 type-line* Q
199	LEAR No, no . . . have] OXFORD; *1 type-line* Q
214–15	Commanded . . . looks] F; leisure	Q
256–9	My . . . course] F; *prose* Q
259	Vengeance . . . confusion] F; *prose* Q
260–1	What . . . wife] OXFORD; *prose* Q; Gloucester, Gloucester	F
267–70	Infirmity . . . forbear] F; *3 lines* Q: health	oppressed	
272–3	To . . . man] F; *1 line* Q
273–4	Death . . . here] OXFORD; *1 line* Q
274–5	This . . . her] F; *1 line* Q
280–1	I . . . you] OXFORD; *1 line* QF
304–8	Nature . . . return] F; *4 lines* Q: confine	discretion	yourself	
319–21	All . . . lameness] F; *2 lines* Q: top	
325–6	O . . . mood] F; me	Q
328–32	Thy . . . train] F; *3 lines* Q: o'er	burn	
347–9	If you . . . part] F; Allow	cause	Q
369–70	Why . . . brought] F; dowerless	Q
381–2	A . . . thee] F; my	Q
388–91	Not . . . passion] F; yet	welcome	those	Q
441–2	No . . . flaws] JENNENS; *2 lines* QF: weeping	

447–8	'Tis . . . folly] OXFORD; rest | QF
457–8	Do . . . bush] F; *1 line* Q
8.1–2	One . . . unquietly] OXFORD; *1 line* QF
22–6	Into . . . far] POPE; *4 lines* Q: negligence | ports | banner |
32–3	And . . . you] JOHNSON; assurance | Q
42–3	Give . . . say] F; *1 line* Q
43–4	Few . . . King] OXFORD; yet | QF
45–6	I'll . . . other] OXFORD; lights | Q; him | F
9.2–9	You . . . man] F; drenched | and | to | head | flat | nature's | make | Q
10–13	O . . . fool] F; *verse* Q: house | door | blessing|
18–24	You . . . foul] F; *6 lines* Q: pleasure | and | servile | joined | white |
25–36	He . . . glass] CAPELL; *prose* Q
42–9	Alas . . . force] F; *9 lines* Q: here | these | of the | caves | fire | groans of | remember | carry |
49–56	Let . . . covert] F; *7 lines* Q: dreadful | now | thee | justice | and | incestuous |
56–8	and . . . guilts] OXFORD; *2 lines* Q: life | ; *2 lines* F: seeming |
61–8	Alack . . . courtesy] F; *prose* Q
71–3	The . . . heart] F; can | Poor | Q
75–8	He . . . day] F; *prose* Q
10.8–19	Go . . . careful] F; *verse* Q: Dukes | received | spoken | injuries | home | landed | and | talk | him | gone | me | is|
20–4	This . . . fall] F; *4 lines* Q: know | deserving | less|
11.1–3	Here . . . endure] F; *prose* Q
3–4	LEAR Let . . . enter] CRAIG; *1 type-line* Q
18–21	In . . . that] F; this | father | lies | Q
43–4	Hast . . . this] OXFORD; *prose* QF
67–8	Judicious . . . daughters] F; flesh | Q
107–11	Swithin . . . witch, aroint thee] CAPELL; *prose* Q
123	Horse . . . wear] F; *prose* Q
129–30	The Prince . . . Mahu] OXFORD; *prose* QF
131–2	Our . . . gets it] POPE; *prose* QF
133–8	Go . . . ready] F; *prose* Q
140–2	My . . . house] OXFORD; *1 line* Q
142–3	I'll . . . study] F; *prose* Q
146–7	Importune . . . unsettle] F; *1 line* Q
155–6	The . . . grace] F; wits | Q
156–7	O . . . company] F; *1 line* Q
159–60	With . . . philosopher] F; *1 line* Q
13.11–12	A king, a . . . them] OXFORD; *prose* Q

21	Come . . . me] CAPELL ; *prose* Q
22–3	Her . . . speak] CAPELL; *1 line* Q
25–7	The foul . . . herring] Q2; *verse* Q1: nightingale |
27–8	Croak . . . thee] *1 verse line* Q; *not in* F
29–30	How . . . cushions] THEOBALD; *prose* Q
31–5	I'll . . . too] POPE; *prose* Q
37–40	Sleepest . . . harm] THEOBALD; *prose* Q
58–9	Tom . . . curs] F (*ambiguously verse or prose*); *1 verse line* Q
60–5	Be . . . wail] F ('Curres, be'); *3 lines* Q: bite | him |
66–9	For . . . dry] F; *prose* Q (*though* 'For' *is capitalized at the beginning of the line, after a comma*)
70–5	Then . . . changed] F; *verse* Q: her | hardness | hundred | say |
83–5	There . . . master] F; *2 lines* Q: friend |
86–9	If . . . provision] F; *3 lines* Q: thine | loss|
92–4	Which . . . behind] THEOBALD; *2 lines* Q: cure |
95–6	When . . . foes] Q2; *prose* Q1
14.1–3	Post . . . Gloucester] BLAYNEY; *2 lines* Q: letter | ; *prose* F
4–5	Leave . . . company] BLAYNEY; *1 line* Q1; *prose* Q2, F
6–9	The . . . like] Q2; *verse* Q1: father | going |
9–10	Our . . . us] *prose* F; *1 verse line* Q
14–18	Some . . . friends] F; *prose* Q (*though* 'Some' *is capitalized at the beginning of a line, after a comma*)
25–6	Shall . . . traitor] F (*setting* 'Who's . . . traitor?' *on a separate line, after the direction*; blame | Q
33–4	By . . . beard] F; *prose* Q
35	REGAN . . . traitor] *same type-line as the end of the preceding speech* Q
36–7	Naughty . . . chin] F; *1 line* Q
43–4	And . . . kingdom] ROWE; *prose* QF
44–5	To . . . Speak] F; *prose* Q
49	CORNWALL . . . Dover] FURNESS; *1 type-line* Q
72–3	But . . . hold] F; *1 line* Q
74–5	If . . . mean] F; *prose* Q
79–80	O . . . O] F; *prose* Q
84–5	Edmund . . . act] F; *1 line* Q
85–8	Out . . . thee] F; *prose* Q
91–2	Go . . . you] F (*setting* 'How . . . you?' *on a separate line after the direction*); *prose* Q
94–6	Turn . . . arm] F; upon | untimely | Q
98–100	If she . . . monsters] THEOBALD; *prose* Q
104–5	Go . . . him] THEOBALD; *prose* Q
15.9–11	O . . . fourscore] JOHNSON; *prose* Q

36–8	How . . . master] F; *prose* Q
54–6	Both . . . fiend] F; *3 verse lines* Q: footpath | wits |
56–61	Five . . . master] POPE; *6 verse lines* Q: once | dumbness |
	Flibbertigibbet of | chambermaids |
63–4	Have . . . still] F; thee | Q
75–6	With . . . need] F; me | Q
77–8	Give . . . thee] F; *1 line* Q
16.3–11	Madam . . . offensive] F; *prose* Q
26–7	My . . . due] F; *1 line* Q
29–30	O . . . wind] F; *1 line* Q
46–7	Send . . . come] MALONE; *1 line* Q
48–9	Humanity . . . deep] POPE; *1 line* Q
51–2	Who . . . know'st] F; *2 lines* Q: honour |
52–5	that . . . land] THEOBALD; *3 lines* Q: pity | mischief |
58–60	See . . . woman] F; *prose* Q
69–71	O . . . Gloucester] F; *prose* Q
77–80	This . . . eye] F; *3 lines* Q: justicers | venge |
80–1	Both . . . answer] F; *1 line* Q
85–6	Upon . . . answer] F; took | Q
93–4	Gloucester . . . King] F; *1 line* Q
17.3–7	Something . . . necessary] STEEVENS; *prose* Q (*but reading* 'So' *after a comma, at the beginning of a type-line*)
14–16	Her . . . o'er her] POPE; *2 lines* Q: passion |
33–4	It . . . conditions] THEOBALD; *1 line* Q
41–2	What . . . daughter] POPE; *1 line* Q
46–8	To . . . Cordelia] JOHNSON; *2 lines* Q: mind |
55–6	Lending . . . me] JENNENS; *1 line* Q
18.9–10	In . . . him] OXFORD; *1 line* QF
16–17	All . . . earth] F; *1 line* Q
21–2	News . . . hitherward] F; *1 line* Q
25–6	It . . . France] JOHNSON; *1 line* Q
19. 2–3	Madam . . . soldier] F; *1 line* Q
12–14	In . . . army] F; *2 lines* Q: life |
12–13	In . . . life] BLAYNEY; *1 line* Q. F *treats* 'His . . . descry' *as one line*
17–18	I . . . business] F; *prose* Q
35–6	I . . . farewell] F; *1 line* Q
20.3–4	Horrible . . . sea] F; *1 line* Q
33–4	Why . . . it] F; *1 line* Q
41–8	Gone . . . sir] F; *prose* Q
81–2	The . . . thus] F; *1 line* Q
83–4	No . . . himself] *prose* Q2, F; *1 verse line* Q1; *2 verse lines* BLAYNEY: I |

104–5	The . . . King] F; *prose* Q
105–9	Ay . . . fly] F; *prose* Q
110–12	Does . . . daughters] *prose* Q; thrive | father | F
113–14	Got . . . dame] *prose* Q; *3 lines* F: sheets | soldiers |
115–27	Whose . . . thee] CAPELL; *prose* QF
129	O . . . world] F; *prose* Q
130	Should . . . me] *prose* Q; *2 lines* F: naught |
133–4	No . . . of't] MUIR; *prose* QF
136–7	I . . . it] *prose* Q; report | F
137–9	And . . . eyes] Q, *which sets Edgar's speech as prose, sets* 'breaks . . . case' *on one type-line.*
154–7	Thou . . . cozener] POPE; *prose* QF
158–60	Through . . . seem] ROWE; *prose* QF
161–2	To . . . So] CAPELL; *prose* QF
163–4	O . . . madness] F; *1 line* Q
165–9	If . . . me] F; *prose* Q
171–3	When . . . shoe] F; *prose* Q
174–5	A . . . kill, kill, kill, kill, kill, kill] OXFORD; *prose* Q; F *adds* 'I'll put't in proof' *after* 'felt', *and divides after* 'proof' *and* 'son-in-laws'
176–7	O . . . dear] F; *1 line* Q
178–81	No . . . brains] F; *prose* Q
183–4	No . . . salt] F; *prose* Q
185	To . . . water-pots] JENNENS; *prose* Q
187–9	I . . . that] OXFORD; *prose* Q; what | king | POPE
193–6	A . . . to] F; *prose* Q
202–3	But . . . army] F; *1 line* Q
216–18	Hearty . . . boot] F; *prose* Q (*though* Qb *divides after* 'heaven')
218–22	A . . . thee] F; *prose* Q
222–3	Now . . . to't] F; *1 line* Q
223–6	Wherefore . . . arm] F; *prose* Q
241–2	To . . . death! Death] F; upon | Q
244–5	As . . . desire] Q2, F; *1 line* Q
247–51	Sit . . . not] F; *4 lines* Q: pockets | friends | deathsman |
276–7	Give . . . drum] Q2, F; *1 line* Q1
21.1–2	O . . . goodness] Q2; *1 line* Q1
6–8	Be . . . off] Q2, F; *2 lines* Q1: those |
11–12	Then . . . King] F; *1 line* Q
12–13	O . . . nature] Q2, F; *1 line* Q1
15–16	So . . . long] F; king | Q
24–6	O . . . sisters] F; *2 lines* Q: lips |
54–5	I feel . . . condition] F; *1 line* Q

55–7	O . . . kneel] Q2, F; *prose* Q1
76–7	Be . . . in him] F; *prose* Q
77–80	and yet . . . settling] THEOBALD; *prose* Q
82–4	You . . . foolish] OXFORD; Q1 *divides after* 'forgive' (*it is unclear whether verse or prose is intended*); Q2 *and* F *divide after* 'me' *and* 'forgive'.
84–5	Holds . . . slain] OXFORD; *1 line* Q
86–7	As . . . Gloucester] CAPELL; *1 line* Q
87–9	They . . . Germany] OXFORD; *prose* Q
89–91	Report . . . apace] OXFORD; *2 lines* Q: about |
91–2	The . . . sir] OXFORD; *1 line* Q
22.13–15	I . . . hers] OXFORD; *prose* Q1; *2 lines* Q2: conjunct |
16–17	I . . . her] F; *1 line* Q
18–19	Fear . . . husband] CAPELL; *1 line* QF
20–1	I . . . me] THEOBALD; *prose* Q
34–5	Let . . . proceedings] F; *prose* Q1; determine | Q2
35–6	EDMUND . . . tent] OXFORD; *same type-line as the end of the preceding speech* Q
50–2	I . . . again] Q2, F; *prose* Q1
57–8	By . . . you] F; *1 line* Q
60–2	Each . . . enjoyed] F; *2 lines* Q: adder |
23.3–4	If . . . comfort] Q2, F; *1 line* Q1
24.3–5	We . . . down] Q2, F; *2 lines* Q1: incurred |
37–8	I . . . do't] OXFORD; oats | Q
45–6	To . . . guard] Q2; *1 line* Q1
51–3	My . . . session] F; tomorrow | hold | Q
53–6	At . . . sharpness] THEOBALD; *3 lines* Q: bleed | quarrels |
59–60	I . . . brother] F; *1 line* Q
65–6	Not . . . himself] F; *prose* Q
67–8	In . . . best] F; *1 line* Q
70–1	Holla . . . asquint] F; *1 line* Q
103–4	All . . . discharge] F; *1 line* Q
116–18	What . . . summons] F; *2 lines* Q: quality |
119	By . . . canker-bit] Q2, F; *2 lines* Q: tooth |
120–1	Yet . . . withal] F; move't | Q
124–5	That . . . mine] F; arm | Q
136–8	This . . . liest] F; *2 lines* Q: spirits |
147–50	This . . . beguiled] F; *3 lines* Q: arms | opposite |
150–3	Stop . . . know't] F; *prose* Q
154–5	Say . . . for't] F; *1 line* Q
155–6	Most . . . paper] CAPELL; *1 line* QF
167–9	Make . . . eyes] F; *2 lines* Q: vicious |
169–70	Thou . . . here] Q2, F; *prose* Q1

173–4	Let . . . father] OXFORD; *1 line* Q
178–86	BY . . . rings] F; lord | told | proclamation | near | death | once | rags | disdained | Q
200–1	For . . . this] Q2, F; *1 line* Q1
201–4	This . . . extremity] THEOBALD; *3 lines* Q: such | much |
218–19	What kind . . . knife] F; *1 line* Q
219–20	It's . . . of] STEEVENS; *1 line* Q
230–1	I . . . night] F; *1 line* Q
249–50	To . . . despair] F; lay | Q
271–3	Did . . . now] F; day | would | Q
290–6	That's . . . honours] F; *prose* Q (*but capitalizing* 'Know' *at the beginning of its second prose line*)
297–8	Have . . . foes] POPE; *prose* Q
299	The . . . see, see] F; *prose* Q
300–2	And . . . more] F; *prose* Q
303–4	Never . . . O, O, O, O] OXFORD; *prose* Q
308–10	Vex . . . longer] F; pass | rack | Q
313–15	Bear . . . sustain] QF; *4 lines* OXFORD *conj.*: hence | woe | kingdom |

INDEX

This is a selective guide to words and expressions annotated and to names in the Introduction and 'The Ballad of King Lear'. Asterisks identify entries that supplement the information given in the *Oxford English Dictionary*.

The
Oxford
World's
Classics
Website

www.worldsclassics.co.uk

- Information about new titles
- Explore the full range of Oxford World's Classics
- Links to other literary sites and the main OUP webpage
- Imaginative competitions, with bookish prizes
- Peruse the Oxford World's Classics Magazine
- Articles by editors
- Extracts from Introductions
- A forum for discussion and feedback on the series
- Special information for teachers and lecturers

www.worldsclassics.co.uk

American Literature

British and Irish Literature

Children's Literature

Classics and Ancient Literature

Colonial Literature

Eastern Literature

European Literature

History

Medieval Literature

Oxford English Drama

Poetry

Philosophy

Politics

Religion

The Oxford Shakespeare

A complete list of Oxford Paperbacks, including Oxford World's Classics, Oxford Shakespeare, Oxford Drama, and Oxford Paperback Reference, is available in the UK from the Academic Division Publicity Department, Oxford University Press, Great Clarendon Street, Oxford OX2 6DP.

In the USA, complete lists are available from the Paperbacks Marketing Manager, Oxford University Press, 198 Madison Avenue, New York, NY 10016.

Oxford Paperbacks are available from all good bookshops. In case of difficulty, customers in the UK can order direct from Oxford University Press Bookshop, Freepost, 116 High Street, Oxford OX1 4BR, enclosing full payment. Please add 10 per cent of published price for postage and packing.